Inside The Walls
& Beyond

My journey through the
federal criminal "in"justice
system

Lynn Espejo

Inside The Walls & Beyond
My journey through the federal criminal "in"justice system

Copyright © 2023 Lynn Espejo

This book is a real-life story about the events that led to the indictment, conviction and imprisonment of Lynn Espejo. Some names and identifying details have been changed or initials of the person have been used.

Book Cover Design: Jim Wheeler of Justina James Designs

All books printed in the United States of America
Published by: Freedom Publishing, LLC

ISBN: 9798852341624

Dedication

I dedicate this book to the many amazing women I met while serving time in federal prison. May God continue to be with you on all your journeys.

Acknowledgments

First and foremost, I thank God for carrying me through all of life's journeys. HE is my lighthouse in the storm. But most importantly, I thank God for sending HIS son to die on the cross, so that I, and everyone who comes to have a relationship with HIM, can know the true meaning of FREEDOM.

To the love of my life, my husband Pancho, no words can express my gratitude for you. Your loyalty through this journey has been unequaled. There is no way I could have made it through this life storm, without your ever-present support and love for me. You stood beside me, when the storm raged out of control, around me. It is unfair the disruptions to your life my criminal case caused, yet you never wavered. When I lost my way, you were there. When I was a wreck and hard to live with many times, you remained steady. Inside those walls, you were my sanity. I am truly blessed to be your wife. Thank you for standing by my side, and holding me up, when I felt like I would fall. Thank you for keeping our home in order, while I was away. Thank you for providing me with the best life. I love you more than you will ever know. You continue to tell me how strong I am, but it is you, who is the strongest. I look forward to all that we have left ahead of us, and all the new chapters we will write, on this journey we call life. Lastly, thank you for always encouraging me to tell my story. I would not have written this book, without you continuously pushing me, to do so.

To my three sons, Joseph, JT, and Timothy, I love you to the moon and back. You are my biggest blessings. I am sorry for the times your lives were affected, due to my long fight with the federal government. Thank you for your love, support, and for being my reason to go on, even when at times, I wanted to give up. I am so proud of all three of you. May you continue to do great things.

To Pastor Rod Loy, thank you for always being an example of how we should treat *all* people. Thank you for your steady guidance, encouragement, advice, and prayers. Your love for my family and me, during this life storm, was constant. Thank you for counseling me, both before, and after, prison. Your wisdom has echoed in my head many times, when I am faced with decisions, I feel unequipped to make.

To my friend Kathy Skrdlant, thank you for your many years of friendship. Thank you for your love and support. You took on the enormous responsibility of posting for me on my blog, *Inside The Walls*, and kept it moving forward, during my time in prison. My voice would not have been heard, from *inside the walls*, without your dedication to my story.

To my family, friends, and church friends. Thank you for standing by me, and encouraging me, through one of my most challenging journeys. Your love and kindness will never be forgotten.

To everyone who sent cards, letters, books, photos, and emails to me, during my time in prison, you will never know how those acts of kindness made a huge difference, during a very difficult time in my life. Hearing my name at the nightly mail call, assured me that I was not forgotten, or alone, on this journey. It was often the very words in your email, card, or letter that I needed to hear, at that moment. God used you, to be HIS messengers, during some of my darkest days.

To everyone who spent time out of their busy lives, driving eight hours one way, to visit me in prison, thank you. Your visits meant more to me than you can ever know. Thank you for sitting in plastic chairs, and eating bad junk food from vending machines, just so I could have a few hours of reprieve from prison life.

To all the women and men, I have met along this journey, who have also found themselves in the crosshairs of the federal government, I commend you for continuing to move forward. I value your friendships. Your stories are invaluable to the changes needed in our nation's criminal "in"justice system. May the Lord richly bless each one of you.

To all the criminal justice advocates, who fight daily, to expose the flaws in our criminal justice system, and work hard to bring about needed changes and reform, thank you for all your hard work. You have made an enormous difference in my journey, and many of you have become invaluable life-long friends. Never give up the good fight.

To my bunkie, Rhonda Rosales, who remains inside the walls, thank you for being a huge part of my journey. There is not a day that goes by, that I don't think about you, or pray for your continued journey. I will never stop fighting the good fight, until you, and many others, are free again. I will continue to speak out on your behalf, until changes have been made, to our broken criminal "in"justice system. I love and miss you. I can't wait until I can give you a hug, on this side of the walls.

A special thank you to United States Probation Officer, Victoria F. Thank you for always encouraging me to complete this journey. I wish everyone could be lucky enough to have you as their probation officer. Thank you for always standing up for what is right and just, and for being a supportive voice before, during, and after my supervised release. May God continue to bless you and your family.

Many thanks to Jim Wheeler, of Justina James Designs, for his kindness in volunteering to design my book cover.

Finally, to my friend Sam Bent, aka DoingFedTime, who helped me with the publishing of this book. And to my dear friend Retta, who provided me with needed encouragement, along the way. Because of you, this book came to fruition. I am forever grateful for your input and encouragement. Your friendships mean the world to me. I wish both of you many blessings on your own journeys.

FORWARD

This book is about my story as I journeyed through our federal criminal "in"justice system. It's not a story of winning, but it's certainly not a story of losing either. Although at times during this journey, I did lose a lot.

This book is a cautionary tale of sorts. A tale about how my selfish motives, and choosing to turn a blind eye to the wrongdoings of others, wrecked not only my own life, but at times, the lives of my family, as well. It is a story about how trusting in man, more than God, took me totally off HIS path for my life, and left me with disastrous results. And how I allowed my anger to gain a foothold over my entire being, ultimately costing me my peace and happiness, for years to come.

But my story is so much bigger than any of that. It is also a story of redemption, and learning to move past my anger, with God's help. Most importantly, my story is about how God's grace and mercy took the most broken of pieces, and made them whole again. It is the story of how I found forgiveness, in the face of great adversity. Forgiveness for myself, and those who had wronged me. Even though sometimes I still struggle with what has happened to my family and me.

It is not a story about being a victim, although I may have felt like one, many times along this journey. It is not a story about beating the government. Although, I wish I could have proven the truth at trial and won. The real victory in my story happened, only after I allowed healing through Jesus Christ.

However, this book is also about our federal criminal "in"justice system, and the unfairness that many face daily. It is a story about my journey through a storm that has raged on for over twelve years, as I finish writing this book. And how

I finally found peace, regardless that the storm still rages around me at times. Peace through God our Father–even when it was HIM that I was angry with at times.

The hardest part of writing this book was truthfully telling my story, while still honoring God in a way that I wanted to do. I hope that this comes across to the readers. I prayed a lot about how to glorify HIM, without diluting what happened in my case, or during my time in prison. I remind the reader that this book is my story. And the opinions expressed here, are my views of what happened along this journey. Many of the stories were memorialized in my blog, *Inside The Walls*, and then rewritten and expanded upon for this book.

I am not a perfect person, nor are the other people you will read about in this book. However, I can only speak for the part I played in this tragedy. Only through HIS grace am I saved. I still fail daily, but I continue to move forward with HIS love. And I continue to learn daily from my mistakes. I hope that my faith is conveyed to my readers, in a way that would encourage others to allow God's grace and mercy, to work in their own lives–just like HE has in mine.

1 Corinthians 15:10 "But by the grace of God I am what I am, and his grace toward me was not in vain."

Table of Contents

Chapter One
Are You A Strong Person?

The following is taken directly from a blog post I wrote in February 2018, shortly before I self-surrendered to federal prison. The original word "blog" has been changed to "book" in the last paragraph.

Are you a strong person? I get that question a lot when people find out about my criminal case, and how long it dragged on before I went to trial. I've had many people say, "I could never make it through something like that." I suspect that is not the case at all. You see, when faced with one of life's storms, we have really only two choices: 1. We can lie down and die—basically give up, or 2. We can get up daily and keep moving forward—living life the best we can during life's struggles.

My wise pastor, fondly known to everyone who loves him as P. Rod, summed it up like this, "What choice do you have?" His words have resonated with me since the day he asked me that question in his office on February 12, 2017—just four days after I had been through an excruciating eight-day jury trial, where I had been found guilty on all counts. I had already spent the last four days wallowing in my pain, basically wasting four of the few days I would have left at home with my family, before I would be forced to report to federal prison.

What WOULD I do now? What would others' view of me be as I walked this path? What example would I set for my children during this process? What example would I set as a Christian to my fellow brothers and sisters in Christ, or even to non-believers who may be watching from the outside? How could I bring glory to God in this and every situation?

I'm naturally a controlling person—I want to be in control of EVERYTHING in my life! This has been one of the hardest things for me to fully turn over to God. I'm a work in progress. We all are. The one thing this journey has brought me to understand, is that the sooner we submit to God's plan for our life, and get off of our own plan, the more peace we find, and the better our life becomes. And who doesn't want peace? You see, life really is a choice, and while we may not have a choice in a lot of things in this life—such as the fairness of what happens to us at times. We do have a choice in how we react to those things.

If we put our trust in God—fully turning everything over to HIM and allowing HIM to lead us—HE will see us through what may seem like the valley of death. With HIS help, we can leave the valley and continue on the journey to what HE has planned for our life. God can and will move mountains. And while valleys always seem so dark and dreary, everyone knows that the view from atop the mountain is always breathtaking!

So how would I climb back up? What could I do to move forward from this dark and dreary valley I found myself in? And what steps would I take to glorify God along the way? And what if God didn't move this mountain? What then? How would I continue to honor and put my trust in HIM?

At the time of my trial in January 2017, I had been fighting the federal government for roughly seven years. I wish I had been stronger at times. I wish I had limited my reactions and held my tongue more. I wish I had allowed HIM to guide me more, and had trusted HIS plan, more than my own.

Unfortunately, these are life lessons that you learn along the way. I fully believe that God allows adversity, anguish, and heartache to be valuable lessons in our lives. These trials and tribulations can bring us to a higher level of insight and understanding about who we are as a person. It can bring about changes in our own behavior and our perception or view of the world in which we live. Most importantly, the adversaries of life can change our perception regarding our relationship with HIM, and can teach us to trust HIM even more.

The bible in 1 Peter 5:10 tells us this, "after you have suffered a little while, the God of all grace, who has called you to his eternal glory in Christ, will himself restore, confirm, strengthen, and establish you."

Isn't God's mercy, grace, and love amazing? My prayer is that everyone reading this book will come to truly know HIM and allow HIM to guide your path. HE is my strength daily. HE will be your strength too, if only you allow HIM!

Chapter Two
Life Before Indictment

What would I do now? What would others' view of me be as I walked this path? What example would I set for my children during this process? What example would I set as a Christian to my fellow brothers and sisters in Christ, or even to non-believers who may be watching from the outside? How could I bring glory to God in this and every situation? These are hard questions when you are in a "feel sorry for yourself" mood. Reflecting back to my blog post from February 2018, I see how badly I failed, many times, in all of those areas.

It's not that I did not take heed of what my pastor said on that cold February afternoon in 2017. I was aware of what the Bible commanded me to do. I knew that my struggles should keep me nearer the cross, and that I needed to allow God to lead me. I had been in church for most of my life. I understood the gravity of my situation, and how my actions going forward could make the situation much worse. And I did try my best to live out my Christian values, trying hard to put my trust in God. After all, I had seen what trusting myself and man had done for me.

But as I look back now, to the last year I was home before federal prison, I do so with a lot more clarity. At the time, I lived in constant dread of what lay ahead. Instead of being still, and listening to HIS voice. I let fear grab ahold of my entire being. Fear of the unknown–federal prison. It gnawed at me, my every waking moment. It haunted my dreams when I went to bed at night. I knew at the time it was not biblical to feel that way, but I couldn't help myself, no matter how hard I tried, or I prayed. From February 2017, to February 2018, felt like an eternity! An eternity where I continued to allow my anger to take deeper root. I believe this was a time of immense grief for both me and my husband.

I was grieving life as I knew it. After all, my freedom was about to be taken from me. It's hard to reconcile that you are a convicted felon, and about to go to federal prison, especially for a crime you know you did not commit. And I realize now that I was angry at God for what I saw as HIM allowing this to happen. Afterall, HE knew the whole truth, and nothing but the truth, even if the jury never had the chance to hear it. My husband, Pancho, was struggling with the loss he was about to experience, with me being gone for almost four years, and all the extra responsibilities that would come his way in my absence. As we prepared for him to take over those extra responsibilities, I could tell he was also feeling the weight of what was about to happen.

My children were dealing with their own feelings, as well as the change in my behavior, which was many times driven by the anger I felt in those moments. It was a stressful time for all of us. Our youngest son, Timothy, who still lived at home, unfortunately received the most harm, from this season of my life. He was a junior in High School when I left for prison.

Honestly, I can't even remember most of that last year at home. Maybe my mind blocked it out? From the moment I heard the guilty verdict read on February 8, 2017, until a time that did not arrive for many years in the future, my life was shattered by what our federal government had done to me. But mostly by what I allowed the anger inside of me to do. I held on to those feelings for all they were worth, which turns out to be a lot of heartache and pain, mostly from my own actions. Heartache and pain to the ones I love the most, as well as those I met along this journey, but mostly to myself.

And my control issues continued to try to control situations, that I should have turned over to God. I knew HE was the only one that could carry me through this journey. Yet, as I reflect back now, I see how I continued to try to take things into my own hands, throughout the entire process.

But long before I found myself a convicted felon, or federal prisoner number 26304-009, I was just a typical American, living in my own little world. Never thinking about our criminal justice system, unless it had to do with a speeding ticket. Unfortunately, I've had a few of those in my time. My story was nothing special. It started out like many middle-class Americans. While my family was not wealthy, we certainly were not poor. My parents had me on March 11, 1964, when they were just 16 and 17 years old. One year to the day later, on March 11, 1965, my sister Kay was born. It is not surprising that my parents divorced when I was only four years old.

Afterward, my sister and I went to live with my maternal grandparents. My grandfather was a farmer, so we were raised on the farm. My grandmother, Nanny, as we called her, was the epitome of the southern housewife, and grandmother. I still miss her fudge candy, chicken and dressing, and many other dishes she cooked for me as a child. Nanny was not all fluff though; and her peach tree switches would certainly sting your legs when you did wrong. But it is her love that I remember the most.

Growing up on the farm was not glamorous, and in my younger years I remember not liking it very much. For starters, there were not many other children around to play with. I remember preferring to be at my other grandparents' house in town, because there was more to do there. Many summer days were spent riding my banana seat bike with the pink and white basket on the front. I always pretended I was Jan Brady, even though I had long light brown hair, not blonde like hers. During the summers, I enjoyed swimming at the local swimming pool, and we always had seasonal passes to go as much as we wanted. I played softball on a team each summer, even though admittedly, I was not very good at it.

My sister and I attended Vacation Bible School and went to several church camps during the summer. I also attended majorette and cheerleading camp. My junior year of high school, I was one of two girls, from my high school selected to attend Girls State. We often took vacations with both sets of grandparents.

Looking back, my time on the farm is certainly some of my fondest memories from my childhood. If I concentrate hard enough, I can still smell the freshly baled hay, and feel the warmth of the sun shining brightly on my back, as I rode my horse across the fields. I believe growing up on the farm is why Fall is still my most favorite season. It takes me back to a time that was innocent.

I remember walking through the side road that ran between the fields that separated our house from my great grandparents' house. The crisp Fall air would be blowing on my face. Once there, my great grandmother would give me a hot dog wrapped in aluminum foil, and a Hershey with almonds chocolate bar. I would eat it as I walked back home.

I remember the Fall carnivals at my school, and bobbing for apples. I couldn't wait each year to pick out my Halloween costume and go trick or treating. My grandfather allowed us to have all our friends over each October for a hayride and weenie roast. In this way, my childhood was actually magical, even if I didn't realize it at the time.

I grew up in a loving home with grandparents that nurtured and cared for my every need. I led a sheltered life. I attended a small public school, where I had many friends. We were raised in the church, and taught to do good things for our fellow man. Both sets of my grandparents raised us with strong Christian values. Values that have served me well throughout my entire life. They led by example, and it was a great example to follow. I learned to treat others with care and respect, because my grandparents modeled these acts daily.

My mother taught me how to be acceptive of others, as she has always had many friends, from all walks of life. I've lived by her example in this area of my life as well. It's probably one of the main reasons I survived prison. Accepting and treating others well, even those who may be different from me.

I was popular in school. I was involved in many activities, including being a majorette, cheerleader, on the homecoming court, and in almost every club at my school. You could certainly say that I grew up privileged. But my life was not without heartache and adversity. When I was 15 years old, my father committed suicide. I look back years later and see how traumatic this event was. At the time I was still too young to fully comprehend, how it would haunt me throughout my lifetime.

I have a good relationship with my mother. However, most likely due to the young age at which she gave birth to me, she has always been more like a friend, than a mother.

My Nanny Howell and my Grandmother Denton were the people I considered to be mother figures in my life. I remember a recurring dream I would have as a young child. In the dream, my Nanny would be swallowed up by a hole as she walked in different areas of the farm. Sometimes she would be on the road in front of our house. Other times she was walking in one of our fields, when the dream occurred. I remember how vivid and frightening those dreams were to me at the time. I think as a child I may have suffered from separation anxiety. Of course, I never told anyone about these dreams, until now.

In August 1992, I was blessed to have my only biological child. I was 28 years old at the time of his birth. During my pregnancy it was found that I had female cancer, and I had to have a complete hysterectomy a few years later.

While that killed my dreams of having three children, I was excited and nervous, about the one child God had given me. My son's name is Joseph, named after my dad, and he will be 31 years old this year. At the time of his birth, my then-husband, his dad, was in the Marines. We were stationed at Camp Pendleton in California.

We lived in San Clemente, a small beach town, in Southern California. And our apartment was just three blocks from the beach. When Joseph was only six weeks old, we moved back to Arkansas. After twelve years of marriage, we divorced.

After returning to Arkansas, I worked as a manager for a well- known trucking company, and later as the general manager for a locally owned oil company. When Joseph was about five years old, I went back to college. My then husband, was a mailman, in the small Arkansas town where we lived. I did not realize that by putting so much pressure on myself to get an A in every class, that I would be forced to spend so much time studying, that it would ultimately impact my marriage.

Well maybe it was that, or it might have been the fact that my ex-husband found someone else he liked better on his mail route? I'll never know what caused our divorce. I take full responsibility for my part in its demise—I admit that my studying and taking care of a small child—regardless that I intended to better our family—did take a toll on it. I like to compare it to "two ships passing in the night," as my husband and I, became more like roommates at that time, than soulmates for life.

Shortly after the divorce, I graduated with my Bachelors of Business Administration with a double major in Accounting and Finance. After graduation, I briefly worked for Lockheed Martin as a cost accountant for the PAC3 Missile Program, where I had a government security clearance. A few years after my divorce, I decided living in the same small town with my ex-husband was just not healthy for me. I had not wanted the divorce, and I struggled with moving forward, while still living in the same small town. So, Joseph and I moved two and a half hours north, to North Little Rock, Arkansas.

At the time my mother was living in Little Rock, Arkansas, just across the river. It felt like it was a way to have a new beginning, and to get away from the hurt and pain I still felt from the divorce. And it was a chance to finally be close to my mother.

I purchased a house, and took on the task of remodeling it. However, a few months after my relocation, my mother's real mother passed away, leaving her a house in another town. So, my mom relocated an hour away from me. Let me clarify, my grandparents that raised me, actually adopted my mother when she was fifteen months old. However, we had contact with my mom's birth mother.

After my relocation, I met my current husband, Pancho, who is a Certified Public Accountant (CPA). Having recently graduated with my accounting degree, we had things in common. He was also recently divorced. While our relationship started out as friends, and I actually tried to fix him up with a few of my girlfriends, we ended up falling in love. We were married on February 14, 2004. To say he is my biggest supporter, would be an understatement. One does not realize just how loyal someone is, until you go through what I have been through the last twelve years with the federal government. This is not to say, that we haven't had our fair share of troubles, just like many marriages do.

But leading up to my incarceration, one of my biggest fears was that he would leave me, while I served time in federal prison. I had read so many stories of this happening to other women, that I had a lot of angst about it for no reason, leading up to my self-surrender to prison. In the end, it was our mutual love and respect for each other, along with learning to put God at the center of everything we do, that has been the glue that has held our marriage together, even in the hard times. He is undoubtedly my best friend.

I've also been a big supporter of him as well. A few years into our marriage, we were granted custody of his two sons. While I could write a book about the reason for the change of custody, that is not the topic of this book. What I will say on the subject is this; JT and Timothy came to live with us in 2006, at very young ages, after a custody battle that went on for years, and continued, until the judge finally took away the rights of one parent.

It was a storm that I was thrust into when I married Pancho. And maybe it was God's way of preparing me for the storms that would later come my way? Regardless, of all the challenges, we made the best of it, and formed a blended family.

And I helped raise JT and Timothy as my own. I could not love them more if I had actually given birth to them. In this way, God allowed me the other two children I had always dreamed of having. While I am not their birth mother, I do share a strong maternal bond with them. I was surprised to find out that many people did not realize I was not their birth mother, until my criminal case was made public. Fortunately, Joseph, JT, and Timothy, became close as they grew up. They consider each other their "real" brother. We stopped using the word *step,* to denote the difference in blood relations, a long time ago.

JT graduated from college in 2018 while I was in prison. He got married in 2019, also while I was in prison. He is now 26 years old, is a missionary pastor, and he and his wife live in Africa. Timothy is 22 years old, has graduated with his undergraduate degree and his master's degree. He works as a pastor at our church, and still lives at home with us. Joseph graduated from college in 2013, in between my first and second indictment, and currently lives and works in Seattle, Washington.

He has always been a very responsible young man. Since graduating from college, he has also lived and worked in Chicago, and New York City. He has done well for himself; all of our sons have. Since his college graduation, Joseph has worked with many well-known people, as well as some highly recognizable businesses. We are very proud of all three of our sons. They have all been supportive of me throughout my criminal case, which I realize has dramatically impacted their lives, regardless of how I wish it had not.

Before my indictment, saying my family and I were blind to the criminal justice system in this country would be an understatement. While we had spent our fair share of years in family court, dealing with the situation with JT and Timothy's mom, we knew nothing about criminal matters.

Before this experience, we truly believed that only bad people were indicted. We believed an individual had to be breaking the law to go to prison. We believed that innocent people did not get charged with crimes, and those who won in court were not guilty. Anyone who did lose at trial was guilty of the crimes they were charged with. And honestly, we probably didn't think about our criminal justice system much at all, if any.

Once upon a time, I believed a jury of my peers existed, and that juries and trials were fair. I believed in our government, and our criminal justice system. I thought only noble people worked at the Federal Bureau of Investigations (FBI), Secret Service, Internal Revenue Service (IRS), Department of Justice (DOJ), Bureau of Prisons (BOP), and the United States Attorney's Office (AUSAs). I never thought about capital punishment, or prison reform. I never wondered why the United States has the highest prison population per capita in the world. I was naïve. Nobody in my family had ever been to prison. I had no clue about the prison system, nor did I care. It didn't affect my family or me. I was a typical American with my head in the sand.

Then March 2, 2011, happened. That was the date of my first indictment. And so began my journey through our federal criminal "in"justice system.

Chapter Three
Working or The Doctors

Instead of using the doctors' real names in this book, I have decided to give them pseudonyms. Not because I believe they deserve protection—certainly not after all the lies they told on my husband and me. But because this is my story— not theirs.

From March 2007-September 2010, I worked for eight physicians as their Clinic Administrator. After I married Pancho, I worked for several years in public accounting. He and I worked at the same firm. This is where I met one of the doctors, Dr. Rascal Jones, while I was his accountant. Dr. Jones found me very helpful to his practice, and begged me to leave my job in public accounting, to work for the group of doctors he had recently joined. I was not even looking for a job at the time.

Little did I know how meeting him would change the rest of my life. I was not aware that Dr. Jones had many secrets in his past. I was certainly not aware that he had been asked to leave the previous group where he had practiced medicine, due to his unscrupulous practices—practices that would eventually impact my life in nefarious ways. In this book, I have used the first name Rascal for the doctor I refer to as Dr. Jones. It certainly fits him well. As it turns out, he was indeed a rascal. And honestly, that would be putting it nicely when describing him.

But not knowing these things, I agreed to an interview with four of the eight doctors, to see if we could agree on me coming to work for their clinic. When I first started interviewing for the job, four of the eight doctors (Rascal Jones, Jack Thatch, Butch Swan, and Sam Boring) were meeting behind closed doors.

Apparently, they were plotting to overthrow what they called their Executive Board. Dr. Jones told me about these meetings. The board consisted of the other doctors in the group (Pete Zorick, Todd Korker, and John Moon), who were currently operating as President, Vice-President, and Secretary/Treasurer of the Executive Board. The group also included Dr. Charles Black, who was not a voting member of the group, due to some sort of membership fee he had not yet paid to the other doctors.

The four doctors meeting behind closed doors planned to force out the current officers, and elect three of the four of themselves (Swan, Boring and Thatch), to the executive offices. They then planned to fire their current office manager, who they claimed was too loyal to Dr. Korker. After they fired her, they wanted to hire me. I was not interested in the position, and I told them so. However, after I met with them, several of the doctors kept putting pressure on me to take the job. They even insisted that I meet with Dr. Thatch's wife, so she could try to convince me they needed me to run their clinic.

I was offered $25,000 per year above what I was already being paid at my current position in public accounting, most likely to entice me into taking the position. The four doctors (Swan, Jones, Boring, and Thatch) even had several secret meetings with me after hours. The other four doctors (Zorick, Korker, Moon, and Black) were unaware that any of this was going on.

At the time, doctors Swan, Jones, Boring and Thatch, were accusing the current office manager of stealing money from the practice. They also believed she was billing them for part of Dr. Korker's clinic bills. I never found any evidence of this, and it did not appear from the accounting records that anything of the sort had taken place.

As part of my job duties, I would later be asked to find what she had taken. Doctors Swan, Boring, Thatch, and Jones wished to use it as leverage to take away all the employee benefits they would owe her when she was fired. Regardless of how they pressured me to do so, I never found anything she had taken, and I told them as much.

All I ever found was some accounting errors she made, which appeared to be honest mistakes. There was absolutely no proof that she was cheating other doctors to help Dr. Korker. Regardless that she had done nothing of the sort, they voted to take her benefits from her anyway, when they fired her.

As planned, in February 2007, the four doctors overthrew their current Executive Board, voting them out, and electing themselves to the offices. I was hired a few weeks later. Dr. Swan became the President and my direct supervisor, Dr. Boring became Vice-President, and Dr. Thatch became the Secretary/Treasurer of the group. There was much dissension between all the doctors, except for Dr. Black, who was not part of the group, and had no vote, or say, about what happened.

All of the meetings and plotting behind closed doors should have been my first *red flag*, and I should have run in the opposite direction as fast as my legs would carry me. Instead, I ignored the evidence clearly in front of me, and proceeded to take the job anyway.

As President, Dr. Swan was to oversee the business's day-to-day activities, monitor the bank statements, and co-sign the checks to be mailed from the *zero*-balance checking account. The same account I helped to oversee. During the bulk of my employment (with the exception of the last two months), Dr. Swan was the President of the Executive Board, and my direct supervisor. At the time of my employment, I thought Dr. Swan was a kind, older fatherly figure, a true gentleman. Little did I know, it would later be his refusal to take responsibility for his own actions, that would cause me to end up in federal prison.

The way the group was set up, the office manager answered to the President for the most part, unless he was out of the office. Then the office manager was to go to one of the other executive board members. I found that none of the other members wanted to be bothered, and they were frustrated when the President was not around to handle things.

In one of the monthly meetings, the rule was established that any new *shared expense* over $1000, had to be voted on by all doctors, before approval. Still, the President approved everything else. This new rule happened after the doctors could not agree on the purchase of something as simple as an ice machine. Several doctors argued that they did not use the ice machine as much as some of the other doctors in the group. The ice machine was to cost roughly $1200.

These were silly arguments as all the employees of the office used the ice machine equally. However, because Dr. Swan did cosmetic procedures such as fillers and Botox, he used the ice for patients as well. Given that some of the other doctors did not like him, they wanted him to pay more of the cost of the ice machine. The $1000 rule continued to be problematic because none of the doctors could get along or agree, and most of them seemed to hate each other, unless they needed something.

I would watch in disbelief as they would often vote against a shared expense for items needed to keep the clinic running, if a doctor thought the new item would benefit another doctor's practice more than his own. Nobody wanted to play nice in the sand-box.

The practice also presented many other issues. It was a unique setup, at least as far as accounting and Medicare practices go. The doctors did not actually operate as a group. They merely split some overhead expenses, payroll for shared employees, as well as shared rent for the suite they shared.

They each had their own individual practice and staff, and most made it clear that the other doctors were not to know about, or see, any of *their* business. They were also aware that they had Medicare fraud issues with the way they billed, especially since they also owned the inhouse lab, but each of them personally billed for the lab expenses to insurance companies and Medicare.

I had tried to point these problems out to them many times. As their Clinic Administrator, I brought in two attorneys who specialized in Medicare and Stark II billing issues, so experts could explain to them how they were committing fraud. Each time, the doctors choose to ignore the advice of the attorneys, and continue operating as they already were. Another *red flag*, I choose to ignore.

Every two weeks it was my job to present the doctors with what was referred to as Settlement Statements. These statements showed each doctor's direct and shared expenses owed. The statements included copies of invoices as backup documentation, for what the doctors were being asked to pay. The invoices were given to me by other staff members in the clinic, and accounted for the purchase of drugs, supplies, and other operational expenses, ordered for that particular doctor's practice. Those bills were called direct expenses.

That doctor's staff ordered the supplies, and approved the invoice, *before* it was given to me, to add to the next settlement statement. There were also direct and shared payroll expenses verified by the attached payroll reports, that broke out each employee's pay, and payroll taxes. After the doctor reviewed his settlement statement, he had five days to write a check for his portion of the bills. The doctors' personal checks were deposited into a checking account (the *zero-balance account*), that I oversaw with the President of the Executive Board, Dr. Swan. I would, in turn, pay the employees and the bills, with the approval of the President,

Dr. Swan, who signed off on everything I did, including being the second signature on the checks. This system was in place before my tenure. I made no changes to it during the time I worked for the doctors.

As the Clinic Administrator, I was not responsible for the doctors' patient insurance billing, or revenue collection. Other employees within the clinic handled all the billing, collections, insurance claims, patient co-pays, and the deposits of revenues for the individual doctors. Some of the doctors even had outside billing services that handled these tasks. Any revenue collected, was deposited directly by the billers, or the outside billing service, into each doctor's individual bank accounts.

I never had access to the doctors' personal business bank accounts, or any of their revenues. I only had access to the *zero*-balance account, which accounted for the expenses of the clinic. The only way money got into the *zero*-balance account was through checks written by the individual doctors that paid their settlement statements, which in turn were deposited into the *zero*-balance account, and then used to pay the clinic expenses–the doctors' bills and payroll.

Working at the doctor's clinic was like nothing I had ever experienced. There was constant drama with the doctors, nurses, and other staff members. It felt more like running a daycare center, than a doctor's office. I soon learned that what I had previously thought about doctors, and their professionalism, was not the case—well, at least not with the group I worked for. Don't get me wrong, several of them genuinely did seem to care about their patients, and displayed a degree of compassion. However, the bulk of them only saw dollar signs. And again, none of them liked each other. I guess it's hard to have that many egos all in one place.

They would constantly argue amongst themselves. It was nothing for them to cuss each other out, and fight over petty things. I recall Dr. Boring and Dr. Moon in the hallway of the clinic, yelling the F word at each other, regardless that patients were present, and could hear them at the time.

We also had monthly meetings with just the doctors and myself. I dreaded those meetings, because what happened in them felt more like a circus, than an actual business meeting. I had come to the job from a very structured public accounting position. I had worked at many other professional jobs in the past, many of them in management positions. *Red flag* number two.

Rascal Jones turned out to be a boisterous tyrant. He was in his early 40s, during the time I worked at the clinic. When I was his accountant, before coming to work at the clinic, he had been pushy but never mean. However, once I became employed at the clinic, I saw him in a much different light. I found him to be overbearing, and a micromanager. He was also disrespectful to women. He spent a lot of time trying to find out about the other doctors' business.

He constantly badgered me to tell him what other doctors were making. Honestly, I had no idea, since I did not handle their billing, nor did I see any of their revenues, and he was aware of this fact. I could not have told him, even if I knew, by the doctors' own agreements. But that did not stop him from asking me anyway. However, he was very secretive about his own business. The worst part about him was his demeaning behavior directed at me, as well as other women who worked in the clinic, and even at female drug reps that frequented the clinic. Honestly, as time went on, he gave me the *heebie jeebies,* with his inappropriate comments towards me, and other women.

Dr. Jones was married and had seven children. One of them had been killed several years before I met him, in what was said to be a tragic accident, that I never found out the details of. He wanted to be the top dog in the group, even though he was the newest member, and didn't have the clout to do so. I found it odd that his wife, who was a stay-at-home mom, was intimately involved in the clinic's business. At one point, I was made to provide the Office Depot bills to her so she could audit them. The last year I worked at the clinic, he built a mansion that was estimated to cost millions, and included an over $200,000 swimming pool.

Years later, during his criminal case, I would be asked to cooperate with the federal government regarding his accounting practices, when federal agents were gathering information to seize his home. This was after he was indicted as the ringleader in a large drug ring. I kindly refused the government's request, as by this time, I was indicted for a second time, myself.

Sam Boring had never married. He was about ten years older than me, small in stature, with graying hair. He had remained at home, living with his mother, until she passed away, a few years before I came to work for the practice. He now lived alone; in the home they had once shared. I found it strange that each year he took his nurse and her husband on vacation with him. It seemed he could never be far from his nurse. He spent a lot of time dining out with her and her husband. I never knew him to date. If he had been female, he would have been referred to as a spinster. I found him to be judgmental; and his personality appeared to be underdeveloped for his age.

However, he was an amazing photographer, and many of his photographs were framed and hung around the clinic. He also had a few disturbing traits about him, such as the way he was always sneaking around the clinic, peering into everything, like a child looking through a glass window at a candy store. Putting his ears up to closed office doors, attempting to listen in to the conversations on the other side. He was certainly the oddest duck in the group.

Butch Swan had an eccentric personality. He was married, and had two grown children. His wife traveled a lot, leaving him at home with their two small designer dogs. He was an older gentleman. However, it was hard to know his real age, due to the amount of work that had been done to his face. He was probably in his mid to late 60s, when I went to work for the group. However, he did not look a day over 50. He was tall, thin, and kept his hair dyed jet black. Every now and then I could see the gray peeking through, but not for long, as he was very vain about his looks. He would dress in expensive clothing, and liked to talk about his world travels.

He was certainly one for keeping up with the Joneses. Of course, not the Rascal Joneses, since the two of them did not get along. He enjoyed dropping the names of well-known people, connections he said he had. He lived the country club lifestyle. Ads for his clinic were often run in local trendy publications, since some years earlier, he had started moving his practice away from internal medicine, to cosmetic medicine. This change may have been out of necessity, since some years earlier, after an insurance audit, he had been banned from accepting certain mainstream insurances, due to what the insurance companies claimed were questionable billing practices.

Dr. Swan liked to brag that his patients were high end. He relished that the other doctors did not have the same type of clientele he had. Indeed, the other doctors were practicing internal medicine, not injecting fillers and Botox into patients.

Jack Thatch was also a tall gentleman with bad scarring on his face, from what appeared to be acne from his younger years. He was roughly my same age. He and his wife both worked at the clinic. She ran their drug trial site that was located inside his practice.

The wife liked to gossip and constantly told anyone who listened, about the doctors' meetings, and other clinic business. From all accounts, Dr. Thatch and his wife had a rocky past, or so the clinic gossip went. Apparently after being caught having an affair at a hospital where he worked as a doctor, and she as a nurse, they married. After filing for bankruptcy, they had briefly moved up North, so he could practice medicine there.

Their son-in-law, who also worked at the clinic, liked to spin tall tales about their past escapades. One such tall tale was a story about how Mrs. Thatch had caused the death of her previous husband, in order to be with Dr. Thatch. What I noticed the most was that Dr. Thatch, and his wife, badly wanted to keep up with the Joneses, including Dr. Rascal Jones. They were constantly trying to figure out ways to obtain luxury items, cars, and a house. Due to their credit issues, and past bankruptcy, they could not even purchase a new car from a car dealership, and were forced to buy from "anyone is financed" car lots, at high interest rates. Given that he was a doctor, I always felt this embarrassed them, and they constantly tried to find ways around it.

Todd Korker was the tallest of the bunch, bald, and was somewhere between the ages of Dr. Boring and Dr. Swan. He and Dr. Swan had an on-going love/hate relationship with each other. I found Dr. Korker to be an intelligent man. From our few conversations, I could tell he had great respect for his wife of many years. While he and I were not close, given my relationship with Dr. Swan, I did like Dr. Korker.

He was however a gruff man, with a suspicious personality. He did not like many of the things that went on at the clinic, including the hiring of me as his Clinic Administrator, since he was very fond of the previous office manager.

And I would years later find out, from the discovery in my criminal case, that he had been reading and printing my, as well as the other doctors, emails. These were not emails through a clinic server; these were emails from our personal email addresses, through private servers. How he had accomplished this, I never found out? But I saw the proof, that he had in fact done so, in the discovery provided to us by the federal government, during my second indictment.

Pete Zorick, was a gray-haired man who was probably in his mid to late 60s, when I became his office manager. He was my absolute favorite out of all the doctors. I found him to be honest, gentle, and to have a true bedside manner. It was obvious he cared greatly about his patients. He was also level headed, and did not get involved in the clinic drama that many of the other doctors seemed to enjoy. I admired him greatly. He was the one I would seek out when the other doctors would fight amongst themselves. He was the voice of reason for the group.

I found him to be a true family man. His children were grown, and he and his wife liked to travel to see them. I enjoyed his pleasant personality. I also trusted him. I would later find out that my trust in him was not necessarily misplaced. However, his memory certainly failed him at times, when he was on the witness stand, during my jury trial.

Charles Black was a young African American gentleman, and the only non-white doctor of the group. We called him the black Doogie Howser. He was probably in his late 30s, or early 40s? He was struggling financially, and I felt that some of this was because he tried to live out of his means. He had allowed one of his nurses to do his patient billing, in order to warrant paying her extra money. Unfortunately, the nurse did not understand medical billing, which constantly caused insurance claims to be rejected, resulting in him not being paid. His accounting firm talked with me many times about his financial situation.

He was the only non-member of the group, and was often treated like the step-child, by the other doctors. He and Dr. Korker were very close. Dr. Black often made weekend rounds for Dr. Swan, so that Dr. Swan could go to his lake house, and do whatever it was he did there. I liked Dr. Black. I tried many times to help him budget better, and get on his feet. I tried my best to get him to use a billing company, instead of his nurse. But he was loyal to his staff, regardless that it was hurting him financially.

I always felt he got the short end of the stick by the other doctors, due to being the only non-voting member of the group. Later the government would tell my attorney that I was the reason this doctor went bankrupt. Obviously, this was untrue, and the government knew it. Regardless of the government's lies, they never brought up Dr. Black's bankruptcy at my trial, nor did they call him as a witness.

John Moon was an older gentleman, and very close to retirement age, when I went to work for the clinic. He was standoffish, therefore, I never got to know him very well. He left the practice roughly two years into my tenure there. He was short, had gray hair, and was reclusive. However, he did have a feisty side, as he often argued with other doctors in the group. He had no problem standing his ground. I found him to be a little abrasive. However, he was always pleasant to me, and treated me respectfully.

Shortly after I began working for the doctors, Dr. Swan made it a point to befriend me. He would stop in at my office every morning, for a chat. He made me aware that he would protect my job, and that he was the one in charge. At the time, I didn't know what my job needed protecting from? However, in this way, he groomed me into thinking he was on my side, and in essence, got me to do what he wanted in the long run. We often prayed together in my office, regarding the situation with JT and Timothy's mother.

In this way, he gained my trust. He was also kind enough to send me flowers on my birthday, and give gifts to my children, on theirs. I confided in him about my dad's suicide, which I never share. After that, he always told me I was like a daughter to him. I now realize this was just him grooming me, and using manipulation, to play on a very vulnerable part of my life. At the time, I didn't recognize it as such. It wasn't too long into my tenure, as his office manager, that Dr. Swan, and a few of the other doctors, started requesting that I pick up things for them, using my personal credit card, and be reimbursed for these items, when I was paid by the clinic, every two weeks. While this started on a small scale, Dr. Swan soon took full advantage of it.

Within a few months, I was leaving work often, sometimes several times a day, and even being called on the weekend, and after hours, to do things of a personal nature for him. From the previous accounting records, I could tell that he had done something very similar in the past, with one of the previous office managers. I could also see evidence from the past financial records, of him paying his personal bills through the clinic. Many of the things Dr. Swan requested that I purchase for him, were of a personal nature. Let's just say that Dr. Swan had a secret lifestyle that he enjoyed outside of his medical practice. And it was not a secret to those who worked in the clinic.

Dr. Swan spent a lot of time at his lake house, living out this secret life, with his male friends. He often used the excuse "I'm hiding money from my wife," to keep me charging things on my personal credit cards for him. At the time, my husband and I were dealing with his custody issues with his ex-wife, and the transition of JT and Timothy, having recently come to live with us. My personal life was somewhat chaotic, due to everything going on at our home, with the change of custody.

Admittedly, I was just trying to get through life in those moments. It was a hard time for us in our own family. I honestly didn't care about what Dr. Swan did in his own personal life. I honestly gave it no thought, as I had my own issues to deal with. And I've never been a judgmental person anyway. I went along with whatever he told me, and charged whatever he asked. However, at the end of my first year of employment, I faced a moral dilemma. Dr. Swan wanted me to go into the QuickBooks accounting software, and reclassify the personal items I had picked up for him, as business expenses. *Red flag* number three.

At first, I was reluctant to do so, and my conscience went back and forth, in an argument with myself. In the end, I was already in too deep, and it was hard to say no at that point, so I came around to Dr. Swan's way of thinking. I justified it, by reminding myself, that I was not his accountant, nor responsible for his tax work. From my previous work in public accounting, I knew that many clients try to sneak in personal expenses, as business expenses. I had never known a client to be charged with tax fraud. However, I did think at the time, "if Dr. Swan ever gets audited, he will have a lot of penalties and interest to pay." But I knew from my past public accounting work, that more than likely, his accountant would reclassify these expenses, when his tax work was done anyway.

I blindly told myself that it was not my place to police him, or his business practices. And right then and there, I got off God's plan, and onto Dr. Swan's plan. I sold my ethics and morals, to keep my job, and to make my direct supervisor happy. And honestly, I did not give it much thought, as I had my own personal life to deal with. At the time, my family and

I was constantly dealing with family court, and custody issues, as well as blending a family.

And, Dr. Swan made it easy for me to see things his way, as he constantly did nice things for me. And because of all the nice things he did, I went along with what he wanted. Most likely, for my own selfish reasons. One of the things he approved as President was for me to arrive at work at 6:00 a.m., and leave at 3:00 p.m. This schedule worked out great for me, since it allowed Pancho to drop the boys off at school in the morning, and allowed me to pick them up in the afternoon.

I was able to take them to sports practices, help them with homework, and cook dinner for them. recognize now how Dr. Swan was able to groom me into thinking he was on my side, which led to me doing whatever he wanted me to do for him. However, it would be unfair for me not to acknowledge my own selfish motives, motives that helped lead me down this path of no return. It was the easy road I chose to take, never giving any thought to how my poor choices would end up harming my family.

As time went on, Dr. Swan began to tell me that he was keeping me from getting fired. It made sense at the time. I had heard rumblings of the other doctors complaining to the billing staff about me being gone so much from work, due to running personal errands for Dr. Swan. Apparently, the other doctors thought he monopolized my time. And truthfully, they were correct. These complaints got so bad that one day Dr. Swan had me figure out my salary to the minute, based on the amount of time I was gone the previous day, doing personal errands for him.

He then proceeded to have me go down to the bank, and cash a personal check he wrote. He instructed me to get the exact amount in change, owed to each of the other doctors, for their part of my time he had used the previous day. He had me place the change (quarters, dimes, nickels, and pennies) in seven envelopes, representing the amount of time he owed, to the other seven doctors. He then instructed me to pass the envelopes out. Of course, I was the one the other doctors got angry with, not Dr. Swan.

This is just one example of the dysfunction that plagued the practice, and affected my job, as well as the other shared clinic employees, on a daily basis. The jealousy between the doctors was always a factor. Everyone found a personal gripe with the other members of the group. At the time, I was more focused on our family's drama, which was continuously playing out in family court.

And as time went on, Dr. Swan became more and more dependent on me being his Girl Friday, and I charged more and more personal expenses for him, on my credit cards. After a while, it seemed like it was just part of my everyday job, and I didn't even see it as odd any longer. Yet something was always there nagging at me, my conscience.

My husband, however, did not see these errands as part of my job, and began to resent the interruptions to our life. Dr. Swan often called me at home, to ask me to run errands for him. These calls took place after hours, and on the weekends, and did not sit well with my husband. Admittedly, we had enough going-on at our own home, on the weekends at the time. And because of Pancho's increasing annoyance with the issue, I failed to disclose to him that it was our personal credit cards paying for Dr. Swan' errands, or that he was reimbursing me as employee expense reimbursement, through electronic payroll.

I certainly did not tell my CPA husband that at Dr. Swan's request and prompting, I had recorded personal purchases I made for Dr. Swan, to business expenses in the QuickBooks I kept for the practice. Repayment for these expenses also became an issue for me, as time went on, when Dr. Swan started dragging his reimbursement payments to me out, longer and longer each time. Sometimes he would allow himself to owe me for months, until the amounts became rather large, before he would reimburse me. This was frustrating, as he was depositing the amounts of monies he owed me, into the *zero-balance* account, with his every two weeks settlement statement. The money was just sitting there, but he would not authorize me to reimburse myself.

It became frustrating that he would not authorize reimbursement payments to me in a timely manner. And this made me incur interest on my personal credit cards, that I eventually started adding to the balance he owed me. At the time, I could not understand why he was dragging it out. I now realize that larger payments were most likely more convincing to his accountant, since he was having me classify most of the expenses as drug expenses.

By the time he started doing things this way, I was too afraid to approach him about it, because he had convinced me that he was protecting my job. And in all honesty, I didn't want to deal with it, mainly because I had too much to deal with at home, given the continued family court, and custody issues that were in high swing, during the time I worked for the doctors. Crossing Dr. Swan was not something I cared to do, so I continued the status quo. And in reality, it had already gone on for too long, for me to turn back now. Most days, I never even gave it a thought.

Several years into my tenure, another issue arose, when Dr. Jones found out what I was doing for Dr. Swan, and wanted me to do the same thing for him. I had already purchased business related things in the past for him, as well as for many of the other doctors, and been reimbursed by them. But now Dr. Jones saw it as a way to hide income. He was not happy when I told him I could not do it. There was no way I could charge that much on my personal credit cards, for two doctors.

And this was long after Dr. Swan had started being slow to pay me, and I was already accruing interest on my credit cards, due to his slow to pay attitude. When I refused, Dr. Jones was angered, and he and Dr. Swan had words. This also started discussions amongst the other doctors about outing Dr. Swan as President—as many of the doctors felt he was monopolizing my time as their clinic administrator. Another coup to overthrow the Executive Board was brewing.

This time I was not a participant in the behind closed-door meetings. I was the topic of those meetings, as I would later read about, in the discovery in my criminal case.

The best my first attorney and I could piece together, from the discovery we received from the government, was that originally some of the doctors wanted to overthrow Dr. Swan as President, because they suspected that I was somehow in a plot with him, to cheat them in some manner. The doctors thought I was somehow billing them for part of Dr. Swan' bills. Why they thought this, is unbeknownst to me?

The doctors had received settlement statements every two weeks, with the supporting documents attached. These statements clearly showed they were not being cheated. However, it was very similar to what they had accused the previous office manager of doing with Dr. Korker. History repeating itself. Maybe the doctors just weren't very good at math? I must admit, that even I was taken aback, when I first saw the amounts in the wire fraud counts, in my first indictment.

The wire fraud represented the reimbursements from Dr. Swan, for what I had charged on my personal credit cards. Even I was shocked to see that over my four years working for the doctors, I had been reimbursed $611,000.00. At first, I thought this had to be a mistake, surely the math was incorrect?

However, after I went back, and got my credit card records for my attorney, we soon saw that this was undoubtedly the case. Actually, I had charged even more than the $611,000, as I left the practice, with Dr. Swan still owing money to me, for personal items I had charged for him, that I was never reimbursed .

Chapter Four
Beginning of the End

On June 18, 2010, I went to work just like every other Friday. Little did I realize that it would be a day that would haunt me, probably for the rest of my life. As another benefit, for being his Girl Friday, Dr. Swan allowed me to leave at noon on Fridays. Looking back now, that feels more like manipulation, than a benefit.

But at the time, I saw it as a benefit, in my blind selfishness, and took full advantage of it. On this particular Friday, I was to be treated at noon by Dr. Jones for my torn rotator cuff. The treatment was the same as many times before, as I had suffered from the torn rotator cuff since early 2009. On that day, I was to get the same type of steroid shot that Dr. Jones had given me many times in the past.

I was looking forward to leaving work after the shot, and heading home for the weekend. I don't remember my family's specific plans. However, I do remember that I felt good that day, and the sun was shining brightly outside. I remember feeling happy. My husband and I were in the process of building a new home. We had secured a construction loan in late 2009, and were close to being finished with the building of that house. It was taking shape, and I had enjoyed helping to design, and pick out every last detail, of the paint, flooring, and other aesthetics for the home.

What seemed like a typical day, would turn out much different than I ever expected. And it would be the last time I felt true happiness, for a very long time. I should have listened to that little voice in my head, but as had become commonplace for me during this season of my life, I ignored the *red flags*. I set myself on a course that would forever change my life, and the lives of those who loved me, mainly my husband, and children.

For starters, Dr. Jones had made many past remarks to me that were sexual in nature, making me feel very uncomfortable. But I had chosen to ignore them—thinking because I was not interested in pursuing them, there was no harm. While it was degrading to be asked if my breasts were natural—in his words, "you have a nice rack, are those real?" I didn't want to lose my good job with all the benefits. I told myself that I could handle the degrading comments to keep my job, and if I ignored them, they would just go away. I ignored the damage these remarks were doing to my psyche, and the disrespect I was allowing of myself. Looking back now, I'm confused as to why I was allowing him to treat my shoulder in the first place, given everything else that was already going on with him. But as was that season of my life, I was just doing whatever it took to get by at my job, and in my home life as well.

Dr. Jones was already being sued, as were the other doctors of the practice, by an ex-employee. A nurse, who worked directly for Dr. Jones had alleged that he had sexually harassed her, and that the other doctors in the clinic had covered for him. Her allegation was that Dr. Jones had sexually harassed her with degrading comments, and even inappropriate touching, during an exam of her breasts.

The lawsuit said that when the nurse complained about him, he and the other doctors in the clinic got revenge by firing her. And that after her firing, the doctors reported her to the nursing licensing board, reporting that she wrote prescriptions, without Dr. Jones' permission. This in turn, caused her to be placed on probation, with her nursing license. She was not the only nurse that had made complaints, as similar complaints had been made in the past against the doctors.

And she was not the only nurse, who had lost their license, because of the doctors' unfounded reports on them. Huge *red flags*, once again, ignored by me. And enough *red flags*, that I should not have allowed Doctor Jones to treat any of my medical needs.

There were many other *red flags* that I also chose to ignore. I had felt uncomfortable many times when Dr. Jones was in my office, and would come around to my side of the desk. He would accidentally, so I thought at the time, rub himself up against me, and invade my personal space. He also often told me inappropriate jokes that I did not care to hear. As well as made many inappropriate remarks, besides the ones about my breasts.

I would later find out that I was not the only female he had done this to. I should have spoken up about these things, but as many women do in the workplace, I remained silent and took the abuse. And again, I had selfish motives for wanting to stay at my job, due to the extra benefits provided by Dr. Swan, as well as the $75,000 a year I was being paid at the time.

But on that particular Friday in June 2010, everything changed—all those *red flags* I had previously ignored, came full circle. During my exam for my rotator cuff, I was knocked out briefly, by the steroid shot, I was given by Dr. Jones. I was alone with him in the exam room, which is clearly against protocol, when a female patient is being treated by a male physician. When I woke up, I was being sexually assaulted. The details are still too raw, and too private, so I have decided not to include them in this book.

I will clarify that I was not raped, but I was physically touched inappropriately, which is considered sexual assault. I believe Dr. Jones put something in the shot that day that made me pass out. I had been getting the same shots for over a year, without any previous issues. I now realize that the comments and invasion of my personal space were Dr. Jones' way of warming up, to do what he did that day. *Red flags* I choose to ignore.

I left work that day, and drove home. I pretended that nothing had happened. I was numb and sick. I remember feeling dirty. I could not wait to take a shower, and wash off the disgust I felt. I didn't even tell my husband at first. I was scared, but most of all, I wanted to pretend it had not happened. Maybe if I pretended hard enough, the pain would disappear, and I'd never have to face it? Maybe I would wake up, and find out that it was just a bad dream? And selfishly, I still wanted to keep my job.

I have since learned that this is a perfectly normal response to what happened to me that day, but at the time, I felt lost. It was like an out-of-body experience, and I felt like I was looking down on myself, as if I were someone else. I kept asking myself, "What did I do to deserve this?" "Did I say or do something for him to think it was okay to do this to me?" "Was I naïve to trust him when there were so many *red flags*?" "Was I the stupid one?" I was unaware at the time that he had previously done this to other patients, who would later come forward, but not for many years down the road.

There are so many emotions that come in waves when you go through a traumatic event. You go from numb, to angry, to sad, to angry again, and then back to numb. The cycle just keeps repeating itself. It's probably a lot like grieving, from the sudden loss, of someone close to you. I could not sleep. I had to be medicated to stay asleep. I did everything I could do not to think about it, but the thoughts would not leave me. I would wake up screaming, in full-blown panic/anxiety attack mode, at night.

I still have nights like this, where I have nightmares that wake me up in a panic. I don't like being alone with strange men. And one of my biggest fears before I reported to federal prison, was being handcuffed by a male guard, or being placed in a vulnerable position with one.

A few weeks went by, and I was still forced to work with Dr. Jones. I confided in Dr. Swan, about the incident, on the Monday after it happened. He said he would speak to the other doctors and get back to me. He assured me it would be handled, and that I would not have to work with Dr. Jones ever again. He assured me that Dr. Jones would be gone from the clinic. Dr. Swan didn't like him anyway. Now he had a reason to have him removed from the group.

I requested meetings with the other doctors and confided in Dr. Thatch's wife, who also worked at the clinic. Nothing happened. I could not get away from Dr. Jones. He continued to say inappropriate things to me. These statements made my skin crawl, just being in his presence, made my skin crawl. Dr. Swan wrote me a prescription for Xanax, an anti-anxiety medicine. I was dependent on it to make me numb during the day, just so I could make it through the stress of it all, and also to get to sleep at night.

My anxiety was through the roof, and the panic attacks escalated. I was finally forced to tell my husband what had happened. We were very close to closing on our permanent loan, for the home we had just built, and it was not the time for me to quit my job. And we were hopeful that the other doctors would do something to rectify the situation.

But the situation continued to get worse for me at work. I kept some of the da- to-day details from my husband, because I did not want him to pressure me to quit my job. I did however start looking for another job, but I was in no shape mentally, to get serious about job interviews. And my selfish motives, wanted to stay at the job I was at, due to Dr. Swan's extra benefit of allowing me to leave work early each day. And truthfully, I just didn't have it in me to change jobs at the time. Reflecting back, my life was spiraling out of control, but I didn't even recognize it. I was just going through the motions, and not thinking straight at all.

A few weeks after I was assaulted, and while waiting on the other doctors to do something about the situation, Dr. Jones cornered me up in an exam room. He was invading my personal space, saying things to me about my complaints to the other doctors. He actually had me backed into a corner, where I had no way out of the room, except through him. I was scared, but trying hard not to panic. At that very moment, Dr. Thatch walked past the exam room, as he made his way down the hallway. I knew he saw what was going on. I yelled for him to help me. I knew he was aware of what had happened on that day in June, because it was his wife I had confided in, and she told me she had alerted him to the incident. And I had every reason to believe Dr. Swan, that the other doctors were already in discussions to get rid of Dr. Jones. To my surprise, Dr. Thatch yelled back, "You're on your own," as he continued to walk down the hallway, making no efforts to help me.

That was the day I decided enough was enough! I contacted an attorney's office for advice. At first, I refused to give them my name. I only spoke to them under anonymity. I was still scared. We were about to close on the house we had built, and at the time, I thought I needed to protect my job. Finally, after a few weeks of talking to the attorney, I was forced to disclose my name, because I had to hire her to represent me, since I was still being forced to work with Dr. Jones.

It had become apparent that the other doctors were not about to do anything to him, as it came down to money. They did not want to pick up his part of the shared expenses. Since it was not my intent to file a lawsuit, the attorney suggested that I schedule a meeting with the doctors' Executive Board, to discuss the matter. I tried for weeks to do so, to no avail.

In early August 2010, I took off work on a Friday, so I could take Joseph to college, and help him move into his college dormitory room. It was his first semester of college. When I returned the following Monday, I found a memo that had been slid under the door to my office, on the previous Friday. The memo simply said that a new Executive Board had been elected. And just like that I had a new boss, the new President, Dr. Boring.

I text messaged Dr. Swan, and he replied back that "Brucie will return with a butcher knife." And said, "The pay for the job was not very good anyway." He told me to "Learn how to do billing so we can leave this place." He informed me that he was planning on leaving the practice, and wanted to take me with him. He instructed me to get busy finding him a billing software, to use at his new location.

I immediately wrote a memo to the new President,

requesting a meeting with the Executive Board, regarding my complaints on Dr. Jones. Nothing happened. I was frustrated. But mostly, I was just scared, and stressed out. Every day I was forced to deal with Dr. Jones, and he became more aggressive, as the days went on. He had become brazen with his advances toward me.

One day, he demanded that I come downstairs to the parking deck, to his truck, to get his settlement statement payment check, for his portion of the bills. When I refused, he told me I would be fired for disobeying him. I continued to request meetings with the Executive Board. Dr. Swan started blaming the lack of getting a meeting on the new President, probably more manipulation to keep me thinking he was on my side. And maybe he still was at the time? Dr. Swan also began to talk daily to me, about leaving the practice, and wanting me to go with him.

About a month after the new President took office, I was out for a few days, when Timothy was sick. I was in phone conversations with Dr. Swan during the few days I was at home. He had me consulting with the billing software sales representative, during this time. He was finalizing plans to leave the practice for sure, now that he was voted out as the President, and was no longer in charge.

He was putting pressure on me to move with him. He wanted me to be his office manager. We were in discussions regarding my pay, and if he could afford financially, to pay my salary by himself. He felt confident he could pay me what I was already making, if I would learn his billing. I was hesitant. I felt Medicare fraud was a real possibility, with how the doctors billed. As their office manager, I had brought in two attorneys to show them the error of their billing practices, only each time to be shut down, as they voted to continue the status quo, even though attorneys had advised that what they were doing was Medicare and Stark II violations.

However, I was desperate to get away from Dr. Jones. As the Clinic Administrator, I did not touch billing at my current position. Although, I had turned a blind eye to the *red flags* regarding the doctors' billing, and knew they were most likely breaking the law. Again, allowing selfishness, to rule over ethics, and morals. I had blindly told myself that since I did not touch billing, I was not the one doing wrong, although, as the Office Manager, I did supervise all the clinic staff, including the ladies who did the billing. Even though in reality, I knew nothing about billing, or the job, the billers actually did.

Regardless, it was always at the back of my mind. What if the doctors got caught, and blamed me? I had heard of bookkeepers having to pay payroll taxes that were not paid in by their employer. This was one reason, that I had always put my foot down, when the doctors had tried to late pay the payroll taxes, at the clinic. I was not about to get the blame for that, especially since I was responsible for doing the payroll, with the President's approval, and signing off on it. What if the blame game worked the same for Medicare? I was not willing to take that chance!

Because of the need for me to do billing for Dr. Swan, for him to warrant my pay, I told him that I would continue to pray about the job. I said I would think about leaving the clinic, to go with him. Part of me wanted to go, but the other part was just buying time, until I could find another job. I had started getting serious about other employment, and had sent my resume out to several other places. While I desperately wanted to get away from Dr. Jones, I was scared to work for Dr. Swan.

It's one thing, to turn a blind eye to something like Medicare fraud, but it would be another, to take part in it, by participating in the billing process. And while Dr. Swan did very little internal medicine, as he was phasing out of that practice, he did enough that I did not want to take the chance. I knew that all the patients he still had were old, and most likely, all of them had Medicare. And I did not want to leave the clinic, before I could get something done about Dr. Rascal Jones. I feared if I did not stand up, he would continue to do what he did to me, to other women. I felt guilty that I had not defended the nurse better. At the time, I was still not aware of what he had already done to other patients.

Fortunately, the decision was made for me, without me ever having to make it. I feel confident, at that point in my life, I would have made the wrong one, and been in even deeper trouble, than I already was at that point. When I returned to work the following Monday, I could not get my key to work to get into the clinic door.

I called the ladies that worked for me. I could see them through the glass door of the front entrance of the clinic, but they would not answer their cell phones, or the clinic phone. I called several of the doctors' cell phones, including Dr. Swan, but none of them answered. I had no choice, but to leave a message on the doctors' voicemails, and return home. Later that same morning, I received a call from Dr. Boring, the new President. The Executive Board was willing to meet with me at noon that day. I instructed him that I would bring my attorney with me.

I knew the doctors were not happy about the attorney I had hired, because she also represented the nurse that was already suing them, for Dr. Jones' sexual harassment. But she was the only employment attorney I knew to call at the time. Dr. Boring would not tell me why I was locked out of the clinic, but I assumed I was being fired, since I had complained so much about the sexual assault. After all, I had seen what the doctors did to other employees, who dared to cross them. It was not surprising, and I had sort of brought it on myself, by ignoring all those *red flags* along the way.

At noon on September 20, 2010, I met my attorney in the parking lot, and we proceeded to the meeting we had been requesting for months. The Executive Board and their attorney were present. However, to our surprise, they were not willing to discuss the sexual assault, but instead were accusing me of wrongdoing. I was in shock.

I immediately offered to cooperate. I suggested they have a financial audit. I knew I had done nothing wrong, and was anxious to get this matter cleared up. During the meeting, it was decided that I would be placed on administrative leave with pay. My attorney and I, accompanied the Executive Board and their attorney, back to my office, where I found out they had also changed the lock to my office door, and locked me out of my work computer, by changing my password, on the previous Friday, when I had been off work.

I was only allowed to take a few of my personal items from my office. While accompanied by my attorney, I also showed Dr. Boring, and their attorney, where all the financial documents were kept, including all the copies of settlement statements, and the backup documentation, for the current, and past years. I knew they would need this information to conduct the financial audit I had suggested.

In the presence of the doctors' attorney, I also gave the Executive Board President, Dr. Boring, the keys to the storage closet, that housed the boxes upon boxes, stacked all the way to the ceiling, of financial documents. I took him, and his attorney, to the storage closet, and opened it with the key, so they could see all the boxes. I also pulled out all the file cabinet drawers in my office, and showed them the most current financial records. I gave him all the other keys to the clinic I had in my possession.

My attorney requested that the doctors' attorney preserve all the financial documents, and my work computer. She and the other attorney were talking in legal language, which I did not understand at the time. I stood there numb and in shock. I was barely aware of my surroundings at all. I felt sick. All I could think was why? Why were they accusing me of wrongdoing? I never saw it coming, because I never wanted to address the *red flags*. Deep down, I knew what they did to employees, that dared to cross them.

All I had wanted was for them to put a stop to Dr. Jones. I never threatened them, or planned to sue them. I had made that clear from the beginning. I had not gone to the police, or made any reports against them, or Dr. Jones. I just needed them to protect me. Obviously, the doctors had other plans.

I wanted to resign immediately, and I discussed this with my attorney. However, my husband and I were about to close on the final loan for the house we had built, and I felt that I needed to stay employed until we closed in a few weeks. It was not a time for our household to lose $75,000 a year in income. We had two excellent incomes when we took out the construction loan, so we assumed we would need both of those incomes, to close on the permanent financing.

After all, it was a rather large mortgage loan amount. I would later find out this was not the case, and that my husband's income alone qualified us for the loan. But at the time, I stayed employed by the doctors, to assure our loan was closed. I would not be required to come into the office during this time anyway, since I was on administrative leave, so I would not be forced to deal with Dr. Jones.

I was still in phone talks with Dr. Swan, and he was still wanting me to work for him. He called me many times, during the time I was on administrative leave. He even had me figure out his monthly sales tax report for him. He was in the dark about what was going on, since he had been voted out as President, or so he said. He assured me it would all be fixed, and that "the other doctors would then have egg on their faces." There were many text messages to me from him, stating as much. Text messages he would later lie about at my trial. Until my attorney showed him the proof.

My husband and I closed the permanent loan for the house we built, on September 30, 2010. The following day, October 1, 2010, I resigned. My attorney sent my resignation letter directly to the doctors' attorney. I felt I could never go back to work for the doctors. They had basically accused me of theft. I also felt they were doing so, because of the sexual assault, and my insistence that they do something about it. I never wanted to see Dr. Jones again, and I could no longer take the stress of working with him. It was apparent that the other doctors planned on protecting him, not me.

They had surrounded the camp with the wagons, just like they had done when the nurse reported the sexual harassment, by the same doctor. And I knew from her experience and others, that they would do anything to protect their own.

After I quit, I never heard from the doctors again, except for Dr. Swan, who continued to call me, for a few weeks after my resignation. He still said he wanted me to come to work for him. But soon, even his calls stopped, and honestly, I was happy I didn't have to deal with him either. At the time, he still owed me money for things I had charged for him, but I was willing to just write that off, in order to move on with my life. The less I had to focus on the past, the better.

I was never contacted or asked any questions by the doctors' Certified Public Accountant, whom I assumed was doing an audit. Even though my attorney had sent the doctors' attorney a letter, reminding him to preserve all the evidence, and reaffirming my willingness to cooperate with the audit, we heard nothing.

I assumed that the audit had shown what had really happened, that I had done nothing wrong, and the doctors had moved on with their lives. I was scared to report the sexual assault, because I had already seen what the doctors did to employees who crossed them. I did not want to be prevented from getting future employment. Truthfully, I had hoped I could just forget about it, and move on with my own life.

Little did I know what the doctors really had up their sleeves, or that they had already put the wheels of "in"justice into motion. I would later find out, after I was indicted the first time, that Dr. Boring had actually reported me to the Federal Bureau of Investigations (FBI) on November 28, 2010, for theft, and later to the Little Rock Police Department (LRPD), when the FBI had no interest in the case. The reporting of me to the LRPD, is how the Secret Service became involved.

Shortly before my first indictment, President Obama had appointed federal agents to work with local police departments on a federal task force. The LRPD had a brand-new agent, who had just been hired by the Secret Service, one month previously. The agent was newly part of the Obama Task Force at the LRPD. Now my case has come to his attention. And he had discovered that we had money in our checking and savings accounts, that he could use the *Patriot Act* to seize. My attorney believes this is why I was indicted so quickly, and without any investigation, into the allegations against me. I would soon find out that asset seizure, and forfeitures, are big money for government agencies.

After I resigned, I tried to move on with my life, but it was hard. I was angry, scared, sad, and disappointed in myself, and others, along with many other emotions that consume your life, when faced with trauma. My husband was supportive, but he had no idea what to do to help me. I sought counseling, and medicine, for depression and anxiety. I struggled to forget the assault. Christmas came and went, and a new year, 2011, began. In February 2011, we bought a new puppy, and named her Olivia. I was busy trying to housebreak her, and find a new job.

This kept my mind occupied for most of the day. It was a nice distraction. But the pain of what had happened was still raw, and I continued to need medicine just to sleep, and make it through some days. The nights were the hardest. I dreaded going to sleep, because I did not want to dream about the assault.

I believe a sexual assault is one of the hardest things that a person can go through, or recover from. If you find yourself dealing with a situation like mine, my advice is to go directly to the police, and make a report. Do not try to handle the situation yourself, or pretend it did not occur. You will need support, and professional help, to get through the pain and trauma. And, the person who assaulted you, should be held accountable. Medication does not work long term. Do not allow others to bully you into thinking that you should just walk away, and turn a blind eye to what has happened. I later found out that Dr. Jones had assaulted many other patients, not just me. The other doctors had covered it up, and had even lied to protect him during the police investigation. If only I hadn't ignored all those *red flags*.

A local newspaper editor, Gwen Moritz, wrote a story on September 3, 2012, *Little Rock Internist Rascal Jones Subject of Renewed Police Investigation* (real name of doctor changed to Rascal Jones), in the *Arkansas Business,* detailing the accusations, by multiple patients, that Dr. Jones had sexually assaulted them. In the article, she interviewed the detective that was investigating the case. This was the same detective that told my attorney and me that the doctors had lied to him during the investigation to protect Dr. Jones.

Of course, the story in the *Arkansas Business* was two years after I quit working for the doctors. The same reporter wrote another story on the same day, *Doctor Has Twice Reported Nurses Who Complained*. That article, detailed actions taken by Dr. Jones, against nurses' licenses when they dared to speak out against him, confirming that the nurse who sued the doctors, was not the only employee, who had their nursing license attacked for speaking out.

Several years later, after Dr. Jones pled guilty for being the ring leader in a drug conspiracy case, another article appeared in *Arkansas Business* on August 30, 2017, detailing the nine years Dr. Jones had been sentenced to federal prison for selling fraudulent painkiller prescriptions. While the following quote from the August 30th article has nothing to do with my criminal case, I share it as additional information, because I believe it is relevant to Dr. Jones' state of mind, regarding his assault of patients, including me. Dr. Jones' comments to the judge at his sentencing hearing are quoted in the article. "I'm not the same man I was two years ago," he said, describing a period of psychological treatment and religious meditation" (real name of doctor changed to Dr. Jones).

While serving time at FPC Bryan, I met another person who had also been charged in the painkiller prescription drug conspiracy with Dr. Jones. She told me a story about how he had made her uncomfortable with his sexual remarks toward her. She said, "He is a very sick man." I couldn't agree more. I now pray for him and his family. However, I have to admit that there was a time that I hated him for what he had done to me, and at times he still haunts my dreams.

With God's help, I have been able to heal from this nightmare. I know HE sustains me. Our God is mighty. HE can restore all things! HE is always there walking this path with us, if only we allow HIM. Turn to HIM with your heartache and grief. Pray to HIM to restore your soul. Jeremiah 17:14 "Heal me, O Lord, and I shall be healed; save me, and I shall be saved, for you are my praise.

Chapter Five
Ignoring RED Flags-
Indictment #1

The song *Even If* by the group Mercy Me, contains some incredibly accurate lyrics. "They say sometimes you win some, sometimes you lose some. And right now, right now I'm losing bad. It's easy to sing when there's nothing to bring me down. But what will I say when I'm held to the flame like I am right now?"

Looking back to March 5, 2011, it's hard to believe I've made it this far, but I know that would not be the case, without God's grace and mercy. March 5, 2011, was the day I went to my mailbox, and retrieved a letter that told me I had been indicted on March 2, 2011, just three days earlier, by a grand jury, in the Eastern District of Arkansas. You may be wondering why nobody came to arrest me? Did I know I was being investigated? Did I expect the letter? The answer to all of those questions would be NO! I had no idea. There was no raid of my home by the FBI, or any other government agency, and none of the things you read about in the news, or see on TV shows, happened to me.

I was never questioned by detective, a federal agent, or any other law enforcement personnel. I was never asked or allowed to tell my side of the story. I didn't even know I was under investigation. The letter had been sent to me by the District Court, from the United States Probation Office (USPO), pretrial division. The letter only instructed me to call their office and make an appointment. It didn't even tell me what I had been indicted for, or any other pertinent information. My husband was out of town at a client's location, and not due to be home for a few days. I was confused and scared. But I did not want to tell him about this over the phone. When we got home from the airport that Friday evening, I told him. He was as confused as I was.

As crazy as it sounds, when you are federally indicted, you are on pretrial probation, which strips you of all your civil liberties, before you have even been convicted of a crime. I have found that in our criminal justice system, you are "guilty until proven innocent," not the other way around. This is especially true in federal cases, where there is no "guilt beyond a reasonable doubt," like in state cases. In the federal system, your guilt is decided upon, by the "preponderance of the evidence." There is a massive difference.

While on pretrial, you are required to turn over your passport, take drug screenings, regardless if you have a history of drug use or not, allow your house to be checked by a pretrial officer any time, day or night. They can just show up unannounced, and look in any closet, drawer, or another part of your home, if they so choose. And not just your stuff. Your family has to submit to these searches of their private home, and belongings, if they want you to be able to continue to live with them. While I found the pretrial officers to be friendly, and none of them ever came to my home unannounced, nor did they go through my belongings, or my family's belongings, it was still unnerving, living with the threat of someone coming to your home, anytime they wanted, to rifle through your stuff.

While under indictment, you must tell the pretrial officer where you work, and report any changes in employment immediately. You must agree that the United States Probation Office (USPO) may come to your work, and discuss your case with your current employer, even though you have only been charged with a crime, not found guilty of one. You must not move without your probation officer's permission. You are not allowed to have a gun in your home.

You must report to them in person, by phone, or by electronic monitoring, at whatever increments they require of you. Along with many other rules, such as allowing them access to your medical records, and informing them of any prescription drugs you are prescribed. You are also required to get permission from them, before you are allowed to travel, or go outside of the county in which you live. They can even dictate what type of job you are allowed to work at, while on pretrial release. Pretrial release means remaining free, while awaiting the outcome of your case.

When I read the letter from the USPO's office, my first thought was that my past employers had finally been caught committing Stark II and Medicare Fraud. The chance of my employers being charged with Medicare fraud, had been one of my biggest fears, when I worked for them. I chose to ignore a huge *red flag* when I stayed employed for doctors, I saw being unethical at every turn. After all, I had been in those meetings where I watched the doctors vote to continue their fraudulent billing practices, when both times the attorneys I brought in to advise them, told them it was a fraud, and fixable. Regardless, even knowing this, I carried on, and selfishly kept my job, not considering that doing so, could cost my family and me so much more in the long run, than just the loss of a job.

Once I read the letter, I had just retrieved from my mailbox that day, I stood in shock for what seemed like forever, then, I picked up the phone and called the attorney who represented me during the sexual assault incident with Dr. Jones. She was as stunned as I was, that I had been indicted. Nobody had reached out to her, and like me, she had assumed that the audit had revealed the truth that I had done nothing wrong, and the doctors had moved on. In fact, we thought they were just accusing me of wrongdoing, to make me go away, due to the sexual assault.

When she looked up my indictment on pacer, she asked, "Lynn, are you sitting down?" I responded, "I can if I need to." She then advised me that I had been indicted for wire fraud for stealing $611,000 from the doctors. I immediately fell to my knees on my kitchen floor. I couldn't move or breathe. I was in shock. How could this be? There had to be a mistake!

I would later find out that what had happened on March 2,

2011, was that the LRPD Task Force Secret Service Agent, along with an Assistant United States Attorney (AUSA–government prosecutor), had told a grand jury, that I had inflated invoices, and stolen $611,000 from the doctors, through the *zero*-balance checking account. The indictment alleged that this had happened through wire transfers, those wire transfers, were reimbursements through electronic payroll, for the items I had charged for Dr. Swan, and a couple of the other doctors.

In one of the pretrial hearings, it would be discovered that neither the Agent, nor the AUSA, had reviewed any invoices to verify that I had done what I was being accused of. Nor did they show the grand jury any physical proof of what they told them I had done to be charged. Instead, the government took the doctors' word for it, went to the grand jury, and indicted me.

In our judiciary system, the grand jury is supposed to be a check and balance between the prosecutor and the person being charged. Members of the grand jury are supposed to see evidence that a crime has been committed for there to be a true bill returned. I would later find out that the doctors had also caused all of their financial documents to be shredded by a company called Shred-It, on February 18, 2011, just a few weeks before I would be indicted for the first time. They also had my work computer hauled away, and destroyed. Everything that would have proven my innocence, had been hauled away and destroyed, or shredded.

On the flip side, that same evidence would have proven my guilt, if what I had been accused, was actually true, and the government had failed to take possession of this evidence, when they got involved in the case! And if that wasn't bad enough, every dime in my joint bank accounts, held jointly with my husband, had been seized by a Little Rock Police detective, on the date of my indictment, at the direction of the same Secret Service Agent.

All the money we had in the bank was gone, including my husband's entire month's pay, deposited into our checking account, just a few days before the seizure had occurred. And I knew it was punishment for choosing to ignore *red flags,* and continuing to work for unethical doctors. When you get off of God's path, and take things into your own hands, you start down a rabbit hole of no return. You set yourself up for failure, and ultimately hurt your family, and everyone you love, in the process.

You don't just lose some, as Mercy Me's song says, you lose EVERYTHING. You tell yourself lies, to make yourself feel better, such as the lie I told myself, about Dr. Swan's accounting practices not being my concern. And in the process, you ignore every *red flag* in the book. You start living your plan for your life, not HIS plan. While doing so may not land you in a criminal indictment, as I found myself, it could be worse than that, and cost you your eternal home and your soul. The consequences of these actions are grave indeed. They significantly impact your walk with Christ, and our ultimate goal, to live with HIM, in Heaven one day.

I hope my story will inspire readers not to ignore *red flags*. I hope my example warns others not to stray from God's plan. Our plan is never better than the one HE has for our life. And there is no job worth the risk. NOTHING is worth that kind of risk.

Chapter Six
You've Been Indicted

I have chosen to refer to the federal prosecutors, and the IRS agent, discussed in this book, by their real names. I do not feel that it would be fitting to protect their identities, as I expose the unethical behavior I witnessed in my case.

A federal indictment is a very stressful occurrence. I remember my first meeting with my new federal criminal attorney, recommended to me by the attorney who had represented me during the sexual assault. Unfortunately, that attorney only practiced employment law, so she had no idea about criminal law. She was just as shocked by the indictment as I was. We had no indication the doctors really believed I had stolen anything. The day I retrieved the letter from my mailbox, and called her, she referred me to a federal criminal attorney.

At the time, I was still trying to avoid dealing with the sexual assault. Being around strange men was frightening to me. And the attorney, to which she referred me, was male. She assured me that he was the best, and that I could fully trust him. I immediately called him, and made an appointment. It was an awful weekend for my husband and I. We were confused and frightened. I had been told by the attorney to bring him a retainer of $15,000, the following Monday, when we were to meet.

On that Sunday, I went to our online bank accounts to transfer $15,000 from our savings, to our checking account. That is when I found out that all of our bank accounts had been frozen. We had no money. It was shocking. We didn't know what to do. I called my new attorney, and he advised me that most likely, the government had seized our funds. He also scolded me for calling his cell phone after hours.

I went to the attorney's office on Monday, March 7, 2011, so we could meet, and discuss my case. The Secret Service, and a LRPD Detective, the one I would later find out had seized our bank accounts, had already been there, and served him with the forfeiture paperwork, on our seized funds. The attorney could not understand how I was indicted in federal criminal court, yet it was the LRPD, who had seized our bank accounts? My attorney opined, "No state case gave the LRPD detective the authority to do so." He had consulted other attorneys, and they agreed. He told me the first thing he would work on was getting our money back, so that I could pay him. The seized money was the least of my concerns. I was more worried about the crime, I was now accused, which I knew I had not committed.

In the meantime, the attorney said, I could give him a credit card, for the $15,000 retainer fee I was required to pay, for him to even start working on my case. I wondered what people who had no credit card with at least a $15,000 limit did in this case? Luckily, my husband and I had good credit, and paid our credit card balances at the end of each month. I handed over my credit card to the attorney's secretary. I was scared and emotional.

This was the first time I heard of the *Federal Sentencing Guidelines*. A large book, which tells you how long you are going to prison, for the crime you have been charged with. The attorney showed me the chart, and explained that I would spend only two years in federal prison, since I was charged with 57 counts of wire fraud. I was in shock. How could a good citizen be put in prison? I had not done what I was accused of! I did not belong there! ONLY TWO years, he made it sound so normal.

I would soon realize that attorneys who practice in the federal arena are so jaded, that two years sounds like nothing to them. They believe that defendants will be forced to take a plea deal and never go to trial anyway. And most defendants will find that they did break some law, since there are so many available at the federal prosecutor's disposal that can be used to charge a defendant.

I would learn that there are thousands upon thousands of laws in our federal system. These laws make it easy for you, or someone you know, to be charged with a federal crime. And attorneys know that going to trial will only get a defendant more time, than taking a plea deal. That is another flaw in our criminal justice system. It is a system that punishes those who dare to exercise their constitutional rights to a jury trial. This is often referred to as the *trial penalty,* because it penalizes those who go to trial, with more time in prison.

Not to mention trials are unfair. They are one-sided, with the one side in favor of the federal government. Attorneys that practice in federal court know that a defendant will most likely not beat the United States Attorney's office. However, they don't tell you this upfront. And what they do tell you about the system, will scare you to death. Federal criminal attorneys don't seem to have much of a bedside manner. They are not there to be your therapist. Don't expect them to be too concerned about your feelings, or your family members' feelings.

While they may be sympathetic towards you, they see federal cases every day. It's business as usual for them. They are desensitized to your pain, and the system in general. The book, *One Nation Under Arrest (How Crazy Laws, Rogue Prosecutors, and Activist Judges Threaten Your Liberty),* by authors Rosenzweig and Walsh, shines a spotlight on the problem of overcriminalization, in our federal criminal justice system. I encourage you to read this book, if you are interested in the subject.

My new attorney explained that he would accompany me to court in a few days, for what is called an arraignment. This is where I would enter a plea of guilty or not guilty to the indictment, and get my instructions for pre-trial probation, the conditions of my release. He said everyone pleaded not guilty that day. Then the discovery process starts, and my attorney would be able to see what "they" (meaning the federal government), had on me. I assured him "they" could not have anything on me, because I had not done what I was accused of.

What I didn't know at the time, is that attorneys are jaded, and have heard this "I have done nothing wrong," many times before. He told me everyone says that at first. I was appalled at his lack of trust in his new client. I would later find out that clients have to earn their attorney's trust. The whole system is so backward. He assured me that I would be allowed to remain free until trial, on my own recognizance. He reasoned that I had never been in trouble before, and this was a white-collar case.

In the meantime, he would go with me to the pretrial office to meet with my new probation officer. After the arraignment, he would accompany me to the United States Marshal's office, to be fingerprinted, and have my DNA taken. Fingerprints? DNA? What? This was all so shocking to me. But as I would soon learn, when one is under federal indictment, you are required to do all of this, and much more. Your rights are greatly restricted. The things you took for granted in the past, become luxuries after indictment. All of these things were shocking and scary to me. Your mind plays tricks on you when you go through something like this.

The days seemed dark and dreary. I was a total mess. My husband was a mess. It felt like the walls were closing in. I could not believe I was charged with a crime I had not committed. Wasn't this America? How could this even happen? I was also shocked that the doctors would take it this far. I wanted to contact Dr. Swan. After all, it was him, I had charged all those things for on my credit cards. I knew he could straighten all this out for me, once he told the real story. I still believed that the truth mattered.

My attorney advised me that I would be put in county jail, or held in a small cell at the US Marshal's office, until trial, if I contacted Dr. Swan. He was now considered a victim, of my crimes. Any contact with him would be considered tampering with, or threatening a witness. The AUSA in my case, would jump at the chance to use the government's power, to lock me up until trial. This would put me in no position to defend myself, or work on my case, with my attorney.

I questioned my attorney on all of this, and asked why I had to be on probation, when I was not guilty, and had not been convicted of a crime? Why was I required to submit to DNA testing? Wasn't this a violation of my rights as a citizen? He just laughed and answered, "Because that is the way it is in the federal system." Words I would hear many times during my case, when I would question the unfairness of the entire process. This talk about prison, pretrial probation, and DNA testing was overwhelming. I started researching the federal criminal justice system, and reading about federal trials, which led me to articles about federal prison.

You can get all sorts of misinformation on the Internet. If you are indicted, save yourself the heartache, and don't use Google. Everything I read made me more of a basket case. I ran across a book called *Orange Is The New Black* in my search. This was long before the Netflix series by the same name. The author, Piper Kerman, had served time at Federal Prison Camp Danbury, located in Danbury, Connecticut. The book was her account of her case, and time in prison. I was desperate for answers. I downloaded the book, and read it within hours. This did not help my fears. Nothing gave me peace.

Chapter Seven
Proceeding Through The System

Being indicted for a crime I had not committed made me angry. I questioned God. I felt everything but peace. I had certainly gotten off HIS path, by turning a blind eye, to all the doctors' unethical behavior. I was no better than them. I was struggling with guilt and shame. I realized I had stayed at the job for very selfish reasons, and I had not been honest with my husband about what I was doing for Dr. Swan. I was embarrassed. I had allowed my morals and ethics to be significantly compromised. I knew God was probably disappointed in me, and truthfully, I was disappointed in myself. I also knew my husband was disappointed as well. He could not understand why I would put myself in this situation, by charging personal items for Dr. Swan, on our credit cards. This caused a lot of discord between us at the time.

A federal indictment is hard on everyone. It's hard for family members to understand, or comprehend. People who don't understand the system, question how one could even be charged with a crime they did not commit? Some people just look at you with disbelief, when you proclaim your innocence. Having never experienced this situation themselves, they have no idea.

My advice to anyone in this situation, is to remember your family members are hurting, and confused, just like you. Give them a break if they are not as supportive as you feel they should be, as they are most likely dealing with their own emotions regarding what has happened. They need time to adjust to this new normal, just as you have to adjust. Others who are not supportive, do not matter in the big scheme of things, and God is the only one who can really help you carry this weight.

On March 11, 2011, my forty-seventh birthday, I met my new probation officer. He gave me a copy of the rules of my release, and instructed me to bring him my passport, since as part of my release, I was required to surrender it to the government. It was a scary day for me. The federal building was overwhelming, with its massive security entrance, security checkpoints, and guards. I tried to be brave and strong, as I fought back the tears. I went home after that meeting numb.

On March 17, 2011, I stood before a federal judge, with my new attorney by my side, and pleaded not guilty to the crime of 57 counts of wire fraud. The 57 counts, represented the number of times I had been reimbursed, through electronic payroll, for the items I had charged on my personal credit cards, for Dr. Swan, during the four years I had worked for him. I was now being accused of stealing those amounts. It was a devastating day.

Surprisingly, I was not the only one in the courtroom that day. It was filled with other people who had been indicted on the same day as me, March 2, 2011. Public Defenders were standing around, waiting to be assigned to a client. I was getting a first-hand civics lesson on how the federal criminal justice system operated, whether I wanted one or not.

My attorney gladly shared his knowledge, that the grand jury meets once a month in my district, and indicts everyone the US Attorney's Office brings before them. Cases are paraded before the grand jury members by the various AUSAs (Assistant United States Attorneys—government prosecutors), handling those cases. Remember, the person being indicted is not present, and is not allowed to tell their side of the story to the grand jury. As was the case with me, a defendant may not even know their case was taken before the grand jury that day, or that they were even under investigation.

I learned that there is a saying amongst federal criminal

attorneys, that a federal prosecutor can "indict a ham sandwich." Sadly, after my time in the federal criminal justice system, and all that I have witnessed, I believe this to be 100% true. All of the defendants in court that day, including myself, were being run through the system like cattle lined up for slaughter, at least that is how it felt. None of them looked like criminals, and most appeared like deer in the headlights.

I had the same look. Many of them appeared to be professionals, like myself. There were none of the people you see on the TV crime shows. None of the defendants looked scary, nor what my idea of a criminal was supposed to look like, at least up until that point in my life, since I was now one of those supposed criminals.

I was too frightened to even hear much that day. I remember feeling numb, as my name was called to stand before the judge. My knees wanted to falter, and I had to hold on to the podium, to prevent myself from passing out, or throwing up. Just as my attorney had promised, I was allowed to remain free, and was not made to even post a bond, like some defendants had been required to do, that day. My attorney did most of the talking. I only had to say "not guilty" when asked by the judge how I pleaded. And nod and say "Yes, your honor," when asked if I understood the conditions of my release. Even to myself, my voice was unrecognizable, and it shook when I spoke. I signed a piece of paper, assuring the court that I understood the pretrial release conditions, and walked out with my attorney.

The US Marshal's Office was the next stop on this wild ride, for which I was now a captive audience. The men who took my fingerprints, photo, and DNA were friendly. They did not treat me like a criminal. They were professional, and just had a job to do, and that was it. However, my attorney was not allowed to accompany me to the back of their office, so we parted ways once he showed me where to go. This made me uneasy. I was scared. There were no women around, and I was still very fearful of strange men at this point, due to the sexual assault.

I remained calm and told myself this would all be over with soon. I walked out of the federal courthouse that day, alone. As I got in my car, I began to cry. I could not control it any longer. I sat in my car, in front of the federal courthouse, and wept, for what seemed like forever. Then I drove home, not sure what my future would hold. I still believed in our criminal justice system. I blindly told myself that once the US Attorney's office heard my side of what had happened, this would all be over. That my name would be cleared of any wrongdoing. That could not be further from the truth. I would find through this process that the truth is actually what a federal prosecutor says it is. The real truth doesn't matter much at all.

The following day the pretrial probation officer came to my home to do a walk-through. Again, I was forced to be alone with a strange male. It was stressful, but I had my anti-anxiety medicine to numb the pain and fear. I told myself I could get through this, but inside, I was falling apart. I was determined to be strong, and put on a good front for my family. If only I had been trusting God during this time, instead of trying to go it alone. I know my journey would have still been challenging, but I would have had the peace of knowing HE was guiding me.

However, a few years before my indictment, we had stopped going to church. Which meant, I had relied on God less in those years. The best way for me to describe what took us away from church, would be to call it church hurt. We hadn't stopped believing in God; nor stopped praying, or studying the bible. We just stopped attending church services. This had more to do with JT and Timothy's mom, as well as our good intentions, of trying to keep them at the church they had attended for their whole life, once we were granted custody of them. It turns out that was another failed attempt to fix things, without God's help. And again, that is a story for another book. Maybe I'll write it one day too.

If you are reading this book because you are going through a stressful time in your own life. I beg you to put your trust in God, right this minute. My prayer is that you do not make the same mistakes I made. Do not try to go it alone. Put your faith in the ONLY ONE capable of seeing you through hard times.

Proverbs 3:5-6 says "Trust in the LORD with all your heart, and do not lean on your own understanding. In all your ways acknowledge HIM, and HE will make straight your paths."

Chapter Eight
In The News

The thing about a federal indictment is that it's very public. The United States Attorney's Office, puts out press releases, to alert everyone that you have been charged with a crime, or crimes. These press releases go out to all the national news wires. The local newspapers, and sometimes local television stations, pick up these news releases, and make your plight public knowledge. National news media outlets may also share the story. Sometimes, the media even spins the story, if the government's press release is not juicy enough, to satisfy readers.

And since the government puts out the original press release, it has already put its narrative of the case out for public consumption, to begin with. This narrative generally becomes what everyone believes about your case. It becomes ingrained in every Google search, for years to come, when someone decides to look up your name. Again, the truth is not what matters. The truth is what the government says it is.

For example, one of the government's press releases stated I had purchased a car. Now reading I purchased a car, in the context of a wire fraud case, where I had been accused of stealing $611,000, from my former employers, would cause the reader to believe that I purchased the car with stolen funds. Regardless, that could be further from the truth.

The government failed to mention that the exact car I purchased, had a monthly car note that I paid each month. That same press release also stated that we built a house, which would imply that it was built with stolen money, but fails to mention the construction loan and other financings we had for said house, or the rather large mortgage on said property. Undoubtedly, by the time we got to trial the government had changed its story to claim we built a pool and pool house, instead of a house. Regardless, that all of these things were built at the same time, with the same construction loan, that my husband still pays a hefty mortgage on each month.

I wanted to go on the record and correct all these lies, misstatements that made me, and my CPA husband, look like criminals, but there was nothing I could do. When you are under indictment you *must remain silent,* at the advice of your attorney. Anything you say, can, and will be, used against you. And you can count on the government to twist it, to reflect negatively about you. This was one of the hardest things to wrap my brain around.

I noticed others looking at me in the grocery store, or in other public places. I suspected they were judging me, or talking negatively about me. They probably read all those horrible things in the newspaper; or saw them on the Internet. They most likely thought I was a horrible person, a criminal. My reputation had been tarnished.

I started to become angry and bitter. Maybe some of this was paranoia on my part. It's hard being accused of crimes you know you did not commit. And at the time of those press releases, I was trying hard to deal with the guilt and shame, of what I had really done, that helped get myself in the position I now found myself in.

If you find yourself in a similar situation, I would certainly advise you not to read any of the news releases that are put out about your case. They will only make you sick. I would find myself sitting in front of, and screaming at, my computer in frustration, at what was printed.

And please do yourself an even bigger favor, and NEVER read the comments under those news stories. The comments under news articles, about anyone being charged with a crime, are horrific. People suggest that you should be hung at the courthouse square, so as not to waste taxpayer dollars, receiving a trial. Some commentators believe that we must go back to public executions, and firing squads. Others can't wait to see you go to prison, and add crude remarks about what will happen to you, once you get there.

And some of the comments were obviously from critics, who did not like me personally to begin with, possibly even employees of the clinic, or the doctors themself. They were now taking great delight, at disparaging me, as they hid behind their keyboards. Keyboard warriors on the rampage. While these comments give great insight into our society's mindset, and way of thinking about those accused of a crime, it's hard to be the one that such horrible things are written about.

Unfortunately, once written, those things are forever out on the Internet, for anyone to read, including your family, children, and friends, or worse yet, for those you meet in the future, including future employers. We live in a country with a *guilty until proven innocent* mindset. In the case of a federal indictment, it seems highly unlikely that your innocence will ever be proven, regardless of the truth of the matter.

Two months to the day after I had been indicted, on May 2, 2011, my name appeared in the *Arkansas Business.* This local business newspaper has readers all over the entire state of Arkansas. Their *Whispers* (gossip column) headlines read, *Lynn Espejo Indicted For Stealing $611,000.* I wish I could tell you that was the most unflattering headline I would see during my case. Unfortunately, looking back, it's probably one of the better ones. At the time, it was devastating to both my family and me.

We had not told our children about my case yet, because we wanted to spare them the heartache and worry. JT and Timothy were both relatively young. Joseph was in his first year of college. It didn't seem fair to burden them with it. Of course, after the article came out, we had no choice.

I had found a new job shortly after being indicted. It was a good job, and was paying me close to what I had been making at the doctors' clinic. It was a job I loved, and the people I worked for were nice. I had worked at the job for almost two months, when the article came out. On May 3, 2011, the day after the *Arkansas Business* published its article, I was let go. Unfortunately, with my name plastered all over the Internet and in print, alleging I had stolen over a half-million dollars from my previous employer; the company felt it was not good for their business to have me employed there as an accountant. It did not matter that they believed I was doing a good job, and even told me so. Who could blame them? I probably would have done the same thing, had I been in their shoes.

It's our nature as humans to be distrusting. And I think most of us can be guilty of doing this at times. We judge without thinking about how we would feel, if we were in the same situation, or what the bible says about our actions. In John 7:24 we are commanded "Do not judge by appearances, but judge with right judgment." But many of us fail at this daily.

And if that headline was not bad enough, a new headline was on the horizon shortly thereafter. On June 13, 2011, the headline in *Arkansas Business* read *Lynn Espejo Sued By Her Former Employer.* This same headline ran again on June 27, 2011, for all those who may have missed it the first time. On the Friday before Memorial Day 2011, both my husband and I were served with paperwork, regarding a civil lawsuit that had been filed against us by the doctors. I was served at home, and my husband was served at his place of employment. I had no doubt we were served on a holiday weekend by design, and that the doctors, or their attorney, were the ones who had tipped off the *Arkansas Business*, about the indictment, and the civil lawsuit being filed.

I would later find out that it was the doctor's attorney, who wanted to make the headlines for himself, since he was the attorney filing a civil lawsuit against us on behalf of the doctors. By tipping the paper off to my criminal case, it gave him even more news coverage, since he would be asked for comments on the case, as the doctors' attorney.

The allegations in the civil complaint were even more outrageous than the indictment against me. However, it also incorporated the criminal allegations language as well. Additionally, in the civil suit, the doctors alleged that my husband was their Certified Public Accountant (CPA). And because of this position, he had helped me steal from them.

My husband did not work for the doctors, and they had their own CPA, who didn't even work at the same firm as my husband. The complaint filed against us used words such as unjust enrichment, and other legal terms, we had never heard before.

The civil complaint alleged that my husband and I were a RICO organization. For those of you who are unaware of what RICO stands for, it means organized crime, usually used to refer to the mob, or the mafia. RICO is the abbreviation for Racketeer Influenced and Corrupt Organizations Act. My husband was devastated at the lies in the complaint. He feared he would be fired, and have his CPA license suspended. Civil complaints are public record. Anyone can look them up, and read them. I was too numb at that point to even care. It was devastating. By that time, I had slipped into a deep depression, where I would stay for months.

The civil complaint also alleged that I had stolen 500,000 sheets of copy paper from the doctors' office. YES, you read that correctly. It also alleged that my husband and I had purchased tens of thousands of dollars of electronics, on the doctors' credit cards. Mind you, I had charged everything for the doctors to my personal credit cards, and had never had access to their credit cards.

It didn't matter that we had never purchased tens of thousands of dollars of electronics, even on our own credit cards, nor did we own tens of thousands of dollars of electronics. The largest television in our home then, and to this day, is only 42 inches, and it was purchased at Wal-Mart. We don't even own surround-sound, or the other gadgets I see when I visit my friends' homes, who are electronic geeks.

The allegations in the civil complaint were mind-boggling to me, and I questioned where the doctors were even coming up with this stuff? Did they believe these lies? The complaint even alleged that I had shipped office supplies to my husband's business, and charged them to the doctors' Office Depot Account.

The funny thing is, my husband doesn't even own his own business. He works at a CPA firm that is very capable of purchasing its own office supplies. I'm sure his bosses would have noticed, and questioned it, if Office Depot had been making deliveries of office supplies to my husband at their office, which is what the complaint alleged. I read the accusations in disbelief, and questioned if there were any checks and balances, in our justice system at all?

The complaint requested that a Temporary Restraining Order (TRO) be placed on our home, so we could not sell it, or borrow money against it, to pay attorney fees. I began to believe if you had enough money and power, the truth didn't matter because people just believed anything you said. Sadly, I would later find out just how accurate that belief may be. The attorney who filed the lawsuit on behalf of the doctors, later admitted to my attorney that he had not checked out one fact. He had not viewed one inflated invoice, or even seen an invoice at all, or any financial records belonging to the doctors, for that matter.

He had never seen any electronics charged to the doctors' credit cards, nor the Office Depot bill, where I had supposedly shipped office supplies to my husband. He hadn't tried to verify if my husband was the doctors' CPA, by reviewing tax returns to see what CPA had signed off on them, or even a bill, to prove my husband had worked for the doctors, as their CPA. These things would have been easy to disprove, if only he had looked. He should have questioned these allegations, and checked to see the proof that we had done all these things? But he hadn't.

He had not reviewed any evidence, or document, that would back up what the doctors alleged in their civil complaint. He admitted this to my attorney, many months later, and only after he had caught his clients, the doctors, lying to him, and had fired them as his clients. Regardless, the damage was done, and the lawsuit was already public knowledge, and part of permanent court records.

The doctors' attorney and the US Attorney's office had a lot in common. They both just took the doctors' word, and ran off filing things, making baseless allegations regardless of the truth. One to the grand jury. The other to the county courthouse. Parallel examples of justice gone awry, with no consequences to those who fail to undertake caution, or do their due diligence. Causing devastation and chaos, for those who are falsely accused.

While my husband and I saw the lawsuit as another tragedy, to this story unfolding before our eyes, my attorney was elated with the news that it had been filed. I remember wanting to punch him through the telephone that day, due to the giddiness I could hear in his voice. I wanted to rip the smile right off his face. He was chomping at the bit to get started on the civil case, and could not wait for the holiday weekend to be over, so he could do just that. He used words like discovery, "noticing up" the doctors for depositions, and subpoenaing records, words that were still Greek to me at the time.

He was ecstatic that my husband had been sued along with me. Apparently, the lawsuit opened up the chance to get discovery from the doctors, and take their depositions. And of course, that meant I owed him more in attorney fees. He advised that my husband needed to hire an attorney of his own, to represent his interests.

Since my husband had been sued along with me, and had no Fifth Amendment rights to protect, he could go head-to-head with the doctors, and get all the discovery we needed for my criminal case. Discovery, that we were not allowed to get, under the federal rules of criminal procedure. Surprisingly enough, in a federal criminal case, you are not allowed to take depositions, and the only discovery you get, is what the US Attorney's Office is willing to give you, for the most part.

I would later learn that the government will do everything

in its power to block you, if you try to subpoena things on your own. You most likely will never have access to the grand jury transcripts, or other paperwork, that the government deems as agent field notes, or the government's work product. You aren't allowed to depose those who accuse you of wrongdoing, or for that matter, any government witness at all. It is a one-sided process, from start to finish. Every aspect of it is designed to give the government the upper hand, and make a convicted felon out of all who find themselves caught in the government's crosshairs. No wonder 98% of all federal criminal cases settle out with a plea deal.

It was a miserable Memorial Day weekend, filled with stress and dread. It was a low point for both my husband and me, and there were times we felt like we couldn't take any more stress. We also had children who were now being forced to deal with this tragedy. Joseph was in the second semester of his first year of college, and two children were still at home. JT was in middle school, and Timothy was in grade school. Depression, anxiety, even thoughts of suicide at times, all of these things, alive and well, within our household. Yet we were forced to appear like everything was okay, to shield our children. We did not want to cause them additional stress.

After the doctors sued us, my husband used his forensic accounting skills to go through every bit of our personal finances with a fine-tooth comb. He wanted to make sure what I had told him was the truth about what had happened. Do you blame him? He soon found out just how honest I had been. That revelation made him even angrier, yet relieved him at the same time. His wife was telling him the truth. I think his financial review, accompanied with the fact that now these same doctors were making false accusations against him, in their civil filings, was enough for him to understand whom we were up against. At this juncture, we still did not understand that the government was the real enemy, not the doctors.

I had done none of what I was accused of, and neither had my husband. Yet the system was swallowing us up whole, causing us to spend every extra dime we could get our hands on for attorney fees; cashing in 401K and life insurance policies, running up our credit cards, with no end in sight. A federal indictment is financially crippling by itself. But now, we had a civil lawsuit, to defend as well. The government had seized every dime we had in our bank accounts on March 2, 2011, when I was indicted. We had already started over financially at this point, yet we had to continue to fork out money, and cash in our assets, to pay for attorney fees.

On June 8, 2011, the government superseded the March 2, 2011, indictment, and added more accusations against me. The allegations in the superseding indictment, regarding what I had supposedly done using the QuickBooks accounting software, were not even possible to do using QuickBooks. Therefore, they could not have been true. I would later find out that these allegations were written by the new office manager, hired by the doctors.

She later told me, and my attorney, that the doctors filed the civil lawsuit, assuming we had no money to fight them. They assumed they could file the civil lawsuit, and take our home. Not sure why they would have wanted it, given the rather large mortgage? They assumed that everything else we owned, had already been seized by the government. The doctors believed they could do all this, without us putting up any fight. The saying that *money is the root of all evil,* proved to be the case.

And as Christians, we are warned in the bible, about what happens to those who allow others to lead them astray. The bible says in 1 Corinthians 15:33 "Do not be misled: Bad company corrupts good character." I had allowed myself to be led astray by one of my former bosses, and now my entire family was paying the high price for my mistakes.

Unfortunately, once something like this is made public, the damage has been done. Early on in the civil case, my husband won a *summary judgment* against the doctors, meaning he won, without ever going to trial, because we were able to prove to the Court that there was no evidence/proof of any of the allegations made by the doctors, in their civil complaint. The same allegations that were a mirror image to my federal indictment.

We also were also able to prove that there was no truth to the additional accusations the doctors added to their civil lawsuit that had not appeared in the indictment. Even so, no reporter ever wrote a story about this part of the civil case. If you Google my husband's name, you can still find the article that discusses him being sued, for all kinds of nefarious things.

During the civil case, one of the hardest parts about taking discovery, was being in a conference room all day, with Dr. Swan on the other side of the table. But that was exactly what I was expected to do. On the day we took his deposition, he made eye contact with me, rolled his eyes, and gave me a look of "This is crazy," when the attorneys had begun to argue, at one point during his deposition. It reminded me of the looks he gave me from across the table, during some of the doctors' monthly meetings, when the doctors would argue. It was hard for me to dislike him at this point, as I still had hope that he would come forward with the truth, and save me.

He and I had a close relationship when I worked for him, and I had thought of him as a father figure at the time. I often confided in him about our on-going custody battle with Pancho's ex-wife. He was also the only doctor I had confided in about my dad's suicide, something I rarely talked about at all, even to those who were very close to me. At the time, he would pray with me and tell me "You are like a daughter to me." I had genuinely liked him. But now, he was the enemy, or at least that is what my attorney kept reminding me.

Later, at the trial in my criminal case, when Dr. Swan was on the witness stand, he would once again make eye contact with me, and give me the look of "I'm sorry." "What do you want me to do?" But by that time, I knew he would do nothing, as it was either me, or him, that was going to federal prison. Ultimately, he chose me, with his continued lies.

After we took his deposition that day in the civil case, the doctors' attorney called our attorneys to offer to settle the case with me. The doctors wanted me to pay them $100,000 for them to drop the civil case, and discontinue cooperating with the government against me in the criminal case. I refused immediately.

Since I had been under federal indictment when my husband filed for summary judgment, I had not been able to fight the civil case, or file for summary judgment myself. I had been forced to remain silent. Therefore, the civil case remained open, since both my husband and I, were parties to it. Once the federal indictment against me was dismissed on May 12, 2011 (see Appendix Document 1), I was allowed to start fighting my side of the civil case.

*Note that I was initially indicted on March 2, 2011. Since that indictment was *superseded* (meaning language in the indictment was changed after initial indictment) on June 8, 2011, the dismissal shows for the June 8, 2011, indictment, not the March 2, 2011. indictment. Superseding means the indictment was amended to add language to it. The March 2, 2011 indictment, and the June 8, 2011 indictment, are still the same indictment.

Chapter Nine
The Wheels of Justice Turn Ever So Slowly

After the AUSA handling my criminal case had superseded my original indictment, in June 2011, adding even more absurd accusations regarding QuickBooks, he abruptly retired in December 2011. The rumor, told to my attorney by another AUSA at the US Attorney's office, was that he had realized I had been falsely indicted. He was not about to stick around and get the blame for it. After all, it happened on his watch. Wasn't he the one that had taken this case to the grand jury, without ever seeing an inflated invoice, or any other shred of wrongdoing? But we all know how rumors go, so who knows if that is even the truth?

During this process, another thing I learned is that AUSAs, both current and former, are much like the doctors I worked for; they do not necessarily like each other, and will criticize each other in a heartbeat, given the opportunity. The man was close to retirement anyway, so he jumped ship, and passed my case off to another AUSA, JB (I have chosen to use the initials JB for this AUSA, because he was the only *honest* AUSA I ever met during this entire process).

By the time AUSA JB was assigned my case, it had been continued many times at the government's request; however, the AUSA would request that my attorney file the continuances. This made it look like I had requested them as the defendant. I learned this is because of the *Speedy Trial Act*. Apparently, the government does not want to appear to be violating it. The act guarantees defendants will not have their lives or liberties held up indefinitely. A defendant's trial must commence within 70 days from the date of the indictment. I found nothing speedy about our federal criminal justice system.

Government prosecutors make deals with your attorney to continue your case, regardless of how you, as the defendant, feel about it. The attorney advises you to agree to these things, so as not to make the government mad. As if the government is your friend to start with? And because you, as the defendant, show to be the one requesting these continuances with the Court, you have waived your right to a speedy trial. So, in essence, you have given up your rights, by the government's trickery. Rights you most likely didn't even know you had. And don't expect your attorney to explain these things to you. You must research, and read up on your own, to find this out. Most likely, only after the fact, and after your rights have already been waived. This is why I always advise others to know your own rights. Do your own research. It's your life on the line. Nobody will take care of you, better than you!

My attorney advised me that the new AUSA assigned to my case was a lovely man. He assured me that he knew him personally, and that he was "One of the honest ones." I stupidly asked, "Aren't they all honest?" I did not like the answer I received. My attorney had over 30 years of federal criminal law experience. He had seen a lot of wrongdoing, and underhanded behavior, at the hands of our government, during this time.

Up to that point, I honestly had not realized just how corrupt, and crooked, government prosecutors could be, nor did I realize how much power they wield. I did not fully understand the full implications of my case, and how the grand jury had been lied to in the first place, to even get the indictment against me, or lied to a second time, to get the superseding indictment. These are not things attorneys readily point out to you, probably for fear that you may want your attorney to hold someone accountable for these bad acts. Attorneys already know from years of experience that this will never happen. What I did know was that I was falsely accused. All I cared about was proving my innocence.

Around March or April 2012, my attorney tipped off the new AUSA assigned to my case, that the supposed victims in the case, the doctors, my ex-employers, had caused all the financial documents to be shredded, and my work computer to be destroyed. We were roughly a month from the trial date by this time. We had learned this information in August 2011, from a past employee, one of the billers, named Linda, who had left the clinic, and had called to tell me about the shredding of the financial documents (**see Appendix, Document 3**). She stated that it was her belief that I had not done what I was accused of, based on things she had heard the doctors say after I left, and based on her knowledge of how the clinic worked. This was her reason for passing along this information. At least then, we finally understood why we were being stalled on our requests for discovery, in both the criminal, and civil cases. It's hard to provide something that no longer exists.

She also told a story about a heated conversation between Dr. Jones and Dr. Swan, that had happened in a hallway of the clinic, that she had overheard. They were discussing me charging things for Dr. Swan. This conversation apparently took place before I left the practice. And supposedly happened when Dr. Jones was mad that I refused to charge any more items for him, on my personal credit cards. She also said that Dr. Swan had a "male friend" that would come to pick up many of the items I had purchased on Dr. Swan's behalf.

The gentleman had picked the items up at the front desk where Linda had worked, and she had personally given them to him many times. It was no secret around the clinic that Dr. Swan had an *alternative lifestyle*. Most of the items I purchased for him were most likely directly related to this lifestyle. Unfortunately, by the time my case got to trial, Dr. Thatch had hired the past employee back to work for him to do his billing.

She was now once again loyal to the doctors, and did not wish to be a witness for me, regardless that she had previously signed an affidavit, regarding her knowledge of the shredding of the documents, and been one of two previous employees that met with me, and another attorney, to sign a contract to report the doctors' Medicare fraud, under a Qui Tam Lawsuit. A Qui Tam lawsuit is a whistleblower lawsuit. We were unable to go through with the lawsuit, because the United States Attorney's Office in the Eastern District of Arkansas, refused to take the case.

If you have an inquiring mind, you may wonder why anyone who was accusing a past employee of stealing $611,000, would even do such a thing as destroy all the financial documents, the very evidence that would prove money had been stolen? I knew the answer. If the doctors let those documents get into the hands of anyone, especially a government prosecutor, the documents would not only prove that I had not stolen any money from them, but the same documents would likely implicate Dr. Swan, for the tax fraud I now suspected he had committed.

In fact, at this point, I suspected that Dr. Swan had been adamant about reimbursing me through payroll, instead of writing me a personal check, because of that very reason. Those expenses, charged to my personal credit cards on his behalf, regardless that he had reimbursed me through the business account, should have been noted on his business tax return, as personal expenses, not business expenses. They were not deductions or expenses. By taking those items as business expenses, he would have lowered his business income each year, and to the tune of over $611,000, for the four years I worked for the doctors.

I felt the other doctors were protecting him. But honestly, I'm not even sure if the other doctors knew the truth or not, then or now? Only they know that for sure. And of course, there was the pesky fact, that all the doctors were aware that I knew they had been committing Medicare, and Stark II fraud.

The documents that were shredded, would have also

proven this fraud. And, of course, they had to dispose of my work computer, because it contained the QuickBooks software that I needed to prove my innocence, and all the electronic copies of the settlement statements, and bills that could have proven my innocence, and the doctors' fraud.

After AUSA JB's revelation regarding the destruction of evidence, my attorney and I were extended a prompt invitation to come to the US Attorney's office for a little visit. A very intimidating experience for someone who had never been in any trouble, much less seen the inside of such a place. It was unknown territory. My attorney looked right at home, and it was apparent that he had spent much time there. He was even on a first-name basis with the security guard, who was responsible for x-raying our belongings, before allowing us into the waiting room.

Up to this point, nobody from the government had interviewed me, or heard my side of the story, even though my attorney had offered for the government to do so, many times. I thought that finally I would be heard, and this matter would certainly be cleared up, once and for all. The new AUSA seemed pleasant enough, and it felt like he was rolling out the red carpet, to make us feel welcome that day.

However, once in his office, he got right to the point. Curiously, he wanted me to write on a piece of paper what I was willing to be accused of, in the government's plea offer, which the government wished to extend to me immediately. He slid a yellow legal pad and pen my way, so that I could accomplish this task. I was astounded. I tried to explain to him the truth of what had really happened.

I also informed him about the Medicare fraud I had witnessed, millions of dollars stolen from the federal government by the doctors, along with what I suspected was tax, and pain medicine drug fraud.

I explained that I had simply been charging things on my personal credit cards, and being reimbursed by several of the doctors, but particularly the bulk of the charges had been for mainly one of the doctors, Dr. Swan. He did not want to hear about such things. He informed me that the government was not interested in any crimes I witnessed, or that the doctors may have committed. The fact was, the government was not even interested in hearing my side of the story. None of that mattered at all.

It quickly became apparent that the meeting with me was not to get to the truth of the matter, well at least where the real truth was concerned. The AUSA just wanted to know what felony I was willing to plead guilty to, so the government could put my case to rest. The AUSA would have to get any plea deal, we may agree to, approved by his boss AUSA Harris, the First Assistant United States Attorney in my district, second in command, just under US Attorney Thyer.

I had met AUSA Harris that same day in the hallway, when we had first arrived for our meeting. He shook my hand and smiled, as he welcomed me to their office. He was anxious to make a deal with me, that could put my case to rest. You would have thought we were long-lost friends, and that he was doing me a HUGE favor. At the time I had no idea that AUSA Pat Harris would become my nemesis for years to come.

Since I knew I was innocent, I was not about to plead guilty to any crime I had not committed. I knew of no crime to write on the yellow pad. My only choice was to reject the government's *ever so kind* offer, to write my own ticket out of there. This did not sit well with my attorney, who was fully aware of my innocence, nor with AUSA JB, who had extended the offer of a plea deal.

AUSA JB named off three or four crimes that he asked me to write on the yellow pad. I did as I was instructed. He then asked me to circle whichever crime was appealing to me. There was some discussion of the matter, but I remained firm. I would not be taking a plea deal, for a crime I had not committed. When it became apparent that I was not going to compromise my beliefs, the meeting ended, and I was advised by both my attorney, and the AUSA, that I needed to think about this.

They said a plea deal could make all of this go away, and get my life back to normal. Really? What part of me becoming a felon, for a crime I had not committed, would make my life get back to normal? The AUSA even told me that sometimes you have to "Put the shovel down in situations like this." Looking back now, as sad as it may sound, that seems like solid advice.

When the meeting ended, my attorney and I were allowed to review the discovery in my case, or lack thereof, which I had not been able to see until that point. I found it curious that the settlement notebooks we had received in the small amount of discovery we had obtained in the civil case the doctors had filed; were not the same ones I was reviewing at the US Attorney's office that day. Several were missing. The ones missing were the only ones that contained the very few invoices we had, and which proved the truth, that I had not inflated anything, unlike the indictment alleged.

This was an essential fact, since the only way I could have stolen money, was to have tricked the doctors into putting more money into the *zero*-balance checking account, the only bank account I had access to, while I was their office manager. In my job, I had never had access to any of the doctors' revenues. I had no access to payments from Medicare and private insurances, nor any of the cash co-payments that came through the front desk.

My job was simply to send out to the doctors what was called settlement statements, a recap of their vendor/operational bills, and payroll expenses, every two weeks, and to pay those bills and payroll, out of the *zero*-balance account. The settlement statements included the invoices and payroll records that backed up the amount each doctor owed for their share. Each doctor then wrote a personal check for their share of the bills, from their business checking accounts, where their revenues had been deposited. Business checking accounts I had no access to, as their office manager.

The doctors' individual checks were then deposited into the

zero- balance checking account I oversaw to pay the bills and payroll. It was part of my job to print out the vendor/bill checks, process payroll, print out the payroll checks, and electronically pay the payroll taxes. The President, Dr. Swan, who was my direct supervisor, oversaw this process, and signed off on, and approved, all of these things. He also signed all the outgoing checks, with me as the second signature, before the checks were mailed to the vendors, or given to employees.

When I took the checks to be signed by Dr. Swan, each check had the invoice or other documentation attached behind it, for his review. These were additional checks and balances, most likely put in place to prevent theft. This was done so the President, Dr. Swan, could verify that the amount the check had been written for, matched the amount on the invoice, or payroll record. It was a straightforward setup and one that left very little room for anyone to steal.

And there was nothing to steal anyway! It was a *zero-balance* account. The President was the person I was charging things for on my personal credit cards. He was reimbursing me through electronic payroll using employee expense reimbursement. Expense reimbursements that he approved. He was also the only doctor that saw, and reviewed, the bank statements for the *zero*-balance account. He would later claim he never reviewed the bank statements. I beg to differ. He got them each month, sent directly from the bank, to him.

Since there was no extra money deposited in the *zero*-balance checking account for me to steal, if I had not inflated the bills (invoices), then the only other option for theft, would have been for me to have not paid the vendor bills, payroll taxes, or employee payroll checks, and then have diverted those funds to myself. However, this would have caused employee paychecks, vendor bills, or payroll taxes to go unpaid, and in this case, that would have been to the tune of $611,000, the amount I was accused of stealing in the indictment.

During depositions in the civil case, the doctors had already admitted that all the vendor bills, payroll taxes, and employee payroll had been paid. They would later also admit this at trial, during their witness testimony. But on this day, the government was yet to know about this admittance by the doctors. I whispered all of this to my attorney. However, I don't think AUSA JB cared about anything I was saying to my attorney anyway. I'm sure that he felt confident I would come around to the government's way of thinking on a plea deal, as 98% of all federal defendants do. I probably could have just spoken it out loud in his office, or screamed it from the rooftop at the US Attorney's office, that day. The truth did not matter anyway.

Days rocked on, and we were getting closer to trial. I was more than ever determined to prove the truth. My attorney was more than ever determined to get me to sign the plea deal (**see Appendix Link 1**), that he and AUSA JB had come up with, along with AUSA Harris' stamp of approval. A *sweet deal* he called it. He even had the attorney that represented me during the sexual assault trying to get me to take the plea deal. As she told me, I would always be looking over my shoulder, if I did not do so. Looking back now, the plea deal does seem sort of sweet, considering what ultimately happened at trial.

Regardless of how sweet a deal my attorney said it was, it was not the truth. I was determined that the justice system I had been taught about in school existed, and that the truth did matter. Of course, that was then, and this is now. My opinion has certainly changed over time. The plea agreement offered by the government was for me to plead guilty, to conspiring with two unnamed, and unindicted doctors, in order to hide their income. The plea deal said that the doctors had paid me a bonus, that I had failed to report on my personal income taxes. Therefore, I had conspired to defraud the federal government, and I owed the Internal Revenue Service $29,960, in back taxes.

In return for my guilty plea, the government would submit

that I was a minor participant in the conspiracy. For my minor role, I would get a two-point deduction off of my sentence, under the Federal Sentencing Guidelines, and another 2-3 points off for taking responsibility for my crime, and being remorseful. I would give up my rights to appeal my conviction, to Freedom of Information Act (FOIA) any records related to the case, and the right to sue the federal government, or any of its employees (AUSAs, Secret Service, etc.). I would become a convicted felon, for life. Also, nothing would happen to the two unnamed and unindicted doctors, who were supposedly my co-conspirators. The government only wanted to put this case to rest, and move on.

However, there was a silver lining to the looming doom and gloom, so my attorney touted. I would be considered at the 0-6 months prison time level, on the Federal Sentencing Guidelines Chart, the most confusing chart you have ever seen. A chart that clearly believes amounts and quantities, should dictate the amount of time a person spends in prison, regardless that they may have been accused, or convicted, of the same crime as the next person, who may have had a lower dollar amount, or who was caught with fewer drugs. And AUSAs dictate how much dollar amount and drug quantities go into the plea deal, therefore having complete control of the amount of time a defendant will be sent to prison. It is a one-sided system with government prosecutors controlling most of the outcome.

Navigating the federal sentencing guidelines is brutal. And don't even try to wrap your brain around the grouping of charges, enhancements, or other legal maneuvers that government prosecutors have in their bag of tricks. The whole process is ridiculously complicated and designed to keep a defendant guessing as to how much time they will spend in prison. I had already paid approximately $60,000 in attorney fees up to this point, money that was supposed to pay my attorney to go to trial with me, to prove my innocence. The trial he had not even started preparing for, that would be occurring in a matter of weeks.

The exact attorney that was now telling me that all I needed to do was go before a federal judge, and flat out LIE under oath in federal court, about crimes I had not committed; and ALL of this would be over with. Now wait a minute here, isn't lying on the record in court perjury? Isn't that a crime? The irony. To take a plea deal, think about this for a minute, you must throw logic out the window, and be willing to lie under oath, to a federal judge no less, because the federal government, which is already prosecuting you for crimes it says you committed, tells you to do so.

This is just one of the many reasons I know our criminal justice system is broken. To make my case go away, I would be required to admit I did all these things that never happened, and then lie under oath to a federal judge about them. For doing so, I could walk out of the courtroom a convicted felon for life, and owe the IRS a small sum, well, small, compared to the $611,000 the government said I stole in the indictment. Based on that confusing Federal Sentencing Guidelines chart, I would most likely get probation, home confinement, or halfway house time for the maximum amount of 6 months. However, per my attorney and AUSA JB, it was highly likely that I would just be put on probation for six months. And AUSA JB was happy at sentencing to suggest this to the judge in my case. I more than likely would never see the inside of a prison.

Now, suppose you are a logical person, or have even the smallest amount of common sense. In that case, you may be asking yourself several questions, right about now. If the government thought there was even the slightest chance that I had stolen $611,000, from the doctors, why would I be allowed to plead guilty to such a minor role and crime? This would in fact penalize the doctors, because they would not get restitution for the $611,000, I was accused of stealing from them. Instead, the government wanted me to pay the IRS, another government agency, $29,960 for the back taxes, it said I owed, for a bonus that I never received.

And how could there be two unnamed and unindicted co-

conspirators who were not charged? Shouldn't the main participants be charged, if I was just the minor participant in this so-called conspiracy? Doesn't it take more than one person to even make a conspiracy? Are you starting to see the injustice yet? And what happens to the AUSA, and secret service agent, who lied to the grand jury in the first place, to get the false indictment? Absolutely nothing, because they are untouchable. Remember that little clause in the plea agreement where you gave up your rights to sue the federal government? Not to mention the immunity federal prosecutors, and government agents, enjoy.

I prayed about the plea deal offer, sought other counsel's advice, and talked to family members, but I received no good answers. I told my attorney that I would consider pleading guilty to a misdemeanor charge, to just get this over with, but I would not become a felon for life, for a crime I had not committed. Per AUSA JB, United States Attorney Thyer said, "No misdemeanor convictions out of this office, only felony convictions." I was angered at US Attorney Thyer's statement.

Only felony convictions? Didn't he take an oath to uphold justice, not railroad defendants? I refused the government's plea deal, against the very strong advice of my attorney, to take it. One week before we were scheduled to go to trial, on May 12, 2012, the government filed a motion to dismiss its indictment. And so, it would begin, my seven-year battle with the federal government, and AUSA Harris, who had approved the "sweet plea deal," and whom I had greatly angered, when I refused to settle my case, by pleading guilty to a crime I had not committed.

After the dismissal of the first indictment, my attorney immediately sent discovery to the doctors in the civil case. Because the indictment was dismissed, I was now able to file for a summary judgment against the doctors, like my husband had done. But first my attorney needed the doctors to answer questions to be used in my summary judgment filing. My attorney sent what is called a set of interrogatories to the doctors. Interrogatories are a discovery document of questions that the doctors were required to answer truthfully, by the law.

However, we would soon find out that the doctors did not wish to answer the questions posed to them, in the interrogatories. Apparently, the thought of answering questions about their Medicare fraud, tax fraud, prescription drug fraud, my sexual assault, as well as what really happened from 2007-2010, when I charged items for Dr. Swan on my personal credit cards, and was reimbursed by him through payroll, was not appealing to the doctors to answer. Or maybe they were not willing to risk that their answers would become public record in a Motion for Summary Judgment? Then the whole world would know what liars they are.

The doctors, through their attorney, objected to the interrogatories. My attorney threatened to file a motion with the court, for contempt of court, to force them to answer, since they were required to do so by law. It was almost as if they had forgotten that they had actually sued us, not the other way around. Almost immediately, the doctors decided to dismiss their civil case, so they would not be required to proceed with discovery, nor answer those pesky interrogatory questions regarding their Medicare fraud, and the shredding of documents. However, before they could do so, their attorney abruptly fired them as clients. Later, he would tell my attorney that he had caught them being *less than honest* with him. Shocker!

The doctors were forced to hire another attorney, to file the motion required for them to dismiss the civil case against me. That attorney put in the motion to dismiss, that he entered the case, to represent the doctors for dismissal purposes only, meaning he wasn't taking their case on, should they decide to sue us again. But by now, our reputations had been permanently tarnished, regardless that the indictment, and the civil case had been dismissed. You can still Google our names and find the news articles. Even after dismissal, the media would not take the news articles down, even though I requested the *Arkansas Business to* do so, many times, and told them how devastating those articles are to our reputations, and my husband's career.

Chapter Ten
The Fight Is Not Over

After my first indictment was ordered dismissed on May 15, 2012, AUSA Harris began threatening to recharge me, if I did not fork over my claims to the $50,000 the government stole, opps, I mean seized, from our bank accounts on the day of my first indictment. While my family and I were trying to recover, and move forward from the publicity caused by my first indictment, AUSA Harris was putting pressure on AUSA JB, who had dismissed the first indictment, to charge me again.

This was due to AUSA Harris wanting to keep the $50,000 the government had seized using the *Patriot Act.* AUSA JB told my attorney that AUSA Harris was mad, that I had refused the government's generous offer of a plea deal, forcing them to dismiss the indictment, without getting a conviction. However, it later became clear to me that AUSA Harris just wanted the seized funds. He didn't care anything about justice, it would seem.

AUSA Harris was determined to show me who was the boss, the United States Attorney's Office in the Eastern District of Arkansas. Within weeks of the first indictment being dismissed, AUSA JB contacted my attorney to inform him that he had written a memo, detailing the reasons why I should not be prosecuted. But he also warned my attorney, that AUSA Harris, was bound and determined to charge me again anyway. Because of this, my attorney requested to meet with AUSA Harris. I believe this was the worst mistake my first attorney made in my case.

The meeting took place at my attorney's office, in Little Rock, Arkansas. I understood from my attorney that when he met with AUSA Harris; he showed him my credit card statements for the items I had charged for Dr. Swan. He also showed him the few settlement statement notebooks we were able to obtain, during discovery in the civil lawsuit. Those settlement notebooks contained invoices that proved I had not inflated the invoices, or the settlement statements. Unfortunately, we did not have settlement statements for all of the years I had worked for the doctors, since those documents had been destroyed. We did have settlement statements that belonged to Dr. Korker, who had left the clinic in 2009, and had taken his personal settlement statements with him. These statements contained this particular doctor's direct bills, and the bills he shared with all the other doctors, for January 2007-September 2009.

I had been the office manager from March 2007-October 2010. Unfortunately, there was a little over a year of statements missing. Dr. Korker's settlement statements clearly showed that nothing had been inflated to get money into the *zero*-balance checking account. Therefore, there would have been no extra money in that account to steal. The settlement statements clearly showed that no shared bills had been inflated, shared bills that included all doctors, for January 2007-September 2009. Because we only had Dr. Korker's direct bills during this same timeframe, we could only prove that his direct bills had not been inflated. We did not have the other doctors' statements for their direct bills, and no settlement statements at all for Dr. Swan, and of course none ever materialized, during my case. Those statements had been destroyed.

However, since the indictment had alleged a continuing scheme, this certainly proved that it would have been impossible for me to have done this. It did not leave much room for someone to have been able to get an extra $611,000, into the *zero*-balance bank account, since the settlement statements we did have in our possession, proved that all the shared bills were not inflated for 2007-September 2009. And Dr. Korker's direct bills had the highest direct bill amounts, out of any of the doctors in the clinic, leaving even less room, for a chance to sneak an extra $611,000, onto the settlement statements.

This information did not impress AUSA Harris, nor deter him from trying to find something else, to indict me for. He was blind to real justice, and only wanted a conviction. He continued to threaten to indict me, and even to indict my husband, unless we gave up claim to the money from our bank accounts, the government had seized. I honestly did not believe someone could be indicted twice for a crime they did not commit. I still believed in an honest and just criminal justice system. I held firm. And I started making complaints to the Department of Justice (DOJ), and the Office of Inspector General (OIG), in Washington, D.C. Those complaints were made against AUSA Harris.

In early 2014, AUSA Harris filed a motion with the judge presiding over the grand jury in my district. In the government's motion, AUSA Harris accused me of many things, one of which was being the author of a blog site that AUSA Harris alleged had been set up, to criticize AUSA Harris, and then United States Attorney Thyer. I assume AUSA Harris thought he had the power to control someone's freedom of speech, as well as hold an indictment, over their head. I would later come to realize that the US Attorney's office isn't the only government agency that thinks it can violate the First Amendment rights of individuals. But that revelation didn't happen until I found myself sitting in a federal prison.

I knew AUSA Harris was just mad, because I had been complaining about his unethical behavior to other government agencies in Washington, D.C. My attorney had told me so, even though he was no longer representing me, at the time. However, AUSA Harris was still sending him emails, with threats to indict me. I was considered a pro se defendant, since counsel did not represent me, and therefore, I was acting as my own attorney.

My attorney thought it best that I file an answer to the

complaints in the government's motion. He felt that AUSA Harris was looking unhinged to the judge, filing motions about blog sites. In my pro se answer to AUSA Harris' made-up allegations, I pointed out my constitutional right to freedom of speech. I noted that even if I were the author of a blog site that criticized the government, so what? Was that illegal? The judge did nothing in regards to AUSA Harris' motion. What could he do? I would later have similar discussions with the Bureau of Prisons Staff, as well as with City of Faith Halfway House staff, regarding the blog about my case, that I started in 2018. It seems many government entities forget that even those charged with or convicted of a crime, still have certain rights, including the constitutional right to freedom of speech.

At the time of the government's filing, I searched for the blog site ASUA Harris had alleged I had started, but never found it. I wanted to read it myself. This was long before I truly understood the full depths of AUSA Harris' unethical behavior, or corruption. I find it ironic that I started my blog, *Inside The Walls*, to blog about the trial in my case, and am now writing this book. Both to expose the government's corruption, and defend myself, from the conviction of crimes, I never committed. And I guess you could say that my blog, and this book, indeed criticizes the government, including AUSA Harris. But at the time, I was doing none of the things AUSA Harris accused me of, in the government's motion.

My first attorney had high hopes that AUSA Harris would see the error of his ways, if we showed him enough of the truth, so my attorney had given my entire defense to the government, on a silver platter. Why would this be a problem, you may be asking, if I did nothing wrong? It's a problem because, in reality, the truth does not matter to most government prosecutors, and it certainly did not matter to AUSA Harris. You may not be aware that government prosecutors receive promotions, based on convictions, the amount of time they put a defendant in prison for the crime the government says has been committed, and the dollar amount of the restitution ordered, or the amounts of drugs the defendant is alleged to have had.

It is a win-at-all-costs mentality, as hard as it is for most people to wrap their brains around. By the time I met AUSA Harris, he had been a United States prosecutor for probably more than 30 years. The culture was already ingrained in him by this time, but I was not yet privy to any of this, at the time.

By telling AUSA Harris my defense, it gave the government a heads up on what my defense would be at trial. This allowed the government to develop a dog and pony show that twisted the evidence, and went directly against what it knew my defense would be, regardless of the truth. And that was precisely what ultimately happened at trial.

Believe me, I have realized that anything can be twisted. if you have enough PowerPoint slides, and government agents to testify to it! Unfortunately, most people who sit on a jury cannot understand accounting principles, much less the definition of schemes, statutes, elements of a crime, or any of the other things they are presented with, during an eight-day jury trial. It's overwhelming to them. And federal trials are not quick. Most federal jury trials go on for days, sometimes weeks, or even months. Jurors believe that the government would never charge anyone with a crime that was not committed. Why would they? If only jurors knew.

During the years 2013-2014, I received many target letters from AUSA Harris. My attorney received many phone calls and emails from him, threatening indictment. The long laundry list of charges, and crimes, AUSA Harris said I had committed, and was being investigated for, by the federal government, before the grand jury, was like a revolving door. It made my head spin. My attorney surmised that "AUSA Harris just makes them up as he goes along." "Throwing everything up against the wall, and hoping something will stick." Hearing this made my anger rage.

In March of 2013, AUSA Harris sent an email to my attorney that said I was under investigation for tax fraud for the years 2007-2013. I pointed out to my attorney that 2013 taxes would not even be filed until 2014, basically well over a year away. How could I have committed tax fraud, in a year that had not even ended yet, and for which no tax return had been filed? It was all such a mockery of what I thought our justice system was supposed to be. Prosecutors take an oath to uphold truth and justice. The irony was thick. I was in disbelief at the number of resources, and taxpayer dollars, AUSA Harris was willing to waste on this case. I knew I was innocent. It was frustrating for my husband, and me.

During this same timeframe, AUSA Harris also sent an email to my attorney that said I was under investigation for a law that we could not even find existed. Apparently, we have so many laws in this country, that sometimes even a federal prosecutor can become confused, on the difference between what laws are real, and the ones that are just a figment of their own imagination. And because I still believed that truth would always win, I called the government out on these things, which did not sit well with AUSA Harris.

Reflecting back, I realize now that this was when most of my anger started to take deep root. It was one thing for the government to be misled by the doctors, and mistakenly indict me the first time. But now, even knowing the truth, AUSA Harris did not stop. The longer it went on, the angrier I became. It's hard not to be able to live your life, without the constant fear of indictment. It wears on you. I had been living this nightmare for over three years at that point.

I would eventually find out that most government prosecutors do not like to be told they are wrong. They aren't going to agree with you, or admit to it anyway. This calling out of AUSA Harris, fueled my long battle with him, and the United States Attorney's Office in the Eastern District of Arkansas. It got so bad at one point, that AUSA Harris refused to even tell me what I was under investigation for.

Or maybe he didn't even know himself? He sent me a target letter in July 2014, inviting me to the grand jury, but refused to disclose what crimes the grand jury was investigating. During this same time, I was making complaints on AUSA Harris for his unethical conduct, and abuse of grand jury subpoenas to the Department of Justice (DOJ), in Washington, DC, the Attorney General's office (AG), the Office of Inspector General (OIG), the federal judge that was presiding over grand jury proceedings in my district at the time, United States Attorney Thyer, and to the local office of attorney professional conduct.

I also requested that someone investigate why our $50,000 was still being held hostage by the government, when the indictment had already been dismissed. The dismissed indictment was the mirror image of the same language found in the government's civil forfeiture case. I felt robbed by my own government. I was angry that I had to deal with this, and that my life was put on hold, as well as my family's life to some extent.

Also, during the same 2013-2014 timeframe, AUSA Harris used grand jury subpoenas to subpoena all our joint bank accounts for 2007-2010, even though the government had already subpoenaed these same documents, during the first indictment. As well as credit card statements, during the time period I worked for the doctors, and even dates before and after that timeframe. AUSA Harris even used grand jury subpoenas to get records for timeframes outside of any statute of limitations, for any crime the government could have possibly been investigating me for. Most of these records had already been subpoenaed during the first indictment.

The grand jury subpoenas caused our bank to close our bank accounts, and several of our credit cards were canceled, for no reason at all. I suspected it was because of the grand jury subpoenas, regarding those credit card statements. There was no other apparent reason good customers would have their accounts closed. We didn't even have balances on the accounts the credit card companies closed, and had never missed a payment on them. In fact, most times we paid the balances off in full, each month.

Grand jury subpoenas were also used to get financial

documents related to mortgages on houses that we had owned years before, even the ones my husband had owed with his ex-wife, and I had owned with my ex-husband, as well as the houses both of us had owned while we were single. None of these records could have been used to charge me with anything, since it would have been way past the statute of limitations.

The records for our current home were also subpoenaed, the one we built in 2010. records the government had already subpoenaed during the first indictment, and two other homes we had owned together, since our marriage. I had only worked for the doctors from 2007-2010. Anything outside that time frame, was just AUSA Harris, abusing his grand jury subpoena power, to look through all of our personal finances, in what I believe, was his hopes of finding something, anything, that I had really done wrong, with which to charge me.

AUSA Harris also used grand jury subpoenas to subpoena my tax returns from the State of Arkansas, not the IRS, or federal government, for whom he worked, which appears to have been a HUGE abuse of grand jury subpoenas, and possibly even illegal actions on his part. I would later find out that federal prosecutors are supposed to get permission from the DOJ Tax Division, before they can subpoena tax returns, or investigate tax fraud. Tax returns are highly protected documents.

But that didn't stop AUSA Harris, he went directly around this requirement, using a grand jury subpoena, and subpoenaed the state tax returns. The federal government couldn't even prosecute me on a state tax fraud charge, had he actually found anything wrong with my tax returns, filed with the State of Arkansas. Of course, he knew that the state returns would also include the same information that would have appeared on my federal return. In this way, he skirted the DOJ requirements to ask permission to investigate tax fraud.

AUSA Harris even subpoenaed my business banking

account records, and tax returns, from the State of Arkansas, for a business I started in 2013, over three years after I stopped working for the doctors. There was no justification for him getting this information. It was undoubtedly an abuse of the grand jury process, in the eyes of my attorney, as well as AUSA JB, and a former acting United States Attorney, all of whom were so angered by AUSA Harris' unethical behavior, that they were helping my attorney in the background, with my case. Both of these former federal prosecutors, who had worked directly with AUSA Harris in the past, stated they were aware of his unethical conduct in many other cases.

AUSA Harris even went way out of bounds, and used a grand jury subpoena, to subpoena my mother's banking records. My mother shared no assets with me, and neither one of us had ever had access to the other's bank accounts. We didn't even live in the same town. It made no sense why AUSA Harris would need to see this information?

It was abuse, and harassment, as well as prosecutorial overreach. AUSA Harris used grand jury subpoenas to harass the CPA firm where my husband worked, even threatening the firm, at one point, that it *may* be under investigation. AUSA Harris sent IRS agents several times to serve grand jury subpoenas on the public accounting firm where my husband worked as a CPA. The subpoenas requested my husband's bosses to turn over our tax returns. My husband's work had not prepared our tax returns, my husband had, and his work did not even have access to our tax returns.

My husband voluntarily gave our tax returns to the attorney representing the firm where he worked, so the firm did not have trouble with the government. We were not trying to hide anything about our tax returns anyway, and my husband wanted to keep his job. My attorney and I believed that AUSA Harris' serving of grand jury subpoenas on my husband's work was purely an attempt to get my husband fired. Most likely, so that I would no longer have money to pay an attorney to represent me, and as an effort to pressure me into taking the government's plea deal. When the government shows up, people get scared, regardless if they have done anything wrong, or not. Nobody wants to pay attorney fees, to deal with the federal government, especially for a case they aren't involved in personally. My attorney said "If getting Pancho fired is not the motive, then it is an attempt to outright intimidate you and Pancho." It was harassment at the highest levels.

IRS and Secret Service Agents went to my sister-in-law's work, and harassed her, even though she knew nothing about our finances, or my work for the doctors. Secret service and IRS agents, sent by AUSA Harris, served subpoenas on my husband at his work. And AUSA Harris personally left several messages on my husband's voicemail at his work extension, and on his cell phone. He sent my husband emails requesting that my husband call, and meet with him. Basically, the government combed through my, and my husband's, entire life, trying to find anything with which to charge me.

It was unbelievable the amount of time, and taxpayer dollars, being spent on this case, and the waste of resources used to do so. The government never found one thing to charge me with, because we were not committing crimes, so AUSA Harris had no choice but to go back to the original trumped-up charges, from the first indictment. This is the type of government overreach that should be stopped. It's corruption, and harassment, at the highest levels. A federal prosecutor is very powerful, especially one who does not play by the rulebook. I have realized that many of them do not. And nothing will happen to them, and they know it.

Even if it is later found that they falsely convicted someone, hid evidence to do so, or knowingly put witnesses on the stand to perjure themselves, in order to get a conviction, they are untouchable! This is because federal prosecutors have sovereign immunity. A greater chance that they will abuse their power comes from this knowing disregard for the rights of others, and the fact that they can't be held accountable even if caught. Government prosecutors know nothing can touch them, for their unethical actions, even when they are found to be in the wrong. And with the advancement of their careers so highly dependent on convictions, and asset seizure, it opens up the door for so many abuses of power, and a win at all costs attitude, which I saw firsthand in my case.

This is just one of the many areas of our criminal justice system that needs reform. I suspect if we started holding prosecutors liable for their actions, we would see a decrease in the over incarceration rates in this country. And most likely, false convictions would decrease as well.

In July 2014, AUSA Harris sent a target letter to my husband, and threatened me that he would indict my husband if I did not give up our claim to the $50,000 the government had seized from our bank accounts. I was still proceeding pro se, so he communicated this directly to me, through IRS Agent Shortway. I continued to maintain my innocence. I requested meetings with AUSA Harris, and United States Attorney Thyer.

I requested that I be allowed to participate in the IRS investigation. I offered to cooperate. I wanted to prove my innocence. I was denied the right to do so. This was after I sent requests to IRS Agent Shortway's supervisor, and that supervisor's supervisor, in another state, and was even refused by them, to participate in the IRS investigation, regardless that all my research verified that it is customary for this to be allowed, if requested by the person being investigated.

In a meeting at the US Attorney's office with AUSA Harris, IRS Agent Shortway, and Agent Shortway's supervisor; AUSA Harris informed IRS Agent Shortway, the agent we would later discover had illegally shared our tax returns with my husband's employer by way of email, that he was not allowed to talk to me, or hear my side of what had transpired. I suspect, looking back, that Agent Shortway had no interest in my side of the story anyway. He and AUSA Harris were thicker than thieves, it would later turn out. To this day, I have *never* been interviewed by any government official, even though I have offered to cooperate repeatedly. I believe this is because the government doesn't care about the truth!

During the years of 2013-2014, we were forced to spend even more money on attorney fees, and to hire a former DOJ Tax Division AUSA from Dallas, Texas, to help us navigate the DOJ tax policies. Little did we know, we were just throwing good money to bad. I don't for one minute, knowing what I know now, believe that he could have helped us prevent the approval needed by AUSA Harris from the DOJ Tax Division, to charge us with a tax crime. It's the good ole boy system, where a higher up within the DOJ, or in another division, just rubber-stamps, whatever is asked of them, by another AUSA.

And because AUSA Harris was the First Assistant US Attorney in our district, directly under the US Attorney, he had so much more power, and clout, than just a regular AUSA, who would have had to answer to someone else, for everything he was doing. But at the time, we believed we needed to hire another attorney to protect my husband. His career was on the line. Looking back, it was all just a waste of time, and money, trying to prove the truth. I would have been better off just sitting back, and waiting for the second indictment to be handed down, instead of spending money trying to prevent it.

However, anyone that knows me, knows I'm a fighter for the truth, then and now, and you could have never told me to stop fighting for the truth, at the time. While I now recognized the corruption in our system, I did not understand at the time the depths it went. I still believed that truth mattered, and that justice was real. I believed innocent people did not go to prison, or could be indicted twice, for a crime they had not committed. I did not believe innocent people lost at trial.

Somehow, I still had faith in my government, and was confident that the truth would make a difference. I wanted to believe somewhere in this process, that there were still honest people working for my government, that would do the right thing.   Besides AUSA JB, who dismissed the first indictment, I never met one. And with each passing day, my anger was fueled even more.

Chapter Eleven
The New Office Manager Speaks

On August 1, 2012, three months after the dismissal of the first indictment, the woman who had taken my place at the doctors' clinic as their new office manager, contacted me. I had met her once, during the depositions in the civil case. She called our home telephone, to apparently clear her conscience. She told a story about how she had been putting the criminal case, now dismissed, together for the government, as well as the civil case, also now dismissed, together for the doctors' civil attorney, but had finally refused to keep doing so, because she could not find one penny I had stolen. Duh! As if I wasn't already aware that no pennies were missing! When I found out it was her calling, I first told her I had nothing to say to her, but she insisted that I listen to what she had to say. We would have many of these same conversations, in the years to come.

She told a story about how she had reported to the doctors' Executive Board that she was unable to find any money I had taken. She said that Dr. Boring had demanded she keep looking, and find something anyway. She said she had refused to continue to put a case against me together, and that she was fired by the doctors, a few days later.

She also stated that Dr. Swan had approached her many times during her employment, and asked her to purchase personal items for him using her own credit cards, but she had refused. He told her that he would reimburse her through payroll expense reimbursement. I was not surprised. By this point, neither was my attorney. He had come to believe in my innocence, after everything he had seen in my case.

In that same phone call, she stated that she had even been the person to come up with the language, in the superseding indictment, filed by the government on June 8, 2011. I didn't believe her. There is no way the government had an office manager craft the language in a legal document. She was adamant that she had emails, between her and the original AUSA assigned to my case, to prove it. I was floored. To convince me she was telling the truth, she immediately forwarded me the emails, between her and the government, as proof that what she was saying was, in fact, the truth (**see Appendix, Document 3**).

No wonder the indictment had never made any sense? The charges were absurd, let alone that I knew nothing in the indictment could possibly be true, given that I was innocent of the crime. But now, to find out that the government, my government, had allowed a non-lawyer to do its job, and write the language in the indictment? It was almost too much to hear! What kind of operation were they running at the US Attorney's office in the Eastern District of Arkansas?

By this time, the first indictment had been dismissed. The civil case had also been dismissed. I immediately conferenced my attorney on the call with her. After listening to what she had to say, we agreed to meet with her the following day, at another attorney's office. The other attorney was a friend of my first attorney. He would represent the office manager for free, since my attorney could not represent both of us.

She agreed to meet with AUSA JB, who had dismissed the indictment against me. We wanted her to tell him what she had told us. AUSA JB had been keeping my attorney abreast of AUSA Harris' continued demands that I be indicted again. We knew from those conversations that AUSA JB had written a memo for my case file, outlining why I should not be charged. He was not happy with the pressure he was receiving from AUSA Harris. It made him angry that he was being asked to indict me for a second time, when there was no proof of any wrongdoing.

On Friday, August 3, 2012, the office manager, accompanied by the other attorney, went to the US Attorney's office to meet with AUSA JB, and the secret service agent, who had been working on my case, the one who had seized our money. AUSA Harris was not aware that this meeting was to occur, and was not present. The new office manager told the government, what she had previously told us, about Dr. Swan, asking her to purchase stuff for him, on her credit cards, and offering to reimburse her through payroll. She also stated that Dr. Swan had explained his reasoning for asking her to charge personal items for him, and had told her that there are "Lots of gray areas in the tax law that he liked to take advantage of."

She reported that Dr. Swan once bragged that he had not filed taxes at one point in the past, for five consecutive years. When he became worried about an audit, he had self-reported it to the IRS before he could be caught. He blamed the lack of filing tax returns on his then CPA, who had to pay the back taxes Dr. Swan owed, for the five years of unpaid taxes.

She said Dr. Swan smugly touted, "The IRS will never come after me, or even look at my taxes, since I self-reported the five years of not filing," and for this reason, it was his belief that he could do whatever he wanted, and not get caught. Dr. Swan had sued his previous CPA, for damages regarding the lack of filing a tax return for five years, almost costing him his career.

He had made similar claims to me, during my tenure at the clinic, when I would become hesitant to continue charging things for him, and when I would point out to him that reporting personal expenses, on his taxes, as business expenses, could cost him huge penalties and interest, if the IRS audited him. I never even thought about how what he was doing was actually a federal crime. I had previously worked in public accounting, I knew about audits, penalties, and interest. Another *red flag,* I chose to ignore at the time.

On November 1, 2004, *Arkansas Business* published the article *Doctor Sues Accountant for Last-minute Filings,* which discussed the lawsuit filed by Dr. Swan, against his former CPA. The article stated that Dr. Swan sued for one million dollars in damages, from the CPA, and the Certified Public Accounting firm he worked for. The lawsuit alleged that the CPA had not filed Dr. Swan's tax returns for several years. The article said it had cost "more than $100,000 to pay off the penalties, interest and cover the accounting fees." The article further reported that "The accounting firm's attorney said the complaint is without merit, and indicated that *Swan* is responsible for tax returns, not getting filed properly" (name changed to Swan to hide the true identity of the doctor). That case later settled out of court.

The new office manager also relayed to AUSA JB, and the secret service agent, that when she had told the Executive Board about Dr. Swan' request for her to charge personal items for him on her credit cards, the other doctors told her, "Do not do that, that is what Lynn Espejo did that started all of this mess." She repeated the details of the story she had told me and my attorney, about when she failed to find anything I had stolen, while putting the case together for both the feds and the civil attorney, that the doctors on the Executive Board had ordered her to "Make something up."

Further, she said that immediately upon her being hired as the office manager in February 2011, the doctors advised that her first duty was to destroy a room full of boxes of old records. She described the urgency in their request. These records would include the financial documents that would have cleared my name of any wrongdoing. She said it was the new President, Dr. Boring, who had directed her to destroy the records. He had been with her when these documents were given to the Shred-It Company (**see Appendix, Link 2**).

She said it was actually Dr. Boring who had decided which records were to be destroyed. Doctor Boring was one of the doctors present at the meeting in September 2010. He was one of the doctors, whom I had shown the location of the financial documents, on my last day in the office. The day my attorney and I had met with the Executive Board, and the doctors' attorney. He was also the doctor I had given the key to the closet that housed those records, with his attorney present as a witness.

The new office manager described how all of this had taken place. She said that she and Dr. Boring, had met on a Saturday morning at the clinic, to accomplish the destruction of documents. She had brought her daughter with her to help. They carefully went through all the boxes in one area of the room. Dr. Boring gave specific instructions on what items in each box were to be shredded. However, when they got to the closet that required a key to open it, Dr. Boring opened the door with the key and said "ALL of these," without going through any of the boxes, or allowing her to see what was in them. She described how Shred-It then hauled all the boxes away.

I knew what she was describing was the financial document closet. It was the only closet that needed a key to open. And the only closet that would have had that many boxes in it. The documents were all there, right up until a few weeks, before the government indicted me. Why had the government not taken control of the evidence?

She further advised that the computer I had worked on, which was brand new, having been purchased in May 2010, had also been hauled away and destroyed. Obviously, the doctors had systematically destroyed any evidence that could prove my innocence. And the government had facilitated it, by not doing its job, and not taking control of the evidence, before indicting me!

During the meeting between the office manager, and AUSA JB, the secret service agent became angry when he saw she was going against the government's case. He then exposed the fact that he had found out, around the time she was hired by the doctors, about her previous seventeen (17) state felony convictions. Unfortunately, she had not disclosed this information to us before the meeting. Apparently, the secret service agent had run a criminal background check on her, when she became employed by the doctors. My attorney was not even sure it was legal for him to do so? But it was still problematic for the government, since the office manager, a Seventeen-time convicted felon, had actually written the language in the superseding indictment against me, and helped put the government's case together for the AUSA.

But by now, that indictment had been dismissed. What was most disturbing to me, was that the government had purposely withheld her felony convictions from us, a possible Jenks violation, since she was the star witness, in their first indictment against me. The indictment had been dismissed anyway, so we had no reason to alert the court to the government's dirty deeds. It probably would not have mattered anyway.

We were blindsided regarding her felony convictions, because she had failed to disclose them to us, when we had met with her, a few days earlier. Her felony convictions would be problematic for the defense, because her credibility would be questioned, due to her being a convicted felon. And since AUSA Harris was still threatening another indictment, I was saddened that she most likely would not be able to let the jury know that she too, had been approached by Dr. Swan to purchase things for him on her credit cards, and also told that she would be reimbursed through electronic payroll, since that was precisely what I had done!

It was confirmation that I was telling the truth! Or at least that it was still happening! AUSA Harris would later claim that I knew her, and had told her to apply for the position at the clinic. I had never seen this lady in my life, until the day of the first deposition in the civil case. And of course, the government never made those allegations publicly. AUSA Harris only used them in an attempt to make me give up claims to the money the government had sized. Again, the truth does not matter.

The US Attorney's Office meeting took place on Friday,

August 5, 2012. On Monday, August 8, 2012, the doctors made a police report against the office manager to LRPD (**see Appendix, Link 3**). The police report alleged that she had stolen $100,000, from the doctors, in less than a year, of working as their office manager. It also alleged that she had charged electronics to the doctors, just like they had alleged my husband and I had done, in their civil complaint against us. It was my attorney's belief that the secret service agent had tipped off the doctors about the meeting with her that had taken place on that Friday in the US Attorney's office, and alerted them that she was going against their story about me.

True to their corrupt nature, the doctors ran out, and filed a police report against her, in order to discredit what she had to say. It is highly likely, that the Secret Service Agent told the doctors to make the report. What I have found on this journey, is that oftentimes, federal agents and federal prosecutors work hand in hand, and are actually on the same team, with the same goals. And in my case in particular, I saw federal agents lie multiple times to get the end goal, both in court, and to the grand jury.

I guess it is possible that the timing could have just been a fluke, given the doctors' penchant for making false reports, on any ex-employee they suspected might cross them. Regardless, she became the third office manager in a row that the doctors would allege had stolen money from them. Yet, I was the only one, who had been charged with a crime. I feel confident that had I not been adamant that the office manager, previous to my tenure, had not taken anything from them, she too would have been reported to the police.

After she was fired, she reported the doctors to the EEOC, for what she claimed was age discrimination. I never found out the outcome of that investigation. But what I do know is that I could never find anything she taken from the doctors, regardless that the doctors continued to claim she had. And I had stood firm against the doctors falsely accusing her, and had refused to make up anything against her. She had escaped their wrath at the time, mainly because of my ethics.

The ethics I had when I went to work for the group, before I allowed those ethics to be compromised by Dr. Swan.

Another odd thing to me personally, having worked in the accounting field, was that I knew it would be common practice for any business to put additional measures into place, to protect assets, especially after any suspected theft. More checks and balances, so to speak. Common sense says that anyone who truly believed they had $611,000 stolen by their previous office manager, would certainly NOT hire someone with seventeen felony convictions, consisting of forgery, and other types of fraud, to replace the previous office manager, who had supposedly stolen large sums of money from them. And surely their CPA would have advised them to put practices into place to prevent a future office manager from being able to steal from them.

Yet here we were, less than two years after my departure, and the doctors were once again, claiming that a large sum of money had been stolen by an office manager. We would later find out that the doctors had sued the employment agency that had found the new office manager for them, for the amount they said she had stolen, as well as other damages. That case was settled out of court.

Beginning shortly after the August 2012 meeting, the office manager had with AUSA JB, she would intermittently call my attorney or me, in a panic, to report many examples of what appeared to be harassment by AUSA Harris, and government agents. She said AUSA Harris kept threatening her with an indictment, due to the doctors' complaint that she had stolen money from them. He wanted her to be a witness for the government, not me.

She told stories of government agents showing up at her home, and place of employment, to harass her, which often cost her jobs. She said the agents were putting pressure on her to go against me. The indictment had been dismissed, but the government apparently intended to indict me again. I knew it was because the government wanted the money it had seized.

I had already read way too many horror stories on the Internet, of others claiming similar harassment, at the hands of our government. She said an agent even told her at one of the visits, that "AUSA Harris wants Lynn Espejo, not you." And that all she had to do was "Take back what you said in the meeting with AUSA JB in August 2012, and you will not be bothered by the federal government, or charged with a crime."

She claimed federal agents came to her mom's house, and scared her mom, with their threats against her. She claimed that agents forced meetings with her, by having her state probation officer call her into his office. Then a federal agent would be sprung on her, at the meeting, and she would be forced to meet with them. She told a story, about how a state trooper had stopped her car, for no apparent reason, and then took her into custody and to the Little Rock Police Department (LRPD). Once there, a federal agent waited to force a meeting with her.

This was after she said she had refused to talk to that same agent, a few days earlier, when he had shown up at her home unannounced. She told stories about how AUSA Harris, and Agent Shortway, had visited her at the Lonoke County Jail, to try to make a deal with her, to go against me. If she agreed to cooperate with them, they would make the LRPD report against her go away. Many of these stories we had on tape, as after a while, my attorney and I both started taping our conversations with her.

At one point she showed us an email, where during her tenure as the doctors' office manager, she had reported the doctors for their Medicare fraud. She never knew what transpired after her report, or if the doctors were told it was her that made the report? I was stunned.

To this day, nothing ever came of the police report made against the office manager by the doctors, for the alleged theft of over $100,000. She was never charged with any crime related to that matter by AUSA Harris, or any other law - enforcement official.

However, the government did manage to scare her into submission. She was worthless as a witness in my case, by the time it got to trial three years later. It was beyond frustrating, and just another example, of the power wielded by federal prosecutors and federal agents.

Chapter Twelve
Indictment #2

Finally, after waiting two and a half years for the statute of limitations to run on the 2007-September 2009 timeframe for the wire fraud charges from the first indictment, on October 8, 2014, AUSA Harris indicted me for the second time. True to AUSA Harris' threats, he stuck it to me. He charged me with wire fraud for the time period of October 2009-September 2010, the exact time period my attorney had shown him we had no settlement statement notebooks from Dr. Korker, with which to prove my innocence. He also indicted me for money laundering and tax fraud. In the indictment, he alleged a continuing scheme to defraud that went all the way back to 2007, which was the first date I went to work for the doctors. Because it was alleged to be continuous in nature, the scheme covered the entire time I worked for the doctors, and had charged items on my credit cards for Dr. Swan, the entire $611,000.

And for every check written out of my personal bank account to subcontractors during the building of our home, that was over $10,000, AUSA Harris charged me with one count of money laundering. It didn't matter that we had a construction loan that paid for the building of our home, that was easily documented with the bank.

The truth, once again, was irrelevant. The second indictment, just like the first, alleged that I stole $611,000 from the doctors. Yet, the new indictment took it a step further, charging that I had failed to report the stolen money on my taxes, as illegal income, for the 2007-2010 tax years. Therefore, I was also charged with four counts of tax fraud, for those four years. And, the second indictment also incorporated the $50,000 seized from our bank accounts in March 2011, during the first indictment, as a criminal forfeiture. This meant that I could no longer try to prove the money was innocent.

All the government needed to do was convict me of any of the alleged indictment crimes, and the money would automatically be forfeited to the government. And the federal prosecutors, and secret service agents, would get to keep it for their budgets and 401K plans. Yet, the government did not dismiss the civil forfeiture case that had been ongoing since March 2011. I assume just in case, by some sheer miracle, I won at trial, or the government had to dismiss the second indictment, it could still hold on to our money, and have one more trick left in the government's bag of tricks.

Apparently, the government could have it both ways, and there was nothing we could do about it. It is a very one-sided system, designed to give government prosecutors the upper hand, at every turn. I was devastated. My husband was a basket case. We still did not know if he would soon be indicted, right along with me. After all, the government had been threatening to do so, for the last two years, if I did not play ball its way, which I hadn't. And we had filed joint tax returns, and I was now indicted on tax fraud.

What would happen if he was indicted? We would have no way to pay our bills, or take care of our children, much less have money to pay attorney fees. The attorney, who had represented me during the first indictment, was so angered by the second indictment, that he signed on to represent me in the second indictment, for *free*.

Shortly after the second indictment had been handed down, on October 8, 2014, AUSA Harris sent my attorney an email, on November 22, 2014, that said the office manager had changed her mind about my innocence, and the statements she had given to AUSA JB, in the meeting at the US Attorney's Office on August 5, 2012 (**see Appendix, Document 4**).

This email arrived on a Saturday morning. I remember my

attorney calling me that morning. I was up on a ladder, decorating our family Christmas tree. I cannot describe the anger I felt that day, as my attorney read the email out loud to me, over the phone. The government had finally succeeded at getting the new office manager to buckle.

However, in her next phone call to me, she would firmly deny that she had recanted what she had told the US Attorney's Office, in the August 2012 meeting. I was no longer the trusting soul I had been in the past. I had taped the phone call, at the advice of my attorney, as proof. On tape, she can be heard making the same statements she made in August 2012, and denying that she had recanted these statements to AUSA Harris, or any of the government agents.

Regardless, she would be hounded so much by federal agents, and AUSA Harris, that by the time my case went to trial in January 2017, she had become so fearful, that there was no way she could be trusted to testify on my behalf at trial. The last time I spoke to her, sometime in 2015, when she called me crying, she stated that her probation officer had contacted her again, and was putting pressure on her not to cooperate with my defense attorney. She feared AUSA Harris would indict her. She had always maintained her innocence to us, regarding the doctors' complaints to LRPD, that she had stolen money from them.

I don't know if she was telling the truth or not? It was another million-dollar question, in the ongoing saga, that was my criminal case. Her criminal history indicates that she has a penchant for defrauding others. However, I also know that the doctors have a penchant for lying about having money stolen from them. It's a toss-up, as to who is telling the truth?

The week of my trial, the office manager was under a federal subpoena to testify, that had been served on her by my second attorney. She ignored the subpoena, and was a no show that day. I suspected the government told her to do so, but of course we had no proof of that. The judge offered to send the US Marshal to pick her up, and bring her to court, but my attorney refused the offer, after he made a call to her probation officer. From that conversation, it was evident that the government had once again won.

My attorney advised me that she would ultimately hurt me, not help me, since he felt she would lie for the government, and had most likely made a side deal with them, not to testify on my behalf. The government had already done this with another witness, who had told us about the shredded documents. AUSA Mazzanti approached my attorney at trial regarding the other witness, the biller named Linda, to say the government had spoken to her, and she did not want to testify, even though she was also under subpoena. Regardless that she had previously signed an affidavit regarding the shredding of the documents, **(see Appendix, Document 2)**, she was now willing to lie for the government, at my trial.

The jury never got to hear what either of these witnesses had to say. Evidence, that had they been willing to tell the truth, would have helped my case. But we couldn't put them on the stand, because my attorney was adamant that we could never trust them to be honest. And due to the office manager's 17 or more felony convictions, she would have been discredited anyway, by the government, had we used her as a witness. The government actually could have it both ways.

Chapter Thirteen
Who Wrote This Indictment?

When I first saw the second indictment handed down by the grand jury, on October 8, 2014, I was amazed at how many ways the alleged crime could be charged. It is not uncommon for the government to overcharge in an indictment, in order to force a person to take a plea deal. This is actually common practice. I was also shocked, at the common-sense errors, the indictment contained, apparent errors, even to me, a non-legal mind. And I knew that nothing in the indictment was true, because I had not committed the crimes, for which I had been charged with, for a second time now.

For example, Count 22, of the money laundering charges, alleged that on October 1, 2010, I had written a check to R.C. for $16,500. The indictment alleged that I had written the check to purchase a car, and used stolen money from the alleged wire fraud, to do so. I was able to go directly to my bank statements, the same bank statements that had been provided to us in discovery by the government, during both indictments, and immediately show my attorney that the check, the government said was *written from me to R.C.* for $16,500, was actually a check *written from R.C. to me* (**see Appendix, Document 5**), that had been deposited into our bank account on October 1, 2010. R.C. (Russell Chevrolet) had written the check to me on September 27, 2010, for a 2005 model Honda, that I sold back to the dealership. A car I had purchased in 2005, two years before I went to work for the doctors in 2007. I had deposited this check into our savings account, the same bank account the government had seized in March 2011, when I was indicted the first time.

Count 21 of the indictment alleged that I had committed money laundering, by stealing money, the wire fraud charges, and then writing a check to B.M. for $23,785 (**see Appendix, Document 6**). Again, taking the identical banking records, the ones the government had subpoenaed from my bank, not once, but twice, I was able to show my attorney that on August 6, 2010, we closed on the home we sold on West Lake Circle, and received a check for $82,744.65 (**see Appendix, Document 7**), which we then deposited into our bank account. Instead of drawing on the construction loan we had for the building of the new home (**see Appendix, Link 4**), we used part of the money that we had deposited from the closing of the West Lake Circle house, to write a $23,785 check to our builder B.M., on August 9, 2010.

The check was for money owed to the builder for the new house we were building, and in fact, as noted on the Memo of the check, this was our final payment to the builder. The money paid to BM, had come directly from the closing of our old home. Our bank records clearly showed this paper trail, and proved it was not stolen money, nor proceeds from the alleged wire fraud.

B.M. deposited the check into his bank account, and it cleared our bank on August 11, 2010. We used the remaining money from the sale of the old house, the remainder of the $82,744.65, for the pool house, which was the last thing to be built, and was actually a shed, or small shop plan, like our other neighbors have on their property. Because we put up extra walls to have a bedroom and bathroom, we deemed it the pool house.

However, the government would, over and over again, in their narrative of my alleged crimes, continue to state that I stole money, and used it to build a pool and pool house, all of which was built at the same time as our home, using the same construction loan, and proceeds from the sale of our previous home, and is part of the $2,600 mortgage payment, my husband pays monthly, to this day.

This process of showing my attorney, what the government

said in its indictment, was just not the case, would be repeated, as I showed my attorney that none of the money laundering charges alleged by the government could possibly be true. The construction loan, and our banking records, proved otherwise. Regardless, I was convicted of all counts in the indictment at trial, including the money laundering charges.

Count 24 of the indictment, alleged that I had committed tax fraud, by not reporting the correct amount of *adjusted gross receipts,* on our Federal Individual 1040 income tax return, for 2007-2010. There were several problems with this allegation. First, the number listed in the indictment by the government, as the *adjusted gross receipts* number for 2008, did not appear on our 2008 Federal Individual 1040 Income Tax Return, which was the only return we had filed for the year 2008. In fact, the number in the indictment did not appear on *any* of our tax returns, for the years 2007-2010, the years the government alleged, in the indictment, that I had committed tax fraud. I assumed the government had just pulled the number out of thin air. The truth really didn't matter anyway!

And because my husband and I were both W2 employees, there would have been no *adjusted gross receipts* to report, on our 2007-2010 Federal Individual 1040 Income Tax Returns, to begin with. This brings me to my next point; the government obviously did not understand the difference between *adjusted gross income*, income that gets reported on a Federal Individual 1040 Income Tax Return vs. *adjusted gross receipts,* income that gets reported on Federal Business Income Tax Returns 1120, 1120S, or 1065.

A *gross receipt* is a term used in accounting, and by the IRS, to represent the total amounts an organization or business received from all sources, during its annual accounting period, without subtracting any costs or expenses. *Adjusted gross receipts* are *gross receipts* for a business, after *subtracting costs and expenses,* for the year. As W2 employees, we did not own our own business at the time, and therefore, did not have *adjusted gross receipts,* of any kind. The indictment did not make sense.

A Schedule C reports sole proprietorship business income on a Federal Individual 1040 Tax Return. Still, even a Schedule C, did not apply to the government's allegations in the indictment. And, my husband had reported extra money he made from doing accounting work, outside of his regular job, on a Schedule C, on our Federal 1040 income tax return.

The IRS does require stolen money, from illegal activities, such as from drugs, embezzlement, illegal gambling, and other illegal activities, to be reported on Line 21, of an individual federal income tax return. Yes, the IRS requires that illegal income be reported on an income tax return.

Since the indictment did not make the government's accusations clear, we could only surmise that what the government was really trying to allege, in the indictment, was that I had not reported money from illegal sources, the alleged wire fraud, on my 2007-2010 tax returns. Yet, nowhere in the indictment was it alleged that I had not reported stolen funds on my tax returns, even though that is precisely what the government said at trial that I had done.

The language in the indictment made it clear that neither IRS Agent Shortway, or AUSA Harris, who had jointly written the indictment, to be presented to the grand jury, understood general accounting terms, nor did they understand tax terminology, related to the filing of Individual Tax Return vs. a Business Tax return.

And even worse yet, based on Count 22 of the indictment, the R.C. money laundering charge, it appeared that neither AUSA Harris, nor Agent Shortway, could tell the difference between a check vs. a deposit, when reviewing bank statements. And the government had certainly not looked at the deposit from the sale of our home, the proceeds used to pay the $23,785 to our builder, which appeared in Count 21 of the indictment.

What was illegal about any of these transactions? The government never did correct the language in the indictment, for the alleged tax fraud counts. Still, AUSA Harris, was ever so kind, as to dismiss Count 22 of the money laundering charges, the R.C. check, shortly after my attorney pointed this mistake out, in our Motion to Dismiss.

When the government did dismiss this charge, its motion to dismiss stated that "the $16,500 check was from the sale of an asset that had been paid for with stolen money from wire fraud, but that the government would just dismiss it anyway." Regardless, the real truth was, that I had purchased this car two whole years, before ever working for the doctors. Once again, proving my point, that the government will never admit its mistakes. And from what I have seen in my case alone, federal prosecutors, and federal agents, make a lot of mistakes! And sadly, there were many other issues with the indictment that I quickly pointed out to my attorney.

The indictment made allegations about the QuickBooks accounting program that I had used at the doctors' office, to create the settlement statements, and pay their bills and payroll. The allegations in the indictment were ridiculous, since the program itself was not even capable of doing such things. Doing a quick search of the QuickBooks website, I was able to pull up information, to show my attorney. Information, which quickly proved that the language in the indictment, could not be correct, regarding what the government said I had done, in the QuickBooks.

Surely the IRS Agent should have understood these things? Didn't he have an accounting degree? And a CPA license? How could he not understand how QuickBooks, a popular accounting software, worked? But none of this mattered. My attorney didn't really understand accounting either. I would come to understand that nobody involved in my case understood accounting. And this is how the government was able to allege anything it wanted against me.

And if those mistakes were not enough, there were even more issues with the indictment language. Certainly, an indicted citizen could expect that any IRS agent, or a government prosecutor, would be competent enough, to tell the difference between, an earnest money deposit vs. money considered income from another source, that should be reported on an income tax return. Primarily since the same IRS agent, and AUSA, had used grand jury subpoenas, to get the closing documents for the house, we had sold in 2010, when we built our new home. The name on the check written to us for $1000 (**see Appendix, Document 8**), as an earnest money deposit on the house we sold on West Lake Circle, clearly matched the buyer's name on the closing paperwork for the sale of that home (**see Appendix, Link 5**), and the $1000 was listed as a *deposit or earnest money,* subtracted on line 201 of the HUD-1 closing document, the exact closing document, that the government had used a grand jury subpoena, to get from the title company, not once, but twice.

However, it turns out that all of my expectations would actually be expecting way too much from our federal government. In the discovery given to us by the government, one of the government's exhibits showed that I had failed to report $1000 in taxable income, on our 2010 tax return, the year we sold the West Lake Circle house. The government listed the source of the unreported income, as the name of the person whom we had sold our house on West Lake Circle. And that check had not even been written to me. It was written to my husband. And most disturbing, is that even non-accounting people have enough common sense to know that a deposit on a house you are selling is not a taxable event, because it's not income. But that did not stop my government from charging me with a crime for the $1000.

And I really wish I could say these were all of the mistakes I found in the indictment. Unfortunately, there were many, many others. It was appalling that this was my government. These are the people who are entrusted with decisions that can ruin a person's life. Federal prosecutors choose who is prosecuted and for which crimes they are prosecuted. They should be held to a higher standard.

Yet, these two government employees, one a criminal investigator for the IRS, and the other, the First Assistant US

Attorney in the Eastern District of Arkansas, the next in charge directly under the US Attorney in my district, who had been a federal prosecutor for 30+ years, obviously did not even understand simple financial transactions, that even laypersons understood. No wonder these people could not be trusted to care about the truth of what really happened in my case, or even understand what had happened to begin with!

Even simple math was over their heads. How were they expected to understand the difference between a reimbursement through payroll for things I charged for my boss, vs. wire fraud? Or was the real truth that they knew the difference, but placed these allegations in the indictment anyway? I was so mad! My anger turned into hatred toward these two individuals, and took an even deeper root inside me.

The statute of limitations had run on part of the original 57 counts of wire fraud that appeared in the first indictment; however, in the second indictment, the government used language of a "continuing scheme," to bring in the entire $611, 000, I had charged for Dr. Swan, on my personal credit cards, into the second indictment.

The government only had to make a case from October 2009-September 2010 timeframe to a jury, the exact timeframe, AUSA Harris had been told by my first attorney, that we had no records from. Regardless, it could make allegations of a "continuing scheme," all the way back from 2007 forward, as far as a restitution number goes, and cover the entire amount of wire fraud charges from the first indictment.

And by doing so, they could drive up the amount of prison time I would receive, based on the Federal Sentencing Guidelines, should I be convicted. It would be as good as getting a conviction for the entire $611,000, the government had alleged in the first indictment. And AUSA Harris knew I had no way to defend the 2009-2010 time-frame, because we were missing all the financial evidence from that time frame, since Dr. Korker's settlement statements were the only ones not destroyed.

The second indictment had alleged a $285,000 wire fraud scheme. My attorney suspected this was by design for several reasons. 1. The government could incorporate their original indictment in its entirety, even though the government had dismissed that indictment, and waited two and a half years to indict me again, on basically the exact charges available to them in 2011. And because AUSA Harris knew I did not have settlement notebooks for October 2009-September 2010, thanks to my attorney, it would be an easy conviction for the government. It was a win, win for AUSA Harris. 2. This also allowed the government to charge 2007-2010, regardless that the government had failed to get complete banking records, for part of those years. The bank statements were no longer available for 2007-2008, because the bank no longer had them. But by only charging October 2009-September 2010, in the new indictment, the government could claim it had given us complete banking records for all the wire fraud charges found in the second indictment.

While not having the complete banking records helped the prosecution's case, it hurt my case. I needed the deposits to show which doctor put money into the *zero*-balance bank account, to be able to prove that Dr. Swan had, in fact, been the person who put the $611,000, into the bank account, which was then reimbursed to me. I could not show who had deposited funds, because the deposit records were unavailable. I wondered how we were now on a second indictment, yet, the government was just now figuring out that it had incomplete banking records, and only after we had pointed it out in one of our motions.

I could feel the walls closing in. I knew I was innocent. My anger at the government grew with each passing day. I should have been praying, and asking God to help give me peace during this time. But I was so fueled by anger, that I was just lost. And how much of this was a mistake, on the part of the government, or actually by design? I would never know. It is well documented by criminal defense attorneys that often government agents do not subpoena records they feel may hurt the government's case. It is a way around the Brady laws. The amount of incompetence and corruption was unbelievable.

Not only had the doctors shredded all the financial documents, and destroyed my work computer, but also the government, my government, had failed to get records that would help to prove my innocence. How was I supposed to prove the truth of what happened, with no documents to back up my defense? And unfortunately, that would not be all the evidence the government had lost in my case.

During the course of my case, we received many copies of a QuickBooks backup, from the government, in the discovery process. None of which we could open, to view the data. Each time we filed a motion with the Court, to get a correct copy, the government delivered yet another copy of the QuickBooks. Supposedly these backups had come from my work computer, now destroyed. Shockingly, the government did not know the password to open any of the copies it gave us. How had the government made allegations regarding my tampering with QuickBooks, in the current indictment, just like there had been in the first indictment, but nobody from the government had ever even opened a copy of the QuickBooks to look at it?

I wondered out loud at my attorney's office, "Who are these people?" "Barney Fife?" "The Keystone Cops?" This was on the day that the IRS agent had come to my attorney's office, to show off what he proudly touted, was "His hacking skills." Agent Shortway actually bragged about these skills, and seemed quite proud of them. He used his hacking skills to "break into the QuickBooks," so we could finally review the data. This was, of course, many months into the second indictment. Proof that the government had never looked at the QuickBooks data, before either indictment, since Agent Shortway had to *hack* into it, for us to even get access to the data.

Again, I questioned how there was language in the indictment, alleging I had manipulated the QuickBooks entries, when nobody at the government had even looked at the QuickBooks? Who made these accusations? Or even verified them to be true? I was just the proverbial government *ham sandwich*.

What we saw, once we gained access to the data in the QuickBooks, was equally as shocking. Entries clearly showed that someone had been working in the latest copy, given to us by the government, well past the last date of my employment with the doctors. In fact, there were entries, several years past the time, I had been employed at the doctors' clinic. It was apparent things had been changed in the QuickBooks as well.

I could immediately tell that this was not the copy of QuickBooks I had used. I showed my attorney, using the bank statements we had, bank statements that included photocopies of vendor checks, that the cleared checks did not match the data contained in the QuickBooks copy we had received from the government. Something was amiss. There was no way we had been given a copy of the QuickBooks data that those checks could not have been printed out of? I knew so, because I knew, that the QuickBooks program automatically records checks when printed, and the copy we had, did not contain the correct data.

Further disturbing, there were no electronic payroll records reflected in the copy of QuickBooks, which we had been given by the government. Electronic payroll is an automatic download, from the QuickBooks program, when the payroll is processed. The user of the QuickBooks program, which would have been me during my employment with the doctors, does not control this process. I was disgusted.

We had no hard copies of the payroll records, because those had been destroyed by the doctors, when they destroyed all of their financial documents, in February 2011, just a few weeks before the first indictment in my case. And the QuickBooks copy we had been given by the government, did not show the electronic payroll records. We would later find out that the doctors' CPA claimed he had actually backed up a copy of the QuickBooks, the week I left employment with the doctors, in September 2010, and had given that flash drive to either the IRS, or Secret Service agent, at the time. Nobody in the government could produce the flash drive.

My attorney had been to the same CPA's office months earlier, shortly after the handing down of the second indictment, trying to get a copy of the QuickBooks data files. I wanted the copy so I could prove what had really happened. The funny thing was, when the CPA and my attorney looked at all the computers in the CPA's office, no copy of the QuickBooks could be found on any of the computers.

However, when AUSA Harris, and Agent Shortway, went to the same CPA's office months later, a copy appeared, on one of the same computers, my attorney had already looked at with the CPA, months earlier, that contained no copies of the QuickBooks. I was suspicious of this. I knew that one of the doctors' previous office managers now worked for the CPA. This office manager was still very close with all the doctors, and had often visited the clinic, when I worked there. Of course, one could not go about alleging such things. Otherwise, they would be no better than our federal government, and its false allegations. I also suspected that Agent Shortway may have planted the copy of the QuickBooks, on the computer, with his hacking skills.

We never were able to get a copy of the flash drive that supposedly existed, and that was reportedly downloaded by the CPA, a few days after I left employment with the doctors. That flash drive had conveniently been lost by the government, and the government never found it. And the Court did not even hold the government responsible for its loss of crucial evidence.

Regardless of the apparent chain of custody issues, the Judge allowed the copy of the QuickBooks, which the government claimed had been retrieved from the CPA's computer, to be entered into evidence at trial. My first attorney believed the chain of custody could not be verified for the QuickBooks. However, my second attorney did not make any argument that made sense, to explain this to the judge, or to prevent the wrong copy of QuickBooks from being entered into the record, at my trial.

He instead argued that as long as the office manager, the one who went to work for the doctors after me, with the 17 felony convictions, had not touched the copy the government wanted to enter into evidence, that we had no objections to it. I was shocked by my attorney's argument. And that is how the government got by with these things, repeatedly at trial. Leaving me with really no way to defend myself from the allegations in the indictment, regardless of the truth.

The government failed to secure the financial documents when they became involved in the case, which allowed the doctors time to have them shredded. It had also lost crucial forensic evidence, the QuickBooks flash drive, given to them by the doctors' CPA. Not to mention the incomplete banking records. And if that was not enough, my work computer had also been destroyed by the doctors, after the government failed to even make a backup copy of that computer, which is standard practice in a federal investigation. The sloppiness of this investigation was incredible. Yet I sat indicted for a second time, for crimes I had not committed.

It would later come to our attention that IRS Agent Shortway had also illegally shared our tax return, with my husband's boss, before I was charged in the second indictment. This was illegal, because my husband's boss had no legal right to see our tax return. Tax returns are highly protected documents.

Even people who work for the IRS, can't view your tax return, without a valid reason. But that did not stop Agent Shortway from violating the law. Sometime in 2014, IRS Agent Shortway served a subpoena, on my husband's work, that requested any tax returns, belonging to us, that could be found on my husband's computer, to be turned over to the federal government.

My husband had willingly given our tax returns to his bosses' attorney, to prevent losing his job, even though he was not required to do so. Regardless, this didn't give the IRS agent the legal right to share our tax returns with my husband's boss. And it did not make any sense to begin with, since by law, a return has to have been *filed* with the IRS to even qualify as fraudulent, should the return be found to be incorrect.

Anything on my husband's computer would not be proof of fraudulent tax returns anyway. And remember the allegation the government was lodging, was that I did not report stolen money on our tax return, not that we had not reported income from legal sources.

When asked about sharing our tax return, during testimony at one of the pretrial hearings, Agent Shortway lied on the stand. He denied that he had emailed a copy of our tax return, and a password to view the return, to my husband's boss. My husband's boss had kept the email that proved the agent had emailed him a copy of our joint tax return, with a password to view it. He had given all this information to my attorney, so we had the proof of what my attorney was asking Agent Shortway about, in sworn testimony. Agent Shortway also testified that personal tax returns on my husband's work computer contained errors. As soon as Agent Shortway left the witness stand, my attorney called my husband's boss to the stand to testify.

His testimony clearly proved that Agent Shortway had sent him our tax return, that he had no right to view. He admitted that the email we entered into evidence that day, was sent to him by Agent Shortway, and also testified that he knew nothing about our finances, in which to comment on our tax return, or its correctness, so there was no reason for him to view the return. In the government's cross-examination, the government's line of questioning tried to push him to say he knew about our finances. But he did now waiver during his testimony.

My husband's boss further testified that CPAs often keep old tax returns on their computer from previous years, in order to do tax planning for the current tax year, not just for their personal returns, but that this practice is commonly used for client tax planning, as well. These returns would show as errors in the accounting software system, because the returns would not be complete, and would not be able to be electronically filed, or printed from the software to be filed by mail, due to showing errors on the return.

The chances of the government getting one of those returns, never meant to be filed, from my husband's work computer, was great, since my husband is a CPA, and would have used our old tax returns from previous years, to do our current tax year planning. In fact, the agent's email to my husband's boss, where he had shared our tax return, suggested that the government believed there was one of our state tax returns, on my husband's work computer, that did contain errors.

How did the agent know what was on my husband's work computer? The government had never been given access to that computer. You make your own decision about that! When you are considering your options, remember that this is the same IRS agent, who bragged about his "hacking skill," the day he broke into the QuickBooks at my attorney's office. One thing is for certain, it's not a crime to have a partly completed return on your computer, or even one used for tax planning, that may contain mistakes/errors. The crime does not happen, until you file the return with the IRS, that contains the errors. And even then, the government has to prove that you knew that the errors existed when you filed the return, and had criminal intent in doing so.

Something, even the IRS agent had to admit in court during the pretrial hearing that day. The return on my husband's computer had not been filed, so even if it had contained errors, the government could not have entered it into evidence anyway. So why was the government trying to use grand jury subpoenas to get them?

My attorney felt that the email to my husband's boss by the government, was clearly harassment on the part of the IRS agent, in an attempt to make my husband's boss suspect that my husband was using the firm's accounting software, and work computer, to create false tax returns. Up to that point, the government had served several grand jury subpoenas on my husband's work. All before the email from the Agent Shortway, that included our tax return.

The government had also called my husband's bosses to a meeting with AUSA Harris, and Agent Shortway, at the US Attorney's office. The government had hinted in that meeting that the government *may* be investigating the accounting firm where my husband worked. A scare tactic commonly used by the government to intimidate people.

I would see this happen over and over again in my case. The government used this tactic, to get people to say whatever the government needed them to say, or not to say. In this manner, the government intimidated witnesses, when what the witness had to say would likely undermine the government's narrative of the case.

But trying to give the government the benefit of the doubt here, maybe it was as simple as Agent Shortway not knowing enough about accounting practices, to even know that CPAs use old returns, to do tax planning? Given all the errors in the indictment itself, it was obvious to me that the agent knew nothing about accounting.

The email (**see Appendix, Link 6**), sent to my husband's boss, clearly proves that Agent Shortway sent our tax return to someone who had no legal right to view it, and for no apparent reason, since the IRS agent already had certified copies of our filed tax returns from both the State of Arkansas, and the IRS for the years of 2007-2010. Testimony further showed that Agent Shortway had just committed perjury when testified, "I did not send an email to or share the Espejo's joint tax return with Mr. Espejo's boss." Regardless, the judge did not reprimand the agent. I also reported this illegal sharing of our tax return to the Inspector General's office. However, to my knowledge, nothing happened to the agent as he was still working for the IRS, at least as of the week of my trial, which was several years after my reporting of his sharing of our tax return.

Chapter Fourteen
The Games Prosecutors Play

Federal criminal proceedings are complicated indeed. There are many confusing legal terms, for example, Jencks Act materials. Jencks Act materials include documents such as field notes used by the FBI, IRS, and other government agents, to record what *the agent says* is the content of their conversations with a witness, as they do not record these conversations.

There are also grand jury transcripts, Brady Material, 404(b) Evidence, Touhy Requests, and a hoard of other legal terms, and rules of criminal procedure, that are both confusing, and complicated. For example, a defendant cannot get copies of Jencks Act materials, or grand jury transcripts, in discovery. You may only see this information at trial, and only IF the government calls a person as a witness, that was interviewed by the agent, or put before the grand jury.

Therefore, the defendant may never know that a witness actually said something favorable to their defense, unless the prosecution is honest, and provides you with this information in discovery, or allows pretrial viewing of said information, at the US Attorney's Office. And the viewing of this information, is at the prosecutor's discretion, unless the witness is called at trial.

In the case of defendants that take a plea deal, the information would never become available to the defendant. If the government fails to provide information favorable to the defendant in discovery, and the defendant can *prove* this failure has occurred, the prosecutor has withheld exculpatory evidence, better known as Brady Evidence. But, how does one *prove* they did not get evidence, if they never knew about the evidence to begin with?

The Jencks Act, 18 U.S.C. § 3500, provides that the government prosecutor must produce a statement, or report, made by a government witness, or prospective government witness, other than the defendant, but only after the witness has testified at trial. Jencks Act material is evidence used in the course of a federal criminal prosecution in the United States. A Brady disclosure consists of exculpatory, or impeaching information and evidence, that is material to the guilt, or innocence, or to a defendant's punishment. The term comes from the U.S. Supreme Court case, *Brady v. Maryland*. The Supreme Court ruled that suppression by the prosecution, of evidence favorable to a defendant, who has requested it, violates due process.

In my case, we caught AUSA Harris, red-handed on the record, hiding Brady Material, but again, nothing happened to him. Not even a tongue lashing from the judge, or a sanction to the government. Nothing! These acts and laws, basically the rules of federal criminal procedure, are all dependent, on a federal prosecutor being honest, in the discovery process. The same prosecutor who wants to win their case at all costs.

This is a *considerable* disadvantage for the defendant, the person trying to prove their innocence. Take the Jencks Act Material as an example; at trial, your attorney needs to listen to direct examination of a witness by the prosecution, so they know what to ask on cross-examination. However, the attorney also needs to be able to review the Jencks materials, at the same time, to make sure the witness does not change any statement previously given, and for other information relevant to the defense, for the charges in the indictment. And since the defendant isn't allowed to see the material until the witness is on the stand, it's a double-edged sword.

Once again, the government has the upper hand. The process is very one-sided, with everything being in favor of the government, which already has a considerable advantage anyway. Government prosecutors have many resources

156

available to them. They have numerous staff support and an unlimited budget. The government basically controls every aspect of the entire process from start to finish.

And what if the prosecutor withheld exculpatory evidence? While the hiding of the evidence significantly damages a defendant's chances of proving their innocence, or making a complete defense to the charges, nothing happens to the prosecutor who hid the evidence. Such as in my case, with AUSA Harris, making it even more advantageous for a prosecutor to operate in this manner. Even if the prosecutor gets caught; he will not be punished. The most that may happen, is that a defendant uses this hiding of evidence, to get a new trial, but that will be years down the road, and the chances are very slim. It is a moral dilemma that is all too often abused, and one you will read about more, than you would like to, if you follow many criminal cases. Yet, as the defendant, you can do nothing to the prosecutor, to hold him accountable due to his immunity. It is a broken system.

This is just one area, of many areas, that badly need to be reformed, in our criminal justice system. The system is supposed to be fair, and give the defendant every opportunity to prove their innocence. Yet, I found it to be precisely the opposite. And when the government is caught, its excuse is always, "We thought we had previously turned over all the evidence," or "That evidence is not exculpatory," so no harm, no foul. An interesting example of prosecutors hiding evidence, and committing Brady violations, gained widespread attention in the late Senator Ted Stevens' case.

Given that Senator Stevens' case was very public, one would think prosecutors would have been on their best behavior, especially given the media attention the case received. Yet, that did not stop government prosecutors from hiding evidence, and playing dirty, in that case as well.

Considering the Stevens example, what would prevent a prosecutor from hiding evidence in a run-of-the-mill case, as are most cases, that work their way through the system? Unfortunately, the hiding of evidence happens in many cases that do not get reported, because the defendant never knows about it.

The study, *Harmful Error*, found 223 prosecutors around the nation had been cited by judges, for two or more cases of unfair conduct, but only two prosecutors had been disbarred, in the past 33 years, for mishandling criminal cases." And in a January 4, 2014, news article in the *New York Times*, Judge Alex Kozinski, who was the chief judge of the United States Court of Appeals, for the Ninth Circuit, at the time, is quoted as saying, "There is an epidemic of Brady violations abroad in the land, and the lack of professional consequences for failing to disclose exculpatory evidence only makes the breach of duty more likely." "Some prosecutors don't care about Brady because courts don't *make* them care."

Getting back to my case, after we started getting discovery in the second indictment, it became apparent that AUSA Harris liked to piecemeal discovery to us. My attorney opined that AUSA Harris was obviously, "A fly by the seat of his pants kind of guy," or "Is possibly trying to get some sort of strategic advantage from doing so." We would receive the same documents repeatedly, and in many different formats. We received the same evidence/documents on cd disk, as printed hard copies, and in electronic form, by way of emails, from AUSA Harris.

We were forced to look at each page we received, regardless of the format we received it, to make sure we had seen all the documents, and were not missing anything new, that may be included in the new copy we received. This was very time-consuming. And remember, my attorney was working for free on my case during the second indictment, because he believed so strongly in my innocence.

I'm not talking about a few hundred pages either; I'm speaking to well over 200,000 pages of documents, mostly bank statements, and emails between the doctors. This was another area, where the government's incompetence surprised me. One would expect that with all the staff, and other resources at its disposal, it would be a seamless process. That was not what I witnessed at all. And maybe again, this was by design, to keep the defense with their lack of resources, bogged down in so much discovery, that the attorney couldn't prepare for trial?

But we could not take the risk that the government would sneak an extra page into the discovery, so we were forced to review the same documents, repeatedly. This is one of the jobs my attorney assigned to me. And each time I went through this process, my anger was fueled even more, and continued to take deeper root within me.

During the first indictment, we reviewed settlement statement notebooks, in AUSA JB's office, at the US Attorney's office. We reviewed them in the civil case, at the doctors' attorney's office. But we did not receive these notebooks in discovery from AUSA Harris, during the discovery phase of the second indictment. Regardless of how many emails my attorney sent to AUSA Harris, or how many motions he filed with the court, nobody at the US Attorney's office could produce these notebooks. These were substantial white notebooks, full of paper. Twelve to fifteen of them, to be exact. That amount of evidence, could not have evaporated into thin air? Or could it? What had the government done with these notebooks?

My attorney filed several pretrial motions that requested these notebooks be produced, and also requested that a correct backup copy of the QuickBooks be produced. The government, specifically AUSA Harris, kept denying that the government had the settlement notebooks, and claimed it had already given us the QuickBooks. We knew this was not correct. The now-retired, AUSA JB, who had dismissed my first indictment, continued to tell my attorney that there was no way AUSA Harris was being honest. In fact, he had pushed a cart full of the discovery in my case, down the hall to AUSA Harris' office, himself, which mainly consisted of the settlement notebooks, when he refused to indict me for a second time, even though AUSA Harris was demanding he do so.

Per my attorney's conversations with the retired AUSA, he felt certain that AUSA Harris was purposely hiding this evidence, and not turning it over in discovery. It was Brady Material. AUSA Harris kept denying that he had the notebooks, even denying this fact in court on the record, while standing in front of a federal judge. Because we needed retired AUSA JB to tell the court otherwise, my attorney sent what was called a Touhy Request to Washington, D.C. via a FAX message. This request alerted the government that retired AUSA JB would be coming to court at a pretrial hearing, to testify as a witness for the defense, about giving the notebooks directly to AUSA Harris (see Appendix, Link 7).

At the same time, my attorney also sent an email to US Attorney Thyer, and all the other AUSAs on my case, including AUSA Harris, alerting them that a Touhy Request had been sent to the DOJ in Washington, D.C. (see Appendix, Document 9). Within an hour of the DOJ in Washington, D.C. receiving the Touhy request, and the local US Attorney's Office receiving the email, sent to them regarding this request being sent to Washington, D. C.; my attorney received an email from another AUSA, now assigned to my case, AUSA Mazzanti, who was now working with AUSA Harris. AUSA Mazzanti's email alerted us that the government had the settlement notebooks and would produce them (see Appendix, Document 10).

A few days later, we received another email from the government, after my attorney continued to press the government for an answer as to how these notebooks had "suddenly been found," after months of us asking the government for them, and filing multiple pleadings with the court to try to get them (see Appendix, Document 11).

Please note that the government's position was that AUSA Harris *thought* we had the notebooks, from the first indictment, because he *thought* he saw them in my attorney's office. Yet, at no time, during the months of back-and-forth emails with the government, or the many motions we filed with the court, trying to get these records, had AUSA Harris ever brought up this point.

And regardless if AUSA Harris thought we had them in the first indictment or not, that indictment was dismissed, so discovery started over. This was a new indictment. The Court's orders, and the Brady laws, required the government to produce discovery. And why would we waste all that time asking for them, if we had them? It was hogwash! And the government knew it!

On the date of the July 2015 pretrial hearing, we were prepared to put former AUSA JB on the stand, to testify that "He had given the notebooks directly to AUSA Harris." But before he could be brought to the stand, AUSA Harris suddenly was willing to admit on the record that he had basically lied to a federal judge at the previous pretrial hearing, and in pleadings before the Court, about the government "never having these notebooks." We knew he did so to prevent AUSA JB from taking the stand in court that day.

On the record, AUSA Harris admitted, that he had left the court the day of the last pretrial hearing in May 2015, had gone back to the US Attorney's office, and put his hands directly on the notebooks, yet had not alerted my attorney, or the court, about the existence of the notebooks. We were now two months past the previous pretrial hearing, and we were just now finding this out!

Basically, the government had been able to withhold these documents for an additional two months. We could have been using the notebooks in our trial prep. Yet, AUSA Harris was now willing to admit this on the record, to prevent testimony from the retired AUSA who had dismissed my first indictment, and who was sitting outside the courtroom, waiting to testify about giving the notebooks directly to AUSA Harris.

Whatever the retired AUSA had on AUSA Harris, he was scared of him. Apparently, whatever it was, AUSA Harris didn't want the information put on record, in federal court. That much was obvious. AUSA Harris, turned white as a ghost in court that day, when he thought the judge might be about to rule in favor of allowing retired AUSA JB to testify. Regardless that we had now proven, that AUSA Harris had not only lied to the court many times on the record, as well as wasted months of the court's time going back and forth about these notebooks, and had actually hidden exculpatory evidence, Brady material, no sanctions were handed down by the judge, to the government that day. AUSA Harris did not even receive a reprimand, or tongue lashing, from the judge. The only thing that happened was that AUSA Harris disappeared from prosecuting my case, after that day in court.

It was frustrating, and disappointing, to say the least. Regardless that the entire process is already favored toward the government from start to finish, this is obviously not enough for an overzealous prosecutor. They still want more. The book *Licensed To Lie (Exposing Corruption In The Department Of Justice)*, written by Sidney Powell, a 10-year veteran of the United States Attorney's Office, is an excellent read. Ms. Powell's book details horror stories of the corruption she personally witnessed, when she was an AUSA, working for the DOJ, and later when she has represented defendants in criminal cases against the government.

Another seemingly unethical move by AUSA Harris came, when he had continued to have grand jury subpoenas served to my sister-in-law, by IRS and Secret Service agents, at her place of business, prior to my second indictment. She was subpoenaed to the grand jury, as a witness against me, many times. Each time, the government canceled those subpoenas, the day she was to appear before the grand jury, to testify. Then a few days later, an agent would call, or come by her work, to ask her if she would be willing to have a meeting with AUSA Harris instead. There was no reason for this, except for pure harassment of my family, at the hands of the government.

She knew nothing about my case, or our finances. On the last date that she was subpoenaed to the grand jury, in March

2014, she swore that she had testified, and even recited to my attorney, the questions she was asked by AUSA Harris. Since we knew, if true, that my sister-in-law should have a grand jury transcript, from her appearance at the grand jury, we kept requesting to review the grand jury transcript, at the US Attorney's office.

A defendant cannot get copies of these transcripts in the discovery process, so the only way to see them is to go to the government's office to review them in person. Another way the government keeps the upper hand, and forces defense attorneys to jump through government hoops.

The government kept telling us that my sister-in-law had not testified before the grand jury, therefore there was no transcript to review. My sister-in-law continued to maintain that she had. As it would turn out, AUSA Harris had once again abused his grand jury subpoena power. He used a grand jury subpoena to force my sister-in-law to have a meeting with the government, after she had refused to do so many times. AUSA Harris had accomplished this feat, under the guise of telling my sister-in-law, that she was testifying before the grand jury, when she was actually in a meeting with AUSA Harris, and Agent Shortway. The very meeting, she claimed she had refused to have, regardless of the government's many requests.

When we finally got to the bottom of the matter, we found that AUSA Harris, and IRS Agent Shortway, had been the only ones in the room with my sister-in-law. She had not actually testified before the grand jury at all. There was no transcript of this meeting, and the government said there were no meeting notes, kept by Agent Shortway, or AUSA Harris. Therefore, it was the government's word, against my sister-in-law's word, about what was said in that meeting. The two accounts did not agree.

Further, by being underhanded in this manner, AUSA Harris, had denied my sister-in-law her legal right to be represented by an attorney, at the meeting. When a person is called before the grand jury as a witness, they may not take an attorney in with them. You may have one waiting outside to consult with, if you wish to leave the grand jury, which most people do not wish to do, since this gives the appearance that the witness is hiding something.

However, in a meeting with the government, you are afforded by law to be represented by counsel at the meeting, if you so choose to bring an attorney with you. No person is required by law to meet with a prosecutor, or government agent, unless that person so chooses. Many people who are approached by the government do not realize this. Many believe that if they cooperate, and just tell the truth, that all will be well, but instead, end up being charged with the crime of "lying to a government agent," should their side of what was said in that meeting differ from the government, which nine times out of ten it will.

Remember Martha Stewart? Lying to a government agent was the crime for which she served time in federal prison. The same can be said most recently, about Michael Flynn. And there are many stories of people being ambushed at their homes, by federal agents, and then ending up in trouble after speaking to them, without an attorney present. This is how the government charges people, for which it can find nothing else with which to charge them.

My advice is never to trust the government. I know how it feels to be someone who is convicted of a crime I did not commit, and I would hate to see anyone put their liberties at stake. Unfortunately, a federal agent is not your friend, no matter how nice they seem, when they show up at your front door. They are looking to charge someone with a crime, and any statement you give them will become your word against their word, about what was said. I hope I don't need to explain to you, who will the judge, or jury, believe?

My sister-in-law claimed she had refused to meet with AUSA Harris many times. She had every right to deny those meetings. However, because she was not the target of an investigation, she did not have a choice, in regards to appearing, under a grand jury subpoena to testify.

The target, the person the government is investigating, at a grand jury investigation, may refuse a grand jury subpoena to testify, and cannot be held in contempt of court, should they refuse, because they have a Fifth Amendment right to remain silent. But a non-target, of an investigation, must testify if subpoenaed, and can be held in contempt of court, should they refuse.

By federal criminal procedures, AUSA Harris would have had to put my sister-in-law before the grand jury, to force her to testify. It was apparent that AUSA Harris only wanted a meeting with my sister-in-law, most likely so that no record of what was said would be recorded, in case the government did not like what she had to say, or so the government could later twist her words. But if the government did like what she had to say, then they would call her before the grand jury, to testify against me. Again, the government wanted to have it both ways!

Whereas at the grand jury, a court reporter types every word. And a transcript is available, to memorialize what was said, during testimony, and would be available to use in my defense. So corrupt AUSA Harris, just tricked my sister-in-law into a meeting, by using a grand jury subpoena to get her to the government's offices. She claimed she believed she was before the grand jury, and did not know the difference.

This was a massive abuse of power, and an abuse of a grand jury subpoena, to allow her to believe she was forced under subpoena to testify, when she was only in a meeting with the government. Again, my attorney made the judge aware of this apparent prosecutorial misconduct. My sister-in-law testified in Court about it, at one of the pretrial hearings. But once again, the judge did nothing!

In our personal conversations, my sister-in-law was swooning over IRS Agent Shortway, who she thought was good-looking. This made me sick to my stomach! He looked more like a greasy hair drifter to me. And at the time, this made me angry at my sister-in-law. How dare she have a crush on the person trying to. put me in prison? Not to the fact that she was already married. I was disgusted at the entire situation.

The amount of underhanded, and just downright dirty games, played by AUSA Harris, was incredible. Obviously, he did not believe in justice, and it was a win at all costs, game to him. The amount of unethical behavior was sickening. I'm sorry to say that even after AUSA Harris was caught lying on the record about hiding evidence in this case, and was either removed from my case, because I complained against him, or removed himself from the case, after he had been called out on the record, the situation did not improve.

AUSA Mazzanti, was no better than AUSA Harris. And the truth did not matter to her either, I would soon find out, after she became the lead government attorney, on my case. She was just as unethical and corrupt as AUSA Harris had been.

Chapter Fifteen

Proceeding Pro Se: Going Head-to-Head with the US Attorney's Office in the Eastern District of Arkansas

On March 9, 2015, my attorney filed a Motion to Dismiss the second indictment. The motion was 50 pages long, and had 32 exhibits. The 32 exhibits from that filing, back up a lot of what I've been reporting in this book, regarding the faulty indictment language, the unethical behavior by the government, and the destruction of documents by the doctors. We had worked for months on it, with the other volunteer attorneys, and former AUSAs, that had been helping with my case, in the background. I had done most of the paralegal work on it myself.

In the filing, we tried hard to make the judge understand that the destroyed evidence basically left me with no way to defend myself, against the charges. We worked hard to show the court just how dirty AUSA Harris, and the government, had operated in my case. I was being prosecuted because I had angered the government, mainly AUSA Harris, not because I had actually committed a crime. Along with the federal government still wanting to keep the $50,000, it had seized from our bank accounts in March 2011.

After a long, and hard-fought battle, with many pretrial filings, and court appearances, my relationship with my first attorney, who was working on my case for free, was strained. It was frustrating to everyone on my legal team, that the judge simply could not seem to understand the issues in my case.

Especially that I had nothing with which to make a defense, or defend myself at trial, to the allegations in the indictment, due to all the evidence being systematically destroyed by the doctors, or mysteriously lost by the government. It was a stressful time for everyone on my legal team. Especially given they were all volunteer members, and working for free. And honestly, by this time, I was becoming belligerent, due to my increased anger at the situation. The strain of a second indictment was wearing on me, and my deep seeded anger at the government was causing me to lash out at those trying to help me.

My attorney knew my case well. He had been with me since the beginning. I knew he felt confident in my innocence. He had several other attorneys in the background helping, and consulting with him, including retired AUSA JB, the AUSA who had dismissed my first indictment, a former acting US Attorney, who was now a law professor at the local law school, and who at one time had worked with AUSA Harris, and a hoard of other local federal criminal defense attorneys, who saw my case for what it was, an overreach by the federal government, and a travesty of justice.

These attorneys were frankly fed up with AUSA Harris' years of unethical behavior, in many other cases, besides just mine, and often helped each other with cases, behind the scenes. And they were all working for free on my behalf.

I didn't really want to fire my attorney. I respected him. However, at the time, he had many personal problems of his own. I had become more of a counselor to him, than a client, sometimes causing me to be on the phone with him for hours, discussing his personal issues. This was stressful, as I already had my own stress to deal with.

Not to mention, the increasing anger I was feeling at the government. I was also helping to do the bulk of the legal research in my case, and was responsible for writing the draft, of all the pleadings we had filed to date. Being the defendant, and your own paralegal, is taxing on a person. And at the same time, I had my own small business to run, my family to take care of, and I was in graduate school pursuing my master's degree in Clinical and Mental Health Counseling. Plus, I was once again, putting added pressure on myself, with my goal of making straight As in my classes.

All of that, accompanied by the emotional drain of being under federal indictment for many years, became too much for me to bear. In court during the pretrial hearings, my attorney had many times depended on me to tell him what to argue before the court. At times he would have to ask the judge to allow him to leave the podium mid-argument, to consult with me. He would come back to the defense table, to consult with me, about what he was supposed to be arguing, regarding specific issues in my case, as well as what case law he should argue, regarding those issues.

This was because I was the one doing most of the research in my case. And at the time, his drinking had gotten out of control, and he was not himself. Further compounding my stress was the fact that he did not understand accounting, or how QuickBooks worked. This made me overly anxious. Because he was representing me for free, I knew that in reality, he could not spend the amount of time he needed to on my case.

I would later find out that the judge saw my angst in the courtroom, during these defense table consultations, as me mistreating this attorney. That could not have been further from the truth. I loved this man. He had become a good friend, more like family, given everything we had been through in my case, and I had tried hard to help him, with his own personal problems. We had been through a lot by this time. Still, we were starting to have disagreements, due to the stress of this situation, most likely caused by my deep-rooted anger, at the situation I found myself in, for the second time. Admittedly, I contributed heavily to this discord.

It's hard to fight the government, with its staff and unlimited resources. The government's many pleadings keep a defense attorney jumping through hoops to respond. My attorney had other clients paying him, and he was responsible for doing the work in those cases. He made many comments about how my case could be a full-time job. And while we had other attorneys helping in the background, the work ultimately fell on me and my attorney. The other attorneys were more of sounding boards, and second opinions, mainly because they too did not care for AUSA Harris' ways, and saw how the government prosecutor operated in our district.

Also, one of those attorneys, who had been helping in the background on my case, had started to make me distrustful, due to some of his actions and comments. I did not feel he had my best interests at heart. At the time, he too was being looked at by the same US Attorney's office, for a possible tax fraud charge himself. I started getting the feeling that he was trying to undermine my relationship with my attorney, because he did not like that my attorney was going after AUSA Harris for the prosecutorial misconduct we knew was happening in my case.

I understood why he may have wanted my attorney to back off. Afterall, it was AUSA Harris' wife who was the AUSA on his own case. If my attorney got crossways with AUSA Harris, it could cause an issue with my attorney getting a good deal for him with that office. And AUSA Harris at his high rank inside the US Attorney's office would have to approve any plea deal this attorney would be able to get.

I would not know until after I got home from federal prison that my attorney did, in fact, secure a very good deal for that attorney, in August 2018, after I was already serving time in federal prison. He was charged with a *misdemeanor* tax fraud charge by AUSA Harris' wife, for his failure to pay taxes on unreported income for 2010-2012, in the total amount, per the court transcript, of $1,193,308, in unreported income. Yet the government agreed he could plead guilty to a *misdemeanor* plea deal for one count of tax fraud that covered only the year of 2012. He would owe restitution to the IRS in the amount of $344,162.00.

Remember, AUSA JB told my attorney and I, in 2012, that US Attorney Chris Thyer said "no misdemeanor plea deals out of that office." At the time we were asking for basically the same thing to settle my case, a misdemeanor tax charge since the government wanted me to pay the IRS restitution. Yet that is exactly what this attorney pled guilty to in November 2018, and received three-years of probation for this guilty plea.

According to a newspaper article, and my reading on pacer, of the sentencing transcript in his case, the judge questioned the government about the plea deal in open court, the day this attorney pled guilty to the information he agreed to plead to. An information, does not require the grand jury to be involved. It is a way around indictment. The defendant simply admits they are guilty, and allows the government to charge them. The judge was obviously disconcerted with the deal the government was giving to this well-connected attorney, even stating so on the record.

He noted that as a former public defender, himself, he had never seen any of his clients get this kind of deal. And that per the defendant's PSR, that the attorney had failed to file taxes from other years not listed in the plea agreement. In fact, he had not filed taxes since 2007. It was not just the three years charged in the plea deal. Speaking of *sweet deals*. No wonder he wanted to cause discord between my attorney and I. He and my attorney had actually become very good friends during this time.

And I certainly do believe he was a big part of the reason my attorney and I started having problems. I fully believe he planted a lot of the discord that seemed to be brewing at the time with my attorney, in order to help himself in his own case. But it was certainly not the only thing going on between us.

By the time August 2015 rolled around, I felt it was a good time for us to part ways anyways. The stress of the case was taking a toll on us. And another attorney, who was a mutual friend of both my attorney and I, kept pushing me to fire my first attorney, as well. She was very aware of all of his personal issues. She told me over and over again, "He will end you up in federal prison," when referring to my attorney's personal problems. This constantly wore on my sanity, and even made me distrust my first attorney, at times, even more.

Admittedly, I was not in a good place, myself at the time, both emotionally and mentally. I had previously mentioned to him about getting off my case several times in the past, but each time, he still wanted to stay on the case.

However, after a massive blow up one day, after the judge had once again ruled against us, he agreed with me that it was time for him to get off the case. But this was only after the other attorney who I had begun to distrust, had put his two cents in, and disagreed with how I wanted to proceed as the client. I believe his constant meddling and planting discord had been partially responsible for the blow up. And because I did not trust the other attorney, I was getting tired of my attorney listening to him, and had told him so on this particular day, when I ultimately fired him.

We were due for trial in September 2015. But my attorney was about to be forced to file another continuance, due to the government continuing to give us discovery documents, that we had not had time to review. These documents mainly were bank statements, my credit card records, and the very few settlement statement notebooks, we had already seen.

However, because the government used a Bates numbering system, for document numbering on the discovery documents, and kept assigning different numbers to the same documents, we had no choice, but to review the documents, each time they were sent. Bates numbering, also known as Bates stamping, Bates branding, Bates coding, or Bates labeling, is used in legal, medical, and business fields, to place identifying numbers and/or date/time-marks on images and documents as they are scanned or processed.

For example, during the discovery stage of preparations for trial, or as a way of identifying business receipts. All of this repeated review of thousands of pages of documents was time-consuming, and wasteful. Still, not being able to trust the government, we were forced to review those documents repeatedly. Since we had previously caught AUSA Harris hiding evidence, there was no way to trust that there may be something else the government had not given us.

My attorney felt the government may try to sneak a document in amongst the repeat documents. Up to this point, we had also been given many electronic backup copies of the QuickBooks, after Agent Shortway hacked into the one copy at my attorney's office. Somehow copies just kept being found by the government, which also required us to look at each copy, to see if changes had been made. It was frustrating. I was ready to get this over with, but my attorney was not prepared for trial, and there was no way he would be, by the September trial date.

I filed a sealed motion with the court, which described the reasons I wanted to fire my attorney. I filed the motion sealed, because I did not want to embarrass my attorney, or make his personal problems public record. He had come to court unprepared many times, but I could never be upset, because he was working for free. But I also knew that he had more issues going on than I was capable of helping him with.

The other issue was one of the reasons the other attorney kept telling me I would end up in prison, if I did not fire him. She understood about his personal issues all too well, as they were also friends. My motion requested that I be allowed to proceed pro se; basically, I wanted to be my own attorney. However, I did ask the judge to allow my attorney to remain on the case, in the background, to help me.

After my motion was filed requesting to represent myself pro se, the following morning, my attorney filed a motion requesting to be removed from my case, just to cover himself with the court. He used language attorneys use to get off a case, stating that the attorney-client relationship had broken down. This was the only way he could be assured that the judge would let him off my case, so close to the trial date. And in all honesty, the relationship had broken down, so it was not a lie. Contributing to this breakdown was what had become my uncontrollable anger at this point, and my attorney's personal issues, and pending divorce. He also brought another attorney, who was his friend of his, to represent him in court that day.

It felt odd sitting across the table from my attorney that day in court, and being on opposite sides of an issue. I was used to him being on my team. And in all honesty, I valued him as a friend, and confident. To this day, I miss his presence in my life. He had become family to me by this time. However, I have not spoken to him again, since that day in court. Just one of the many heartbreaking things in my case.

The judge granted my attorney's motion to be removed from my case. However, she would not allow him to remain on my case in the background, as I had requested in my motion. I was now going head-to-head, with the federal government, on my own. It was a scary time, but I still somehow falsely believed that the system was honest. And I had my anger to push me forward, and fuel my drive.

Regardless, that in the past, I had always tried to find the positive in everything, by this time in my case, that positivity had been squelched by my anger. Even so, I was positive towards the next phase of my case, the trial phase, because I genuinely believed a jury would see through the government's facade.

Even so, I was shaken to my core due to all I had been through, and I could feel my candle burning dimmer and dimmer as the days went on. But while my candle may have been growing dimmer, my anger was growing brighter, with each breath I took. I no longer had my rock, my first attorney, there to fight with me. He had been a great advocate for me, and I trusted him. I felt nervous, but at the same time relieved, that the stress that had started ruining our friendship, was no longer an issue. Letting my first attorney get off my case is most likely the worst mistake I ever made, and possibly one of the biggest reasons that I am a convicted felon today.

My first attorney had represented me well during my first indictment, and had worked hard trying to get the second indictment dismissed. Working many hours on my case for free, and I am forever thankful for his pursuit of justice. I should have never fired him. But in that season of my life, I was confused, angry, and lost. I was not allowing God to lead me, even though I was aware that my actions were not biblical. And I was a fool to still believe that justice would prevail, after all I had seen proceeding through our criminal justice system. I should have known better by then. I was now on my second indictment, and four years into dealing with this case. I would not find out just how dirty government prosecutors really are, until I started going it alone.

In true corrupt fashion, the government would later claim that I had filed many continuances, and fired my attorney, to delay my case. That could not be the farthest thing from the truth! It was the government not turning over discovery, and continuing to give the same discovery documents repeatedly, that caused the delays, during the second indictment. And remember, the government was the one that had asked us to file continuances, during the first indictment. The minute I became my own attorney, the government was required to communicate with me, just like they would any other attorney, who may be representing me. The main form of communication used by the US Attorney's office was email.

Shortly after I proceeded pro se, the government accidentally copied me on an email chain, that should have been an interoffice-only email, about my case. The email was sent to AUSA Mazzanti and another AUSA assigned to my case, and I was of course somehow mistakenly copied on the email. It was from their boss, AUSA White, the head of the criminal division, of the US Attorney's Office in the Eastern District of Arkansas. The email was a strategy email, discussing me and my case, and it directed the AUSAs to start filing Motions In Limine, in my case, to prevent me from presenting certain evidence, about the doctors, and other witnesses. Things that would hurt the government's case should I be allowed to get them before a jury.

A motion in limine (lim-in-nay) n., Latin for "threshold," is a motion made at the start of a trial requesting that the judge rule that specific evidence may not be introduced at trial. This is most common in criminal trials, where evidence is subject to constitutional limitations, such as statements made without the Miranda warnings (reading the suspect their rights).

Basically, these motions were to be filed, to block me from telling the jury my complete defense, including about the destruction of documents, the sexual assault, the drug and Medicare fraud committed by the doctors, and many other truths, that showed what really happened while I was employed by the doctors, as well as to prevent character assassinations, calling out bad acts, of witnesses the government wanted to testify at trial.

Most of what the government wanted to exclude from trial was things my first attorney had honestly told AUSA Harris about, when he attempted to show AUSA Harris, the error of the government's ways, in between my first indictment and the second indictment. Now the government wanted to block me from telling the truth, the whole truth, and nothing but the truth, at trial.

The government's motions also wanted to block me from using reverse 404(b) evidence, evidence of wrongdoings of the doctors, such as the lawsuit filed against Dr. Swan' CPA, when five years of income tax returns had not been filed, as well as block me from bringing up wrongdoings of witnesses. These motions were filed by the government as *sealed* motions, therefore, anyone reviewing my case would not be able to see how the government was trying to prevent the truth from coming out at trial.

Unfortunately, since those motions remain sealed even today, I cannot give the full details, or share them, in this book. The filing of sealed motions by the government is another trick it uses, to prevent reporters, and the public, from seeing everything that goes on in a case.

Especially if the information is not favorable to the government's theory, or narrative, of the case. And by filing *motions,* I do mean *plural.* The motions were coming at me like daggers. There were two AUSAs in my case, and of course, they had a host of staff attorneys at their disposal.

Obviously, the government was doing this, to intimidate me, in hopes I would accept its plea deal. That offer came shortly thereafter. AUSA Mazzanti sent me an email, with a plea deal offer, for me to plead guilty to one count of tax fraud. If I agreed, the other charges in the indictment would be dismissed by the government. In order to take the plea deal, I would agree to plead guilty to one count of tax fraud for 2010, and owe the IRS restitution in the amount of $207,000.

Again, just like the previous plea deal offer in the first indictment, nowhere in the current plea deal, was I asked to plead guilty to stealing any money from the doctors, much less $611,000. I was furious when I read the government's latest offer! The email stated that I only had a few days to decide if I would accept the government's plea deal offer, or it would be withdrawn. In her email **(see Appendix, Link 8)**, AUSA Mazzanti said *IF* I did not accept the government's plea deal **(see Appendix, Link 9)** that the government would be requesting 8-13 years of prison time for me, by adding enhancements to the charges in the indictment, should I lose at trial.

If I accepted the government's plea deal, I would owe restitution to a government agency, the IRS, for tax fraud. However, nowhere in the email or plea offer, did it say exactly what I did that constituted tax fraud. The indictment had charged that I stole $611,000 from the doctors, and had not reported the stolen money on my taxes, which constituted tax fraud. Curiously, the amount of restitution I would owe to the IRS, if I agreed to the plea offer of tax fraud, is the exact amount of taxes owed on the $611,000, had Dr. Swan paid the taxes on that amount.

Basically, the government was asking me to pay the taxes, on what was most likely tax fraud by Dr. Swan. Dr. Swan had most likely committed tax fraud by claiming the $611,000 as business expenses, when they were clearly personal expenses. The amount represented the dollar amount, for the items I had charged on my personal credit cards for him, in the four years I had worked at the clinic, and been reimbursed. Those items were mostly of a personal nature to Dr. Swan. I was outraged! It was past the statute of limitations for the government to be able to charge any of the doctors, so I felt once again, I was being made their scapegoat! My anger seethed.

But how was I guilty of tax fraud if I didn't steal the $611,000? The plea deal would also require that I give up claims to the $50,000, the government had seized from our bank accounts, during the first indictment. Up to this point, in my case, I had never heard of enhancements. I immediately researched it, since I no longer had an attorney to ask.

My research found that there are many aggravating factors, a prosecutor can try to add to your alleged crime, AFTER you are found guilty at trial, or take a plea deal. These enhancements can actually cause you to serve more time in federal prison. Aggravating factors increase the severity, or culpability, of a criminal act, including, but not limited to, the heinousness of the crime, lack of remorse, and prior conviction of another crime. Just more ammo in the government's never-ending arsenal.

AUSA Mazzanti listed three enhancements in her email, that she said, the government would be adding to my crimes, IF I did not accept her plea offer, and instead proceeded to trial. I had three days to decide.

In a fit of anger, I not so kindly told her that there was no need for the government to wait for an answer, until its offer expired. The answer was NO! See you in court! I brazenly inquired, how she thought her career would advance, once a pro se defendant beat the government at trial? This was probably not one of my finest moments, nor was it a smart move, but I was fed up! We were now roughly five years into this case, yet the government continued to move the ball, and change the rules, while violating my rights with each step. It was obvious that even AUSA Mazzanti knew I had not stolen $611,000 from my past employer.

And this was now the second plea offer from the government, that did not require me to plead guilty to wire fraud, or stealing $611,000, the main charge in both the first, and second indictment. In the current indictment, the tax fraud charges stemmed from what the government said was me not reporting the illegal income from the wire fraud, a specified unlawful activity, the government said occurred when I stole $611,000 from the doctors. The money laundering charges also depended on me being found guilty of wire fraud.

How could I have laundered stolen money, if there was no stolen money? The money laundering, and tax fraud charges, depended on me being found guilty of wire fraud, if my case went to trial. If I didn't steal the money, which constituted wire fraud, why did I owe income taxes on unreported stolen money to the IRS? Obviously, the government only wanted to steal our seized $50,000, that it was still holding, and make a convicted felon out of me, for crimes it knew full well, I had not committed. I'm ashamed to say that the above example would not be the only time I pushed the government's buttons. It would be unfair to call out the wrong actions of others, and not admit to my own shortcomings in this book.

On the contrary, I made complaints to Washington, D.C. on AUSA Harris, and Agent Shortway, for their unethical and illegal acts, including the abuse of grand jury subpoenas in my case, the hiding of exculpatory evidence, and the sharing of my tax returns illegally with my husband's bosses. I was not a fan of AUSA Harris, and was determined to expose his dirty deeds. Not to mention the hatred I felt for him, due to all the anger that was raging inside of me at the time.

I had tried many times to meet with the government to no avail. During my first indictment, I tried hard to meet with the United States Attorney in my district, US Attorney Thyer. I sent him letters and emails requesting meetings. When he finally answered, and refused to meet, in another fit of rage, I referred to him in my reply email, as an "unethical coward." This was after I had been requesting to meet with him, to discuss my side of what had happened in my case, and what

I felt was AUSA Harris' abuse of grand jury subpoenas. Not one of my finest moments, for sure. An example of another time I allowed my anger to get the best of me, instead of just praying to God for peace, and allowing HIM to lead me in those moments.

While I was representing myself, pro se, I marched up to the US Attorney's office, and personally served AUSA Harris, with a subpoena for him to be a witness, at another upcoming pretrial hearing, and at the same time told him I had a present for him. I had taken him a copy of Sidney Powell's book *Licensed to Lie: Exposing Corruption in the Department of Justice.* Sidney Powell, a former AUSA, had written about the reasons she quit being a prosecutor, and had become a defense attorney. In her book, she detailed the corruption she had seen in United States Attorney's Offices across the country. Many of her complaints discussed the hiding of Brady evidence. On this day, the receptionist called AUSA Harris to the lobby where I stood, subpoena and book in hand. When I served the subpoena on AUSA Harris, he would not even open his mouth.

He simply signed for the subpoena, and used hand motions, to communicate with me. Maybe he was afraid I would use whatever he said against him? Or maybe he knew I saw through his lies? Or maybe he was actually afraid of me? I was rather unhinged in these moments. I don't know what he was thinking, but it was one of the weirdest encounters I've ever had with anyone. On that day, he was certainly not the bully I had seen in the past. He was like a cowardly lion, instead. It was a very strange encounter with him.

When AUSA Harris hand motioned that he would not take the book from me, I warned him that the next time he saw a book detailing government corruption, I would be the author, and he would be the subject matter. But let me clarify, this is not the book I promised him I would write that day. My anger no longer fuels me to do so. This book is my story, not the governments. However, marching up to the US Attorney's office, and putting on such a show, was not in my best interests. My anger was taking over, and I had no peace in these moments. The government had created a monster in me. A monster that would follow me throughout my entire case.

I also served a Touhy request on the DOJ in Washington, D.C.. I served a subpoena to the original secret service agent in my case, to testify as a witness, at a pretrial hearing. I hunted him down at his new job. This was the same agent who had seized our $50,000, during the first indictment. Obviously, these acts would make the government want to go after me even more. By the time these acts occurred, I'm not sure they could have done much more to me anyway, and truthfully,

I really didn't care. I was angry, and tired, of trying to prove my innocence. I was fed up with the government's dirty deeds. I wanted to expose them at all costs. Little did I know, the costs would be all mine. I was only angering the government more, and enticing government prosecutors to show me who was boss. Reflecting back, it was not a smart move at all. These were the people that held my fate in their hands.

My advice to anyone reading this book is this, when you find yourself under this much stress, turn it over to God, and pray, pray, pray. It is probably best to seek therapy to vent. Do not take matters into your own hands, by going after the government. I still get emotional when I am forced to relive these moments, even now as I am typing these paragraphs, in this book.

And I am still deeply ashamed of my actions, in many of the examples, I have written about in this book. I should have held myself to a higher standard. I should have shown the love of Christ, instead of lashing out at those who persecuted me. Even with God's help in this area, I still struggle at times. Of course, it's easy to look back now, and see all that went wrong, during this time. But in those moments, the anger, that had taken such a deep root within my very soul, reared its ugly head, each and every time.

After I refused the government's newest plea offer, in what I truly believe was an act of harassment, for my refusal of that offer, AUSA Mazzanti immediately asked for a pretrial hearing, and the judge granted it. I received an email late one afternoon from the judge's law clerk, instructing me to appear in court the following morning. This particular law clerk was the brother of the acting US Attorney, in the Western District of Arkansas. I had always felt he was why we could not win anything in my case that we filed. By all accounts from the former AUSAs who helped with my case, my second indictment should have been dismissed.

However, because law clerks are assigned to perform the research in cases, and possibly write the orders, for the judge to review and sign, we felt he was finding case law that argued against us. But on this particular day, the government had filed a Motion for a Protection Order, to be placed on all the discovery in my case. This motion attempted to block me from sharing any of the discovery documents in my case with others, now that I was operating pro se.

Basically, the government did not want to risk me getting help from anyone with my case, as I proceeded pro se, and wanted to prevent me from showing any of the discovery documents to other attorneys, or anyone else for that matter. Maybe they suspected my first attorney was still helping me? He had done so in the background, between the first and second indictments, and the government was most likely aware this had happened.

I was served with the government's motion late that afternoon, via email. I filed my pro se answer the following morning, before proceeding to the courtroom, for the hearing. I served the government AUSAs with my answer, once in the courtroom. I then alerted the judge's law clerk, to its electronic filing, that had taken place, when I caused it to be filed with the court clerk that morning.

Acting as my own attorney, I argued before the Court that it was too late for the government to make this request. The same discovery had already been through a previous indictment, and a civil case, both now dismissed. Still, I had no way to know how many other people had copies of the same discovery documents. I argued that I should not be held accountable for how many people it had been shared with, or risk being penalized, should the government blame me for sharing it, if the government's motion were to be granted by the judge.

Further, we were already almost two years into a second indictment, with the same discovery shared by my attorney, with many other attorneys who had consulted on my case. The government should have asked for a protection order before starting the discovery process, if it felt it was necessary to protect the documents. The government knew this. AUSA Mazzanti was just attempting to harass me. Believe it or not, the judge actually ruled in my favor (**see Appendix, Link 10**).

In my case, this win in court would be only one, of two motions, ever won, and I'm proud to say that I actually wrote both of them. During the hearing, I noticed a lady I did not recognize had come into the courtroom, and was sitting on a bench behind me. I had assumed she was just another reporter the government had tipped off about the sideshow that would go down in federal court that morning. The government had a habit of tipping off reporters to show up at hearings, especially when the government thought the judge would most certainly rule in its favor, and that I would look bad in the eyes of the media.

However, after the judge ruled in my favor on the protection motion, the judge advised that the lady I had noticed in the courtroom, was actually a federal public defender, that the judge was appointing to my case. I had not requested a public defender, yet, I was not given the option to say no, to having one appointed. This appointment was due to me requesting that my previous attorney be allowed to continue to help me, and maybe the judge felt sorry for me, knowing what was yet to come, at the hands of government prosecutors? After the hearing, the public defender met with me in a small room off the courtroom.

Her first question to me was "Where did you graduate from law school?" I answered, "I have never been to law school", and told her that I didn't have any formal legal training, except all the work I had done on my own case. She was surprised. She told me that when she watched me argue my case before the judge that morning, she had felt confident I was an attorney. After witnessing how I had gone up against AUSA Mazzanti, so passionately, she was surprised that I wasn't an attorney, due to the way I had argued for my rights against the government's motion for a protection order. I promptly answered, "I am just someone who is fed up with the government, and am trying to prove my innocence." She assured me "You are not the only one fed up with government prosecutors" "We will get along just fine."

I informed the federal defender that I planned on hiring a paid attorney to represent me, and that I had been interviewing several firms in the last few weeks, as I had been proceeding pro se. We agreed to keep in touch until I could do so. Looking back now, I really wish I had allowed her to stay on my case. Hiring another attorney, just wasted more of our hard-earned money.

But you know what they say, live and learn. Hindsight is 20/20. I have learned some tough lessons at the hands of my own government, and even by my own hands, given my anger in these moments. Life lessons learned, at times because of my own bad choices, some of them made in moments of rage, stress, and extreme anger, during this process.

But most importantly, I have learned that I must trust God, to lead me in the right direction. Taking things into my own hands, will only get me into more troubled waters. I would certainly not advise anyone to go against the government as a pro se defendant. It is a road less traveled, for an excellent reason.

Chapter Sixteen
Ignoring That Little Voice In Your Head-Taking Bad Attorney Advice: 404(b) Evidence

After I was charged in the first indictment, and the doctors filed their civil lawsuit against my husband and me, I obviously needed to get a job ASAP, like yesterday, to help pay for some of the attorney fees that were increasing at a rapid pace. My family was down to just my husband's income from his job, to pay bills that had previously been paid, with two excellent incomes. And now we had two sets of attorney fees, we had to pay for the criminal, and civil cases. And remember, the government had seized *all* of our savings in March 2011, when they indicted me the first time.

I had been unable to obtain employment, and had been let go from the job I was hired for after I had left the doctors' employment, when the indictment had been made public. My name had appeared in the *Arkansas Business* newspaper and on the Internet. On top of that, now my husband's job, and his professional license, were at risk, because both of our names were in the newspaper, due to the civil lawsuit. As allegations of fraud were being lodged by the doctors, against my husband as well. Nobody wants an accountant accused of theft, fraud, and RICO. It was a legitimate concern that he could lose his license or job.

No matter how many times I applied for jobs, nor that I was the most qualified applicant, or even over qualified, I could not get a job. I mean, it's not like the last name Espejo is a common name, well, at least not in Arkansas. One day when I met with my attorney, he said he had come up with what he called "a marvelous idea."

He advised me that I should legally change my last name, and he suggested that he file paperwork to have my last name restored to my maiden name. I asked him if this was legal? He replied, "of course it is." "What crime is it to change your last name?" He also advised me *not* to inform prospective employers that I was currently under indictment. And I shouldn't put the doctors' office job on my past employment history. Again, I questioned if this was legal, and he assured me that it was. My gut was telling me otherwise. Another *red flag* I choose to ignore.

That little voice in my head said, "Don't do it, this isn't ethical," but I did as my attorney advised, feeling very shady the entire time. I promise you, this would come back to bite me later, but not until my case finally made it to trial. And something that was actually legal, yet probably not very ethical or moral, would end up being twisted in a nefarious manner by the government. And I knew better! I was already under indictment for turning a blind eye to wrongdoing, and participating in unethical and immoral behavior. I'm not sure what I was thinking? But I blindly followed my attorney's advice.

I would later find out that in the federal criminal justice system, there is something called 404(b) evidence. This evidence is where the government, once again having the upper hand, is allowed to bring evidence before the jury at a trial of the defendant's supposed *other bad acts.* Per federal rules of criminal procedure, "404(b) evidence is a rule of criminal evidence to show other wrongs, acts, or crimes. However, this evidence is **not** to be submitted *to prove the bad character of a person".* Well, at least in theory, since that is how the law reads. In practice, in federal criminal proceedings, things turn out quite differently.

And it is the judge that decides if the 404(b) evidence will get into the trial, which nine times out of ten, it is allowed, regardless if it is just to *"bash the character of the person"* on trial.

After changing my last name, I did as my attorney instructed, and applied for a job using my new last name. I also followed his advice, and did not list my past employment with the doctors, on the application. *BINGO*, I was hired almost immediately. But as my gut tried to warn me, during this employment, the company owners found out that I was using the wrong last name, or at least that is what they accused me of, regardless that my legal last name had actually been changed to the one I was now using.

And even worse, they found out that I had failed to put on the job application the work I had done at the doctors' clinic, or that I was currently under federal criminal indictment, accused of stealing $611,000 from those same past employers.

The day the owners called me into a meeting to confront me about all of this, I had nothing I could say for myself. I felt guilty and ashamed, and did not blame them for being upset about it. I was, of course, fired on the spot, and I deserved it. I had misled them on my employment application. I had on purpose, left off information, and intentionally hidden things from them. Things that most likely had they known, would have prevented them from hiring me in the first place. Instead of allowing God to lead my path, I was again on my own plan, or in this case, my attorney's plan.

I ignored that little voice in my head, and followed my attorney's advice, even though I felt what I was doing was wrong, and unethical. Exactly like when I went along with Dr. Swan's requests that I classify personal expenses, as business expenses, in the QuickBooks program. Once again, it came back to bite me big time! During its investigation in the second indictment, or maybe the first, who really knows, the government sent the secret service agent to visit this past employer.

Now I have no way to know what the government may, or may not, have discussed with this past employer, as there is no record of those conversations. Considering how the government harassed my husband, his bosses, the office manager who worked for the doctors after me, and my sister-in-law, there seems to be a pattern here of putting pressure on witnesses to say what the government wishes to hear. And I do know the company I had worked for, had already had their own run-in with the federal government, some years prior, when their office was raided. All their financial records, had been seized as evidence, in another criminal case, which had to do with an attorney they had hired to set up their retirement plans. And like many companies I had done bookkeeping for in the past, I was aware that many of their personal expenses had been paid through the business.

Given this knowledge, it is not a stretch to believe, they were probably already afraid of crossing the government. And when the government comes knocking, people tend to panic, regardless if they are doing wrong, or not. Even those without prior dealings with agents get nervous. One can only imagine how someone who had already had all their financial documents seized in a previous matter, would react to a government agent, showing up at their place of business? I would assume they would want to cooperate, and say whatever the government needed them to say, as nobody wants to cross the federal government. Federal agents certainly know how to intimidate.

What I do know for sure, is this, by the time my case went to trial, the owners were brought in to testify against me under the 404(b) Evidence rule. My attorney did not believe the 404(b) evidence the government wanted to put into the record was being done for any other reason except to *bash my character*, the exact opposite of what 404(b) evidence is legally allowed to be presented at trial for. However, the government's arguments to the judge, was that it was evidence that would show "lack of mistake" on my part, that connected the current charges with this other "bad act," and the government wanted to have the owners testify to it in court.

Of course, the judge ruled in favor of the government, and allowed the 404(b) evidence into evidence anyway. When the owners, all three of them, were paraded into court at trial, one by one, by the government, to take the stand, and testify against me at trial, the story went something like this.

When asked by the government to identify the defendant, Mrs. Espejo, each owner made sure they let the jury know that Espejo was not the last name they knew me by. I'm not sure they understood that my legal last name had actually not been Espejo when I worked for them? On direct examination by the government, they told a story of how they had become suspicious of me. They believed that I had failed to take a $600 cash deposit to the bank. Mind you, this never happened! I rarely was even asked to take a deposit to the bank, and always returned with the deposit slip, when I was asked.

While under cross-examination from my attorney, they admitted their suspicion was only after they had found out that I was indicted. I had told my attorney about the cameras in the office. On cross- examination, they had to admit that the cameras would have shown me getting money out of the register for a deposit, had I been the one supposed to make the $600 deposit. However, they claimed that the cameras were not working on the day they said "I failed to take the $600 deposit to the bank." While I worked there, it was well known that they had cameras that made a daily recording digitally. It made no sense that they did not have a file to go back and review to see who had made a deposit that day?

And anyway, I was rarely the person who made deposits. The owners admitted that they had never made any police report against me, nor reported me to any law enforcement agency, regarding the supposed $600 deposit that I had allegedly failed to make.

Yet, the government now had them on the witness stand, accusing me of not taking a cash deposit to the bank. Under cross-examination, in their defense of not reporting this supposed crime, they claimed that they were just too busy at the time to make a report to the police.

Regardless, what they said about the bank deposit could not have been further from the truth. But I honestly can't say that I blame them for thinking I was shady, and becoming suspicious of me. And maybe had I been more upfront with them about who I was, when they hired me, they would have thought better of me. I get it. I probably would have felt the same way, had I been in their shoes. I suspect the government hounded, and harassed them, too, like it had my husband's bosses, my sister-in-law, and the office manager that took my place at the doctors' office. I'm certain, their earlier run-in with the federal government, made them understand, that they should just do whatever the government wanted. Obviously, they knew to be cooperative.

And who wants to get their financial records seized again due to someone else's indictment? Or maybe the agent planted a seed of suspicion, and the owners really started believing there was a $600 deposit that was never taken to the bank, during my employment? I'll never know the truth, because I burned my bridge with this company, by not doing what was proper, and ethical to begin with. And as hard as it is to type all this, and expose what truly was unethical behavior on my own part, I certainly want to take responsibility for my own failings. I am human, and I am flawed. Only by God's grace and mercy, am I worthy.

Had I listened to my gut, which was God trying to warn me, and not taken my first attorney's bad advice, the owners may not have felt how they did about me. I had a choice. The moral of the story is if you hear God telling you it is wrong, it does not matter what advice you are receiving from an attorney, or anyone else for that matter, don't do it. Stay on the right path. Stay on the path that God would want you to be on. Listen for his voice and pray for his guidance in everything. Things like this have a way of coming back, and biting you.

I feel horrible that the owners think of me the way they must. I violated their trust. I fully deserve the way they feel. I make no excuses for my behavior, and I hope to apologize to them, and ask forgiveness one day. And I have learned to listen to that little voice in my head! And only to follow God's plan, not man's plan. This example alone taught me a valuable life lesson.

As you can only imagine, there was no way to overcome something like this in the eyes of the jury. It's hard for a jury to reconcile that this testimony was not a crime that I had committed, or to understand that I took my attorney's advice to change my last name, because they never heard that part of the story. The jury never knew that on the date the owners said that I had not taken the $600 deposit to the bank, I was waiting patiently for the government to dismiss the first indictment, and would have been stupid, to do anything to prevent that from happening.

In my defense, they would not hear these things, because we were not allowed to tell these things to the jury at trial. The government used the story of a $600 deposit to put a nail in my coffin for conviction. The jury likely thought I was just a common criminal, going from job to job, stealing from anyone I worked for, and who could blame them? That is how it looks in light of what the government told them. 404(b) evidence is just one of the many one-sided manipulations the government can use at a criminal trial.

This supposed evidence, should have never been allowed into trial against me, because it was used for nothing but the purpose of character assassination, which goes directly against the letter of the language of the law, as at no time did the government show how this evidence showed lack of mistake, or tied to my case in any way. And of course, the judge ruled against me, and I was not allowed to bring in testimony of reverse 404(b) evidence, regarding the doctors' "bad acts," or put it into evidence.

This reverse evidence would have included the shredding of all the financial documents, the sexual assault, the doctors' Medicare, and drug fraud, and that Dr. Swan failed to file his income taxes for five years, and blamed his former CPA.

Before we could even file our motion requesting to do so, the government filed a Motion in Limine to prevent this testimony, which was granted by the judge. All of our motions, and in court arguments, to enter reverse 404(b) evidence into the trial, were denied.

It was AUSA Harris who originally filed the motion to enter the 404(b) evidence into trial against me. This happened within days of us filing motions against the government, exposing the hiding of the evidence done by AUSA Harris. Bottom line, I ignored *red flags* and then paid the high price at trial. The high price of getting off God's plan, and getting onto my own plan. It is a *high* price indeed.

Chapter Seventeen
Doesn't He Know About Spousal Immunity?

Doesn't he know about spousal immunity? That would be a very sarcastic question, posed to me on March 24, 2015, by the former acting US Attorney, who was now a law professor, and helping behind the scenes on my legal team. He asked this question when he found out that AUSA Harris' latest filing, was a Motion for Court-Authorized Immunity **(Appendix, Link 11)**, requesting the court grant my husband immunity, in return for his testifying for the government, against me at trial. We filed our 50-page Motion to Dismiss against the government on March 9, 2015. That Motion also contained 32 Exhibits, most of which were not very flattering, to AUSA Harris personally, including some brazen emails he had sent, along with the allegations, that he was hiding exculpatory evidence from us in discovery. We were calling the government out!

My legal team was sure that the Motion for Court-Authorized Immunity for my husband was just AUSA Harris' way of retaliating against us, due to our Motion to Dismiss. We would see this same pattern of behavior, over and over again, when we would file motions regarding the exculpatory material that AUSA Harris had hidden, and then lied on the record about. As well as when we would file motions, requesting the court to force the government to follow the discovery order, and give us a good copy of the QuickBooks backup. Each time, in response, AUSA Harris would either serve a subpoena on my husband, another family member, or my husband's boss, or he would file another motion against me.

It was a win at all costs game the government was playing, and as I have said many times before, *the truth is what the federal prosecutor says the truth is*. The real truth does not really matter much at all. Each time I became angered at how my family was being treated. I wanted to protect them from this nightmare.

It made my legal team angry that AUSA Harris was abusing the system like this. It made me furious! Several attorneys, consulting with my attorney in the background, had worked with AUSA Harris at the US Attorney's Office. In many other cases, they had witnessed his unethical behavior, and they were not fans. The former acting US Attorney, now law professor, called AUSA Harris "A threat to justice and the entire criminal justice system." Honest prosecutors do not like dishonest ones. Many other attorneys that my attorney consulted with, had the same concerns about AUSA Harris' ethics. I would cringe at the stories I heard.

Unfortunately, none of them were willing to make official complaints, to call AUSA Harris out on his bad behavior. I saw this over and over again. They talk, but they won't put their neck on the line, to bring about change. That is why dishonest prosecutors continue to get by, with unethical behavior. Those who witness unethical behavior most often remain silent. After all, it is not their family, or them being harassed, nor their liberties being threatened. It felt more like an unspoken code to me. They claimed, reporting AUSA Harris' bad behavior, would not do any good. The DOJ in Washington, D.C., would most likely never do a thing to AUSA Harris. In fact, they may reward him for it. This disgusted me. It confirmed once again to me just how dishonest the system really is.

And the request for my husband to testify was actually comical, considering he didn't know anything that could help the government's case against me anyway. There wasn't anything to know! And legally, the government had no leg to stand on with this request, since both my husband and I had a right to spousal immunity.

I had a right to file for the marriage confidential communications privilege, since either spouse has that right. The United States Supreme Court in 1934 held that "The basis of the immunity given to communications between husband and wife is the protection of marital confidences, regarded as so essential to the preservation of the marriage relationship, as to outweigh the disadvantages to the administration of justice, which the privilege entails." Wolfe v. United States, 291 U.S. 7, 14 (1934). My husband had two rights. He was afforded the right to the marriage confidential communications privilege that I had, and he also had what is called adverse spousal testimony privilege.

Again, it was just plain and simple harassment, in the highest form, and another abuse of power from AUSA Harris. He knew the spousal immunity laws, before he filed the motion. My husband had already told the government many times that he was not willing to meet with AUSA Harris, nor testify against me at trial. He had told the Secret Service agent this same thing, each time he served my husband with a subpoena, at his place of business. The secret service agent even apologized to my husband that he kept having to serve him. It would seem that even the secret service agent knew the law, and was fed up with being AUSA Harris' messenger boy.

Regardless, anything my husband could have testified to, would have only bolstered my defense. Looking back, we should have just allowed him to testify for the government. Strategically, it would have been good for me in the long-run. He could have gained immunity, and then the government would not have been able to force him to give up our $50,000 with their threats, after I was found guilty. But at the time, my anger at the government for continuing to go after my husband, made me view the situation much differently. And the situation had a strong irony, given that AUSA Harris had sent my husband a target letter in July 2014, telling him that he was, in fact, a target of the grand jury, for tax fraud on our joint tax returns, filed in the years 2007-2010.

This letter invited my husband to testify at the grand jury. A target letter means the government is looking to indict you. The government's claims that I had stolen $611,000 using wire fraud, and had failed to report my illegal gains on our tax returns as income, constituted tax fraud. My husband could also be found guilty because we had filed joint tax returns. To indict someone on tax fraud, a prosecutor must gain permission from the DOJ Tax Division.

This is supposed to be another check and balance, between an overzealous prosecutor, and a defendant. But just like the grand jury, the DOJ Tax Division, turned out to be just another formality. A federal prosecutor has unlimited power. The DOJ Tax Division in Dallas, Texas, Unfortunately, another spineless division of the DOJ, had rubber-stamped AUSA Harris' request for approval, to charge my husband, and me, with tax fraud, on October 1, 2014. We still do not know why AUSA Harris failed to indict my husband, on October 8, 2014, the day he indicted me, in the second indictment.

Maybe the grand jury actually denied AUSA Harris' request for a true bill against my husband? That's doubtful, given the "ham sandwich" theory, and what I saw with the grand jury, in both the first and second indictment. Reading the transcript of testimony from IRS Agent Shortway, from the grand jury on October 8, 2014, I do not believe the government tried to indict my husband. Getting approval to do so was just more arrogance on behalf of AUSA Harris. He did it because he could.

There had been no exhibits shared with the grand jury, on the date of my second indictment, that proved I had done anything illegal. It was simply the IRS agent's word alone that AUSA Harris used to indict me the second time, much like the Secret Service agent's testimony, had been used the first time. That's certainly not the checks and balances between a party and the government, the grand jury is designed to be. If I were a betting woman, I would guess that AUSA Harris never had any intention of indicting my husband.

I suspect that in July 2014, his target letter was just another form of harassment, used to harass us, just like he had harassed my husband, at his place of business, and harassed my husband's bosses, the office manager, and my sister-in-law. It was just another way AUSA Harris tried to force me, to make a deal with the devil, and give up my claim to the $50,000, stolen by the federal government out of our bank accounts, in March 2011.

In hindsight, I wish we would have ignored AUSA Harris' immunity motion, and let my husband testify. But at the time, I was angry and even more determined to show the government that it could not push innocent people around. I just wanted to show the government that it could not keep harassing the people I loved. And an Order in our favor would prevent AUSA Harris from serving future subpoenas on my husband at his job. I have always believed the government knew I did not commit this crime! After all, government prosecutors had offered me two plea deals up to this point, neither of which involved me pleading guilty to wire fraud, or the theft of $611,000.

My husband's testimony would have helped me. It made no sense for the government to even want my husband to testify on behalf of the government's case in chief. My husband is a CPA with a CFF, which is the forensic accountant designation. He had looked at our financial records back in 2011, to verify that I had been telling the truth, about what happened. And most importantly, he could have testified that we did not have any of the items purchased on my personal credit cards. The items that I had purchased for Dr. Swan.

I think any spouse would have noticed, and questioned where the money was coming from, to pay for such, if their wife had been bringing home $611,000 worth of items, or had been taking trips without him. And the type of items I had charged for Dr. Swan, were certainly unique. My husband knew I never purchased items like those for myself. He could have told the jury all of this.

Strategically it would have been a good move to allow this to happen. However, I didn't want to put my husband through the stress. I'm not even sure the jury would have believed him anyway. They seemed to buy the government's tall tales, hook, line, and sinker.

Since no legal counsel presently represent my husband, we had to decide on which way we wanted to proceed. 1. We could ignore AUSA Harris' motion, and allow my husband to become a witness for the government, should the judge be inclined to grant the government's Motion; 2. We could spend more money, and hire counsel for my husband, to see what they advised, since my attorney could not advise my husband, due to conflict of interest, since he already represented me; 3. We could wait until trial and have my husband take the stand and assert his marital privilege; or 4. We could figure out how to file an answer to AUSA Harris' motion pro se, and ask the judge to deny it, based on the spousal immunity privilege.

I chose number four. I researched and wrote the motion for my husband to file pro se (**see Appendix, Link 12**). The Court granted his pro se motion on August 20, 2015 (**see Appendix, Link 13**). After his motion was granted, he never received another subpoena from the government. It stopped AUSA Harris from sending agents to my husband's work, requesting that he come to meet with AUSA Harris.

At least my husband got a little relief this way. Looking back, it probably hurt me, more than it helped me, at trial. But my husband did not deserve the harassment the government was using to intimidate him. Nor did he deserve to be put on a witness stand, against his wife, when he knew of no crimes I had committed.

Regardless that it most likely hurt me at trial, I'm glad I saved my husband the added trauma of testifying at trial. One thing that I thought of, while writing this book, that my legal team never thought of at the time, was that by having my husband be a witness, he would have not been allowed to sit in the courtroom during my trial. Maybe that was AUSA

Harris' motive? To make it appear that my family did not support me. I'll never know.

Chapter Eighteen
A Jury of My Peers

Let me just cut through the chase, and state right up front, that I no longer believe that there is such a thing as a fair federal trial, or a jury of your peers. I do not feel I had a jury of my peers at my trial. I believe it was just one more thing that hampered my case significantly. During jury selection, I watched in disbelief, as the judge allowed many prospective jurors who had accounting, or financial backgrounds, to leave the jury selection room, for what is referred to as *cause*. This means they had some type of personal hardship that would possibly hamper their serving on a jury. However, a few of them only stated work obligations as cause, which I felt was not a good excuse, considering the few accounting and financial background prospective jurors had to pick from. And doesn't most everyone have work responsibilities?

After the judge released many of the jurors, I watched as the federal prosecutors voted off the rest of the prospective jurors, who had accounting and financial experience, as well as all the independent thinkers in the pool. You might be curious why the government would vote off financially minded jurors, given the fact that I was charged with wire fraud, money laundering, and tax fraud, all financial crimes?

It surprised me too! But as I sat horrified on the first day of my trial, January 30, 2017, and watched the jury be seated, I realized the federal prosecutors had, in essence, done just that. I was left with medical personnel, school teachers, housewives, and a guy who kept falling asleep during witness testimony. It indeed was not a jury of my peers, and certainly not a jury who would be able to understand a complicated financial fraud case.

Again, I felt a lot of emotion about this, and great anger. The process continued to feel so one-sided, and it seemed to always be in favor of the government. But I also think this goes directly to the fact that the government was unsure about their case against me. Therefore, they could not risk financially minded people sitting on the jury. I will always believe that the government prosecutors knew I had not committed these crimes. But it is relevant to understand that the government structures cases to be in its favor at every turn, in the broken process. Its case is built on its "theory" of the case, not actual facts of what happened.

And criminal law is fascinating. My first attorney spent a lot of time talking to me about his past cases, and explaining the process in general. He loved to talk, and told me many *war stories*, as he called them, about past criminal cases he had been involved in. He had been involved in some high-profile cases in his earlier years, specifically during the Clinton era, think Kenneth Starr and Whitewater. However, I would have enjoyed these stories a lot better, had I not been the one preparing for trial soon. At the time, I just wanted to talk about my case. How was he going to defend me?

Nonetheless, the stories were interesting, and I learned a lot from him. I'm not sure many attorneys take the time to give their clients these valuable civic lessons, and I appreciated him doing so. And as I have said, one of my biggest regrets in this process, has been that I fired him, during the second indictment. He had been with me since my case's inception, he believed in my innocence, and was willing to fight for me. He probably understood my case better than other attorneys, because we had gone through the trenches together, trying to find the needed evidence to prove my innocence.

Looking back, firing him was a grave mistake on my part

for sure. I often tortured myself by thinking about how things may have turned out, had I kept him on the case, or even the federal defender lady. During my time in federal prison, I had plenty of idle time to relive every moment. Rethinking every decision, I ever made. Allowing the devil to use doubt, and self-loathing, against me, each time I thought about it. Thus, fueling my already angry soul even more.

My first attorney also taught me that picking a jury is a mixture of psychology, sociology, human nature, body language, and what sounded like a lot of stereotyping of people. The government wants jurors that favor law enforcement, believe strongly in our government, and who have not had any unfavorable experiences with law enforcement, or in court proceedings. They like jurors who can easily be misled, and overwhelmed, with PowerPoint slides, and agent testimony, exactly what I saw at my trial.

On the other hand, the defense wants open-minded people, who can look past their own biases, who may not be the biggest fan of our government, and who are not easily manipulated. The process would be easy, if jurors just came to the jury selection box, wearing a sign around their necks, that listed their personality traits, opinions, and biases. Of course, that does not happen. An attorney must either be good at identifying, and weeding out these human traits, during voir dire, or hire a professional jury selection consultant. The latter costs a lot of money, and if you have a client like myself, who can't afford to spend that kind of money, an attorney must go it alone, and rely on their gut instincts.

Attorneys know that jury selection is one of the most crucial things they undertake at trial. If you pick the wrong jury, you have already lost. As I saw in my case, the government is busy voting off most of the jurors, the defense is trying to seat, so it's more complicated than it sounds. The process in which a jury is seated, is called voir dire, and is French in its origin. Voir dire generally refers to the process in which prospective jurors are questioned about their backgrounds, and potential biases, before being chosen to sit on the jury.

Voir Dire is how attorneys select, or perhaps more appropriately, reject, certain jurors to hear a case. Each side gets strikes, which they can use to vote off a prospective juror. On the first morning of trial, the judge went through questions with the jury. The courtroom was full of prospective jurors, who were allowed to raise their hands to answer the judge's questions, posed to them, and were allowed to approach the bench, if they wished to speak in private to the judge, regarding their answer. The attorneys were also allowed to approach the bench, so they could listen to what was being said in private, between the prospective juror, and the judge. The rest of us had to watch from a distance.

As prospective jurors are excused for cause, other prospective jurors keep moving into the jury box from the audience, until there are twelve jurors, and several alternates, seated in the jury box. After those jurors are seated, the prosecution, and the defense, get roughly ten votes, to vote jurors off the jury that they do not like. This is what is called striking a juror. After a strike, the next juror in the audience moves up to the jury box, until the jury is seated. The prosecution, and the defense, can ask questions of the prospective jurors in the box.

I was fascinated by the first question asked by the AUSA that morning. She told the prospective jurors a story, about two children sitting at the kitchen table. Their mother had told the children that they were not allowed to eat Cheetos, you know, the orange chips that get the Cheetos dust all over your fingers. When the mother returned to the room, she saw the Cheetos had been eaten, and that one child had orange Cheetos dust on their fingers. The other child did not. When the mother asked who had eaten the Cheetos, the child who had the Cheetos dust on their fingers, pointed at the other child. The prosecutor then asked the jurors to raise their hand, if they believed the child with the Cheetos dust on their fingers was the child guilty of eating the Cheetos.

More prospective jurors than not, raised their hand,

indicating basically, that it would not take much evidence, for them to believe someone was guilty. At least that was my opinion of someone being that quick to assume the worst, without needing further proof. The AUSA then asked the prospective jurors to raise their hands if they needed more information/proof, before deciding who had actually eaten the Cheetos.

One lady raised her hand quickly, and from her body language, she was adamant about her position. She was basically bouncing in her seat. The prosecutor then asked her a few more questions. I knew from her answers, that she was a free thinker, and would never make it to be seated on the jury. I was correct.

When the AUSA asked, "If anyone had ever been charged with a crime?" A middle-aged African American gentleman raised his hand and said he had been falsely accused of a crime in the past. He stated that he had not been found guilty of that crime. He never said what the crime was that he had been charged with, but I knew immediately he would be voted off the jury pool by the government. Again, I was correct. Another man I immediately knew the government would strike from the jury, stated his wife worked as a local attorney. Each time the government proved me correct, and none of those individuals ended up on my jury.

Jury oversite is another area of our criminal justice system that I feel needs reform. Going through the criminal justice process, both in the area of the grand jury and at trial, I came to realize that a *jury of your peers* is certainly a metaphor. It is a long-forgotten fairness that has lost its way over time, in our broken system. There needs to be a better system, where the jury pool consists of people, who have education or technical knowledge, about the case being tried, or put before the grand jury. The sobering fact is, the the prosecution can just vote jurors off, even those who have the very knowledge needed, for the case that is about to be tried, is another unfair flaw in the system. A system designed to give the government the upper hand, at every stage of the process.

Another fault in this area is that most laypersons cannot understand schemes, elements of the crime, and other legal terminology that comes with our overly complicated federal criminal justice system. As crazy as this may sound, my opinion is that there needs to be a career for professional jurors. Career jurors would go to school, and learn jury duty, as a professional trade. These individuals would be taught the law. They would specialize in certain areas of the law, and then serve at the grand jury, or at trials, on cases that pertained to these areas of the law, that they had been specifically trained in.

Most importantly, they would serve as neutral parties, much like expert witnesses, who are highly trained, to decide a case based on the evidence, and the facts, alone. They could not be misled, by either side, with trickery, excel spreadsheets, or PowerPoint slides, that distort the truth.

These jurors would be trained accountants, lawyers, or other highly trained undergraduates. Those versed in wire fraud, mail fraud, bank fraud, tax fraud, money laundering, or other white-collar crimes, would sit on those types of cases. Other jurors would be trained in personal injury, conspiracy for drug crimes, and other types of cases. The qualified jurors would be trained to understand the information presented to them at trial, and could decide, based on facts and the law, not hype, or government theories of the case, which is not factual. I wish our country could go to a system like this. I think it would hold the system more accountable, especially government prosecutors, and help prevent innocent people from ending up convicted criminals, serving prison time.

It took one-half of the first day of trial for us to seat the jury, in my case. I have read of other trials, where it takes days or even weeks, to seat a jury. It is a very stressful process if you are the defendant. It is a sobering thought that the people sitting in that box will decide your fate.

If you choose to go to trial, which I do not really recommend, unless we see changes to our legal system, be prepared for the jury selection process, and how stressful it can be. Read up on the process, and familiarize yourself with the ins, and outs, to avoid being caught off guard. Understanding the process was helpful to me that morning. This is not something your attorney is going to teach you. I was just very fortunate that my first attorney took so much time explaining these things to me.

And on the first day of trial, remember that God is there with you. Turn your trust and your troubles over to HIM. The bible tells us in Romans 5:3-5, "Not only that, but we rejoice in our sufferings, knowing that suffering produces endurance and that endurance produces character; and character produces hope. And hope does not put us to shame because God's love has been poured out into our hearts through the Holy Spirit, who has been given to us."

Chapter Nineteen
Federal Jury Trial: Not For The Faint Of Heart

Federal jury trials are interesting to observe. Of course, not so much, if you are the defendant, and the one on trial. I don't remember much about the eight days I was on trial in federal court. As the week wore on, and the judge ruled more in favor of the government, at every turn, the more my heart sank. I had honestly believed that it would all be over, once I got to the trial phase of my case. I falsely believed that I would prove my innocence, and then I could actually go back to my life, and so could my family. I had actually dreamed of the celebration I would have, when I won at trial. And I have to admit that in my dream, I dreamed of the awful things I would say to the government prosecutors, when I won! But before my trial, I still believed in this part of our criminal justice system. I had every reason to believe that the truth would prevail in court. The jury would be the great equalizer, between the United States of America, and myself. I could not have been more wrong or misguided.

Going through security at the Federal Courthouse morning, after morning, was overwhelming. Knowing newspaper reporters are recording your every move is maddening. You feel like you are living in a fishbowl, and to some extent, you are. I remember the first morning when we pulled up at the Federal Courthouse, and I had to get out of my attorney's car. I was asked to help carry some of the boxes of documents. I remember trying to hide behind the boxes, and hoping that the reporters would think I was the attorney's paralegal. I had seen the horrible photographs of defendants plastered all over the newspaper from other cases I had followed.

Once you get to security at the federal courthouse, it is obvious who is the attorney, and who is the defendant. As a defendant, you are not allowed to bring your cell phone into the courtroom, so you are basically stripped of any communication to the outside world. None of your family or friends can text you with encouragement throughout the day. When the court takes a recess, you can't take a mindless social media break, to get your mind off things. As I wrote this chapter of my book, I realized how numb I had become, by the time I got to trial. While I was still full of hate, and anger, towards the government at times, I had also become primarily numb in other areas, in what was probably a coping mechanism, in order to keep my sanity.

Watching the government pack the courtroom with Secret Service, and IRS agents, other AUSAs who showed up for support of their fellow government prosecutors, and the reporters sitting in the audience, on the government's side of the courtroom, of course, was overwhelming. On the first day of trial, I was still optimistic that I could prove the truth. But, as the days waned on, I started to fear that the government was winning. This was mainly because I came to realize that my attorneys had no idea about my case, or my defense.

One of the first things that happened, which made me realize just how much it was a *win at all costs game* for the government, took place immediately after the government gave its opening statements. The courtroom had been packed with other Assistant United States Attorneys (AUSAs). In essence, the prosecutor basically had her own cheering squad. As soon as she finished with the government's opening statements, she walked back to the prosecution table, and immediately got hi-fives from the other AUSAs in the audience. I was in shock, watching this display of camaraderie, take place in a federal courtroom. How did it appear to the jury? And why did the judge allow such to go on in the courtroom?

My attorney could not explain these things to me, except to say "not to worry about it." I was. appalled. And it was displays of unprofessionalism by the government, such as that one, that continued to fuel my already out of control anger. My trial was not a basketball game, or other sporting event. This was my life.

Another thing I quickly noticed is that the government can take the most innocent of events, and twist them into something very sinister at trial. The government is not forced to put on facts with hard evidence. Instead, it can present its *theory of the case*, which eventually becomes fact, in the eyes of the jury. If you tell a jury something so many times, they come to believe it. The government repeatedly told the jury I was a bad person.

The government has an unlimited budget, with which to go after defendants. It has PowerPoint presentations, and staff, whose only job is to hand the AUSA documents, and turn to the next PowerPoint slide, as directed. During the government's dog and pony PowerPoint show, I turned to one of my attorneys and whispered, "If I didn't know the truth about what *really* happened, I would believe what they are showing to the jury in those slides." My attorney just looked at me. He had no response. It was genuine, and he knew there was nothing to say in return.

I feel confident he knew we were losing. Between the evidence being destroyed, being denied the right to tell the jury, the truth, the whole truth, and nothing but the truth, and the government being able to allege whatever it wanted to, it is hard to see how any defendant could win at trial. Maybe this is why attorneys tell you that only two percent of defendants go to trial, and mostly none of them win at trial.

When we would take a break for lunch, or leave court for the day, my attorneys would be frustrated, and even angry. I rode from their office with them to the courthouse every day, therefore, I had no choice, but to listen to their chatter in the car. This made me even more anxious, and scared. And these conversations, actually stoked the burning fire of anger within me. We really didn't have much in the way of defense anyway. As all the financial documents had been shredded, and my work computer had been hauled away. We were even lacking complete bank records, with which to make a defense.

And we never got a good copy of the QuickBooks program from my work computer. It came down to my word, against the government's PowerPoint slides, and an Excel spreadsheet, testified to by an IRS Agent, where the IRS had calculated how much in tax fraud, I had committed for each year, based on how much I had been reimbursed, for items I charged on my personal credit card that year, for Dr. Swan.

And because the judge refused to allow us to put into evidence the sexual assault, that started this entire case, the civil case the doctors had filed against us, with their baseless allegations, the fact that the doctors had caused to be shredded all the financial documents at their office, or that my work computer had been destroyed as well, it was an uphill losing battle.

Adding further insult to injury, we were not allowed to use reverse 404(b) evidence, to discuss Dr. Swan' past issue of not filing his tax returns, for five consecutive years, and then blaming his CPA, nor that I had witnessed all the doctors voting to continue their Medicare billing fraud, or the prescription drug fraud, I had suspected during my tenure as the doctors' office manager. In fact, Dr. Jones had since been indicted in a drug conspiracy for allegedly putting illegal painkillers on the street, which had resulted in at least one overdose death, but we were not allowed to tell the jury about that either.

I was devastated and in shock. The judge was handing the government, my conviction, on a silver platter, as if they didn't already have the upper hand to begin with, after my first attorney had given AUSA Harris my entire defense. The entire process was unfair. I thought my attorneys would lose it, the day the IRS Agent was on the stand, and the judge actually got up from her chair, and poured him a glass of water. Yet when I took the stand, on the last day of trial to testify, and needed water, she told me I could get some without offering me any help. What kind of message did that send to the jury? A federal judge is supposed to be neutral. I'm not accusing her of not being neutral, only pointing out how the act of her getting water for the IRS Agent must have appeared to the jury? My attorneys were furious when this happened.

Not being able to connect the fact that Dr. Swan had previously tried to get out of paying taxes, by accusing his CPA of not filing them, to the fact that I had charged items for him that were personal, and then classified them as business expenses, was detrimental to showing the jury what really happened. Due to all the destruction of documents and my work computer, and the missing deposit slips from the banking records, as well as not having a good copy of the QuickBooks backup file, we were basically stripped of any way to prove the truth.

After the government had rested its case, I would find out that my young attorney, who had never tried a federal jury trial, or possibly any trial, at all, for that matter, had failed to even turn over the limited discovery we did have, to the government. That meant none of the evidence I had given him, that may have had any chance of showing what really happened, or swaying the jury in my favor, or would at least give the jurors a reasonable doubt, could be entered as an exhibit, into evidence at trial.

And if all of that were not bad enough, the icing on the cake came, when the judge allowed the government to add a jury instruction that read, "It does not matter how the money got into the bank account that was transferred, only how it got out of the bank account." This meant the jury should only consider the money that had left the *zero*-balance checking account. They could only consider the money that had been paid to me through electronic payroll, for reimbursements of personal items, I purchased on my personal credit cards for Dr. Swan, the transfers the government said I stole. How could it not matter how the money got in the account? It was a *zero*-balance account. The only money that was ever deposited into the account was checks paid by the doctors for their bills, after being presented with a settlement statement for their share of the expenses. How could the jury not be allowed to consider it? In the end, It came down to my word against the doctors, and the government.

Dr. Swan would be caught lying on the stand several times during cross-examination. This apparently did not matter to the jury. And in closing arguments, my attorney did not tie together Dr. Swan' lies, with the evidence for the jury anyway. Only four, of the eight doctors I had worked for, were called to testify at trial. On the first day of trial, the first witness was Dr. Zorick, whom I respected very much. I had advised my attorneys to ask him as many questions as possible, to prove the truth of what had transpired. I felt he would most likely be the only doctor, who would be honest on the stand. I saw how the other doctors operated after working for them during the four years I was their office manager, and I knew they would do whatever to protect their own hides. As I suspected, Dr. Zorick admitted on the stand that he had gone back through all of his settlement statements, and so had his Certified Public Accountant (CPA).

They had found nothing misleading in them, or that he could say I had stolen. He also admitted that anytime I had made a mistake, during my tenure as the office manager, I had volunteered my mistake, and corrected it immediately. He also volunteered that I had been immediately forthcoming, anytime he asked me for additional financial information. He even admitted that all the bills, payroll, and payroll taxes I was supposed to pay out of the *zero*-balance account, had, in fact, been paid. There were no unpaid bills found after I left the doctors' employment.

Basically, he gave the jury everything they should have needed to understand that there was *nothing* to steal in the *zero*-balance account. His testimony should have clued them in, that there was no way I could have stolen $611,000, because "how was there money in the account to steal," especially if all the bills had been paid.

But unfortunately, none of the jury members had

accounting knowledge. And my attorney never tied any of this testimony together for the jury, during our cross-examination, or in our closing arguments, on the last day of trial. Frankly, because my attorneys did not understand basic accounting themselves. I tried to show them how to tie it all together, but they would not listen. The lead attorney, who had never even spent any time with me, was arrogant, and the one directing the junior attorney, on how to proceed.

The jurors didn't even get the chance to understand how the *zero-* balance account operated, because my attorneys didn't explain it to them, most likely because they didn't understand it themselves. It was all over their heads. I had begged my attorneys early on, to hire an expert witness, who was a CPA, but they would not listen to me, on that point either. The jury was never shown anything that could have helped them understand my case. As I suspected, the other doctors were not as forthcoming on the stand.

Dr. Boring testified that he had not looked over his settlement statements after I left, nor had his CPA checked them for errors, or inflations. Something I knew was a lie, due to statements made during the civil case, but we were not allowed to mention that case, because the judge had blocked us from doing so. Common sense should have told the jury that this would not be true. Who in their right mind suspects that $611,000 has been stolen, but doesn't have their statements checked, to see how much was stolen directly from them?

My attorneys forgot to ask one of the doctors these questions on cross-examination, so who knows what his answer would have been? And Dr. Swan testified that "I had kept his settlement statements for him, so he had no idea if I had done anything wrong or not". Another lie! My attorney later proved that he was lying about me keeping his settlement statements, by way of testimony of a past employee, who had also worked for the doctors during my tenure at the clinic.

That employee, one of the only witnesses called by the

defense to testify on my behalf, admitted on the stand that she, and another employee, were the ones who actually distributed the settlement statements to ALL of the doctors, every two weeks. She testified that Dr. Swan had gotten copies of his settlement statements. Yet my attorney did not do a good job making the jury understand why this testimony was important. My attorney never tied the two witness statements together, for the jury to understand that Dr. Swan was, in fact, caught lying on the stand, which would have made everything else he testified to suspect.

We were able to get the government's QuickBooks expert witness to agree with us, that what the government said I had done in QuickBooks, was not possible for the program to actually do. And that the copy of the QuickBooks the government had put into evidence, could not be the copy actually used for the business.

The government's expert admitted that the copy of QuickBooks the government had entered into evidence, was missing the direct deposit payroll, which is an automatic download directly from QuickBooks, when the payroll is transmitted, and would have shown in the audit trail function of QuickBooks, if it had been manipulated by any user, which was what the government was accusing me of having done, in the QuickBooks. But again, this was not tied together for the jury by my attorneys, most likely because they did not understand it.

My first attorney had tried hard to get a good copy of QuickBooks. The government had misplaced the copy given to them on a flash drive by the doctors' CPA. That copy had supposedly been backed up the week I left the doctors' employment by their CPA, something else we were blocked from telling the jury. The government was allowed to show at trial QuickBooks entries that the government said had been changed, or manipulated by me. What the government showed the jury, really just proved that I, or whoever else had been working in the QuickBooks copy, had made data entry mistakes that had been corrected, and the entries where I had

216

gone back and reclassified expenses, at Dr. Swan's request. Again, my attorney did not help the jury understand any of this.

Even in all his arrogance, he didn't understand QuickBooks, or accounting, any better than the government. During testimony, IRS Agent Shortway, also had to agree with us that the copy of the QuickBooks, put into evidence by the government, could not be the QuickBooks used for payroll. If my attorney had only pressed the agent, he would have had no choice but to admit that what was in the indictment regarding the QuickBooks, was impossible, and that I could not have done it. But the jury was never able to understand how what the agent had just testified to, helped my defense, because my attorney did not understand enough about the QuickBooks program, to ask the additional questions needed to make this point.

I could tell the agent knew where my attorney was going. I could tell from the look on his face. If only my attorney had pressed a little bit further, or had known the right questions to ask, we could have hit a home run, with that line of questioning. I wanted to yell the questions he should be asking from the defense table. It was frustrating. I regretted ever hiring them. They were not prepared for trial, and they knew it too.

This lack of preparedness certainly explained why the night before my jury trial, the senior attorney had tried to bully me into taking a plea deal. He had shown me photos of our patio furniture, and our outdoor fireplace, as proof that I would look bad to the jury. It was a nightmare, and I did not feel that he was in my corner, like I had felt about my first attorney.

The IRS agent looked relieved, when he got off easy, during this line of questioning, and did not have to admit what it was obvious he knew. That I had not manipulated the QuickBooks program, like the indictment alleged. I longed for my old attorney, as I sat at trial that week. He knew my case. He had been a loyal advocate. To this day, I still get high anxiety, and a knot in my stomach, when I'm forced to relive my trial. It is one of the reasons I put off writing this book for so long. Trauma that has not resolved, no matter how hard I've tried to work on it.

On the last day of trial, I took the stand, and testified for over three hours. The government could not trip me up, no matter how hard it tried, on cross-examination. It's hard to trip someone up, when they are actually just telling the truth. At one point, AUSA Mazzanti got so angry that she yelled at me. She wanted me to admit that I had perjured myself in my testimony before the grand jury.

She pointed out that I had answered, "I filed my taxes," while testifying at the grand jury. This was a true statement, and I had said that, in my grand jury testimony. However, she was taking that one statement out of context. The government was trying to twist my testimony, while failing to acknowledge to the jury, what questions I was being asked when I answered this way, during my grand jury testimony.

I called her out on it from the witness stand, and she became furious. She had made the mistake of asking to approach the witness, me, with a copy of the grand jury transcript, and had asked me to read from it. She only wanted me to read the answer I gave, regarding filing my tax returns.

I was reading the questions, asked before the answer I had given that day at the grand jury, which told the whole story, and shed a different light on what AUSA Mazzanti was trying to twist, in the jury's mind. She kept interrupting me, and asking the judge to instruct me to ONLY answer her direct question. There were many side-bars during this testimony. It probably didn't help that I had been giving her evil eyes, and looks of defiance, from the witness stand, before she cross-examined me. Again, my anger was getting the best of me.

Regarding the grand jury testimony in question, AUSA Harris had been pounding me with questions, during my grand jury appearance in 2014. Sometimes, he would not even allow me to finish answering his question, before he pounded me with another one. Unfortunately, this does not come across when you read the grand jury transcript, since the court reporter simply types, precisely what is said, word for word, and nothing else, such as the timing of the questions.

At the time, I was asked questions by AUSA Harris, that led me to believe that I was being accused of not having filed tax returns at all, for the years in question. This was at the point in my case, where AUSA Harris would not disclose what I was even under investigation for, so I had no way to know what he was actually asking me about. The questions seemed geared at trying to imply that I had not filed my taxes for those four years.

This happened in the spring of 2014, when I was invited to the grand jury to testify. I had not even been required to testify at the grand jury, due to my Fifth Amendment rights. I was not subpoenaed to testify; I was given an invitation through a target letter from AUSA Harris. I went because I wanted to prove the truth. I wanted to testify, and tell the grand jurors what really happened. But once there, I was not allowed to do so. AUSA Harris had pounded me with questions that just went in circles. The grand jury testimony had taken place in July 2014, between the first and second indictments.

However, at trial on cross-examination, AUSA Mazzanti had asked me the question differently, by asking who *prepared* our tax returns, and filed them? I honestly answered that my husband had. He is a CPA, and works at a public accounting firm. He had prepared our returns at his work, using their tax accounting software. His name showed as the preparer, and his CPA license number, was on the returns, filed with the IRS. The government had already entered those certified return copies into evidence, in its case in chief, at trial.

Two of the returns had been filed electronically by my husband at work. I had probably never seen these two returns, and had undoubtedly not signed them. In fact, on one of them, the same pin number had been used to sign for both my husband and me, as our electronic signature. This reason alone would have prevented the government from convicting me of tax fraud, for those two years, had I wanted to be dishonest on the stand. However, I told the truth, that I knew those two years had been prepared by my husband, and electronically filed. I had no reason to believe they were incorrect.

I knew my husband did not cheat on our taxes. The other two years' returns were mailed, and showed both of our signatures on them, and my husband's name, and his CPA license, again appeared as the preparer of those returns. But the government already knew all of this, due to its badgering of my husband, and his bosses, before the second indictment.

The government now wanted to twist these two statements, the one at trial, and the one at the grand jury, and take them entirely out of context, to prove that I was a liar, and had perjured myself on the record. In my defense, I think most people use the statement "I filed my taxes," the terms I had used during my grand jury testimony, to infer that a return was filed on their behalf for a given year. This does not necessarily mean they actually personally *prepared* the return, or even caused it to be filed. For example, if you take your taxes to be prepared, and filed, at H&R Block, do you not say, "I filed my taxes?" But does that mean you actually prepared your return, or hit the send button yourself? It was all just a big game with the government, and even the smallest of things could be twisted into something nefarious.

During my sentencing, AUSA Mazzanti would attempt to use this example, of what the government claimed was my dishonesty, to get the judge to give me a two-level enhancement, which would cause me to serve more prison time, for obstruction of justice. Luckily, the judge saw through her tactics, and denied the enhancement.

To prove the government's wire fraud charges, the government put the four doctors on the stand, to state they did not give me permission to "transfer" the electronic payroll reimbursements, to myself. The government continued to use the word "transfer" to confuse the jury. I had actually been reimbursed through electronic payroll reimbursement.

The government used IRS Agent Shortway's testimony, that the money left the bank through electronic "transfers", and was paid to me. Those electronic payroll reimbursement of expenses belonged to Dr. Swan.

Those transfers, as the government liked to call them, were repayment for items I had charged on my personal credit cards. They were expense reimbursements, paid to me, when I received my payroll check every two weeks. But this was never explained to the jury fully. I felt the use of the word "transfers" was very misleading, and probably done by design, to once again, give the government the upper-hand.

I had not actually transferred any money to myself. I had been reimbursed through electronic direct deposit payroll. But because all the payroll records had been destroyed, we could not show this to the jury. However, the government's own QuickBooks expert witness, clearly testified about the direct deposits from payroll going into my bank account. I'm not sure the jury connected the two dots? And three of the four doctors, who got on the stand to say they didn't give me permission to "transfer any money to myself," were actually telling the truth, because they hadn't been the ones to approve payroll.

Only *one doctor* gave me permission to reimburse myself through payroll. The President, Dr. Swan, who I was charging the personal items for on my credit cards. The only doctor responsible for approving the payroll and overseeing the *zero-balance* bank account.

The other doctors probably had no idea, and they too, may have been confused, on what "transfer" really meant? The IRS agent also showed the jury that I had used my personal credit cards, to purchase personal items, for myself. I later admitted this on the stand, when I testified on my own behalf. It was true. Of course, I had. They were my personal credit cards. However, hundreds of thousands of dollars, of other items, were charged on those same personal credit cards, for Dr. Swan.

None of those items were traceable to me, or my use, yet

my attorneys never brought that fact out to the jury, at any time during the trial. The number of things I had charged for myself personally on my credit cards, was few. Before working for the doctors, and after I quit that job, our past credit card history would have shown that I did not typically charge those types of items, or those kinds of amounts on my credit cards. If only my attorneys had done the work to show the jury this, using my past, and present credit card usage. It would have shown a pattern of my normal spending habits, vs. what transpired when I worked for the doctors, and was charging things for Dr. Swan, and others, on my credit cards.

The government wanted to paint a narrative that we were living a high on the hog lifestyle, but they didn't have much in the way to work with. Both my husband and I had good jobs that paid well. We don't own any luxury items at all. There is no beach or lake house, no jet skis, no boats, nothing of the sort. We drive Honda model vehicles. They are newer cars, and we trade every few years, but they also have a car note attached.

We have a swimming pool, but the government and my attorney failed to tell the jury that it is a basic small in ground pool, made of fiberglass, not some on-site built fancy pool. And that the same pool was built at the same time as our house, using the same construction loan. We did go on vacations, but only once a year. During the years I worked for the doctors, we went to an all-inclusive resort, in three of the four years, which cost about $2,600 per trip, including all airfare and food, for the week. Not exactly the "high on the hog" lifestyle, the government wanted to paint.

The last year I worked for the doctors, when we were building a new home, we could not afford to go on a vacation, because we were using all the extra money for the house we were building at the time. Had I really been stealing that much money from the doctors; we could have taken as many vacations as we wanted. None of this added up, but somehow the government sold it to the jury anyway. The only thing the government could really use was that in 2010, the very last year I worked for the doctors, my husband and I had built a new home.

However, even that was hard to twist too far, because we had a construction loan, and cashed in other assets, to pay for the building of said home, all with a paper trail, to prove where the money really came from. Regardless, the government prosecutors tried really hard to paint the picture. We had also sold a home that same year for approximately $270,000, and received over $80,000 in equity that was put towards the building of our new home. The house we sold was purchased brand new in 2005, before I even worked for the doctors. The government's narrative did not make sense, but that did not stop government prosecutors from spinning it to the jury anyway.

The government put an IRS Revenue agent on the stand to state the amount of taxes I owed for each year on the money it said I stole using wire fraud to do so. She simply told the jury I stole $611,000, and did not report it as stolen income on my tax returns.

Therefore, the government alleged it was tax fraud. This proved nothing, but it obviously worked, since I was convicted on all four tax fraud counts, and now owe the IRS restitution of $207,000, in back taxes. The government showed the jury four checks, written for more than $10,000 each to subcontractors, to get me convicted on the money laundering charges.

All of these checks are related to the building of our home. One of the checks was the check written for $23,000 to our builder, that I've already covered in an earlier chapter. That check was written three days after we closed on the home we sold on West Lake Circle, and deposited the over $82,000 check from that closing, into our bank account. A clear paper trail of where the money had come from. But the truth did not matter. The truth was what the government said the truth was.

And I honestly do not believe anyone on the jury understood accounting, given the government voted anyone off, that stated during voir dire, they had financial, or accounting knowledge. In fact, I'm not even sure the federal judge, presiding over my case, understood accounting, based on some of her rulings. Otherwise, how could a federal judge not believe it was relevant, how the money got into a *zero*-balance account, or that the very people accusing me of stealing $611,000, had shredded all the financial documents, that would have proved what really happened? I'm confident my defense attorneys had no clue about accounting, or any other financial matter, that had to do with my defense. But that is our criminal justice system in a nutshell.

And if all of that were not enough. The government had still been offering to settle the case, with the previously offered plea deal, all week long, during my jury trial. My attorney had been trying to intimidate me into taking it, by telling me "The judge hates you," and "You are going to prison for 8-13 years if you don't take the government's plea deal."

I'm sure my attorneys had hoped I would get scared, and take the government's plea deal, before they were forced to put forth my side of the case. They knew they were not prepared for trial, and probably wanted to save face. They had to be aware that they had failed to turn over discovery to the government. Why they had not corrected this on the first day of trial, is beyond me? And maybe the lead attorney had not noticed it until it was too late. I unfortunately did not find this out until I tried suggesting documents to put forth as exhibits, when it was my turn to put on a defense.

At the end of my trial, it came down to a jury instruction that told the jury to consider "only the money that had gone out of the zero-balance bank account," and all the other stuff was just my word against the doctors, and the government. And they had denied on the stand that I had permission to reimburse myself through electronic payroll, "the transfers".

However, on the stand, Dr. Swan did admit that he had been "Hiding money from his wife," and had "Paid some personal bills through the business account." I guess none of that even mattered to the jury, or the government. It was all so unbelievable! To get a conviction for wire fraud, the government should have had to prove that there was a "scheme to defraud," and several other elements, required to commit the crime of wire fraud, but they hadn't.

The things I had charged on my personal credit cards for the doctors were not a federal crime. Even classifying personal expenses, as business expenses, in the QuickBooks, was not a federal crime. If the government had charged Dr. Swan with the tax fraud he most likely committed, then maybe the government would have had a conspiracy case against me.

In the end, the jury voted with the government, and since the defendant is not allowed to even question the jury on why they voted, the way they did, it was a done deal. When the jury came back into the courtroom the morning the verdict was read, it was apparent that one of the jurors, a lady, had been crying. Did that have something to do with my case, or the verdict? I will never know.

Once the verdict started being read, and I had been found guilty on count one, I just laid my head down on the defense table. I laid there numb, as I listened to the rest of the counts being read, and the jury foreperson saying guilty to each count. I don't remember much of anything said after that in court, except the judge saying I could continue to remain free until sentencing, on pretrial release. I did not cry, or show any emotion. I was too drained, and numb, to care anymore. I had lost over 20 pounds, the week of the trial, just from stress. My clothes didn't even fit any longer.

I do remember hearing my husband, who was sitting behind me, sniffle a little when the verdict was read, but I did not dare look around at him, for fear I would lose it. My friend, Katherine, who was sitting with him, could be heard sobbing. She later told me that my husband had turned white, when the verdict was read, and she had feared that he would pass out. Hearing that made me glad I did not look back at him.

Immediately after the verdict was read, I was whisked away to report to the United States Marshal's office, to take another round of DNA, and fingerprints, as if the first two sets had somehow managed to change, after being found guilty. Afterward, my husband and I drove home. I don't even remember our conversation that day. It is all a blur. I just remember having a knot in my stomach, and feeling like I could not go on.

We quickly informed JT and Timothy about what had happened. We had chosen to protect them when the second indictment was filed, by not telling them, since we had seen the stress, the first indictment, had caused them. They were obviously confused, and maybe a little hurt, that we had kept them in the dark. I understood. But we had actually done so, because we felt it best for their lives, at the time.

Then, we drove across the highway, to my husband's parents' home, to tell them. We wanted them to hear it from me, before they could hear it from anyone else, or on the news. I had called my mom, and my sister, on the way home from the courthouse. And I waited to call Joseph, who at the time lived in New York City, until later that afternoon, after I knew he would be off work. I then proceeded to stay in bed, wallowing in my disbelief and grief, for the next four days, because I was too sick, and in shock, to even get up.

My husband had no choice but to work, and in fact, he had to leave to go out of state, to do a client audit, the day after I was found guilty. He could not even be there to console me. I'm not sure I really needed him anyway. I was exhausted.

Family and friends called to check on me, and many offered to come to my home to console me, or bring me food. I honestly just wanted to be alone. Our whole world was falling apart, but I really didn't care. I went from being angry, to feeling numb. I had so many emotions. During my times of anger, I questioned God. How could HE allow this to happen? HE knew the truth! Why was this happening to me, and to my family? And I tortured myself, by constantly reflecting back, to all the ways the government had been unfair. How could the AUSAs not see the truth? Did it not bother them to convict an innocent person? I wondered if their careers were that important to them? I'll never know the answer to those questions, but I do know that God punishes those that do wrong.

And what about Dr. Swan? He had lied to save his own skin. Yet, I forgave him, but not until years later, when I would finally let go of all the anger I felt. And not until God showed me that I could not hold on to those feelings any longer, because I could not be whole, or heal, if I continued to do so. But right after my conviction, those feelings continued to fuel my growing anger. I would also learn later, how to forgive Dr. Jones, who had sexually assaulted me. But again, it was a long time before any of that happened, and only after I allowed God to heal me. Shortly after my trial, Dr. Jones pleaded guilty, in his own prosecution, to writing fraudulent prescriptions for painkillers to patients. The prescriptions he wrote were linked to the death of a twenty five-year old man. I often wonder about him. Has he found the forgiveness that only God can provide?

Does it still hurt me knowing what the doctors did to me? Of course, but I can't allow my degree of pain to dictate my degree of forgiveness. That would not be biblical. In Luke 6:37, the bible tells us, "Judge not, and you will not be judged; condemn not, and you will not be condemned; forgive, and you will be forgiven."

My forgiveness of doctors Swan, and Jones, has honestly been one of the hardest things for me to do. It was not just a matter of being obedient to God, but it was also the only way I could move forward, and to heal from all of the pain and deeply rooted anger. They are the ones that will have to answer for what they have done. I only have to answer for my own actions. As they haven't always been appropriate, throughout this nightmare either.

In fact, I've even forgiven AUSA Harris, for his bad actions. While writing this book has caused many emotional moments. And at times, I could feel myself getting angry all over again, reliving traumas, and would sometimes have to stop in mid paragraph, and pray for God's peace, to overtake me. But one thing I have learned on this journey, is to keep pushing forward, with God's mercy, and grace.

With continued prayer in this area, and the seeking of God first, I have been able to keep moving in the right direction. My prayer for each of my readers is that you find the peace that only a true relationship with God can give you. I still struggle at times, with all that has happened to my family, and me, but I'm making it one day at a time, and only with God's love, forgiveness, and continued grace!

Chapter Twenty
Firing of My Second Attorneys

After the trial, I became more and more disgruntled with the two attorneys that represented me at trial. Finding out the week of my trial, that they had failed to turn over discovery to the government, had been hard to stomach. I genuinely believe it was an honest mistake on the young attorney's part. After all, it was his first federal trial. But the fact remains, that his mistake, had contributed to my loss of freedom, for a crime I knew I had not committed.

He also gave me bad advice, regarding what I needed to tell the probation officer, during the PSR report. This report follows you around from sentencing, to the BOP, through halfway house time, and supervised release. It is also the most important document that the judge uses at sentencing. Not correcting misinformation can make a big difference, but this is not something my attorney told me.

In fact, he advised me to answer questions as briefly as possible. Therefore, I never argued things that were not correct, that the PO had been told by the government, and left out arguments about what had really happened, at my attorney's advice. And admittedly, I was tired and broken, by this point. I really didn't care anymore after my trial. I didn't want to address these things anyway.

As it got closer to time for sentencing, I kept asking him about filing a Pre-Sentence Memorandum. I knew it was customary to file one of these motions, on behalf of the defendant, from all the research I had done myself. It is basically a motion with the court to argue against enhancements, or other tricks the government uses, in order to add more time to your sentence, and to ask the judge to give a specific sentence. I knew about these motions from working as my own paralegal, helping my first attorney, and from all the research I had done for my own case.

My second attorney, and his boss, the senior attorney, kept telling me that filing one of these memorandums would tip off the government to our arguments. I knew this was not the case, and did not want to risk arguing these points in open court, on the day of my sentencing. After all, I saw how unprepared these two attorneys were at my trial. And in reality, there are only so many arguments you could make anyway.

I knew that we needed to argue against the government's enhancements, and those arguments would have been well-founded in case law. The government would have been aware of these arguments, regardless if we let them know ahead of time, in a motion, or not. This was just my attorneys being lazy. Additionally, the government had to know that an attorney for the defendant would ask the judge for a lower sentence, than the government requested. This is really no secret!

My distrust for my attorney, but mainly for his boss, the senior attorney, who liked to try to bully me, grew and grew. And admittedly, I was worn out mentally at this point, from fighting the government, and the trial. And I constantly relived how my attorneys were not prepared for my jury trial. I constantly thought about how the night before trial, and during the week of trial, they kept trying to bully me into taking a plea deal. I wished I had alerted the judge the week of trial to the fact that my attorneys were unprepared, but at the time I was scared to do so. I was now on my second attorney. I didn't want the government to claim I was trying to stall the trial again.

Looking back, I should have spoken up. My very freedom was at stake. Every time I thought about these things, my anger would almost consume me. By this point, my anger was so out of control, that I could feel it take over my entire body. I could actually feel the anger wash hot over me. I reflected on my trial and the questions the attorneys asked the government witnesses, and how they wasted the only two witnesses they called on my behalf.

I knew they did not understand my case, and had spent very little time, basically the week before trial, preparing. And because I had helped my first attorney so much, and been so intricately involved in my case, I understood much more about the law than most clients. They were not pulling the wool over my eyes. And the young attorney seemed to understand it too. The day the guilty verdict was read, he told me to file an ineffective counsel motion, called a 2255, with the court against him. I think he got bad advice from the senior attorney, who was supposed to be guiding him, and he realized he had failed as my attorney.

I truly believe he felt terrible about what happened to me at trial. I saw it on his face. My understanding is that he no longer works with the senior attorney. However, I am not sure what the reason is for them parting ways. He was not much older than my oldest son, and I do not blame him for any of this. When I hired their firm, I met with him, and the senior attorney several times. I honestly thought I hired the senior attorney, based on our conversations. I should have known better, given that I never saw him until the week of trial, and it was apparent he knew nothing about my case at all, or at least very little.

And, there were many *red flags* that I had ignored along the way. Meetings were canceled with me almost every time they were scheduled. There were several times I got all the way to their office, in another town, to be told they could not meet with me, or got within blocks of their office for a scheduled meeting time, and would receive a phone call from their office staff, telling me they were tied up in court. I understand this happens sometimes, but every time? I had tried to explain to them that this was a case full of accounting, and that we needed an expert. We talked with a CPA, but the guy knew nothing about QuickBooks payroll. I had been a certified QuickBooks expert during my years in public accounting, so I recognized his lack of knowledge immediately.

What the government was alleging in the indictment, QuickBooks could not do. The CPA we met with only understood QuickBooks cloud payroll, which was not the software I had used at the doctors' clinic. He argued QuickBooks could do those things. My research told me he did not know what he was talking about, and even the government's own QuickBooks expert, had agreed with me at trial.

Regardless, the lead attorney would not listen, and no expert was hired. I most likely could not have afforded one anyway. But all of these things kept replaying in my mind, after the trial. I had personally tried to show my attorneys how QuickBooks worked.

I owned a small business, and used direct deposit payroll, for my own employees. I took my laptop to their office several times to show them how it worked, and why what the government had alleged could not have happened. Each time I was dismissed, the attorneys were not interested in seeing it. The senior attorney even told me, "Stop talking about QuickBooks." At one point he even suggested that I lie on the stand about the QuickBooks program, I refused.

In the scheme to defraud on the wire fraud charges, the QuickBooks was being used as part of the scheme. This was the central element of the wire fraud charge that we could defeat, if only I had been allowed to show the jury how QuickBooks really worked. I could not have done what the indictment alleged. And if there was no wire fraud, then there could be no illegal gains that I had money laundered, and not reported on my taxes. This would, in essence, have beaten the government's entire case.

But I have to admit. that I was not as proactive, as I should have been during this time. This case had been ongoing for over five years, and I was beaten down and tired. I should have been more persistent, but I was not. I told myself that I needed to t rust the attorneys I had paid, that they were the ones with the law degrees, not me. So, I gladly took a break from the case, and tried to live my life, as best I could.

As we got closer and closer to my first sentencing date of August 24, 2017, I could no longer ignore the *red flags*. I knew in my heart that if I allowed those attorneys to represent me at the sentencing hearing, I would get more prison time. The government asked that I be sentenced to 8-13 years. The senior attorney had repeatedly told me, "The judge hates you." He said it would not matter if they filed the pre-sentencing memo or not. He told me, "The judge is going to stick it to you regardless." "You are going to prison for at least eight years, because you would not listen, and take the plea deal." He said they would argue these issues in court at the sentencing hearing.

I knew that we needed to argue them in a Pre-Sentence memorandum. I had done my research. This was my life! I saw how taking his advice, and waiting to argue against the government's motions in limine, when we got to trial, had turned out. It had cost me a lot, possibly my freedom. And I had come to realize that the judge liked to have time to look over things, and consider them. I had witnessed that each time she had to make a hasty decision, she ultimately ruled with the government. And while I felt she may not be my biggest fan, I did not believe that a federal judge hated me, or any other defendant. I guess I still had a little faith left in our criminal justice system.

I had 165 character-reference letters written by people, some of whom had known me for as long as 40+ years. I was being told by the senior attorney that they would only turn in 10 of these for the judge to read. I wanted her to read them all. They all detailed my excellent life-long character of helping others, and my many years of volunteer work with the homeless, Salvation Army, food pantries, at my church, and other charity organizations. In the end, I couldn't take that risk. It was just too great. However, that meant we had to spend between $10,000-$20,000, to get another attorney to represent me at sentencing.

We had already paid my second attorney in full at this point. And if the government still got its way, which my second attorney told me would most certainly happen, then another $10,000-$20,000 would be more money wasted, and taken away from my family, just continuing to fight a losing battle. We had spent approximately $160,000, already fighting this case. But what was the cost of getting many extra years spent in prison, for a crime I knew I had not committed? I felt I had to roll the dice, one more time.

My husband and I discussed it. He agreed that we could not take the risk of me going to prison for 8-13 years, for crimes we knew I had not committed. So, I fired my second set of attorneys. On the day I fired them, the senior attorney sent me an email stating they would file a Pre-Sentence Memo that weekend. I guess they were trying to save face. I advised them they had best not file anything else in my case, as I had just fired them. In the end, I hired another attorney to represent me at sentencing. We paid their firm $10,000. They immediately filed a Pre-Sentence Memorandum, and delivered all 165 character-reference letters to the judge, that same week.

Chapter Twenty-One
You Thought What?

The bible tells us in James 1:12 "Blessed is the man who remains steadfast under trial, for when he has stood the test he will receive the crown of life, which God has promised to those who love him."

By November 3, 2017, the day when my sentencing hearing finally took place, I was just ready to get all this over with. I was still optimistic that the judge would see the truth and possibly give me probation. I felt that my new attorneys had made some good arguments toward it, in our memorandum to the court, and had provided case law I had researched, that could have allowed her to do so. My attorneys were not inclined to be that positive. They felt 24-36 months would be more like it.

I was initially supposed to be sentenced on August 25, 2017. Because I fired my second attorney, that hearing was rescheduled until September 22, 2017. The government tried to say that I fired my second attorney to stall the sentencing date. Really? Did they really think we had an extra $10,000 lying around, just so that I could stall the inevitable for one month? That was the furthest thing from the truth. In all honesty, even I was ready to get it over with. But who wants to go to sentencing with attorneys who don't do their job? How could I trust them to look out for my best interests after they didn't at trial?

And it was apparent they never even understood my case in the first place. The damage was already done, I was already convicted of crimes I had not committed, but I didn't trust them to represent my interests at sentencing. And they had been refusing to file a Pre-Sentence Memorandum, using the excuse that they wanted to surprise the government in court, which I knew to be an outright farse.

I knew the surprise would be on me. Unfortunately, it is the defendant who gets penalized, not the attorney. I knew the government would exploit the fact that I was firing my second attorney. But I could not in good faith risk being sentenced to 8-13 years in prison, due to their lack of knowledge, even if it gave the government one more negative thing to use against me.

On September 18, 2017, my new attorneys filed a Pre-Sentence Memorandum in my case. They hand-delivered the 165 character- reference letters to the Judge's office, and the government. The government waited until after the close of business on September 21, 2017, the day before sentencing, to file objections to the Pre-Sentence Memorandum.

The Judge did not appear happy with this underhanded maneuver, when we got to court the following morning. Personally, all I had seen was underhanded maneuvers on the part of the government, throughout my entire case, so I was not even the slightest bit shocked at this point. Yet, this was the first time it seemed to disturb the judge, after all these years.

The courtroom was packed that day with my husband, sons, mother, sister, other family members, friends, fellow church members, and my lead pastor. They had all come to support me, and I was thankful for each, and every one, of them. God has truly blessed me with a wonderful support group. My attorney argued against the three enhancements the government was trying to get added to my sentence, in order to require me to serve more time in prison.

My attorney also called the government on the carpet. He demanded they tell the Court "What false reports I had made on Agent Shortway and AUSA Harris," since the government had added a statement accusing me of this in my Pre-Sentence Report (PSR), and was requesting that I receive more time in prison because of it. The same PSR that my second attorneys had told me not to argue.

I reported AUSA Harris, for his many unethical actions, such as the abuse of grand jury subpoenas, hiding of Brady evidence, and other unethical acts. I had also complained to the Office of Inspector General (OIG) on Agent Shortway, for sharing our tax returns with my husband's boss. All of this within my legal rights to do so. The government obviously did not want to get into all this at sentencing. Who can blame AUSA Mazzanti? If she could have just added this to my PSR, and caused me additional time, AUSA Mazzanti was all for it. Once the judge required the government to state precisely on the record what was false about the complaints I had made, the government withdrew its request.

I truly believe that had my second attorney been representing me, instead of my third, the government would have gotten by with this last-minute maneuver, and I would have received a longer sentence. The truth was, that AUSA Mazzanti really didn't want to remind the judge about the government's bad actions in my case. She only wanted to use it if she could sneak it in without being questioned, and have it impact my sentence. Once called on the carpet, she withdrew the request. Smart move. Because my new attorney was undoubtedly ready to remind the judge about it, if push came to shove.

Two of the doctors, Korker and Thatch, were present to give victim impact statements. Who could blame them? They were most likely as angry at me, as I was at them. By this time, Dr. Korker would be aware that in 2012, my first attorney had me make a telephone call to him, which was recorded. This happened after the dismissal of the first indictment, but before the doctors dismissed their civil case against me. In the recording, Dr. Korker talks about why he was not part of the civil case with the other doctors, including discussing several of the other doctors' unscrupulous business practices. He also admits his fears that the Medicare fraud the doctors had committed, would be found out. We were not allowed to enter the tape into evidence during my trial, because the judge blocked us from telling the jury about the doctors' Medicare fraud.

However, the government had listened to the tape at my attorney's office several times. It is almost certain the government told Dr. Korker about the tape, and invited him to speak at my sentencing. Around the same time the tape was made, my attorney had also advised the doctors' attorney in the civil case, that Dr. Thatch's employees had told me all about the illegal tasks they were asked to do for his clinical drug trial business. He and his wife jointly owned this business. It was located inside the clinic, where I had worked for all the doctors.

And of course, he would be aware of my knowledge of all his unscrupulous business practices, while I was his office manager. As many times he and his wife tried to get me to do things that I did not feel comfortable doing. As an example, they requested me to make up a fake W2 for Mrs. Thatch's son, so that he would be able to buy a car. I politely refused to do so.

Another time, they had asked me to write a letter stating that Dr. Thatch made more money through the clinic than he really made, in order for them to qualify to purchase a home. Again, I refused. While we were not allowed to enter this information into evidence in my case for the jury to hear. I had documented it in discovery, that the government had viewed, at my attorney's office. The cat was out of the bag regardless, so to speak.

Curiously, Dr. Swan, the doctor I had charged things for on my personal credit cards, was nowhere to be found! Dr. Korker's name never came up during my trial, as the government, nor my attorneys, called him as a witness. And since he left the practice several years before I was indicted, I was confused as to why he was even allowed to speak. Of course, we did not object to it. He told the judge that I had the office manager before me fired. Why would he say this? He knew I didn't even work at the practice when she was fired. In fact, the doctors fired her, and immediately hired me to take her place. Again, the truth was nowhere to be found.

In Dr. Thatch's victim impact statement, he claimed that "I had lied about the doctors throughout my case." I thought to myself, if I had lied, it could have been on only one doctor, Dr. Swan. He was the only one that I testified that I had charged things for on my personal credit cards, and been reimbursed for. My defense to the charges against me. Dr. Swan was nowhere to be found in the courtroom. I'm not sure what lies Dr. Thatch thought I had said something about him, or the other doctors?

And, of course, he never told the judge during his statement, what it was that I had lied about. He gave a 20 or so minute long speech, to the judge, about medical clinics getting stolen from, and how it increases the cost of medicine. It honestly sounded like the government had written it for him. He looked back at me several times, and told me I was not remorseful.

The truth is that I was remorseful for the part I played in this tragedy, but I could not be remorseful for crimes I had not committed. I was, however, undoubtedly remorseful that I had ignored many *red flags* and participated in charging things on my credit cards for Dr. Swan, while eventually suspecting that he was most likely cheating on his taxes.

And the truth is, I was remorseful that I had allowed my ethics to be compromised, by turning a blind eye to the Medicare fraud, and other unscrupulous business practices, of the doctors. I was also ashamed, and remorseful, that I had re-classified personal expenses to business expenses, for Dr. Swan.

My pastor, my mother, and three other friends took the stand to speak on my behalf, regarding my character. And then the judge did something nobody expected. She took it all under advisement, and did not sentence me that day. It was both a gift, and a curse, all wrapped up in a bow. I wanted it over with, but I was also thankful for the extended time with my family.

The new sentencing date was scheduled for November 3,

2017. Again, we packed the courtroom with supporters. We had received an order from the judge, a few days before, and she had ruled in my favor, against allowing the government's request for enhancements. The government did not win that one, thank God. I knew that all the prayers, everyone had been praying on my behalf, had worked! And even though I was still struggling with my anger, I knew that God was faithful!

At sentencing, the judge gave me a two-level variance, for my character reference letters, which got me down to the 41-51 months range, on the Federal Sentencing Guidelines. She then sentenced me to 45 months in prison, with 3 years of supervised release, afterwards. But not before she brought up two bounced checks, and called them, "my other financial crimes," accused me of "being mean to my first attorney," and said that "I had chased a witness out of court during the trial." I was shocked!

One of the returned checks she referred to was when the government seized our funds from our accounts in March 2011. I had asked my second attorney to clarify this in the Pre-Sentence Report (PSR), but he had failed to do so, and had advised me not to argue it. I was tired of arguing with them at the time, and honestly, I was just tired, so I let it go. BIG mistake! Now I was being penalized in the eyes of the judge, and she did not have all the facts.

When the seizure of our bank accounts occurred in March 2011, the first time I was indicted, it had caused several checks that were outstanding to be returned. The government had taken all our money out of the account after the checks had been written. We immediately picked up all the checks that the seizure had caused to be returned, except apparently the one. I would later find out that a check I had written to one of our son's schools was held for several months before they even tried to deposit it.

By that time, I was indicted, and not paying any attention to our old checking account, as it had been closed for several months already. Because the check was returned on a closed account, the returned check was taken straight to the Sherwood Hot Check Office.

The check was only $42, but it cost us over $200 to pick it up from the city. By picking it up, instead of going to court, and explaining to the judge what had happened, I did not realize it would show as a misdemeanor guilty verdict, for a returned check on my record. The other bounced check she referenced, was when I was in college, and frankly not keeping up with my checking account, since my grandfather always put money in my account whenever I asked. I was shocked that the judge was calling these "my other financial crimes," and that she seemed to be penalizing my character for such!

I could not understand how she could have thought that I was mean to my first attorney. I had filed the sealed motion to get him off my case, detailing why I could no longer work with him. However, I was not mean to him, ever. I adored him, and was thankful, for all he had done for me. I'm sure my stress showed, during those pretrial moments, when he would have to leave the podium, and come back to the defense table. Still, I never thought it appeared I was being mean to him. It took me a minute to figure out what the judge meant, when she said that I had chased a witness out of the courtroom during the trial. I had no idea she believed that!

Again, this was another time my second attorney did not make sure something was corrected on the record, and something I never even knew the judge may have believed, until we were sitting there in the courtroom, at my sentencing, hearing her say it. By then, it was too late.

What had actually happened, was that on the last day of trial, I had been on the stand for over three hours. During those three hours, I had to drink a lot of water, because I talked so much that my throat kept getting dry. After my testimony, the government put Dr. Swan back on the stand.

My attorney was able to catch him in a few more lies, and I did not want to risk missing any of his testimony. However, I was about to die to go to the bathroom, due to all the water, I

I had drank earlier that day. The minute Dr. Swan was off the stand, I left the courtroom and went to the bathroom. The bathroom was down the hallway. When I came out of the bathroom, my young attorney was waiting on me, and anxiously asked "What are you doing?" I answered that I was just going to the bathroom. He then told me that I couldn't leave the courtroom like that.

By that time, we were on our seventh day of me being on trial, and this was the first I had ever heard of this! Why had I not been told? I'd never been on trial before; I didn't know the unspoken rules. On the first day of trial, the judge had told the jurors not to pay attention to people moving around, and going in and out of the courtroom, from the prosecution and the defense tables. I was sitting at the defense table, so I assumed she meant me too?

At no time did my attorney explain to me that the judge thought I had chased a witness, Dr. Swan, out of the courtroom. It was not true, and I can assure you that if the government had thought it to be the case, AUSA Mazzanti would have brought more charges against me at the time, I have no doubt. When we got back in the courtroom, from the bathroom, that day at trial, I apologized to the judge for going to the bathroom without permission. The jury was no longer in the courtroom. She never mentioned that she thought I had chased a witness out of the courtroom. She simply said "The rules have not changed since the first day of trial." I just answered "Yes, your honor."

I had no idea what she meant at the time, and my attorney did not jump to my defense to correct the misconception. If the judge thought that was what had happened, then it would make sense that the jury most likely thought the same thing, since they were still in the courtroom when I left to go to the bathroom. I can't imagine how that reflected with them? And it should have been cleared up on the record that day by my attorneys, but it wasn't! Now here we were at sentencing, with two new attorneys, who were not with me at trial, so they were not even privy to any of this! All I could do was just stand there in amazement! We did not argue the point. However, I think this was part of why she sentenced me to 45 months.

Overall, I do believe the judge was fair in her sentencing. She gave me a two-level variance due to my character letters, regardless that it was obvious she was not a fan of mine, from her lecture that day in court. I did not cry that day. I was not about to give the government that. And I didn't want to upset my family, any more than I knew the experience alone was causing them. In reality, I was just numb by that point anyway. It was all too much! I was on my way to federal prison for 45 months, for crimes I had not committed, and there was nothing anyone could do about it.

The $10,000 cost for the new attorneys ended up being worth it when I was only sentenced to 45 months. You may be thinking ONLY 45 months, but that is not a lot, in the big scheme of things, compared to what the government was requesting. It was actually a win for me, as bad as it was.

My new attorneys had made sure that the judge could read all 165 character-reference letters, which the judge commented on several times during sentencing. However, I have to agree with my second attorney on one point, the judge did not seem to have a good opinion of someone who fired two attorneys, and basically said as much in court. Regardless, I would certainly not go as far as saying she hated me. In fact, I think it was more of a case of her not understanding everything that had gone on in my case.

In all fairness, I felt she sentenced me fairly, given that I had been convicted at trial. I had prayed about my decision, and felt that I had followed what God led me to do when I fired my second set of attorneys. And this time, I listened to that little voice in my head, and I believe I avoided ignoring another *red flag* by doing so. I'm learning. I'm a work in progress. My God was with me, and HE was helping me, as I moved forward on the journey.

The judge allowed me to remain out on pretrial release and to self-report to prison. After sentencing, I immediately had to go back upstairs, to the US Marshal's office for more fingerprints, and DNA testing. Again, I wondered why the government thought my fingerprints, or my DNA, were changing during the course of this case.

My husband and I left the US Marshal's office and drove home. All I wanted to do was lay in bed for the rest of the day, maybe even for the rest of my life. I was exhausted. Later that evening, my name was all over the local news, and it was reported in the newspaper the following day. I know this because one of my old neighbors sent me a text photo of the news article, with a question mark.

I didn't even bother to answer her. At least that part of my case was over, and by now, I no longer cared what anyone thought of me anyway. They could judge me all they wanted. I knew the truth, but more importantly, I knew that my family and God knew the truth!

That Sunday at church, a lovely lady came up to me to say she loved me. She did not ask me about my case, or inquire about anything else. She simply told me she loved me. I would have many others do similar acts during that time. They will never know how their kindness mattered in those moments. But not everyone was so kind. On that same Sunday, a couple we rarely talked to, approached me and Pancho, and were anxious to talk to me about what had happened. It was as if they were giddy to find out all the gory details. I knew they were just being nosey, but I was too drained to even care.

And on that same day, I overheard another person at church talking about me. She had her phone open, and was showing the press release of my conviction, to another lady in church. From what I heard, I knew she was discussing the news story that had been posted on the Internet about my sentencing, that they were talking about. I even saw her point at me. I was so hurt.

But the worst hurt came from finding out that Pancho's brother, sister, and sister-in-law were gossiping about me. It's one thing for outsiders to gossip about you, but a whole other issue when family chooses to do so. After all, they knew me personally, and had many years of exposure to my kindness towards them personally. This caused a huge riff between Pancho and his family, because he took up for me. After all, he knew I was innocent.

I would later find out that one of my friends from high school had also gossiped about me and made sure everyone I had attended school with, was sent the articles about me as well. She had forwarded it to them through Facebook. Again, I was hurt, but I had to just keep moving forward. I was too tired at that moment to even fight another day. And explaining myself, or trying to tell others what had really happened, especially to those that only cared to gossip and judge me, would have done no good. I think this was the moment I actually stopped caring about what others thought of me. I had spent my entire life being a good person and helping others. But now none of that even mattered.

Chapter Twenty-Two
What Happened To The $50,000 The Government Seized?

Sadly, the government got to keep the $50,000 it stole out of our joint bank accounts in March 2011. I use the word stole, because that is exactly what the government did. There was no fraud traceable to the money. The bank account clearly showed where every dime came from. All from legal sources. Something even the government had to admit to the judge after trial, in its motion for forfeiture. Yet the government used the *Patriot Act* to keep the money anyway. Because I was convicted, I automatically had to give up my claim to the money, due to the criminal forfeiture, the government placed in the second indictment.

However, my husband still had a claim to his one-half, since it was taken from our joint bank accounts. He alerted the court that he planned on asserting his claim to the money, shortly after, the government had filed a motion that admitted, "The government could not trace the seized money to any fraud," but requested to keep it anyway. The judge granted that motion, and the government sent my husband notice that he had 20 days to file an answer alerting the court if he planned on continuing with his claim against his one-half of the funds.

My husband filed his notice on the 19th day, and alerted the government that he would fight them for the money. The government then filed a motion asking the judge to allow civil discovery to proceed. This was ridiculous since there had been a civil case on-going since 2011. Not once had the government notified my husband, that it wished to take his deposition, or asked for any other form of discovery, even though they could have done so at any time. And what discovery was there anyway? The money was taken from bank accounts, so it was easy to trace where every dime deposited into the accounts had come from, without the need for discovery. It was just more harassment.

In January 2014, before my second indictment, the government had tried to notice me for a deposition. This was when AUSA Mr. Harris tried to find something to indict me for the second time. My attorney objected at the time, since I was still getting target letters threatening a second indictment. Obviously, AUSA Harris was attempting to use civil discovery to get things for a criminal case.

At the time the civil forfeiture case had been ongoing for over three years, and the government had never sought discovery before, on me or my husband. My husband had no Fifth Amendment rights, since he was not charged criminally, so the government could have done so at any time. But now the government wanted to depose him almost seven years later?

Apparently, it was not enough for the government that I had been convicted; they wanted to continue to harass my family members. We honestly did not have money to waste on more attorney fees at this point, to continue to fight for our money back. And after seeing how our justice system really works, we felt it would be wasteful to do so.

We were trying to make this decision when the government noticed my husband for a deposition. When she called my attorney to discuss a date for the deposition of my husband, AUSA Mazzanti made sure to tell the attorney that the government would be taking the deposition, in hopes of finding other crimes with which to charge my husband, or me.

We knew we had done nothing wrong, but that had not stopped the government from indicting the first time, nor again the second time, for which I now stood convicted. It was just too great a risk to take. We knew the government's power, and we certainly believed it would try to charge one of us, to get the money. That much had become perfectly clear.

My husband had no choice but to give up his claim to the money. And that, ladies and gentlemen, is our federal government's power and overreach. It is abusive at every turn. Once the government forced my husband to give up his claim to the money through their threats, they then dismissed their civil forfeiture lawsuit that had been ongoing for almost seven years. The government had effectively held our money hostage since 2011, and had finally found a way to keep it. The supposed victim doctors were not given any of this money, even though the government told a jury that I had stolen it from them. It would seem that since the government claimed the doctors were my victims, they should have been given the money, yet that is not what happened.

Asset seizure is a big deal. It provides additional budgets to government agencies and pads retirement funds for the agency seizing the money, and the US Attorney's office that assists the agency, in doing so. Many people are never charged with a crime, but have their assets seized anyway. This happens a lot when people are caught transporting money across state lines. The money is just taken from the person. Usually, these people have something to hide, so they don't make a claim against the money, and the government gets to keep it under what is referred to as Administrative Asset Seizure.

This law allows government agencies to seize an asset under *The Patriot Act* if they suspect it is traceable to a crime. This act is an Act of Congress signed into law on October 26, 2011, by former President George W. Bush, shortly after 911, and in response to the terrorist acts on that day. Its title is a ten-letter backronym (USA PATRIOT) that stands for *"Uniting and Strengthening America by Providing Appropriate Tools Required to Intercept and Obstruct Terrorism Act of 2001."* In other words, it is supposed to be used against terrorists. However, it is being used against regular US citizens, like my husband and me, to steal our hard-earned money, and other assets.

According to a 2014, *Washington Post* investigation, since the 9/11 attack, nearly 70,000 cash seizures totaling $2.5 billion, occurred without warrants, or indictments. Only one-sixth of them were challenged, and only 41 percent of those had their money returned. Once an asset is seized, it is hard to get it back. For starters, you must hire an attorney who specializes in asset forfeiture. This is very costly, and the person wishing to get their seized asset back has to pay for these costs out of their own pocket.

Most people do not have the funds to do so, especially given that the government has already seized their assets. Secondly, you must prove the asset itself is innocent. While this may sound easy, it is not. The language in the act is convoluted, and is designed to favor the federal government, which has unlimited resources to fight you and keep your assets.

We never got our $50,000 back. Regardless, that the government admitted in legal filings in my criminal case that the money could not be traced to fraud, the very reason that the government should not have been allowed to seize the money to begin with. If you do a Google search, you will find many cases, and articles, that are examples of the government using the *Patriot Act* to steal assets from everyday American citizens. If you care to read more on the subject, I suggest you Google it.

Chapter Twenty-Three
Politically Connected?

Many people have asked me how the doctors were never charged with crimes for committing Medicare and tax fraud? People also ask why no charges were ever brought against Dr. Swan, the main doctor I charged personal things for, on my credit card? My legal team believed they knew the answer to those questions. Arkansas is a relatively small state. I knew Dr. Swan had some political pull. He had told me so himself! He had a life-long friend, who is a well-connected attorney in the state. That friend's son was also a well-connected attorney, and a rising political star, in the Arkansas Democratic Party.

The son had served as Legal Counsel for the Craighead County Democratic Central Committee, and as a member of the Democratic Party of Arkansas State Committee from 2002-2005. The son had also served in the Arkansas House of Representatives, and it was rumored that he would most likely become the next Governor of our state. Well, at least until a certain extra-marital affair came to light, and undermined that dream. He was serving as the Attorney General of Arkansas when the affair was exposed. The problem was not just another politician cheating on his wife. It went much deeper than that. There were allegations that the affair undermined his ability to do his job as Attorney General.

The allegations went something like this, court records showed that the attorney he had the relationship with, had represented parents who had successfully challenged the state's school choice law. The state was appealing the ruling in the case, in which the Attorney General's office represented Arkansas. I do not know anything about that case, and since it has nothing to do with anything that happened in my case, I'll leave it to my readers to Google it, should you wish to know more.

However, it was pointed out by my legal team many times that US Attorney Thyer, a Democrat from Craighead County, had also served in the Arkansas House of Representatives. AUSA Thyer was rumored to be a very close friend of both the Attorney General, and his dad, the life-long friend of Dr. Swan. Can I say for sure this had anything to do with my case? Absolutely NOT. I will clarify that I am not accusing AUSA Thyer, the past Attorney General, or his dad, the attorney friend of Dr. Swan, of anything nefarious. I have no proof of any wrongdoing. However, there was always a suspicion by those who worked on my case, that this certainly could have influenced the US Attorney, who was AUSA Harris' boss.

I ask that you, as the reader, to make your own mind up about what influences, or political affiliations, may or may not have played a part in my case, or the decisions made regarding it. I do know that when my attorney met with AUSA Harris, and US Attorney Thyer, in March 2013, US Attorney Thyer agreed with my attorney that "My case was a mess and should not be prosecuted." However, in early 2014, US Attorney Thyer told my attorney that "He would allow AUSA Harris' case against me to go forward." What changed in that year, I'll never know. It is possible that me going after AUSA Harris for his bad acts, may have been the trigger.

Other rumors were that US Attorney Thyer was just a figurehead at the US Attorney's office. That it was actually AUSA Harris who was running the show. That was how Harris got by with so much unethical behavior. There was really nobody there to slap his hand. Personally, I'm more inclined to believe the latter is what actually happened. But of course, that is just my personal opinion. And when President Trump took office, and Thyer resigned, before he could be ousted by the new President, it was AUSA Harris, who became the acting US Attorney in my district.

Another AUSA reached out to my first attorney, to tell him stories of AUSA Harris' behavior at the US Attorney's office, during my case. The older female AUSA alleged that AUSA Harris had accessed her work computer, and planted documents, in an attempt to cause her to lose her job. Per my attorney, the AUSA believed Harris was attempting to get her fired, due to their differing opinions about cases.

Shortly after my sentencing, my husband and I saw AUSA Harris, and his wife, sitting at the bar at YaYa's restaurant in Little Rock, Arkansas, while we were eating dinner there. It made me sick to see AUSA Harris again. And my anger flared. I honestly wanted to go over, and punch him in the face.

Given that I am not a violent person, nor have I never punched anyone in the face, this is proof of how deeply rooted my anger had become by this time. Instead, I sat and watched, as he and his wife watched a football game on the television at the bar, while they consumed a large amount of alcohol.

AUSA Harris and his wife then left the restaurant, with AUSA Harris driving. I remember holding my cell phone in my hand, with the urge I felt to dial 911, to report their license plate, as drunk drivers. I decided in the end not to do so. It was certainly not my place to judge them. However, I had just watched the AUSA that indicted me for crimes I had not committed, driving a car, after consuming a large amount of alcohol, possibly a criminal act.

Chapter Twenty-Four
Did The Government Interfere In The Sexual Assault Case Of Doctor RJ?

One of the more bothersome questions to me personally about my case, is that it appears that AUSA Harris may have prevented Dr. Rascal Jones, from being charged with the sexual assault crimes of myself, and other patients. The detective investigating the sexual assaults, believed the government, prevented Dr. Jones from being charged, in the sexual assaults. He believed AUSA Harris had put pressure on the local prosecutor's office not to file charges against Dr. Jones. The detective had told not only my attorney this, but a reporter from the *Arkansas Business*, who was also investigating the sexual assaults, and other conduct by the doctors. The detective told my attorney "AUSA Harris had gone to the local prosecutors' office and taken the file on the sexual assaults from them." This infuriated the detective who was trying to get Dr. Jones charged, and off the street. A doctor who was obviously using his profession to prey on patients and assault them.

It was common knowledge that one of the AUSAs that worked closely with AUSA Harris, was married to the Pulaski County Prosecuting Attorney. Also, the detective said "AUSA Harris had questioned him regarding his thoughts on the truthfulness of the women who had reported being sexually assaulted, including me." Please note that after the article in *Arkansas Business* came out about doctor Dr. Jones' sexual assaults of patients, additional victims came forward to report that they too, had been sexually assaulted by him.

Apparently, the problem was much more widespread than we had originally known.

This same detective, would also report that when he went to the doctors' clinic, to interview the other doctors, as well as the doctor's wife I had confided in, regarding my own assault, they had stonewalled him. He felt the doctors and the doctor's wife were covering up for Dr. Jones' crimes, and putting pressure on the clinic employees to do the same. He had caught several of the doctors in what he said were outright "lies," and interviewed employees who could not keep their stories straight. I was not surprised.

I had seen this same type of behavior when I was their office manager, when the nurse had tried to expose the sexual harassment that had happened to her. More *red flags* I chose to ignore at the time. I regret not having stood up for the nurse. Looking back, I should have been stronger. I had selfishly allowed my job, and my loyalty to Dr. Swan, to cloud my judgment at the time. The office manager that had taken my place, would later acknowledge that there had indeed been a cover-up regarding the sexual assaults, and that employees had been instructed not to cooperate. She made that statement to my attorney, and in the August 2012 meeting, with AUSA JB.

My first attorney highly suspected that AUSA Harris had also used his pull to prevent Dr. Jones from being charged in the painkiller prescription drug fraud conspiracy, where he had written illegal prescriptions that were sold on the streets. This is the crime for which he is now serving a nine-year prison sentence in federal prison. Apparently, AUSA Harris also had a reputation for corrupt behavior in other cases.

Many local criminal defense attorneys were aware of this, but chose not to report it. They stated that nothing would be done, and that their reports would only hurt their future clients. They feared that any future clients they may represent would be punished by being offered less than favorable plea deals, from the US Attorney's Office, if they made reports against AUSA Harris for his unethical behavior.

They all knew that the US Attorney's Office in the Eastern District of Arkansas was basically being run by AUSA Harris anyway, since US Attorney Thyer was rarely even at the office to run it. I would later realize just how factual these statements were, when my complaints against AUSA Harris' unethical behavior during my case, went unpunished, and were never even investigated.

Chapter Twenty-Five
Life After Conviction

Because it took over a year between my conviction and my self-surrender date to prison, it took a toll on my mental health. I was in a constant state of anxiety, and depression. And my anger was at an all-time high. Yet, I was still forced to proceed through life, as if all was normal. This was the hardest thing I have ever had to do, and admittedly, I failed nine times out of ten. It's hard to think of others, when you are in so much pain. I know my poor family caught the brunt of it. I don't remember much about those months. I just remember constantly dreading the looming sentencing date, and then the self-surrender date. It felt like I was constantly watching the clock, and that time was flying by at times, and dragging on at others.

Shortly after my conviction, I was asked by my church to help lead the *Share Your Lunch* program. This is an essential program as it provides weekly bags of groceries to those who need food, and weekly backpacks to elementary school-age children, who may not have food at home on the weekend. I was unsure if I should take the position, since I was not in the best frame of mind, and felt that I may only be around for a few more months, before reporting to prison.

I was encouraged by several pastors to take the position anyway. After much prayer, my husband and I signed on as co-leads for the project. In another amazing act, God allowed me to stay at home to see the project through the first 52 weeks. The Sunday before I was to report to federal prison the following day, marked one year of the project. In that first year, we provided over 4,000 bags of groceries to hungry people.

My husband and I are still the leads for this program, and

my husband continued to volunteer as a leader while I served time in prison. We have now supplied over 23,000 bags of groceries to hungry people. Looking back, I never expected to be able to see the project through that first year. Volunteering helped me to focus on others, not myself, during a very hard time, that last year at home. It helped me to fully start to understand God's plan for my own life, even though I was often confused, and angry at God, for what I was going through.

As I waited to go to prison, I continued my volunteerism with the homeless population of Central Arkansas. Again, this took my focus off myself, and placed it on someone else. I have always been a big supporter of the homeless. But my mental health training had made me a more prominent advocate for them, especially in the last few years before prison. I understood their needs even more than in all the other years, approximately 20, that I had been volunteering with them. And my own struggles probably helped me relate to their pain, even more than any other time, in the past.

I had no idea at the time how badly my mental state had deteriorated that last year at home. But apparently it had. Honestly to the point that I don't have memories of many events during that time. I believe that I was in so much pain that I blanked out many of those days. For example, I had no idea that I had become almost unbearable to live with. My youngest son, Timothy, would relate to me, after I returned home from prison, that I had been very strict on him during those last few months.

I assume I was trying to have control over something, as the rest of my life was spinning out of control. He said that I told him "He did not appreciate everything we had done for him" and that I had accused him of "Being disrespectful to me." I have no memory of this, but apparently it affected him since he was only 16, and it certainly harmed our relationship before my reporting to prison.

Since my return home, we have worked on healing those hurts, but I still feel a lot of guilt for what he suffered through, during those last few months, I was at home. Fortunately, my other two sons were already out on their own, and missed my downward spiral for the most part. I remember spending the last few weeks of my time at home mostly just staying in bed with one of our French Bulldogs, Olivia, watching CNN, and feeling like my life was coming to an end. And in ways, it was coming to an end, at least the life I had known before prison.

Obviously, I was very depressed. Looking back, that was such a waste of time. The dread of prison was undoubtedly worse than prison itself. I look back now, and realize that I tortured myself, and my family, in this way. But at the time, I was so angry at everything, and everyone.

I was certainly angry at God, for what I saw as HIM allowing my case to happen. I remember P. Rod telling me "God can handle your questions and anger." I was honestly not in my right mind in those moments. I was angry and looking for someone to blame, anyone to blame. I knew God knew the truth about what had happened, and I had a hard time understanding why HE would allow me to be found guilty of a crime I had not committed.

All these years later, I now understand HIS plan, for all of it. And I would not change it, even if I could, regardless of how crazy that may sound to others. But at the time, I was completely broken. Now, I can clearly see that this journey was HIS plan. I had to go on it for myself, and ultimately to gain the ability to help others, on their own journey. My pain for HIS purpose.

Top Left: *Olivia (2010-2020)- Christmas 2017*
Top Right: *Timothy, JT, Joseph, Lynn-Christmas 2017, Last Christmas Home Before Prison*
Below: *Pancho and Lynn-Christmas 2017*

Chapter Twenty-Six
Self-Surrendering to FPC Bryan

On February 26, 2018, my day started out a little stressful. This was the day that I had to report to federal prison by 2:00 p.m. Our flight had been canceled on Sunday evening, so I had to spend about two hours booking another one. I had to tell the airlines, "I have to report to federal prison, I must have a flight, or the US Marshals will come to get me." We started thinking that we needed to just get in the vehicle and start driving. But once again, God provided, and the airlines managed to get us on another early morning flight, with a different airline.

At 4:00 a.m. we were at the Little Rock airport. I took a photo to memorialize the event. I planned on using it for this very book, (see photo, page 273). Even then, I knew I had to write this book. Our flight was delayed in Dallas that morning due to fog, which was very stressful. I was so afraid something would happen, and I would not get to prison on time. Many people texted me and called me during this time. I knew I had an army praying for us, and I really appreciated everyone loving me through such a hard day. It made the stressful time much easier.

We made it to the College Station airport, and took an Uber to downtown Bryan, Texas. The only place we could find to eat was a Whataburger. I didn't really want my last meal in the free world to be at a Whataburger, but as fate would have it, that was where we ended up that day. I didn't eat much anyway, so it probably did not matter where we ate. My anxiety was so high at the time.

The fear of the unknown is worse than anything. I hardly

remember those last few hours with my husband, before I walked through the gates that held me captive for 24 months. What I didn't know at the time, is that I would later be shipped to FTC Oklahoma, due to my advocacy for myself, and other ladies, at FPC Bryan. I self-surrendered to prison believing I would spend my entire sentence at the camp. But on February 26, 2018, my husband and I stayed for several hours at the Whataburger, before I decided to go check in to prison early.

The feeling of having this next chapter hanging over my head for more than a year had taken its toll on me, and I was honestly just ready to "get the show on the road." So, we called another Uber driver, and off to federal prison we went. The Uber driver was shocked to find out that a federal prison actually existed in the middle of a neighborhood in Bryan, Texas. He kept asking us questions in all his confusion. He asked "Are you going to visit someone?" "Do you work for the prison?" He was even more surprised to learn that I was self-surrendering to prison and that he would be dropping me off there, and then taking Pancho, back to the airport, to fly home without me.

I asked him if I could take his photo with my cell phone. He obliged. He said in a shocked voice, "I had no idea self-surrender to prison was a thing." "They just let you walk into prison?" I hated answering him with a "yes." I certainly wished that it was "not a thing." I certainly would have instead preferred to be almost anywhere else that day. We drove up to the camp and checked in on the phone at the gate. We were immediately yelled at by the female voice on the speaker, and she demanded that we back into a parking spot. Not exactly the way I had wished to start my prison sentence.

In my fear of the voice on the loudspeaker, I quickly said my good-byes to my husband of fourteen years, and got out of the car. I stepped around the metal arm that kept cars out, into the unknown, federal prison. My anxiety level was at the max, but I waited until my husband drove away to let it show. I did not want to upset him any more than I knew he already must be.

And I was worried about how he would be on his flight home. We had purposely flown, so that he would not have the eight-hour drive back home by himself, in the state of mind we assumed he would most likely be in. As I made my way up the hill to the voice on the loudspeaker, I tried to stop and talk to two incarcerated ladies working on the flower beds, down by the gate. I could tell they were prisoners by the ugly khaki uniforms and boots they had on. I had many questions that I wanted to get answered, but this attempted chatting also got me yelled at over the loudspeaker. Looking back now, it is comical. But at the time, I was scared to death of the Correctional Officer (CO) that was yelling at me from a building up the hill.

When I approached the check-in window, the CO immediately wanted my driver's license, or other forms of identification. I had not brought any of these items with me. I had read that the Bureau of Prisons (BOP), often loses incarcerated individuals driver's licenses, and social security cards, and many times BOP staff cannot produce these items once a person's sentence is over, and it is time for them to leave prison. What I had brought was a letter from the United States Marshal Service telling me to report to prison on that date.

The CO immediately began drilling me with questions about my identity. In rapid succession, I was asked for my date of birth, social security number, my mother's maiden name, and many other identifying questions. I flashed back to my time before the grand jury, when I was hammered with questions by AUSA Harris. I thought to myself, do other people often self-surrender to prison for another person? I could not imagine. But I did not dare ask that question out loud. It was illogical to think anyone would show up there, and pretend to be me. Yet, the guard seemed insistent on me somehow proving my identity.

After the CO was satisfied that I was actually the person who was supposed to report to prison that day, I was told to sit in a metal chair that was outside the window, through which the CO had been talking to me. The chair was full of water from rain earlier in the day. Not wanting to get in trouble, or anger the already agitated CO, I sat on the edge of the chair, trying not to get wet from the water in the chair, or the water that was trying to leak from my eyes. After what seemed like forever, another guard from what I would later find out was the R&D Receiving & Discharge building, accompanied by an incarcerated person who apparently worked in R&D, walked across the street to get me.

The CO also asked me questions to verify my identity, as if anyone would check into prison if they weren't required to do so? The incarcerated worker behind her was making faces at me, and mouthing "It's going to be okay." At that moment, I did not think it would be. I actually managed to hold it together until the CO told me I could not have my Bible. I had called the prison several times to verify what I was allowed to bring with me that day. My bible was one of those things.

When she took it from me, I lost it, and began what seemed like a three-hour crying spell. After filling out some paperwork, I was told to stand on a towel, and the dreaded strip search occurred. Believe it or not, it was over quickly, and not near as bad as I had conjured it up in my mind. Humiliating yes, brutal no.

I was processed through R&D, and then a male nurse came to get me to do my TB test, and to inquire if I was "Thinking about harming myself?" That question is designed to see if you are suicidal, which I would later find out, had I answered wrong, would have caused me to be thrown in a cold room with no clothing or blanket, with another incarcerated person sitting and watching me through a glass door. Thank goodness I answered the question correctly. In my counseling training, I knew what the question was designed to do. However, at that moment, I was just going through the motions.

I absolutely did not want to hurt myself. But I certainly was not in a good state of mind. Next, I was required to take a TB test, and was told to report back in a few days to medical to have it checked. The TB test I was given was a stab to my arm. The nurse had no apparent bedside manner, or fear of hurting me. It was actually brutal. And my arm later had a huge bruise on it. I was then told to follow the male nurse to another building.

The thought of going into a room with a strange man made my anxiety hit the roof, but again, I did not allow it to show. I felt like I would pass out, most likely from anxiety, but I just started silently praying to God to give me peace. I was relieved when the male nurse left the door to the room open, and I was able to be many feet away from him. I was never handcuffed during this process, which was also a relief. I then met briefly with another staff member, and got my bedroll. That staff member said "Come with me, I'll take you to the Unit."

Going to the Unit meant being paraded through the compound, wearing the newbie clothing and the blue slide shoes. This walk of shame, alerts everyone on the compound, that you are the "new girl" on the block. When we got to the Units, I noticed two buildings, each housing two units separated by a middle hallway of staff offices. I was assigned to Unit Brazos 1, B1. There were also Units Brazos 2, B2, Madison, and RDAP.

At Unit B1, I was put in the Bus Stop, a large room with approximately ten bunk beds, a few desks, and lockers on the walls and floor. The sign on the wall said "Just Passing Through." In the Bus Stop were seven other ladies, most of whom were also newer arrivals. And a few ladies who apparently had trouble getting along with others, and had to be moved to the Bus Stop as punishment. As well as one lady who snored so loudly that she could not room with others and had been moved to the Bus Stop permanently.

There, I met with a lady called a Big Sister, and she told me that I would get my permanent room assignment in a few weeks. She also advised me I would be allowed to go to the commissary the following morning, and would get my PAC and PIN numbers to set up my computer and phone. This really got to me, and I started to tear up again. It meant that I would not be able to speak to my husband that evening, or even know that he made it home safely. I knew he was most likely going through his own nightmare and trauma, from having just dropped his wife off at federal prison. And all I really wanted was to hear his voice. I needed his voice to reassure me that I would be okay. I didn't feel okay at that moment.

After the 4:00 p.m. count, the Big Sister and her friend took me to dinner. The food wasn't too bad. It wasn't too good either. The cafeteria was serving fried rice that evening. Everyone was talking and laughing. They seemed so normal in this environment. Nothing seemed normal to me. I just wanted to be home with my family. I longed to feel Pancho's arms around me at that moment, and for him to kiss my forehead. I needed to be with my husband. This is actually the worst part of being in prison. Being placed in a foreign environment, and missing the ones you love. After dinner, the Big Sister and her friend took me for a tour of the compound, pointing out all the buildings, and explaining the processes that took place in each building to me.

Later that evening, one of the ladies I had tried to talk to when I first arrived at prison that day, gave me a toothbrush. I was able to take a shower with the sample hygiene items I was given with my bedroll. I had also been given shower shoes by the friend of the Big Sister, who had accompanied me to dinner, and on the tour of the compound. In prison, you have to take showers wearing flip flops, or risk catching many diseases, so the shower shoes were essential.

Another lady gave me a hair tie to tie up my long hair, and another gave me a bottle of water. All of these things, kind gestures from *criminals,* as I had thought of those I would meet in prison, in all my angst up to my self-surrender. Yet here were these ladies doing everything they could to make me feel better about my current situation. Other ladies came to my rescue, and helped me make my bed. I was incredibly thankful for their help. Those *criminals*, mostly turned out to be kind individuals, women that had made a mistake, but were now thrown away by society. They were certainly not the people I had feared before my self-surrender date. And many of them have become lifelong friends.

After dinner, I took my shower and brushed my teeth. I briefly went to sleep about 8:30 p.m., because I was mentally and physically exhausted. I actually jumped up when they called count at 10:00 p.m. This is one of the count times you must be up and standing by your bed. After the count, I tried to go back to sleep, but mostly tossed and turned, for most of the night, as I could not sleep. The mattress looked much like a kindergarten mat, and with my torn rotator cuff and arthritis, it was not a good night's sleep. I was basically just lying on the cold metal bed, and I could feel the cold through the thin mat.

The unit was freezing, and there was no heat. My shoulder and my whole body were actually aching all over, the following day, and for many days to come. All that night, I kept watching the clock across from the bus stop, on the wall outside the bathroom. I remember seeing the COs come around with their flashlights, and do their every few hours count, as all the other ladies, who were already acclimated to prison, slept through the night. It is never completely dark in prison, as lights are left on all night in the bathrooms and walk areas. This took me some time to get used to sleeping through.

But mostly what I remember from that first night in prison was the feeling of loneliness, and the deep longing for my husband, our bed, and our two French bulldogs. My gut ached for Pancho. I just needed to hear my husband tell me it would be alright. I didn't realize how bad I would miss him, or that it would hurt so badly to be away from him. I wished the morning would hurry so I could finally get the PAC number, and call him. I longed for his voice.

Even after being home now for three years, as I write this paragraph, I still get the same anxiety and longing when my husband goes away for business. I dread the days up to his departure. I count down the days until his return. And I do not feel whole until he is with me again. It is additional trauma caused by prison that has still not healed.

At 5:15 a.m. the following morning, the Big Sister came to make sure I was getting up, so we could go to breakfast, and turn in my commissary list, before she took me to the cafeteria. Breakfast was not so good, mainly since the BOP does not serve coffee, except sometimes on the weekends, and I'm a huge coffee drinker. And who really wants oatmeal that looks like slop? Not to mention that many times the oatmeal had weevils or some other type of bug in it.

After breakfast, I went to the laundry, and was issued clothes. I was given three used khaki uniforms, three used khaki t-shirts, five pairs of socks, five pairs of underwear, and five sports bras that resembled a half camisole. I couldn't figure out how that bra held up anything, but I was forced to wear it anyway. It was all I had at the moment. A lovely staff member, Ms. D., also gave me my PAC and PIN numbers at the laundry.

I could not wait to get back to the unit and figure out how to enter everything into CorrLinks, the BOP monitored email system, and then go to the public phones in the hallway, so I could record my voice, and make a phone call to Pancho. I needed to hear his voice, worse than anything else in the world. The longing for him set me off crying again, even though I had promised myself I would not do so. Once I heard his voice, I lost it. He was very calm, and tried to reassure me by telling me how strong I am. He reminded me that I would get through the situation. He told me "You are the strongest person I know."

Actually, he was the strong one in these situations. I was amazed at his strength, since I had always thought of myself as the strong one, in our relationship. But in these situations, he really was a champ. Hearing his voice made me feel better. He would later, during one of his prison visits with me, describe his trip home from dropping me off at prison. He described feeling empty when he drove away, to return to the airport. When he got to the Houston airport, where he flew after he left College Station, he described what sounded like an anxiety/panic attack. He described coming home without me as "It felt like someone died, only they didn't."

When I got back from lunch that day, I already had an email from a friend. I can't tell you how good it felt to hear from someone back home. Getting cards, letters, daily emails, phone calls, and weekly video chats, helped me get through the weeks, and months. Visits were especially helpful. And after each one of our visits, I counted down the days until my husband would be able to visit again.

He was a saint through the entire process. I remember one time when he drove eight hours, leaving home at 3:00 a.m., just to get to Bryan in time to see me graduate from cosmetology classes. He spent two hours with me, and then drove eight hours home. I will never forget his dedication to me during what was the roughest time in both of our lives.

On my first day in prison, I was assigned to work around the unit cleaning, until I could go to medical, and be cleared for kitchen work. FPC Bryan had a rule that everyone had to work in the kitchen for three months, before being allowed to get another job. Later that afternoon, I was called to medical. I came back to the unit crying like a baby after seeing the Physician Assistant (PA). I had never been spoken to like that in my life. There was undoubtedly no bedside manner.

And it was evident that the medical staff cared nothing about my medical needs. The only person nice to me in medical that day, was the X-Ray Tech. I remember thanking her for being so kind, and having her look at me as if she did not know what to say. I was cleared by the PA for kitchen duty, even though this should not have happened by BOP policy, since I have a screw in one of my ankles, and cannot wear the steel-toed boots. It violates OSHA policies to have incarcerated people working in the kitchen with soft shoes, and I had been given a soft shoe pass by the medical staff, due to my ankle issue. Regardless, on that first day I was cleared for kitchen duty, and assigned to the 4:00 a.m. kitchen crew. And so began my prison life.

Later during my incarceration at FPC Bryan, I would write Administrative Remedies, grievances requesting change, against the prison for the OSHA violations in the kitchen. My Administrative Remedies resulted in everyone on a walker being removed from the kitchen, as well as those who could not wear the steel-toed boots. But that was many months down the road. At first, I was just flying under the radar, trying to get through the situation as best I could.

Above: *Timothy, Joseph, Lynn, Pancho, and JT on February 18, 2018, Last Family Photo Before I reported to federal prison*

Left: *At the Little Rock Airport, February 26, 2018, On my way to federal prison*

273

Chapter Twenty-Seven
What Is Federal Prison Camp Really Like?

Three days after I self-surrendered, I was moved into a room with three other ladies. They were nice enough, but I was a newbie, and not precisely skilled at keeping a metal locker with a padlock quiet at 3:30 a.m., when I was required to get up in the almost dark room, and get items out of the metal locker to be ready for work in the kitchen. I eventually learned how to be better at it, but at first, I could tell I was frustrating my roommates. One of them seemed to be particularly aggravated with me.

At this time, I was still falling apart inside from missing my family, so I was certainly not on my A-game, to say the least. And I'm certain that at the time, she was dealing with her own demons, and probably not on her A-game either. Unfortunately, nobody enjoys having a roommate who works in the kitchen on the 4:00 a.m. shift, since nobody else has to be up that early. It was indeed a learning process. And my roommates were already acclimated to prison, and had their own routines.

They already had all the things that make one comfortable in prison, things it takes a newbie time to buy from the commissary, with the monthly spending limit you must adhere to. As we called each other in prison, my roomies, cellmates, or bunkies, already had friends, a routine, and knew how to make the best of prison life. At least as best as any of us ever found to make it.

I was still reeling from the loss of my freedom and my family. My heart hurt, and I longed for Pancho. Just hearing his voice on the phone each day made me feel better in ways, but also made it hurt even more. It is a pain that I had to relive to write this book, and one I do not think I will ever get over. I can still remember the sickness in my stomach, and the anxiety that would come on, just from not having him with me. It is just one of the prison scars, I don't think I will ever get over.

The longing for him would become more manageable as time went on, but was almost unbearably painful at first. It is sort of like grieving the loss of a person. At some point I became numb to all my emotions regarding home, a numbness of emotions that I still suffer from, to some extent, to this day. Having to numb myself to get through the prison experience has changed me forever as a person. Another change I have found in myself, that I first noticed when I was first home from prison, is that most things didn't bother me any longer.

When I was first home, and would see people being emotional, and complaining about the smallest of issues on Facebook, I would just shake my head. If they only knew just how blessed they are, maybe they would not complain so much. I often thought to myself "You need to spend about a week in federal prison." It certainly changes one's perspective. As time has gone on, I have started to heal from this emotional void. But I'm not sure it will ever completely heal.

Prison life was not all bad though. I enjoyed friendships with many women while incarcerated. These friends become more like family when you are surrounded by these people daily, after all, you are seeing them more than your own family. They become the only family you have in close proximity, while you are locked up. I walked the track, taught classes to other ladies on women's value and worth, and self-esteem, as well as taught a QuickBooks class in the education department.

At night when everyone else was watching television, I lay in my bed and read. I did not like all the loud noise in the common area. I still have a hard time being around loud noises and crowds. It makes my anxiety go up. The only time in prison that I would watch television, was when my friend, Sarah, would talk me into it. I despised how the women would stampede down the stairs once the 4:00 p.m. count was called. Grown women would rush to get a spot in front of the different televisions. If you were not careful, they would run you over running to the TVs. Truthfully, I'm just not a big TV watcher anyway.

Because of this, reading was something I did a lot during my time in prison. It took me away from prison life, as I would get wrapped up in the characters in the books. I learned to tune out all the loud noise, and get lost in the book. I bet I read more than 350 books during my 27 months of incarceration. After I returned home, my husband and I tried to go back and figure out how many books he had sent me through Amazon, during that time, but there were so many, we got tired of counting. I traded books with many women I was friendly with, and donated the books Pancho sent me to our unit library, for others to read.

The rooms, cells, at Federal Prison Camp (FPC) Bryan are like small closets, made of concrete blocks. Everything was white and sterile. In each room there were two sets of bunk beds, a desk, four metal fold-up chairs, and four lockers attached to the walls. The rooms are tiny, but we kept them clean. Usually, four ladies share a room. There is no door to the room, just an open space where a door would normally be. However, you are required to stay in the room during certain times of the day, and night. All in all, it was certainly not a bad place. It was not a good place either.

But definitely not what I had envisioned prison would be like. We were able to roam around the compound for most of the day. There were no bars on anything, no locked doors, no barbed wire, except on the top of the fence that surrounded the compound. And I had heard this was to keep the neighbors out, since the camp was located right in the middle of a neighborhood. There were stories about neighbors who had snuck in to eat in the prison cafeteria, before the fence went up. Most likely this was only a prison rumor, I could not imagine anyone wanting to eat what we were fed!

The shower and bathroom were clean, for the most part, except for the black mold that grew in the showers at times, and the black worms that crawled out of the drains during certain times of the year. If you have to be in prison, a camp is not a bad place. However, please be advised that there is no such place as Camp Fed, or Camp Cupcake, as prison camps are often referred to in the media, but it could have been worse. The hardest thing to get used to is the noise. Prison is LOUD. I remember thinking I could never get used to all the noise. It took me months.

Now that I am home, someone can be talking to me, and I don't even hear them. I often tune out everything around me when I am focused on a book, or working on something on my computer. You learn to tune out other noises in prison in order to survive. But once home, these habits are tough to break. You have been changed by the experience. You are no longer the person who reported to prison, but some new version of yourself. Not necessarily a better version, at least not in some aspects.

Eventually, I made friends of my own, and got a job I liked in the reentry department. I established my own routine, and was able to obtain things from the commissary to help make my life as comfortable, in my new surroundings, as possible. I adapted the best I could, and made a prison life for myself. It was not the life I wanted to live, but it was the best I could hope for, until I could again be home with my family. The ladies that became my prison family, I called sisters.

Some individuals created whole families with moms, sisters, daughters, and even pappas. I never did this, but I understood why others did. Especially for those that were going to be "down," meaning locked up, for a long time. We celebrated holidays, birthdays, and other milestones with each other. We threw parties to celebrate these life events. Even giving homemade gifts, or items purchased from the commissary, to each other, on our birthdays, and Christmas.

One year my friend, Sarah, gave me the prettiest knitted booties for my birthday. I really cherished those booties. She was undoubtedly a friend that made my life better in prison.

When I arrived at Bryan, Sarah had already served roughly six years there. I never understood how she could still be upbeat, after that amount of time, but she was. Sarah kept the greeting cards sent to her over the years. At each holiday, she would cut the front part of the card that contained the design away from the rest, to make a new card, and then she would write the sweetest, and most heartfelt notes, to others on these recycled cards.

I was fortunate enough to be someone who was on the receiving end of her cards. I would find them randomly left for me on my bunk, side table, or locker. I still have them. They meant the world to me then, and now. Sarah became a valued friend, and someone I still keep in touch with, even on this side of the walls. In 2022, I was blessed enough to help her write a motion to get off supervised release early. I can't tell you how happy I was for her the day her judge granted the motion. She has done so well for herself since prison, and I'm proud to call her my sister.

At Christmas the units would be turned into magical places from Disney, with decorations that looked like they had been professionally made. There is no way to describe the amount of work I saw women putting into these decorations. There were huge castles, life size dragons, and many other items. And the costumes blew my mind. I could not understand how such beautiful costumes were made out of trash.

It honestly looked like something out of a Broadway play. The unit was transformed into something that would have made Walt Disney proud. And everything was made with cardboard or other trash. Each of the four units were able to put on a play, or musical, written by one of the ladies in the unit. I could not believe the amount of talent. The performances truly were amazing. Each unit got to go to the other units to watch their productions.

Staff members would go around to each unit and watch the

productions, to judge the performances. And then the winner would be announced. The anticipation was always high. Both years I was at Bryan, our unit, B1, won. This meant we were first for the Christmas holiday meal, and the ice cream social, that we had shortly before Christmas. This was a big deal to many of the ladies. Especially since the Christmas meal was actually the best meal served all year long.

And the decorations in our unit certainly helped to camouflage the Charlie Brown Christmas tree we had. It was a very old white artificial tree that, if touched, fell apart. There were no working lights, but the ladies made beautiful decorations out of other trash items, and made it look the best they could. I honestly always hated that tree. It made me sad. It stood at the top of the stairs, I had to climb to get to my cell. In prison, no holiday felt like a holiday, and the same could be said for Christmas. In a way, I believe this was good, as it made things easier.

I usually scheduled a video visit with my family on Christmas Eve, and Christmas Day. Many times, it would just be Pancho and I on Christmas Day, since he and the boys would have already celebrated the night before. It made me sad that Pancho was home alone on Christmas. My heart longed to be with him. But I knew that JT and Timothy would be with their girlfriends' families on Christmas Day. Because of all the activity of plays and decorations, before I knew it, Christmas had come and gone, and a new year was approaching. I was always excited for the new year. It meant I was closer to going home.

But in prison, there were also times of great loss. Often, we had to console each other, when family members passed away. I saw women who lost children while serving time in prison. It was heart-wrenching. But the other women rallied around them, and held them up. One of the hardest things while in prison was seeing other ladies leave.

There is a tradition called "walking someone out" of prison. This happens on the day someone goes home. All their friends walk with them, as far as is allowed, towards the front gate, and then bid their farewells to the person, sending them on their way to the free world. After the person leaving, walks away to R&D, the group of friends stand back and watch, as the person is escorted from R&D to their family, who are waiting in a vehicle just outside the gate.

It was exciting to see what clothes the family had sent their loved one to wear home. The lady leaving was required to change into these clothes once in R&D. Many thoughts were put into these outfits, and ladies planned and talked about them for months, before they went home. It's a joy and a curse to be part of these parting walks. The emotions were always high. It's hard seeing others leave, when you must stay. These women become your friends, so you feel their loss when they go. You miss their presence in your daily life.

On one hand, you are so happy for them that this part of their journey has come to an end, and you know that one day soon, this part of your journey will also be over. Yet on the other hand, it feels like someone has died. You are not able to speak to them, or even know that they are doing okay. Normally when a friend moves on, in the free world, you are able to keep up with them by visiting, or on Facebook, text, email, or phone calls. But in prison all contact has been cut off. The emotional strain is real. Your gut actually hurts. You feel like something important has been ripped from you, and that you will never have it again.

I got close to many women while I served time. I will refer to one of these ladies as Ms. JJ, since that is what I called her while we served time in prison together. Ms. JJ was a bright light, and a joy to be around. I always admired her prison mission to lead other women to Christ. It was my mission too, and regardless of my anger, God was able to use me at times, during my time in prison, to lead others to HIM. But Ms. JJ's dedication was admirable. She chose to work in the kitchen the entire time she was incarcerated, because she felt that is where God wanted her to be. She said it gave her the best opportunity to meet most of the women that came to the camp, due to the requirement that they had to work ninety days in the kitchen, when they first arrived.

I shared many experiences with Ms. JJ while we were at FPC Bryan. We prayed together, and often worshiped together in the Chapel, and she was one of the ladies that I shared the weekly sermons sent to me from my church. One such experience we shared, was when I was going through one of my worst times. It was during the time I was fighting the system, and writing Administrative Remedies against staff. I was fighting to get back into cosmetology programming, after I was removed for refusing to sign fraudulent paperwork that misstated the hours I had been in class.

I remember meeting up with Ms. JJ under the pavilion where the work out equipment was stored. The pavilion was across the street from our units. There we sat, at one of the picnic tables, and she prayed with me. I remember when she took my hand to hold it to pray, she quickly jerked back, and told me that she could feel my anger consuming me. She told me that she could feel the devil using my anger against me. I was a little taken back at the time, but reflecting back now, I know she was being led by God to give me that message. Unfortunately, at the time I was not yet ready to receive it.

I think of Ms. JJ often, and often pray for her. I hope she is doing well. I know she is serving God the same way I saw her do while she was in prison. I miss her greatly, as we lost contact once she left prison. She wrote to me a few times, and I always meant to write her back. However, I just never did. I knew at the time I didn't have anything positive to say, as my anger was still raging inside of me. So, I spared her my vile attitude, and did not return her letters. After a few tries, I guess she gave up, as I stopped receiving cards and letters from her.

Another dear woman I met at FPC Bryan was Mia. She became a friend that I still cherish to this day. While we don't talk as often as I would like, we do still check in on each other periodically. I'll never forget the day we walked her out. That day is seared in my mind forever. It was so emotional.

Unfortunately, Mia was charged by both the state and federal criminal justice systems, for the same crime. Therefore, she was not able to go directly home. By the time she left Bryan, she had already served six years in prison, yet she still had state time to serve as well. As we stood and waited for the Sheriff's office to pick her up the day she left, my heart pounded loudly. I can't explain how it felt to see my friend shackled and handcuffed. It tore me apart.

Little did I know at the time, that I too, would leave FPC Bryan in a similar fashion. Mia did not deserve to be treated in that manner. What purpose does it serve to society for people to serve both state and federal time in prison, for the same crime? Another flaw in our system. What was the purpose for minimum security, non-violent offenders to be shackled and handcuffed? Afterall, she had been at the camp for six years without walking away.

Mia is a wonderful Christian woman who did a lot for me, as well as many other women, during her six years in prison. She was also a bright light, and one of the people that was always there for me, even when I was in my own darkest moments. She was my sounding board, a voice of reason when I needed advice, and a great friend. She was certainly not a threat to society. She was serving time for a white-collar crime, mortgage fraud, if I remember correctly. I knew when she left FPC Bryan that day, that she would go to the state prison and help others.

I knew God was leading her on a different journey, but my heart was still sad to see her leave bound in shackles and chains. I also knew she would do great things on the other side of the walls, once she made it home. She is one of the first people I called after my husband picked me up from prison. She had been in touch with him once she was released from the state prison, a few weeks before I was released from federal prison.

As difficult as it was, I always took great joy in seeing a sister leave prison. I knew they were going home to their family, regardless of how hard it was to let them go. I often wondered what the first thing they had done was when they left prison? What would their first meal be?

I also took joy in knowing that my time was getting shorter. I often thought about my walk out of prison. I could not wait for it to be my turn. I had no idea that I would never be able to receive that same walk. At the time, I didn't know that my journey would eventually take me away from Bryan, to a strange land, where I would be released by myself from the bowels of the federal transfer center in Oklahoma City, Oklahoma, during the height of COVID-19. But that is getting ahead of the story.

A few months into my incarceration, I was in the community bathroom one day after lunch. A young woman I'll refer to as L, was in the bathroom crying. I was still new to prison, and trying to learn prison boundaries. Prison is not like being in the free world. And you do not normally interfere in another's business. I had heard L screaming on the phone earlier, and had heard the anguish in her voice. I did not know L, but it was my understanding that she had been in prison for a long time already.

Regardless, I could feel God tugging at me. Following HIS instruction, I approached her, and asked if there was anything I could do. After she stared at me for a few seconds, causing my heart to jump up into my throat, she told me that she had just found out that her brother had been charged with a murder he had not committed.

Knowing how it feels to be falsely accused, my heart immediately began to pound loudly. I actually felt light headed, and thought I would pass out. The emotion hit me like a tidal wave. I asked L if I could pray with her. At first, she just looked at me, like I was a three headed monster, but then she softened, and said that I could. I placed my hand on her shoulder and prayed out loud for her, her brother, and their family. Then I did something totally out of bounds, I hugged her. I told her that I would continue to pray for her family and ask God for the truth about her brother's case to come to light.

Off and on, for the next year, I prayed for and with her. One evening I was laying in my bunk reading. All of a sudden L came running into my room. She was crying and charging toward my bed. I was at first alarmed, but she immediately started hugging me, and told me that my prayers had worked. She told me that the charges against her brother had been dismissed. She said "God really does make miracles happen." After I gave her a huge hug, we got down by the side of my bed on our knees, and prayed. After that day, I really did see a change in L. She was softer, and treated others with more compassion than I had seen her do in the past. She left to go home a few months later. She is another person I met in prison that I often wonder about. I hope she is doing well.

Experiencing that moment with her, really did convict me, as I was constantly convicted in my own mind. It was God reminding me of my relationship with HIM. The relationship I constantly turned my back on, when I allowed my anger to control me. But, each time, after a few days, my anger took over again. I knew I was not living in God's grace and mercy with my bitterness and anger, but I could not let it go. I prayed to God, but in all honesty, I was not yet ready to let go of it. Therefore, I was unwittingly allowing the devil to use it against me. It was a constant struggle.

Early in my prison sentence, I had a roommate named Mary Jo. She was from Oklahoma. She was a beautiful woman and I loved having her for a cellmate. The stories she told were interesting. She had been an addict and one of the biggest heroin dealers in Oklahoma. Obviously, she was clean when she was my cellmate. But long before she started selling heroin, she was married to a man that was known as the Oklahoma Outlaw. They were sort of a Bonnie and Clyde type of pair. She told me many stories about their time as outlaws. Pancho sent us the books her ex-husband had written about their crimes. It was strange reading about my cellmate and her ex-husband in a book. His book was a tell-all. He had become infamous after he escaped from federal prison, and went on the lam for almost a year, before being recaptured by the US Marshals. Unfortunately, not all my encounters with other incarcerated ladies were positive.

I had several roommates/cellmates that brought heartache into my prison life. It is hard for women to live in a room with four people that is smaller than my walk-in closet. One woman I had as a roommate was obviously mentally ill, or maybe her behavior was caused by the many years of drugs she had used? Regardless, it was hard for her to get along with anyone. She was drama from the get go, and was incapable of getting along with others. She had trouble with most of the other women on the entire compound. The ladies that came with her from the county jail told stories of her troubles there. She was not in the room with me for very long, thank God. I prayed daily for her to be moved.

But the short amount of time she was there, it was a train wreck. It is hard to live in a confined space with someone, that no matter what you do, it is fruitless. No matter what happened in the room, her paranoia caused her to find fault in it. Many people who have long drug histories suffer from paranoia. In that situation, I did try hard to show God's grace and mercy to her. Maybe she wasn't ready to receive it at the time? And admittedly, I was struggling myself. Many messed up people are locked inside the walls. They are not provided counseling or other treatment to help them cope. And due to her drug use, her level of maturity seemed stunted. This does seem to be the case with many long-term drug addicts, especially ones that started using at a very young age.

After she was moved from our room, there was a time this same woman was taken to the Solitary Housing Unit (SHU). She had gotten into a fight with another lady in the unit. I remember feeling sad for her, because when the guard came to pack up her stuff, after she had been taken away, almost the entire unit was clapping, as the guard hauled her stuff from the unit.

Even after I left prison, I would hear stories of this same woman being shipped to the SHU for fighting, or other acts of

286

drama. Apparently, she never got it together. When I sent her a Christmas card after I was home, she had been moved to a facility in another state. Admittedly, the prison did nothing to help her. This is just one of the problems I see with the Bureau of Prisons (BOP). There does not seem to be much rehabilitation happening in our federal prisons nationwide. This saddens me greatly, and something I try to speak out about frequently.

One of the scariest times in my prison experience was when I had a cellmate who worshiped Santa Muerte. A website dedicated to the religion states that "The full name of Santa Muerte is actually Nuestra Señora de la Santa Muerte, which translates to Our Lady of the Holy Death. Researchers consider Santa Muerte to be a "folk saint" whose qualities and origins derive from a range of religious and spiritual traditions. The worship of Santa Muerte typically blends Catholicism and Mexican neo-paganism." The *New York Post* reports that "The Catholic Church has condemned Santa Muerte worship as "blasphemous and Satanic."

It is a religion that has been linked to drug cartels. This particular cellmate had been a mule (transporter of drugs), for the cartel. She received a long sentence for doing so. And truthfully, she had a very evil spirit about her, that could often be seen in her ways and actions. God certainly protected me in this situation. My cellmate had an altar set up in her locker, where she cast spells, and worshiped demons.

Many times, she told us she was casting spells on us. It was unnerving, but I just prayed each time for God to protect our room. She also fed and watered the deity she worshiped, with food and water left under her bunk. We would see the items there in plain sight. We would wake in the middle of the night, to hear her chanting something while she had her head under her covers, with her book light on.

One night at 3:00 a.m. the bible my bunkie, Rhonda, had left on top of her locker, came flying off the locker, and hit the floor, with a loud thud, during one of our cellmate's late night chanting sessions We had been reading the bible and praying together right before lights out, and Rhonda had left it on top of her locker. After that night, I asked my husband to send us a book on Santa Muerte. I wanted to know exactly what I was dealing with.

The day after the bible flew off the locker, Rhonda and my other cellmate came running to get me. I was walking back from the education building, after teaching the QuickBooks class, I taught. They said I had to come to the room immediately. When I got to the room, I heard the story of how Rhonda had been blessing the room with holy oil she had purchased from the commissary. Rhonda was Catholic. Apparently in her blessing of the top bunk belonging to our other cellmate, whose bed was attached to the cellmate that worshiped Santa Muerte, Rhonda had spilled holy oil on the Santa Muerte worshiper's bed below. I could clearly see oil spots on her blanket.

They had come to get me for help. I didn't know what to do. Touching another person's bed in prison was worse than most almost anything else you could do. I knew this would not go over well with our cellmate. Needless to say, it was not a good evening in our room, after the Santa Muerte worshiper returned, and saw the holy oil on her bed. I did not blame her for being upset. It was a violation of her private space.

The following day when I was in the room alone reading, the Santa Muerte worshiper cellmate came into the room. She accused me of being the one to put the holy oil on her bed. She knew that I regularly attended church, and that I read my bible each day, and prayed. She saw the bible verses taped to my bunk, and on my wall beside my bed. I guess she did not realize that I was not Catholic, and would not have had the holy oil to begin with. I sat and listened to her speak ugly to me for a long time.

I just prayed for God to surround me with protection, and give me peace in the situation, and HE did. When she started chanting and telling me she was casting spells on me, I decided that I had had enough. It was scary, but I knew that

I had God's protection. I looked at her from my bunk bed across the room, and loudly said "Poof, you're a frog" as I waved my hand in the air, like a wand. Then I stared at her and said "Oh that didn't work, did it?" "Well, that is about as much as your spells are going to work on me." "I have God's protection from evil." I then left the room and went to my counselor's office. I told him one of us needed to be moved out of that room, and gave him the book my husband had sent me. I quoted the BOP policy that prohibited my cellmate from the worship of this religion. She was moved a few days later.

Months later I would see her on the compound. As she quickly approached me, my anxiety went up. However, she was crying, and needed my help. She had just come from the Chapel where she had been made aware that her son had been in a serious motorcycle accident, and was not expected to live. She wanted me to pray for him. I placed my hand on her shoulder and prayed.

I guess in time of need, she knew that the deity she worshiped was not going to help her. She needed God for that. And so, it was God that we asked to heal her son. I'm not sure what happened with her son, and I never found out if he lived, as she and I did not talk after that. And I was shipped from the compound, a short time later. However, I continued to pray for him and her.

During another bad roommate experience, I had a cellmate that was obviously miserable in her own life. It was written all over her face, and well known on the compound, that she was having personal problems with her husband. I was dealing with my own miseries by this time, as it was about a year into my prison stay. Apparently, my cellmate's husband was cheating on her, and later filed for divorce. I saw this happen over and over, to women I served time with.

It was devastating. I knew how lucky I was to have Pancho, and these situations were constant reminders. I tried everything to be kind to this roommate. At times she was receptive, but at other times, nothing pleased her. My other two roommates would also have the same issue with her, but they choose to talk about her behind her back, as their way of dealing with it. I always tried my hardest to give her the grace and mercy I knew she needed, given her situation with her husband. It was not always easy, as she was hard to live with. Many times, I just ignored her, and we lived in the room the size of a closet, without speaking. It was better than unleashing the anger, I had at the time, on her.

Other women approached me to tell me she was talking negatively about me to others. My roommate was not aware that they were telling me what she had said. I just ignored it. I knew that I was just her punching bag. It was not about me; it was about her. Afterall, I too had made similar mistakes by taking my anger out on others. How could I judge her for doing the same?

Because of what appeared to be my cellmate's jealousy of my relationship with Pancho, or at least that is what others pointed out to me, was the issue; she and her friend, who apparently did not like me either, decided to try and make my prison life hard. The friend was also having marital problems, and her husband had also filed for divorce. So, they were united in their misery, and their dislike of me. I would later find out, that the friend had another reason as well that she did not like me. At one point she and I had walked the compound talking. In our conversation she told me about a civil case her victims had filed against her. In this conversation I told her about the civil case the doctors had filed against Pancho and I. I thought by sharing this she would see that she was not alone. Instead, she took this as me making the conversation about myself, instead of about her and her husband.

In my counseling classes I had been taught to share your own story, when it was related to that of a client. In this way, you could assure them that they were not alone. This technique is called being congruent, and is a way to connect with the client. I was attempting to use this skill to connect with her. Unfortunately, she had taken it the opposite of how I was trying to use it. She told another woman that she had come to me for counseling, which at the time she had not disclosed to me, or I would have refused.

I was struggling myself. I was in no frame of mind to counsel anyone. In her mind, I had not cared about her, only myself. I reminded the other woman when she relayed this to me, that I was not a counselor in this setting, that I was an incarcerated person, just like everyone else. Like everyone else, I was just doing what I could to get through the situation, and helping others when I was able. I said, "If she needs therapy, she needs to go to psychology." "If she needs a friend, I'm here."

Now, this lady and my cellmate had become friends, and apparently had a common interest in wanting to make my life miserable. As relayed to me by other women, for some reason, these two women thought I was having a good prison experience. For the life of me, I can't understand how they thought this? I was dealing with my own anger, the loss of my freedom, as well as the longing to be with my family. Regardless, what they thought could have been furthest from the truth, they decided to go cause me problems anyway. So, they started a rumor about me. They told the lesbian ladies on the compound, that I was writing blogs from prison about them. This was absolutely not true. My blogs never discussed the subject. But these ladies knew that if they told this to Big Jenn, the loud-mouthed lesbian in our unit, that it would indeed cause an issue for me.

One evening when everyone was in their cells awaiting the 10:00 p.m. count, I was sleeping as usual. Most nights I fell asleep before count, and would have to get woken up for the standing count. Rhonda would always wake me up. But this time Rhonda woke me up because Big Jenn was yelling in the unit, to let everyone know that I was blogging about lesbians.

At first, I didn't understand what was going on. Another lady who lived in the cell next to me, and who also had a girlfriend at the time, stepped out of her cell and defended me. She yelled to Big Jenn and told her "She is a nice person and she has always treated me and my girlfriend respectfully."

She yelled out, "I don't believe she would do something like that." My cellmate just looked at me. She knew she was the cause of what was taking place. However, at the time, I was not aware of this fact.

The following day, I was tipped off by my friend Mia, that Big Jenn and her girlfriend, had been told the rumor, and had asked my good prison friend, Carolyn, for the name of my blog. They then had the girlfriend's sister-in-law look up my blog, and email my blog posts to them. Nowhere in them, had I blogged about lesbians. After that, Big Jenn and I never had another issue.

However, I found myself being angry at Carolyn for telling them the name of my blog site. And maybe I was just looking for someone to be angry with at the time. She was someone I had been very close to since she came to prison, a few months after me. We had spent lots of time together, and had many common interests. She was someone I would have been friends with on the outside. But I found myself now being distrustful of her. I started distancing myself from her. I don't think she even understood why, nor did I tell her. And honestly, our relationship was never the same after that, because I was holding on to resentment toward her.

This was certainly not biblical, and I knew it. I felt convicted about it all the time, but my anger kept fueling my feelings. And because I no longer trusted her, distancing myself was the only way I knew to deal with the situation at the time. I realized later, but only years later, that what I was really feeling angry at, was being accused of something I had not done, the blog posts I was accused of writing about lesbians.

This anger came from a very deep place, and had to do with the trauma I suffered due to the lies the doctors had said about me. The same lies that had ended me up in prison, in the first place. Since my trial, I have a hard time being accused of anything I have not said. or done. It makes my anger flare, because of the trauma I have been through in my criminal case. I've had to work hard, to get to a point with God's help, that I am able to control it, instead of allowing it to control me. But at the time of this incident, I was not there yet. While our friendship is not the same as it once was. I am reconnected with the prison friend I once distanced myself from. I realize I let my emotions get the best of me in that situation. Prison is full of people just trying to get through the situation. I was just one of them. Everyone deals with it differently.

During my incarceration, I met many women that had been in prison longer than the sentence I was to serve, and other women who had very long sentences that I could not even imagine serving. One such woman was my bunkie Rhonda, who is serving a thirteen-year sentence, due to her husband's drug addiction. She had been indicted in a separate indictment, when the government could not connect her to her husband's drug conspiracy case. Rhonda's husband was an addict who sold and moved drugs to support his own drug habit. The government had requested Rhonda to cooperate against her husband.

When she refused, as a way to show her who the boss is, the government indicted her in another case. Another example of an overzealous prosecutor, wrecking lives when someone dares to stand up for what is just. Unfortunately, in Rhonda's meeting with a federal agent, she had unwittingly admitted that her husband was an addict, and often brought drugs into their home. Because the government had no case against her, as she was not part of her husband's crime, having not been an addict herself, nor had she helped to sell or move her husband's drugs. The government charged Rhonda in a separate indictment for "running a drug premises," based on her admittance that her husband had brought drugs into the home they shared. Her husband is serving forty years for his crimes.

I began to feel fortunate for my 45-month sentence. After all, had the judge not ruled in my favor on the enhancements the government tried to add to my case, I could also be serving an 8-13- year sentence. But that was not God's plan for me. I was blessed. Being in a horrific situation like prison, makes you realize how blessed you really are.

And after my first month in prison, I have to admit the time did go by rather quickly. Before I knew it, I had been in prison a whole year. I had made it through all the major holidays without my family, and most importantly, I had survived. I had also helped many other women during that first year. I was stronger for having done so. But I was still dealing with the anger that had consumed me for so many years. And due to the added trauma of prison, my anger was growing stronger by the day.

Chapter Twenty-Eight
Prison 101

Prison is a strange place in many ways. It is a world all of its own, with its own vocabulary. For example, if someone is *institutionalized*, they are accustomed to prison and most likely have been in prison for many years, or maybe even had been to prison in the past. They feel comfortable being in prison, and don't question how they are treated by staff. I would hear many institutionalized women say "Well its prison," when we would be mistreated by staff. This made me want to scream, and I often spent time correcting this behavior. I wanted women to understand they had value and worth. That even though they may be in prison, they were not trash. It was disturbing seeing how some of the other women conformed to the mistreatment.

Even more disturbing was that many women considered prison their home. They had basically conformed to prison life. I even witnessed women who were so institutionalized that they were hard to live with. They had set standards on how the cell was to be kept, for example what could be placed on the desk in the cell, how the cell was to be cleaned, and many other self-imposed rules they tried to force upon their cellmates. One cellmate even imposed the rule that those who lived with her were not allowed to have shoes on in the cell. These imposed rules made it hard on other women assigned to the cell with the institutionalized ones. At FPC Bryan we called our cells rooms, because they really were a room with no door.

At FPC Bryan, we had a guard that would say, "*stop acting brand new,*" which meant stop acting like you just got to prison, and didn't know the rules. *ROY* stands for "rumor on the yard," which means a rumor going around the camp about something. *Inmate.com* means information or gossip told to you by another person serving time. *Caught your case* refers to when and where you were charged. You are forced to learn this "new" vocabulary in order to understand what another person may be relaying to you. *Chow Hall* refers to the cafeteria. *The mainline* is the lunch meal where BOP staff are supposed to stand in a line so we could approach them and ask questions, at least in theory that is how it was supposed to work. Usually, staff were just standing around talking to each other, and got snappy when we interrupted those conversations. *Down* means locked up. Inmates often say I've been *down* for X months or years. A *cop-out* is a request to staff made by an incarcerated person on a paper form, or through electronic mail, using the CorrLinks system.

Suited and booted refers to the required times we had to wear our uniform and boots, from 7:00 a.m. to 3:30 p.m. each day. *One day and a wake-up* meant the person only has one day left in prison before going home. *Merry go round* referred to the paperwork a person had to take to the different departments to be signed off on prior to their release. A *Shot* or *Write Up* refers to an incident report that someone is given by a staff member when they break the rules, or when staff wants to target a prisoner. Many false shots are written by staff. *Rack Up* means go to your room for the daily counts. The rack the officer is referring to is your bunk bed. *Count Time* refers to stand-up counts, where you are required to stand by your bed, remain silent, and look straight ahead, while a count is taken by the staff. Two officers take the count.

When officers can't agree on the count, they must count repeatedly. After so many failed counts, the lieutenant on duty must come to conduct the count. I never understood why it was so hard to count people who are standing completely still? But it seemed to happen often.

A *Store* refers to an incarcerated person selling commissary out of their locker for profit. Usually, the items are sold as on *two for one* basis, meaning you must give the store back two, of the same item, when you pay up, for the one item you purchased. *You have a social* means a person from another unit has sent someone into your unit to ask you to come outside (prisoners are not allowed to enter units if they are not housed in that unit, although this rule was often broken). *Pulling Chain* refers to being moved from one institution to another. The chains referred to are the shackles and handcuffs placed on women when they are moved from one institution to another. *Diesel Therapy* refers to being transferred by staff from one institution to another institution, as punishment.

Gay for the stay, straight at the gate referred to women who chose to take a girlfriend in prison, but went back to their normal heterosexual life after their release. I saw many fights in prison, and most of them were related to girlfriend issues. Many girlfriends would be jealous when their girlfriend's husband or boyfriend came for a visit. Jealousy of the girlfriend caused other issues as well. I saw women who fought each other over a girlfriend. Honestly, at the camp when there was a fight, nine times out of ten, it was to do with a girlfriend issue. The other 1 per cent, had to do with women who were mouthy, getting into a disagreement with another woman. Most fights resulted in pulling hair and shoving each other. Toward the end of my time at Bryan though, we did start to see some real violent fights. I believe this was because in order to raise the head count at Bryan, at the request of the Warden, the BOP had placed management variables on women who were not camp status, in order to allow them into the camp.

A *management variable* can be placed to allow someone with a higher security level to come to a lower security level facility. It can also be placed on a lower security level prisoner to move that person to a higher-level security facility. Staff at the BOP have many tricks they can use to manipulate the system, and a management variable is just one of them.

Another strange thing about women's prison, and something that always made me laugh, was that, maxi pads are an all-purpose tool. Since they were readily available in every bathroom, they were used frequently. Women used maxi pads as inserts for boots, the boots that killed the feet of anyone who was forced to wear them, as a dust pad to clean the room, locker, or most anything else that needed to be cleaned, including dishes. They are taken apart and made into earplugs, and there are many other uses that women find for them. I heard the term "ghetto sweeper" used when referring to maxi pads placed on the bottom of one's slides, to be used as a mop to clean the floors in their room. Tampons were also used in a similar fashion as tools for cleaning dishes. I often wondered what incarcerated men used for cleaning supplies, since obviously, they did not have access to women's hygiene items in their bathrooms.

One of the worst things about prison was the constant barrage of rumors. that went around the compound. Many of which were started by staff members. I remember one day when a staff member came in to tell us that the prison was almost out of toilet paper, and would not be getting anymore that month. Of course, this caused panic amongst the masses. I tried to encourage the ladies to calm down. I knew it was against BOP policy not to provide toilet paper to us. Afterall, we were a captive audience. And toilet paper wasn't even sold at the commissary.

Common sense told me this was just an idle threat, being made by a bored, or punitive, staff member. However, shortly after the announcement, not a shred of toilet paper could be found in any of the four bathrooms in our unit. I marched over to the education building, and in plain sight, brought back several rolls of toilet paper to my room. I had to walk across the entire compound carrying the toilet paper.

Other ladies were laughing at me. Many were worried that I would get a *shot* for daring to bring back toilet paper from another building. This was towards the end of my time at FPC Bryan and by then, after all the staff had already put me through, I was no longer afraid. I certainly would have appealed any incident report given to me for bringing toilet

298

paper back to the unit. After the chaos was created by the staff member, toilet paper started reappearing the following day. Just as I had suspected, the staff member was just making things up to agitate the ladies.

I saw many examples of this while serving time in prison. Prisoners referred to this as *staff being messy,* but I personally saw it as another way staff created trauma in those serving time. It was an act of control and mistreatment. I later blogged about the incident, referring to it in my blog as *toilet papergate.* Unfortunately, it is not just staff that are *messy.* Many of the women were *messy* too, mostly because they were bored with nothing else to do, and oftentimes, it was these women who were responsible for the many rumors that often made their way around the compound. Many women are also uninformed about policies and laws. They repeat misinformation that becomes facts amongst the masses.

Another thing about prison is that most things go directly against common sense and logic. I always said that at the BOP "logic is illogical." The saying amongst most prisoners was that the BOP was "Backwards on Purpose." For example, even if you have a college degree, and can have your family fax a copy of your high school diploma, and college transcripts, BOP staff still want to force you to take GED classes. For some reason, BOP staff believe they need your high school transcript, or you are required to take these classes. My high school closed many years ago, so I had no way to produce a high school transcript.

However, my college transcript was readily available. Clearly, it showed I had a high school degree before being admitted to college. Common sense should alert staff that someone who has two college degrees, and was only a few credit hours away from having a graduate degree, would undoubtedly have a high school diploma, or at the very least a GED. But again, logic is illogical, when dealing with staff at the BOP.

Shortly after I self-surrendered to prison, I was made to take the math portion of the GED test to assess my math skills. This was because my high school transcript could not be obtained by the BOP. I had 45 minutes in which to complete the test. It took me 15 minutes. Yet I was told that I would still have to take GED classes, since the prison could not get my high school transcript. Luckily, I remembered that my high school diploma was in an old trunk in our garage. My husband was able to make a copy of it and fax it to the prison. After much protesting on my part, finally, the staff were convinced of my high school education. What a waste of taxpayer dollars to make people, who clearly have a college education, take GED classes.

However, the BOP gets money through yearly government budgets, for each person that takes the GED classes, as well as many of the other supposed programs offered in prison. Money that comes from your tax dollars. I suspect the motive was a way to get more budget for the education department, and was the main factor in trying to force GED classes on those that do not need them. And hence why staff do not like educated white collar offenders. We question too many things, such as the waste, and fraud, we see while serving time in prison. As an example, later I would be asked to take college classes in business to receive a certificate from the local community college.

I already had a four-year accounting and finance degree, but was willing to sign up for the classes anyway, just to have something productive to do. That is until I was told by the staff member not to list my college degree on the application. He told me that the prison could not qualify for funds for me taking the classes if I listed a college education. As I watched him erase my college information from the application, I promptly refused the classes. Another waste of taxpayer dollars.

The BOP receives a yearly budget to provide classes for prisoners. Yet staff manipulates that budget by signing up prisoners that already have a college degree in a similar field, in order to pad the yearly budget. This is just one of the many reasons, I continue to advocate for community confinement; where budgets could be used, to actually teach job skills, or educate those who are serving a sentence.

Speaking of waste. I saw so much waste in prison that it made my head spin. If taxpayers, and lawmakers, only knew how BOP staff were wasting their tax dollars at prisons across this nation, their heads might explode! The previous GED and college class examples are just two of those ways, but there are many, many other examples. At the end of each fiscal year, I saw staff frivolously spending lots of money on unneeded items, because they needed to use up the money budgeted for that year.

When I questioned this, one staff member told me, "If we don't spend the money, we will get a smaller budget next year." Some staff members would even allow their prisoner staff workers to pick unneeded items out of catalogs, so remaining budgetary funds could be spent for the year. A few months into my prison sentence, I saw one department spend over $20,000 for new chairs, when the chairs we had were perfectly fine. Perfectly good educational books could be found in trash bins. And dollies full of perfectly usable items could be seen being hauled away. And many times, staff are allowed to take the old items home, since the items were in the trash, and being tossed out anyway.

Many times. new items purchased for the prison never made it on the compound. At one point, ladies who worked in the warehouse, where items were received into the prison, reported several large televisions they had personally checked in, but that they knew never made it to the units.

These televisions were purchased for the TV areas in the units, using trust fund money that had come from commissary profits, and that was earmarked to be spent on items for prisoners Of course there was nothing we could do, except gossip about these types of incidents. We had no means to fix the issue, and most of the ladies were afraid to speak out against it for fear of retaliation. Since I had personally not witnessed the event, I had no means to report it.

The petty behavior of the staff members was something else that was extremely hard to understand. I could never understand why the staff spent so much time taking away yarn, items that had been crocheted, construction paper, pictures cut from magazines, and other items that the ladies were using to make crafts, and greeting cards, to send home to their children, and other family members. This only caused the ladies to be bored, which resulted in more issues within the unit. There is nothing worse than 250 women in one unit, with not much to do to occupy their time.

Yet, I repeatedly saw staff taking these items as contraband. I remember one time our irons were even taken. This prevented the women from spending time ironing their clothes. I blogged about this in a post titled *Irons, Irons, Who's Got The Irons? Fighting Wrinkles At The BOP.* In the post I wrote "It's been a wrinkled three months here at FPC Bryan thanks to our Unit Team deciding to punish us by taking away our irons."

At the time staff were mad because the unit orderlies who worked all day in the unit, were hiding the irons in their lockers. This was done so the orderlies could use them whenever they wanted, for their side hustle of ironing on the black market. It made no sense to have the entire unit walking around looking like they slept in their uniforms as punishment. What message did this send? Wouldn't the BOP want women to leave prison having pride in their appearance? Not to mention the compound's handbook stated "inmates are required to iron their uniforms."

It took me threatening to file an Administrative Remedy on the unit team, for them to give back the irons. This was shortly before I was to have my monthly visit with Pancho. I was not about to go to visit with my husband looking like a rumpled mess. I pulled our Unit Manager aside, and informed her that I was going to write the issue up, given that the *Female Offender Handbook* states it is mandatory for irons, hair dryers, curling irons, and hair straighteners to be provided by any institution housing females. After our chat, the irons were placed back in the unit the following day. This was another time my Unit Manager looked at me and said "Of course it is policy Espejo, and of course you can quote the policy." "I'll take care of it."

We would have these same conversations when hair dryers, flat irons, and curling irons would not be replaced when they broke. Each time as soon as I went to our unit manager's office, the items would appear. After a while, other ladies would come to me to report broken items in bathrooms, so I could take care of getting them replaced, since staff often refused to do so if they asked the staff for the item. But once I threatened to write an Administrative Remedy, the item would promptly appear.

Honestly it seemed staff thought they personally paid for these items out of their own pockets, when in reality, it was our commissary fund profits that were used to purchase these items for the units, based on the BOP policy I read. And my accounting knowledge came in handy for understanding budgets. At least now I had found a use for those governmental and not for profit accounting classes, I was forced to take as part of my accounting degree.

Another huge waste was food. The amount of food I saw being wasted in prison was unbelievable. I saw so much waste in the kitchen. For one, food being served may have sat in warehouses for years. Why was it purchased to begin with if it was not needed? I suspected it was purchased to use up a yearly budget at the end of a fiscal year.

As an example, cereal that had an expiration date of 2014, was still being served in 2018, to unsuspecting ladies who did not work in the kitchen. Many days the milk would be sour. We had to smell each package before we poured it on cereal or into a glass. Some days it took many tries to get milk that did not smell sour. And I always thought it odd that condiment packages that were left on the tables all day long, were recycled at the end of the day, after being allowed to be at room temperature for hours. These condiments came from boxes that already had expired dates on them.

Ladies who worked in the kitchen knew better than to eat most of the food. And one of the perks of working in the kitchen was that kitchen workers were fed things different from the rest of us. However, many women were still forced to eat the food, because they did not have money on their commissary accounts to purchase commissary food. Frequently, the rice and beans would have some type of bugs, and what looked like maggots in them, and would have to be thrown out. However, sometimes staff made the kitchen workers cook, and serve these items, anyway. Oatmeal had the same issues.

Kitchen workers would send word around the compound, warning the rest of us what not to eat that day. Many times, there were food shortages due to silly arguments between BOP warehouse staff, and the BOP kitchen staff. The staff at the warehouse would refuse to send the needed items to feed us to the kitchen due to these disagreements. Also, at one point, it became so overcrowded at FPC Bryan, that the yearly budget did not allow for the feeding of all the women. The cafeteria would often run out of food before everyone was fed.

Luckily, I had food purchased from the commissary, but many women are not so lucky. I made sure I shared what I had with other ladies. In this way God used me to be a blessing to those women with whom I shared my commissary items.

If you are a curious person, look up the BOP national menu sometime. It can be found on the Internet. While the menu looks good on paper, that would certainly not be the case, once you see it on your plate, or are forced to eat it. And we were fed the same things repeatedly, week after week. When looking over the menu, think of the cheapest cuts of meat, and other ingredients you can imagine that could be used to prepare the food, then take it down a few notches. You now have an understanding of what we ate in prison.

Nothing was healthy. Many processed items from both the kitchen, as well as the commissary food, we were allowed to purchase. I rarely saw anything but apples for our daily fruit. Rarely would we be given oranges or other fruits. And never any fruit juice. Most days, the kitchen workers could make the food taste pretty good, but some days it all went in the garbage.

The sandwich meat we were given many times, and as a sack lunch on holidays, was exceptionally questionable. I could never bring myself to eat it. I remember a blog post I wrote about this meat titled *What's That Meat?* In the post I told a story about the very skinny, starving, pregnant cat that hung around the prison. Many ladies would feed the stray cats that lived on the compound, tuna and other items they purchased from the commissary.

Some ladies would sneak things from their plates out of the cafeteria to give to the cats. I remember seeing a bowl of the holiday sandwich meat another prisoner had left out by the track for the pregnant cat, after one of our Fourth of July holiday sack lunches. The meat stayed there in the bowl for days. The flies would not even get on the meat, and even the starving pregnant cat. refused to eat it. Yet this was what we had been served as our holiday evening dinner.

During my time at Bryan, it was found out that we had also been fed hamburger meat made out of cow hearts, and other parts that were not for human consumption. This information came to light, after two brothers in Texas were indicted, for selling over $2 Million of faulty ground beef to the federal government.

While I can't blame the BOP for this happening, it does show the level of low-quality meats we were fed. I believe the BOP looked to buy from vendors offering the lowest of prices, regardless of the quality of these products. Part of the reason for this, is most likely due to Wardens getting bonuses, based on their bottom line profits each year.

Yes, prison is a business and it is a business of huge profits. The more Wardens can save, the more they personally profit. This is another deeply rooted flaw in the system that should be changed. And lends further credit to the stories I have blogged about, and written about in this book. There is really no excuse for locking humans up, and then treating them in this manner. It is actually hurting society in the long run, because people return home, more traumatized, than when they entered the prison system. This is just one of the many things that needs to be reformed. Prisons should not be for profit.

Not much rehabilitation of the incarcerated seemed to be happening at prisons across our country, either. It does not seem to be much of a priority. The bulk of classes available in prison were taught by other prisoners, and most are not beneficial. There is really not much for someone who is already educated. Another problem is that the classes that can give one a certificate, or career option, only have a few spots each year. For example, cosmetology took only 25 new students per year.

There were over 900 women at FPC Bryan, when I was incarcerated there. Horticulture is the same. They take a small number of people for each class. As do the Blinn Junior College certificate classes. Of course, for women who are already educated, such as myself, most of these classes are not available to take, or even valuable. If the purpose is to help prisoners become better equipped to go back into society, why is that not happening, or being made a priority?

Mostly what I saw was women finding more ways to break the rules, and getting more frustrated with the system. For example, I saw a lot of women who took things from the kitchen. They do so to survive. These women do not have a family that puts money on their commissary accounts, putting money on our books as we called it in prison. These women are forced to make ends meet, by stealing from the kitchen, and selling the items to others, in exchange for commissary items.

Prison jobs start at twelve cents per hour. Women working at these twelve cents per hour jobs are paid roughly $10 or less per month. Even clerk positions, the highest-level job on the compound, paid no more than $50-$60 per month. If someone worked at Unicor, the prison industry, they could make much more. However, white collar prisoners were not allowed to work at Unicor, if anything to do with their crime was done using a computer. Since I was accused of using QuickBooks to commit a crime, I was not allowed to work at Unicor. Ironically, I was asked by the prison staff to teach QuickBooks classes to the other ladies. Go figure! Backwards on Purpose for sure!

I didn't see much in prison that was benefiting society at all. I had family and a home to go back to, so for someone like me, there is hope. I didn't need the classes. In fact, prison caused me to be a worse person, given how the psychological strain of being locked up, and away from my family, played on my mental health. Not to mention, the "rule-breaking," I learned how to do in order to survive. For example, we were only allowed to exchange our sheets and blankets once a month for fresh ones. I change my sheets weekly at home. I found the once-a-month time frame unsanitary.

So, what did I do? I paid $5 to another prisoner who worked in the laundry, with commissary items, to bring me clean sheets, and blankets, every other week. This was actually breaking a rule because you cannot give other prisoners anything of value, the commissary, I exchanged for the sheets and blankets. I broke this same rule of "not giving another inmate anything of value," every time I shared commissary with my roommates, or cooked a meal for them, using items I had purchased from the commissary. Most of these rules are not enforced by staff, and they turn a blind eye.

I also broke the "anything of value rule," because I frequently supported the underground prison economy. I paid $20 per month to have my uniforms ironed. Another $5 was paid for a mop bucket pedicure, and $3 for a commissary bowl manicure. I paid $3 to have my eyebrows threaded. And $5 to have my room cleaned once a month, when it was my week to clean. I could have ironed my own clothes, and cleaned my own room.

However, I knew that by paying to have these things done, I helped other ladies who did not get money on their commissary accounts. I often shared my commissary snacks with many other women, again, breaking a rule. I purchased items for others with my commissary money to give to them, because I did not like seeing ladies do without needed items. Therefore, my kindness towards others was actually breaking the rules. I often bought ice cream for other women, because I felt terrible that they never had commissary money to get their own ice cream. Again, this also breaks a rule.

There isn't a lot to look forward to in prison, but the weekly commissary list was one of those things. It was the highlight of the week for most women. Each week there would be different items to choose from, including snacks and ice cream flavors. When there were new hygiene and beauty items on the list, it was very exciting, even though these times mostly amounted to high price dollar store brands. New styles of tennis shoes that became available were a big deal, as women want to look stylish, even if they are in prison.

And women from one unit often purchased something for their friend in another unit if the item was thought to sell out quickly, and the friend went to the commissary earlier in the week. You just traded out with each other in commissary items, for the amount your friend had purchased for you, earlier in the week. Everyone wanted the new items. It was just something to look forward to. Each unit went to the commissary on a different day of the week. This rotated monthly.

When there were limits placed on commissary items, it was not uncommon for ladies to buy items for each other and trade them. In this way, you could obtain more than one of each item that had a limit. For example, I love Cheetos. When the commissary had Cheetos, I would purchase another type of chip for another lady, to trade them for getting me a bag of Cheetos. I never understood why the prison placed a limit of one on bags of chips? The same thing happened when there were special items that one person may not want, but another lady may want multiples of. You just found someone to buy you the extra item and they told you what to get them on commissary in exchange.

The weekly ice cream flavors were always a highlight of the week for me. It's funny that I'm not a big ice cream eater in the free world, but in prison it was something to look forward to each week. I had friends in the other units on the compound, and we would purchase ice cream for each other. In this way, you were able to have ice cream more than one day a week. We helped each other out in these ways. It really was a sisterhood. A bond amongst women.

Many women I served time with were not as fortunate as me. I knew these women needed a new way of life. They needed to learn a new career that would keep them from reverting back to selling drugs. Unfortunately, I did not see the prison addressing most of these needs. Women often told me when they came back to prison, after being violated from supervised release, that they were forced to go back to selling drugs once they returned home. They had no family support, and no legal means to support themselves. Some women told me that a prison job was the first real job they had ever worked.

And honestly, most of the ladies I met at the camp would have benefited from being at home on an ankle monitor, reporting to a probation officer, working and paying their fines or restitution, and raising their children. Women need job training and there needs to be more job training programs in the community, that would help women learn a skill or a trade, so they can do legal work. These programs could be made to be part of a home confinement sentence. This would actually serve a better purpose for society. Non-violent offenders who are not a threat to society, should not be serving time in prison.

This country should implement more community programs that teach those who commit crimes the needed skills to stay out of prison. The money being wasted housing non-violent people could be used to train them in a career. The CARES Act has proven that home confinement programs actually work. And in a community setting, women can get the needed medical care and mental health treatment many need.

Instead, I saw women locked up with health issues, and psychological issues, that went unaddressed. The mistreatment I witnessed did not make them better people, and certainly did not make society better. Remember, most federal prisoners will evidently be back in society, and will become your neighbors and possibly co-workers. Shouldn't society want better for these individuals? Instead, taxpayers pay approximately $40,000 or more, per year, for each of these women, for the BOP to house them. If you consider the ones in wheelchairs, walkers, getting daily insulin shots, or who have major health issues, the yearly cost is undoubtedly much, much higher.

The BOP is basically a human warehouse. Wouldn't society be better served using the $40,000 per year to educate people using community programs? Our criminal justice system is begging to be reformed. It's a system that is failing both the prisoner and society. Isn't it time we do something different? As a country, we are locking up far too many people, and it is not making our society any safer. I saw it first hand, and data and statistics support what I am saying.

Another thing that seemed backwards on purpose to me, was that BOP staff did not place prisoners in jobs that utilized their skill sets. The obtaining of jobs in prison felt more like a political arrangement, or popularity contest. If you knew someone who worked at a job, they could put in a good word for you to be hired, regardless of your skillset. And many ladies got jobs that only required them to work a few hours a day, or on the weekends only, therefore, wasting lots of time during the week doing nothing but laying around the unit. I felt it was teaching people to be lazy, and non-productive. What a waste of taxpayer dollars.

Prison is full of stress and anxiety. Fortunately, with my counseling training, I used coping skills during my time in prison, to deal with many issues that cause anxiety, and stress, to prisoners. Still yet, to this day, I suffer from the trauma of prison, from things that happened during my incarceration. I came home with high anxiety and PTSD. But what about prisoners who don't have those skills? Many women suffer much worse mental health issues from their time in prison, due to the inability to cope. Prison causes mental and financial strain on the families of those who are incarcerated. Every time a lady showed me photos of their children being raised by others, children whom I knew most likely longed for their parents, I just wanted to cry. My heart hurt so bad for them.

One of the hardest things at visitation was watching children cling to their mothers, and beg them to come with them. And don't expect guards to care, or have any compassion or empathy, for the child. Correctional staff quickly told the woman that they could not hug or hold their children that long. It was hard to watch. I was thankful my children were mostly all grown adults.

When I first got to prison, I often laid in my bed, on my kindergarten mat for a mattress, which caused you to lay directly on steel that hurt every part of your body, causing one's health to go downhill, laying on my threadbare sheets, covered with my threadbare blanket, and leaning up against my very flat pillow made out of some sort of folded pillow made out quilt batting material, and thought about the waste that is prison.

Every time I looked down at the old clothing I was wearing, along with the stretched-out neck on the T-shirts, I tried to imagine how many women had worn those same clothes, or slept on those same sheets and blankets. I wondered if those women also cried or felt sick to their stomachs? I wondered if the medical staff also ignored their medical conditions, and told them that the BOP does not allow prisoners to have certain medicines, such as the anti-inflammatory medicine that I had been on for years, that the BOP would no longer allow me to have.

Or the fact that I showed the BOP staff the ever-changing pre-cancer places on my body, that they choose to ignore, even though my dermatology records told them, that I need to see the doctor, every six months for these places. Places that would later turn out to be skin cancer, when I was finally able to get to the doctor, once I was released to home confinement, and was able to take myself to be treated. I wondered how many women the BOP had made go cold turkey off their anti-depressant medicine, something dangerous, and proven to cause suicidal thoughts, in some. Yet something I saw the BOP do repeatedly when women would arrive at the camp.

I wondered how many other ladies had served time for crimes they did not commit? Or if they got railroaded by some overzealous United States Attorney? I wondered how they felt when guards and other staff members spoke to them as if they did not matter in the world? I wondered if they had family and friends that supported them, or if they were forced to face the nightmare alone? I wondered how many years they were locked up for, having their life go downhill with no hope for their future?

These are sobering questions that I often thought about while serving time. I worried about the other women. I worried about their future. And I knew that when I got out of prison, I had to do something to change the system that enslaves the masses. I would become a voice for the voiceless. I promised myself, and other ladies, that I would expose the system and advocate for them. I would not leave them behind, hopeless, and alone. I wanted better for them, even if some of them did not seem to want better for themselves. Prison is full of broken people.

But while I was enslaved to the system myself, I worked to make my own prison life more comfortable. I purchased bags of poly-fill from the commissary. I used it to stuff my pillow and in between my mattress and sheets. The joke in the unit was that I had a pillow top mattress. Obviously, this took a lot of work. I had to constantly re-fluff the poly-fill, as sleeping on it would mash it flat, and cause it to become balled up in knots. I had about ten bags of the poly-fill in my bed. I also had to work hard to hide it, by making my bed very tight each day. I had it down to a science.

There was no rule that prevented me from using poly-fill in

this manner, but I always worried it would be taken from me by staff, who often just made up their own rules. And had it been found out by a guard, I'm sure it would have been. Somehow, even with all the times my room was shaken down, I never lost my poly-fill. But every time I would hear that our room was being shaken down, or that there was a unit shake down, the first thing I would think about was my bedding.

I did not have any other contraband, except extra blankets. Extra blankets I paid a laundry worker to bring me. There were times it was so cold in our unit that women slept with winter coats and other clothing items on to stay warm. Those blankets made it bearable. The poly-fill and the extra blankets were small comforts that made my prison life better. When I left Bryan, I left the poly-fill to my bunkie, Rhonda, so she could have the same comfortable bed.

Many organizations that fight for prisoner rights send newsletters, or other information into the prison via CorrLinks. Many times, the BOP blocks these organizations, to limit the information a prisoner can receive. The BOP also chooses what news channels are available, and CNN was the one that was constantly on in our unit. On January 3, 2019, I read one of the newsletters I received from an attorney that sent his same newsletter into all the federal prisons. I had almost been in prison for a year by this time. In the newsletter, I saw that my appeal had been denied.

I had not heard this news from my own attorney, nor did I ever hear it from him. But I did get the order a few weeks later, from the Eighth Circuit Court of Appeals. I had appealed the issue of not being allowed to tell the jury that all the financial evidence and my work computer had been destroyed by the doctors. By this time, I really did not care any longer. I had lost hope in proving my innocence, and truthfully, in our criminal justice system as a whole, and honestly, by this point, I was just tired of the fight with the government, and almost emotionally numb anyway.

On that day, I resigned myself to making the most of prison, by helping as many women as I could, while I was still there.

I took my focus off of getting out on appeal, and decided to focus on what changes I could make, for the better of others. I knew that soon, I would walk out from behind those walls, back to my comfortable life. I would be greeted by a husband that cherishes me, and loves me unconditionally. I wanted to leave prison better than I found it, for all the women there, and the many others I knew would come after I was gone.

I prayed about it constantly, and discussed it with my husband, when he would come to visit me. He told me how much he supported my efforts. But at times, he was also scared for me, as I took on the system from the inside. Regardless, we agreed, that I would be an advocate for criminal justice reform, when I returned home.

Chapter Twenty-Nine
Prison Visits

I was fortunate that many people came to visit me in prison. My husband has always been my biggest supporter. He drove the eight hours one way, roughly every four to six weeks, to visit me for Saturday and Sunday. He would take off work on Friday, make the drive down, and stay in a hotel for two nights, just so he could see his wife. This meant sitting on hard plastic chairs, having his every move watched by guards, and eating bad vending machine food, for a few hours of time with his spouse. It also meant agreeing to be searched before entering the prison, if the guards were inclined to do so, and having his rights greatly restricted.

As an example, he was not allowed to have his wallet, cell phone, or other personal items. These items must be left in the car. His clothing choices were also restricted, as he was not allowed to wear khaki pants and many other pieces of clothing of his choice, including a jacket. He was allowed to bring in a clear plastic baggie with only $40 in cash, a credit card, and his driver's license. Even if it was 100 degrees outside, he had to leave his cell phone in the car.

He would usually get to the prison at 8:00 a.m., so I could be the first person up to the visitation room, and have as much time with him as possible. Me coming to the visitation room meant waiting in line, and being searched before being allowed into the visit. Most of the time staff started visitation at least 30 minutes late. Regardless, Pancho was always there waiting to be one of the first people in the gate. He visited from 8:00 a.m. – 5:00 p.m. on Saturday. He would then spend the night in the hotel again. He often went out to dinner, to bookstores, or to the movies on Saturday night.

The following morning, on Sunday, he would be back at the prison early, so I could be one of the first people called to visit.

He started out staying from 8:00 a.m. – 4:00 p.m. on Sunday when I was new to prison, and later from 8:00 a.m. – 2:00 p.m., once I was acclimated to being incarcerated. And then after I had been there for a bit of time, I started making him leave by 11:00 a.m. or 12:00 p.m., at the latest. As my anxiety was always high when he left because I worried about him getting home safely. He had to drive eight-hours back home on Sunday, so he could work on Monday. That meant being on the road by himself, many times after dark, depending on the time of year.

I would have felt guilty had something happened to him while he made those long drives to visit me. Recently on a trip I made to Texas, I made that same drive back from Bryan, I certainly had a new appreciation for my husband that day. It is not a good drive, and some of the roads are less than desirable. It is sad that women are most often housed further than men from home, due to the limited number of facilities housing women in the federal system.

I remember the first time Pancho came to visit. I was so nervous and excited. It actually felt like a first date. Because he dropped me off at prison during the height of tax season, it was over two months before he was able to visit me for the first time. Honestly, I probably needed this time to get acclimated to prison and get myself together, mentally, before he visited.

A few days before my upcoming visit, one of my roommates informed me that she could not allow me to go to visit with my horrible eyebrows. I guess I had not been paying attention, as it was everything I could do at the time, just to make it through the day. She immediately plucked my eyebrows so that I did not look "horrific," as she put it. I laughed as she told me this.

The kindness of women helping other women was something I saw a lot of while serving time. She even loaned me her makeup to put on for the visit, since I had still not purchased any for myself from the commissary. .I was not worried about it. Pancho and I had been married for a long-time, he knew what I looked like without makeup. I was just anxious to see my husband. The makeup was of such a poor quality that it made my face itch, but I wore it anyway. Another lady tried to offer me her uniform that had been altered to fit better. I declined, but the offer was so sweet, it made me tear up.

I was also fortunate to have my children, friends, and church friends, who made the trip to see me. I understood the commitment they were making to support me through a bad situation. After all, I was eight hours from home, which meant hotel rooms, and long drives, to get to where I was being housed. And of course, Joseph was all the way in New York, so the one time he visited me was certainly unexpected. I had fully expected not to see him during my entire prison time. It was weird though, having one of my children purchase things for me out of the vending machine. I was used to purchasing things for them. I was so happy to see him. And sad that the photographer did not show up for photographs that day. This also happened when Pancho, JT, and Timothy came to see me in December 2018. My first Christmas in prison.

When I had left home for prison, I had originally been adamant that there would be no photos at visitation. I did not want to have proof of my prison experience. That soon changed, as the first time my girlfriends came to visit, they talked me into taking a photo. After that, I always had the photo tickets I purchased from the commissary, so that photos could be taken. And after a while, I was sad when I had a visit and could not get a photo. It actually became one of the ways I documented my time in prison, even though I had originally thought I wanted none of that. I always warned my visitors that their photo may end up in this book. And some of them did.

Visits were important, they gave me a glimpse of home. It took my focus off the day-to-day grind of prison life, and made me feel like a normal person again. We laughed and talked, ate lots of junk food, and I got to hear about all the fun things others were doing in the free world. I enjoyed seeing people and catching up. And time with my family was especially precious.

My girlfriends that came to visit me enjoyed hearing about prison life. They wanted me to tell them funny stories. But as time went on, it was hard to think of things to tell them, as it all became so commonplace. Instead of it being an odd environment, it became my everyday life. The things that struck me as comical, or odd at first, became mundane and ordinary, as time went on. But it was always sad when the visits came to an end. After a while I no longer cried as I walked back to the unit. I had become numb, or maybe I had just buried my emotions, so that I didn't have to feel the pain.

Above: *Lynn with girlfriends, Gina, Jennifer, and Claudia—June 2018, Visitation at FPC Bryan*

 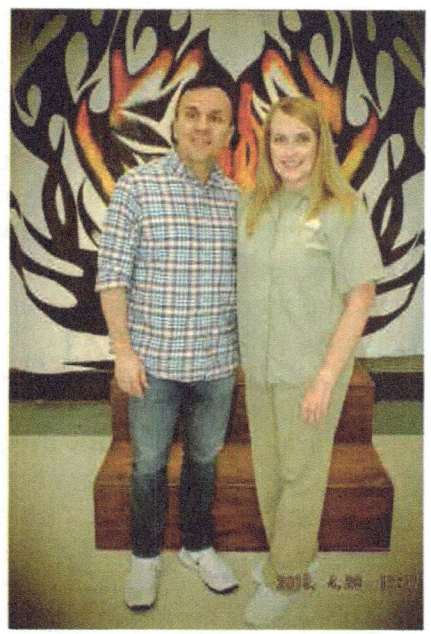

Top Left: *Pancho, Timothy, and Lynn-July 2018, Visitation at FPC Bryan*
Top Right*: Pancho and Lynn-April 2019, Visitation at FPC Bryan*
Below: *Lynn with church friends, Kristy and Tahleigh-January 2019, Visitation at FPC Bryan*

I remember the first time, three of my girlfriends came to visit me, in June, 2018. The three of them that came together. And each one had brought the entire $40 they were allowed to bring into visit with them. They were determined that we were going to eat that much in vending machine food. At the time, it was only my second prison visit. As I had only been in prison a few months, when they came to see me for the first time. It was certainly a fun visit. We laughed so hard that day at all the stories I told them.

And as time went on, and they learned the system, they would have funny things happen at check in with the staff, when they came to visit. One time one of them was made to go change her shoes. These were the same shoes she wore at the previous visit, with no issues. Another time, one of my friends asked the guard "Do you ever smile?" We would often get a good laugh at these things. But it also gave them insight into my new world, when they witnessed things, such as the staff's indifference, to us, and our family, and friends.

As time went on, I stopped crying when Pancho left. I learned to embrace our time together, and look forward to the next visit. It was precious time I spent, just talking for hours with my husband. Something we honestly did not have time to do in the free world, when life seemed so busy. Sitting for roughly nine hours with him on a Saturday, and talking, was magical.

The few minutes outside I could hold his hand was amazing. I honestly believe our relationship grew stronger because of the long talks. As crazy as it may sound, prison made us closer. And I believe the long talks at prison visits contributed to our already strong relationship. We had a good relationship before I left for prison, but I honestly believe it is better now. I'm sure making it through this storm has had a lot to do with that, as well. It changed us, and made us realize just how much we do love each other. It made us appreciate each other more. You know the saying "absence makes the heart grow fonder." I found there really is some truth to that saying, after all.

There was nothing really special about the conversations we had, and they weren't greatly different from free world conversations, but they were focused on each other, with on distractions, unless you count the times I was called away from visitation for count, or when guards would interrupt us to tell me I was not sitting straight forward in the chair. We always talked about where he ate and what he did on Saturday evening, after he left visitation. If he went to the movies, he told me all about the movie he had seen. It was nice hearing about the free world.

Days before his visit, I would email him my list of treats to purchase from the vending machines. This was especially important on Sunday visits, as the vending machines would be low on items to purchase by Sunday, since the machines were only serviced once a week. He always had my microwave popcorn waiting for me when I got to the visit on both mornings.

I love popcorn, and we did not have access to it in prison. It was a special treat, and I would eat it for breakfast during his visits. There were several lunch items I also liked, such as the grilled cheese sandwich, that sold out quickly, so he would have those items waiting for me as well. It is sad to say that vending machine food, equivalent to bad gas station food, brought so much joy to me, but it did. It was something different than what we were fed in the cafeteria, or could purchase on the commissary. And a topic of conversation in the units after visitations was "What did you eat at visit?" Ladies planned their visitation menu, and discussed it with each other. It gave us something to look forward to.

At visitation, Pancho and I often played card games to pass the time, as we were not allowed to talk to other ladies and their families. I always found this so odd, being in a room full of people, maybe even sitting right next to another couple, but not being allowed to speak to them or acknowledge their presence.

If the weather was pretty, we would go outside and walk around, or sit on the picnic tables under the trees. Texas is hot, so it was very uncomfortable for me at times, in the uniforms we were forced to wear, with double shirts, made of non-breathable materials, and long thick khaki pants, and many times it would be too hot for me to stay outside for very long, during the summer months, but I did my best. Being outside meant less guards watching your every move, and I was able to relax a little and enjoy my time with my husband. The visitation rule, once visit ended, was that we were not allowed to look back, wave bye to, or talk to our visitor, if we saw them outside the visitation building. And oftentimes, your visitor would be driving away from the visit, as you were leaving the visitation building, and walking back to the unit.

The parking lot for visitors was next to the visitation building, so depending on how long it took my visitor to get their driver license back, that had to be left with the guard when they checked in to visit, and get to their vehicle, as well as how long it took me to get through the check-out process and get my id back, that was taken from me when I checked in to visit. And depending on how long the line was to leave visitation, or if I was one of the lucky ones, randomly picked to be strip searched, that day. And everyone had to be patted down before they went into, and when they left visitation. But depending on timing, it was possible to see your visitor leaving. If I missed the dreaded strip search, many times I would see my visitor driving away. It was extremely hard not to look at them or wave.

As time went on, I did look back at my husband, and we smiled at each other, and nodded our heads goodbye. At times, I even waved at him as he left. Sometimes, he did not even see me, as I was already down the walkway into the compound, before he made it into my view. I never approached his vehicle though, as this would have been interpreted as an escape attempt, and would have resulted in both of us getting in trouble, as well as my visits taken, or him being banned from visiting me at all. Worse yet, he could have been charged with a federal crime of trying to help me escape.

However, the waving and looking back rule was not actually enforced, as long as you did not get near the vehicle that was leaving, and depending on what staff was on duty at the time. Prison visits kept me sane during my incarceration, they provided needed time with family, and gave me needed glances of home. The strip searches when leaving a visit were worth it to be with my husband, family, and friends.

Chapter Thirty
Personal Losses

I was fortunate to get many cards, letters, books, and photos sent to me while I served time. My neighbor, Pam, who passed away from cancer a few months before I was released, sent me a card every week, up until the last week she was alive. I had not realized how bad her cancer had returned, because nobody had told me. But on the evening, I received her last card, her handwriting was so scribbly, that I could barely read it. I asked Pancho the following morning during our phone call, if she was not doing well? He gave me the sad news that Pam had passed away the night before. I never got to tell her what those cards meant to me in person. But I had sent her a letter before she died, thanking her for her continued support, and telling her how much she meant to me. I looked forward to those cards at mail calls each week, and I felt a huge loss when she died, both from knowing she was gone, and from her encouraging cards.

Before I left home for prison, I was struggling with how to move forward. At that time, Pam told me, "You will be a bright light in a very dark place due to your relationship with Christ." I didn't feel very bright at all. I remember telling her this. Being the very positive person she was, Pam said to me, "Just be a birthday candle until your light can shine bright again." Because of this conversation, she drew a birthday candle in the bottom right-hand corner of the card she sent to me each week. It was a special message just between us. I sure do miss her presence in my life. She was one of a kind. One of the hardest things about prison is being unable to attend special events, such as Pam's funeral. I had no closure when she passed away. I was not able to pay my respects to her, in a normal way, that is meaningful.

During my incarceration, I also missed our youngest son, Timothy's senior year, and high school graduation, our middle son, JT's college graduation, JT and Rachel's engagement, and their wedding, and many other family and special events. These were significantly hard days for me. I am unable to describe the pain I felt in my gut, on days that I knew I was missing major milestones in our children's lives. I wanted to be there to hear Timothy give his Salutatorian speech. I wanted to watch him receive his diploma. I had been there when both Joseph and JT graduated from high school. I was so proud of Timothy. I remember how I cried on the day of his graduation. I felt a great sense of loss, at the exact time I knew he would most likely be receiving his diploma. It felt like someone was punching me in my gut. A prison friend just held my hand, and told me she understood. There was nothing you could really say to each other in those moments.

Prison is full of people suffering their own great losses. I could never compare the things I missed, to women I witnessed lose children while incarcerated. I could not imagine how it would feel, to not be allowed to be at the funeral to say good-bye to one of my children. Yet, my losses were still great to me. JT's college graduation was another day of great loss.

But the loss that hit me the most, was not being at his wedding. I remember the day I received an email from JT, asking me to call him. I felt that he was going to tell me he was getting engaged. I was excited to hear the news. And while that was part of the conversation, he had gotten engaged; there was a second part to the same conversation, that literally left me breathless. They had set a date to get married in September 2019. At the time, I was scheduled to come home in November 2020. I'll never forget the over-whelming sense of loss that came over me in that phone conversation. I felt like someone had taken a knife and stabbed me with it in my stomach. I held it together on the phone, I did not want to upset JT, or rain on his good news.

This was his moment, not mine.

However, the minute I hung up the phone, I broke down in what I can only describe as a gut-wrenching sob. Don't get me wrong, I was extremely happy for him and Rachel. She is an amazing woman, and I was glad that he had found someone that shared the same Christian values as him. And regardless of how I felt, I never let on to JT, just how disappointed I was that he chose to get married before I made it back home. How could I expect their lives not to move forward? Or be put on hold? The pain of knowing I would not be part of that special moment was great, but my love for him was greater. I was happy and broken, all in the same moment. And on the day of his wedding, I felt that great sense of loss and pain again. But all I could do in those moments was pray, and ask God to give me peace.

Pancho tried his best to minimize these losses for me. He was always good about sending me photos, and trying to describe the events to me during our telephone calls, and when he visited. But it was not the same as being there, and I believe it was these moments that started to make me emotionally numb. It is something I still struggle with to this day. I have now been home a little over three years, as I finish writing this book, and I still struggle with my emotional numbness.

I contribute this numbness to being forced to block out so many emotions while in prison, just in order to survive. Otherwise, I don't think I would have made it through prison. My family meant everything to me. It hurt being away from them. Yet these great losses also helped to fuel the anger that continued to grow inside of me. As I felt that these family events had been stolen from me by my own government.

Recently when JT was stuck in the middle of the war that broke out in Sudan, I never cried. I never thought that my son could die. I did not break down, like I would have done, prior to my incarceration. Before prison, I was a person who was emotional, and who wore my feelings on my sleeve. Back then, I still had feelings. In the situation with JT, I remained eerily calm. I even went on an already booked trip to New Orleans regarding my advocacy work, during this same time. I'm sure some people even frowned at me for going. But I felt there was nothing I could do at home, that I could not do from New Orleans. Since all I could do was pray! I do contribute much of most of my calmness to my belief that God would deliver my son from the situation. I trusted God in that moment, and knew he was watching over JT, and the two other pastors, who were stuck in there with him. After all, they were in Sudan, doing God's work. However, I know some of that calmness, can be attributed to the emotional numbness that I still deal with, and may never get over. It is a blessing and a curse. It is trauma from my incarceration.

Of course, Pancho could not remember to tell me everything, while I was away, and he did forget many things. I remember the first time I was allowed to go back to my church, after being released from prison. There were babies I had no idea existed, and marriages I had no idea had taken place. But admittedly, a few minutes a day on the phone, a six-dollar, twenty-five-minute video chat weekly, and monthly in-person visits, did not allow everything to be remembered, or discussed.

But he certainly did his very best. I was only allowed 300 minutes a month to talk on the phone, even though I was required to pay twenty-one cents per minute for the calls. I divided those minutes out by the days of the month, just to make sure I never went a day without hearing Pancho's voice. Hearing his voice each day made the days away from him bearable. But the limited minutes meant we had very little time on the phone to discuss things. Because I was so diligent about planning out my minutes, I never ran out of minutes like many of the women did.

When I returned home, one of the hardest, and most gut-wrenching things for me, was when my family would talk about things they had done while I was away, or that had happened at church while I was gone. It was as if I was living on the outside of my life, like an outsider just looking in. I remember feeling like I was not really part of my family in those moments, because I did not have the same experiences, or the same memories, as they did, for more than two years.

I was happy that their lives had not stopped, but I was sad for myself that I had missed so much and had not been a part of those special memories. I missed two of all the major holidays with them, such as Christmas and Thanksgiving and their birthdays. I missed three Easters, three of JT's birthdays, three mother's days, and three of Pancho's birthdays, as well as many other special events. I made sure I sent cards, and had video chats on major holidays, birthdays, and special life events, but it's not the same.

My family experienced things that I was not a part of, and they share those memories, which I do not have. As time has gone on, we have made new memories together. I try to focus on those, instead of all the ones I missed. But it is still hard sometimes. And I do feel significant losses at not having been at those special events. It's hard seeing the photos and knowing I missed so much.

While I was away, my husband worked hard to keep many of our family traditions alive. He took the obligatory first day of senior year school photo, that I reminded him I must have, and mailed me a copy. He did his best at gifts for special occasions. I had always been the one to handle these things. And he and our children made new traditions without me. For example, while I was away, Timothy decorated for Christmas each year. I remember seeing their trees in our video chats and laughing at their creativity. I was sad I was not there, but happy they lived their lives to the fullest.

I loved hearing the story of how Pancho placed $100 bills on the Christmas tree for the girlfriends to find, as their Christmas presents. I laughed at his ingenious idea. And in this way, I had glimpses of their daily life. I took solace that they were doing well in my absence. Pancho was a supportive father, regardless of what he was dealing with in my absence.

When I left for prison, he was forced to do everything for our home. Tasks that had been handled by two people, now had to be handled by one. I know this was hard on him. And Timothy, at age 16, stepped up and began cooking, and grocery shopping, to help out. I was so thankful at least one of our sons was still living at home. But I was also mindful that Timothy would be leaving for college, before I was released from prison. I constantly worried about how this would affect Pancho, when he found himself truly alone.

I genuinely believe it is harder on the family members left behind, than the person serving the time. Certainly, the daily struggles are much different. I was able to go to a new environment, where nothing there reminded me of my family, or the home we shared. My family was stuck at a house that had been decorated by me, had constant reminders of me everywhere they looked, and even still had all my personal belongings in the closet. They had to go on with everyday life, as if everything was fine, to keep things moving. I was in a strange place with new experiences. I did not have the constant reminders of the person who had been abruptly taken from my life, except the way my heart constantly missed, and longed for them.

I know God brought us through this chapter; this season of life. It is the only way my family would have survived this life storm. God was with us. I am thankful for our strong faith in HIM. I know HE not only walked us through the dark valley, but HE also carried me as I climbed back up the mountain. When I felt I could not go on at times, HE was always there, faithful. Even when I was not. When I was angry, God was still there. When I lashed out at HIM, he stayed.

Colossians 3:15 tells us, "And let the peace of Christ rule in your hearts, to which indeed you were called in one body. And be thankful." My family found ways to have peace in the situation we found thrust upon us, with HIS help. We were thankful for our many blessings, even in the midst of this storm.

We knew that it would come to an end soon enough, and I

would return home. We looked forward to that day. It was always looming just out of reach, but the light at the end of the tunnel shone brighter, as time went on. It was getting closer to the end of my prison journey with each day that passed. And not a day went by that I did not think about my family, and my home. I could not wait to be home with them again.

Chapter Thirty-One
Prison Corruption and Retaliation For Speaking Up

During my time in prison, I became well known for my reporting of, and blogging about, the corruption I saw. However, I even drew the line at reporting, or blogging, about some things. I never wanted to call out things that would hurt another prisoner. Therefore, I saw a lot of staff corruption and rule violations that I never blogged about or reported, for that very reason alone. As an example, I knew that the Head of The Education Department, Ms. V., as well as other educational staff members, such as Mr. C., often brought in food and other goodies from the outside, to give to their prisoner workers.

Ms. V. was even well known for throwing birthday parties for her favorite prisoners. It was not a secret on the compound. By law this could have resulted in the staff member being charged with a federal crime, for introducing contraband into the prison, or at the very least, could have resulted in them losing their cushy federal jobs. Especially, if I had been willing to blog about or report it.

One evening when I went to my shared reentry office in the education building, I caught my good friend Retta with a wing bag from a freshly eaten meal. I did not confront her, even though I knew that Ms. V. had certainly brought her the meal. I didn't ask because I really didn't want to know. In a way, I was a hypocrite in those moments. And because of my commitment not to blog about these things, I often found myself in a dilemma between my desire to expose the staff corruption I saw in federal prison, and the love I had for my fellow prisoners. It was a constant battle of good vs. evil.

I didn't blog or report something, even when it was against the rules and regulations, if doing so would hurt another prisoner. And I didn't care that ladies were provided with special treats that I did not get. I was happy for them. However, I was always angry at the staff that violated the rules. This anger came from deep inside of me.

What they were doing was a crime. They worked for the same federal government that had placed me in prison for crimes I had not committed. Yet, I watched over and over again, as the very individuals responsible for my supposed rehabilitation, broke the rules and committed crimes themselves. The irony was not lost on me. And I struggled greatly in these moments.

Nine months into my incarceration, I was admitted to the cosmetology program. Up until that time, I had worked as a clerk in the reentry department. While in reentry, I had an office to go to each day, with a computer I worked on. It was a retreat from the loud noises in the unit, and I cherished the time away. We only worked from 8:00 a.m. - 10:00 a.m., and then again from 12:30 p.m. - 3:00 p.m., on Monday through Friday, so the weekends were long and boring unless I had a visit. Sometimes our job would be cut short during the week, if the staff member supervising the job was absent from work or left early that day. I looked forward to going to my job. In my job, I was able to help other women with resumes and reentry resources.

I enjoyed helping the other women. I felt God using me in a positive way. I also shared the office with someone who became a wonderful friend. It was nice to share my days with her. Retta and I still talk on the phone most days, even now that we are both home from prison. She and I both have a strong Christian faith, and we often prayed together in that office. On the office television that hung on the wall, we watched Christian movies we checked out from the Chapel library. We shared our faith in God, and discussed my Pastor's sermons that were mailed to me each week, from my church. And we often talked about our plans for the future, about going home. Most everyone in prison talks about going home.

Retta's situation was undoubtedly worse than mine. Her husband was also serving time in prison, having been charged in Retta's case. He, like me, had gone to trial and lost. She could not talk to him on the phone each day or hear his voice, because they were both incarcerated. I understood how hard this must be for her, from just my first night in prison, when I could not call Pancho. But I could not imagine not hearing my husband's voice for years. Some days, the phone calls to Pancho were all that got me through the day. Retta's husband could not come to visit her, or have video chats with her, like I had with Pancho. He was not able to place money on her commissary account. He could only communicate with her by way of letters.

I knew I was fortunate. But hearing other women's stories often made me realize just how blessed I am. And I believe in this way, God often reminded me of everything HE had provided. And many times, HE used me to help and bless other women. Working in the reentry office with Retta, was also a time of healing for me. And because of our shared love of God, during this time in my prison life, HE was the center of my daily focus. I started to feel some of the anger leave me during that time.

One of the coolest things about sharing my pastor's sermons with Retta, was that she also shared them with her husband. She would mail them to him at his prison in South Carolina. He in turn shared them with other prisoners. We heard stories of P. Rod's sermons being mailed to spouses of the men Retta's husband shared with, who were serving time at other prisons, and how the sermons were used for bible studies in many prisons, throughout the BOP. It seemed my pastor was preaching to the masses in the prison system, as Retta was not the only person, I shared them with. There were many ladies that wanted to get a copy.

I spent so much on copy cards, paying for copies, that I finally asked my husband to start sending me six copies each week. I had a black notebook with a sticker on the spine titled *P. Rod's Sermons*, that I kept in the reentry office. Many times, other ladies would check out the notebook to read the weekly message. It often floated around the compound, and was used for bible studies by others. One woman even asked me for a copy of the sermons so she could take them home, to do bible studies with her children, upon her release.

The months I spent in the reentry office with Retta, were the best months of my incarceration. I had mixed feelings about leaving the job to take cosmetology classes. I was sad and nervous to leave the office I shared with her. I felt peace in that space, and felt God used me, and worked in me, in those moments each day. At the same time, I was also excited about the cosmetology classes, and to learn all about hair, having always had an interest in the subject. I did not know what my future would hold, or if I would be readmitted to my graduate classes, once I was released. I wanted a backup plan just in case, a plan B, so to speak. With my previous education, cosmetology was almost the only available program for me in prison.

There were approximately 100 ladies who interviewed in hopes of being accepted to the next class. I was one of the 25 women selected. It was a great opportunity since taking cosmetology classes would cost roughly $15,000, if taken in the free world. The prison received a federal grant to teach the classes to us, which made the classes free for me to take. The hours were being reported to the State of Texas, and I would leave prison with my cosmetology license. I was so excited to be included in the next class.

Unfortunately, only two months into the program, my dreams were shattered when I went to talk to my instructor about the incorrect hours, we were being asked to sign off on paperwork each day, which I knew to be incorrect. I also noticed that the electronic time clock was clocking more hours of class time each day than I knew to be true. I did not feel comfortable participating in this signing-off for hours that I knew I had not actually been in class. I was already serving time for a fraud charge I had not committed. I had learned that ignoring *red flags,* and turning a blind eye to unethical behavior, brought grave consequences. I had vowed to never put myself, and especially not my family, in harm's way again, in this manner.

Because the classes were paid for with federal grant money, I felt confident reporting fraudulent hours was a crime. I also suspected that since the hours were being reported to the State of Texas, some sort of state crime may also be committed, if I signed the fraudulent paperwork. I told the instructor that I did feel comfortable signing off on hours that were not correct, and was afraid that doing so was a crime. The instructor laughed and then advised me, "You have no choice." "That is how the program works." "It's the only way to get enough hours to get your license." She said, "Who will know about the hours unless you tell someone?" "This is how the class has always been run." I was stunned.

I walked away in disbelief. And I knew God would know, regardless if anyone else knew or not. During my time in the reentry office, I focused on trying hard to get my anger under control, to let go of it, and focus on a stronger relationship with HIM. Up to this point, I still had not come to the revelation that I was still holding on to revenge, and non-forgiveness, for those who had wronged me. That revelation would not come until years later.

But I knew that the toll of my last year at home, with prison being held over my head, had truly broken me. I had been angry with God, many times, for what I saw as HIM allowing me to go through that season. I had not been able to understand how HE would allow one of HIS children to be found guilty of a crime that had not been committed. Of course, this was irrational thinking, given what the Bible tells us, and I knew it.

During my time in the reentry office, I had felt God healing me, and my relationship with HIM growing stronger again. Now I faced a new dilemma. Would I turn a blind eye once again to the wrongdoing of others? Or stand up for what I knew was right? What was God trying to teach me? I was so confused. Was HE testing me in some way? I was being presented with a huge obstacle, because going against a staff member was not something a prisoner was supposed to do. But I knew there was no way I was going to go against my morals. I would not compromise on those ever again.

The cosmetology instructor was contracted from outside the prison to teach the classes. I thought maybe there was some mistake, or misunderstanding, on her part. Or maybe I was mistaken on how the hours we clocked worked? As part of our class materials, we had been given the Texas Department of Licensing and Regulation (TDLR) handbook to study. While back at the unit that evening, I scoured the handbook for information and realized that what I had suspected was actually correct.

The reporting of incorrect hours was not an acceptable practice, and to get your license, you had to clock 1500 actual hours in class. I prayed about the situation. I was fearful about reporting this issue to the Head of Education. But the more I prayed, the more I heard God telling me, "Do the right thing and report the issue." A few days later, I talked to the Head of the Education Department, Ms. V., who was the person responsible for the program. I was shocked that she did not care for my views and told me, "Maybe you are not cut out for the class."

A few days after my conversation with Ms. V., the medical department staff told the cosmetology instructor that my rotator cuff issue would preclude me from being in cosmetology. I had the same rotator cuff issue since 2009, over nine years before I was incarcerated. There was no way it was an issue that would prevent me from cutting hair! Never mind that medical staff had signed off, and cleared me medically, before my admittance to the classes. Once again, my anger surged. I knew what was happening.

Staff was protecting other staff in their corruption. Shortly after medical staff made their recommendation, Ms. V. paid me a visit to my unit, where I was informed that I had been removed from the cosmetology program. I was in shock! I chose to do the correct and ethical thing, and what was most likely even the correct legal thing, and I was being penalized. It was another one of my "Why God?" moments, and another time I became angry at HIM, all over again. I couldn't understand.

I prayed about it that night. The following day I went to the education department to talk to Ms. V. to see if she would admit me back to class. She told me she was standing firm in her decision, and had already picked my replacement for the program. I told her right there on the spot that she was leaving me no choice but to report the issue of the fraudulent cosmetology hours to the DOJ, and start an Administrative Remedy to ask the regional office to be put back into the classes. She frankly told me, "You are an inmate, and you will not be believed." I left the education department that day, determined to prove her wrong. Little did I know what all I was about to endure, due to my resolve to not back down.

Sometimes I wonder if all the battles I fought were necessary? In my criminal case, as well as during my time in prison, I let my anger, at being accused of, and convicted of a false crime, cause me to have a distinct need to prove what was right. Most likely due to control issues I had yet to resolve. Many times, my resolve to prove the truth, dictated the decisions I made. But on that day, I walked back to the unit from the education department, determined to take on the battle, intending to prove who was in the right. And I was fueled by great anger in that moment. True to my word, I wrote Ms. V. up, using the Administrative Remedy process available to prisoners.

I also sent an email to the Warden to alert her to the staff fraud taking place under her watch. I made the Warden aware that unless she placed me back in the cosmetology classes, my goal would be to write the compound up three times weekly, for all of its policy violations, and inhumane treatment of prisoners. I'm not sure the Warden believed me. However, she did nothing to correct the situation, so I spent a lot of time in the law library, for the next few months, learning BOP policy.

And I managed most weeks to meet my goal of three Administrative Remedies for policy violations. During this time, I felt a lot of angst. Admittedly, I may have brought this on myself, when I decided to take on this battle. I prayed about the situation, but really felt no peace. I felt far from God, and I probably was during this season. And looking back, maybe I should have just moved on, and not stood up for what I felt was right. But those *red flags* I had ignored in my past, always tugged at my memory. What if I had done things differently then? Maybe I would not be where I am now? That question haunted me.

And because I had turned a blind eye to the fraud and unethical behavior at the doctors' office, and knew what that had cost my family and me, maybe the battles I took on in prison was my way of redeeming myself? Or maybe it was due to my anger at the government? I was undoubtedly conflicted during this time. My resolve to fight the system, certainly came at a significant cost to my daily peace and relationship with God. And because of that resolve, I was retaliated on by staff many times for the battles I was waging.

As an example, staff began to write incident reports on me that they knew to be false. Staff wrote three false "shots,' 'as prisoners refer to incident reports, to me within weeks of each other. The shots accused me of violating rules and were for blogging, being out of bounds while going to the bathroom in the education department, and the most egregious one for "threatening staff." The incident report for threatening staff said I was threatening the writing of Administrative Remedies against Ms. V., the head of the education department, and was signed by her. It was a lie and she and I both knew I never threatened her.

It was true that I was writing administrative remedies, but it was my right by BOP policy to do so. And my anger grew stronger, as I used the BOP's own policy against staff, to beat the false shots. Each time, I won, my room was "shook down," and my personal property was searched and thrown about my cell. I was thrown into the Solitary Housing Unit (SHU), inside the lieutenant's office several times, and berated by staff more times than I care to remember. I would file another Administration Remedy each time this happened, against the staff violating my rights. And my resolve to beat the system, and my anger, grew stronger with each of these incidents.

Unbeknownst to staff, they were creating a monster inside of me. That monster grew, with all my might to expose what was the BOP, and its corruption. This was long before I had decided to be an advocate. This happened in the Fall of 2018. Only nine months into my prison sentence.

I also reported these actions by staff to one of my state senators, John Boozman. My husband even met with the Senator's staff, and provided them with the documents I mailed home. At my request, my husband requested a letter from the orthopedic doctor, who had treated my torn rotator cuff for nine years, before I reported to prison. The letter stated that I had no restrictions, and there was no reason I could not complete a cosmetology course. I used the letter as an exhibit to my Administrative Remedy, regarding my removal from the cosmetology classes. And I was emailing the Senator's staff directly from the BOP monitored CorrLinks email system. I wanted the BOP staff to know everything I was reporting on them. I began to blog frequently about the staff corruption I witnessed, and the staff retaliation against me.

But looking back, this was about more than what I was experiencing in prison. And in reality, I had not yet healed from the long battle I fought against the United States Attorney's Office, in the Eastern District of Arkansas, for seven years, trying to clear my name. The anger I felt at times was all-consuming. And honestly, sometimes I wasn't even sure who I was angry at? Was it God? AUSA Harris? Dr. Swan? Myself? BOP Staff? The system in general? I was certainly conflicted, and lost during these times. I knew my actions were not biblical, but I could not make myself stop, no matter how hard I prayed. The anger had taken control of me. I was angry deep in the core of my very soul. Looking back, I think I wanted vengeance for the wrongs that had been committed against me. I just didn't realize it at the time.

The staff corruption and mistreatment of prisoners that I have reported in this book is honest and real. It happens every day in prisons across our nation. It is certainly something I want to continue speaking out about, and hopefully, help to change. Some days it's a balance when I go to help others battling the exact system, I was caught up in for so many years. And that I still find myself a part of due to the restitution I owe.

As an advocate, I never want to encourage the people I help, to take the route I took while in prison. It was a hard road to hoe. And oftentimes I use the story of my incarceration as a cautionary tale, when I talk to families and prisoners about the battles they choose to take on. But I do believe that sometimes Administrative Remedies is the only way to assure that staff abide by BOP policy. And even then, there is no assurance it will happen. It certainly is a balance, and one I did not have, during my time at FPC Bryan.

And, it would be unfair not to point out the battle that was raging inside my own body, during my time in prison. Looking back, I believe that I felt a strong need to take on the system in a way that was not healthy. I wanted justice. When honestly there is no justice to be found in our federal criminal justice system. At least not in the way it is structured at the present time, for all the reasons I have disclosed in this book. And maybe even what I really wanted was revenge?

During my time in prison, I had no balance between standing up for what was right, and going full force into every battle that came across my path, always fueled with great hatred for the system, and anger at what I had been through. The bible tells us in Romans 12:17, "Never pay back evil with more evil." And in Romans 12:19, "Do not take revenge, my dear friends, but leave room for God's wrath, for it is written:

"It is mine to avenge; I will repay," says the Lord."

Yet there I was again, taking things into my own hands, instead of allowing God to handle them for me. But even in those moments, God was still there trying to reach me. I could always feel HIM, even when I tried not to let him in. And HE always found a way to speak to me, even in my darkest moments. Even when the anger raged deep inside of me, HE kept trying to reach me. I was HIS child, and HE did not leave me.

One night I dreamed that I needed to extend an olive branch to Ms. V. I was conflicted with what I knew was right, and what my anger was telling me to do. But I truly felt like God was speaking to me, through that dream. In the dream, I was to go to her office, and eat crow, so to speak. Something that was extremely challenging for me to do at the time. I was to offer her an apology for how I had been handling the situation, and ask for her forgiveness.

This was a big ask, considering the anger I felt at the time, accompanied with my belief that I was not in the wrong, in my refusal to sign fraudulent paperwork, for hours I was not receiving in cosmetology classes. But reflecting back on that moment now, I realize that God was preparing me for the even bigger ask of forgiveness, that HE would later bring to my table.

At the time, all I could feel was the need for revenge against Ms. V., and I felt the strong need to get it daily. But I was also still trying to rectify my relationship with God. I knew I had gotten off HIS path for my life, and I badly wanted to have the same relationship I had had with HIM in the past. I wanted to feel HIS peace again. The following day, I went to the education department and knocked on Ms. V.'s door.

At first the meeting was not going so well, as Ms. V. was not pleasant to me, so I started to leave her office. That is when I saw God work on her heart as well. Her voice softened, and she asked me to stay. She apologized to me that day for the false incident report she had written on me, the month before. The one that said I threatened her. I had been able to beat the false incident report, but I was still angry and vengeful at her for it. But in that moment, I felt a great peace come over me. God's peace. I accepted her apology. And if I am being honest, I have to say that Ms. V. is not a bad person. We are all sinners, and if not for the grace of God, none of us would be worthy.

I have come to realize that Ms. V. is caught up in a culture that is the BOP. Staff are just human, and they make mistakes too. While I did meet some bad staff during my time in prison, Ms. V. was not actually one of them. She was flawed, just like me. We all make mistakes, we all fall short of God's glory, and HIS plan for our life. From that point forward, I do believe that Ms. V. and I had a better relationship. I believe at that moment, God worked on both of us.

That does not mean that I didn't report the corruption of the cosmetology program when I returned home, as I had promised to do. I felt strongly that I had to report it, if for no other reason, so that women who needed the program would be able to get the hours to actually learn the trade. But I did make peace in that moment, in Ms. V's office, with the situation.

During our conversation that day, in Ms. V.'s office, she told me she did not have a place for me in cosmetology. She promised she would put me back into the classes on the next go around. I told her that in good conscience, I would have to continue my Administrative Remedy to get back in the class. I felt that strongly about it. I had been removed due to no fault of my own. I know she did not like hearing it, but we agreed to just disagree, and find a common ground of respect for each other.

Roughly three months into the process of me writing Administrative Remedies for every little thing the prison was doing wrong, a BOP staff member was sent to "Make a deal with me." She came to the unit one afternoon and called me down to the hallway in front of the staff offices to have a private conversation with me. I respected this staff member, and I have no doubt she was the one given the task of speaking to me for that very reason.

The deal she wanted to make with me was simple: if I was willing to dismiss all my Administrative Remedies, I would be placed back into the cosmetology classes, within days. At the time, I was not aware that the Regional Office of the BOP had ruled in my favor on my Administrative Remedy, and that I would be placed back into the cosmetology classes anyway.

That fact, and paperwork from the Region office, had been withheld from me. So, I agreed to the deal, but only on my terms. I told her that I would receive the original copies of my Administrative Remedies back, and that if anything happened, I would write each one of them again, and there would be no additional deals to dismiss them. I often referred to this conversation as the "deal with the devil." While I greatly respected the staff member who made the deal, the fact that the BOP sent her, knowing I had already won the administrative remedy, was shameful.

And the BOP is certainly the devil for how the staff is allowed to mistreat prisoners. I should have never been removed from the classes to begin with. Even after I made the deal, my anger would often get the best of me. Even though, in the end, I had won. The battle had been mine. But at what great cost?

Sometimes during great fits of anger, I would wish I had just refused the deal, and continued on with my Administrative Remedies against the prison. And in this way, the devil continued to creep into my decisions, in moments of great despair. Looking back now, I see "the deal," as God's way of saving me from myself in that moment. It was HIS mercy and grace that I certainly didn't deserve, but received anyway.

The process of fighting for my rights those months gained me great respect from other ladies on the compound. I became known as the go-to person for BOP policy issues. In this way, God used my knowledge for good, to help women who were in need, and had nobody else to turn to. Many false incident reports, "shots," written to prisoners were beaten using my policy knowledge. Again, this did not sit well with the staff, and I was retaliated against for helping other women. However, I was no longer afraid of the retaliation. The BOP had created a monster in me, and honestly, AUSA Harris had a lot to do with the drive I felt to fight. At that time, I had still not forgiven him either, even though I told myself I had.

And truthfully, I enjoyed learning policy and holding the BOP accountable to its own policy violations. Afterall, I had made the promise to make changes before I left prison. I often had discussions with the Warden, or other staff members, regarding these policies. Often times, these conversations were all it took to bring about change. And I gained the respect of many staff members who saw me as a change maker. Many staff secretly told me I was doing great work, and supported my efforts.

Of course, there were many more staff members that despised my efforts, and did everything in their power to discourage me. I was not deterred by their efforts. I knew I was preparing for the challenges I would take on when I left prison. I was determined to change the system. But for the time being, I promised to do everything I could to hold the BOP accountable for its bad acts, and make changes for the better, before my time inside the walls was done.

Chapter Thirty-Two
Fighting The System From The Inside

Being back in cosmetology classes made my days fly by. I loved learning about hair, and was good with highlights, and several of the haircuts we learned. It gave me purpose for my time, and took me away from prison life, most of the day. The cosmetology room looked and felt like we were at a real salon, that is, until you looked down at the ugly khaki uniform you were wearing.

During this time, I tried to focus on all my blessings. But it was hard because I still saw how corrupt the system was. I often blogged about the corruption, mistreatment, and other policy violations I witnessed. However, I did refrain from writing Administrative Remedies for a few months. Truthfully, I was tired and just needed to rest for a bit.

Even so, I continued to do everything I could to help other women. And so, I continued to be a target of staff, as I fought to change the system from the inside out, and hold staff accountable for the rights of the ladies they violated. I was often thrown in the Solitary Confinement Unit (SHU), that was inside the lieutenant's office, for speaking out. Still, I continued on.

Many of these battles were worth the fight. Many I fought because I could. Many continued to be fueled by my anger at the system. Many of them did bring about needed change, and created positive, and meaningful, policy changes for other women and myself. One of the things I fought for that I am most proud of was a social furlough with my husband. On November 30, 2019, I spent twelve hours with my husband beyond the confines of the prison walls.

Apparently, so the rumor at FPC Bryan goes, I was the first white-collar person known to go on a furlough from the camp. It was a hard-fought battle, but in the end, policy prevailed. My furlough was supported by several staff members, and the Warden. I was surprised when the staff did the correct thing, and followed the policy. However, by this time, I had become well known for winning my Administrative Remedies when staff did violate my rights.

And of course, my furlough created the path for many other women in the same situation, to go on furloughs, with their families too. It felt good in the months that followed, to see other ladies leaving the compound, for a few hours of time with their families. I felt accomplished, knowing that my knowledge of policy forged the way for them to do so. And in this way, many of my battles with the BOP were well worth the heartache, they caused me personally.

I'll never forget the day of my own furlough. On the morning of November 30, 2019, I waited anxiously for my husband to pick me up. I would have twelve hours to be alone with him before I would have to report back to prison. This was the first time I would be alone with my husband since the day he dropped me off at federal prison, on February 26, 2018. It had been one year and nine months, 642 days, and 15,408 hours, since I had been alone with my husband, or in the free world that existed on the other side of the walls, just out of reach from where I had been forced to live. I was actually nervous.

We would only be allowed to be within 150 miles of the prison, so we had already decided to stay in the Bryan/College Station area for the day. I could barely walk, as I was escorted by staff to his car. After being locked up for twenty-one months, I actually got car sick when we first left the prison, and started driving towards the hotel my husband was staying at. I also got overwhelmed at Starbucks, and couldn't figure out what to order. Those who know me personally, know about my Starbucks addiction. My husband was surprised that I only wanted one Grande, medium sized,

Starbucks during the twelve hours. But things of the free world had become foreign to me, and I had actually learned to live without them. Since my return home, I've gotten back to my old habit of frequent Starbucks runs.

Pancho was thoughtful enough to bring me lots of products from home to use for a nice shower, and to shampoo my hair. Just showering in a clean, mold-free shower, using products of my own choice, and my own hair dryer, was an amazing treat. A few hours of peace and quiet was an added bonus. And, of course, there is no replacement for spending twelve hours alone with your spouse. Eating real food was also a treat, and I was even able to find time to get a professional manicure and pedicure that day, in a real nail salon, not a prison bathroom, using a mop bucket, with a contraband trash bag.

I didn't even mind the strip search when I returned to prison that evening. In fact, I demanded it, because I knew it was policy. I was told by staff on duty that it was not necessary. But I would not budge, I did not want it to be used against me later, or against another prisoner to prevent furloughs. It took two hours for a female staff member to be found to do the strip search and urine drug screen.

Unfortunately, not everything about the furlough was positive. Being in the free world has made me realize the level of anxiety I now suffer from. When my husband and I went to the mall that day, I felt out of sorts, and had to leave. Everyday things, like restaurants, had made me anxious.

When I returned to prison that evening, I was refreshed and ready to fight another day. Little did I know at the time, the fight that was about to come my way, in just a few short months. As 2019 ended, and 2020 came into view, I was glad to see another year arrive. It was the year that I would be going home to my family, and it felt so good to know that this part of my journey would be coming to an end in a few short months. I could not wait to be home with my family again. I longed for my church, and couldn't wait to hear one of P. Rod's sermons in person, instead of reading them on paper each week.

In late December 2019 and early January 2020, I began to report and blog about the Prison Rape Elimination Act (PREA) violations I saw happening at FPC Bryan. At the time, our Chaplin, and our Captain, which I did not know about at the time, and many other staff members were having sex with prisoners. This is not only a violation of policy, but is a violation of federal law, since staff are not allowed to have sex with prisoners, even if the act is consensual. And one lady had come to me for my help, and what she described to me made me sick to my stomach. What she described had happened to her, sounded like sexual assault at the hands of our Supervisory Chaplin at the time.

Because of my blogging, I was retaliated against, and my room was again "shook down," several times, with officers taking my commissary and throwing me in the lieutenant's office SHU. I was not deterred. I was no longer afraid of what staff would do to me, so I continued to speak out about the violations, and even contacted the DOJ PREA hotline. I was threatened with "diesel therapy," by staff, if I did not take back my reporting of the PREA violations. Diesel therapy means you are shipped around, passing through county jails, and the federal transfer center.

In the middle of January 2020, one afternoon, right before the 4:00 p.m. count, I was called to the lieutenant's office. Nobody liked hearing their name being called over the loudspeaker to report to the lieutenant's office. This meant trouble for the person being called. Truthfully by this time in my incarceration, I had been summoned there so many times, and threatened for my speaking out against staff, that I was no longer afraid of going, and actually saw it as a challenge. Looking back, I honestly enjoyed the battle in many unhealthy ways due to my anger.

And by this time, I had become well versed in BOP policy. In fact, I probably knew more policy than most of the staff. I had already used policy to beat the three false incident reports written on me, and helped numerous other ladies beat false incident reports. But sadly, my policy knowledge was also often used to taunt staff. As by this time, I honestly enjoyed toying with them with my policy knowledge.

When I arrived at the lieutenant's office that day, I was greeted by a host of various staff members. It looked like a party. Except there was no cake, and I was not a guest. There were several lieutenants, a CO, the Captain's secretary, Shake Down Sally, as she was called by the ladies she had shaken down, and a psychologist. I also noticed, that the captain's door, was open. Therefore, I knew he was listening as well.

When I arrived, the psychologist was leaning up against the wall. She immediately pushed a rolling chair at me, demanding that I sit. At first, she attempted to bully me into taking back the PREA violation reports I had made. She kept telling me, "You are out of line" and "You are making these things up." She said, "You will regret it if you do not take back your report." I allowed her to go on and on for a bit, and when she finished, I kindly informed her, "I will be making a report to the Psychology Licensing Board regarding your behavior, as I know you are a mandated reporter." I also told her, "Shame on you for not protecting other women."

The psychologist was angered by this, and called me a liar. She said, "You have an agenda." And she continued to say there were no PREA violations at FPC Bryan, and accused me of making the whole thing up. I knew she knew better. She had to have known. It was no secret on the compound. But this same tactic is often used to bully those that dare to report staff wrongdoing. Staff protect each other and often bully women into taking back their reporting of PREA. I looked at her dumbfounded. This is when Shake Down Sally got up and left the meeting. I've always wondered if she decided she didn't want to be a witness to what was happening, in case it later was investigated. Or maybe she didn't like what she was seeing? Everyone on the compound, who didn't have blinders on, knew that staff was having sex with prisoners.

When the psychologist couldn't bully me into submission,

the older lieutenant told me, "You realize you can be shipped for doing what you are doing?" He was saying it in a way that felt like he was trying to warn me, more than trying to get me to stop. I let him know that I knew the policy. Since I had not been involved in the actual PREA violations myself, and was only making complaints that it was taking place, he could not ship me, at least not by BOP policy. He half smiled when I said this. He began to ask me questions, "Are you afraid here?" "Do you fear someone will harm you here?" To which I answered NO, each time! I knew what he was doing. Prisoners can be shipped for being in fear of their safety. Staff can also ship you if they claim you are unsafe. It wasn't going to work. I was determined I was going to stay there and keep fighting for the needed change.

After he asked me those questions, the CO who was present said, "Well, there's that," and abruptly left the meeting as well. She would later ask me "Did you know what he was trying to do by asking you those questions?" She said "I did not agree with what was happening in that meeting." And stated "I didn't want to stay and be involved in what was going on, so I left."

When none of the other tactics worked, the younger lieutenant, who was pretty new to the compound at the time, started in on me about my blog. I reminded him that I was allowed to blog by BOP policy, and that I had already beaten a false incident report for blogging. That incident report had happened in November 2018. I told him that the regional office legal team agreed that I could blog, because I still had my fifth amendment rights, regardless of whether I was locked up or not. He responded, "I've been flagging your emails for SIS, the staff that investigates prisoners for wrongdoing, and I've told them about your blog."

By this time in the conversation, I was just fed up with what was happening. Staff were actively trying to cover up PREA violations, and bullying me for daring to report them. I knew the meeting was going nowhere fast. In an attempt to get the meeting over with, I looked at the younger lieutenant and asked, "It wasn't a Russian flag, was it?" "Are you a communist?" The older lieutenant actually laughed at this. But the younger lieutenant got so angry, that he turned red in the face, and slammed his hand on the desk. But as I had wished, the meeting ended with me being yelled at by the younger lieutenant, and told "Go sit on the bench outside the lieutenant's office." As I left the meeting, I loudly blurted out, "I've already reported this to the DOJ PREA hotline." The office went silent.

As I sat on the bench outside the lieutenant's office, I saw other staff coming and going, in and out of the lieutenant's office. The gentleman who was the head of the psychology department was called over. He looked at me as he opened the office door, as if to say, you are in big trouble missy. I knew they were discussing what to do about me.

I felt I was about to be shipped, and actually, at that moment in time, I was hoping staff would be dumb enough to pull that move. I knew then I could really get FPC Bryan investigated, if I could get off the compound. I was aware that by BOP policy, if I were shipped for being fearful, I would receive a visit from an investigator at the regional level, or possibly from the Office of Attorney General (OIG). I knew with my security level, community custody, the lowest security level a prisoner can have, that staff would have to use the fearful move to warrant shipping me, or place a management variable on me for security reasons, to be able to ship me to the real SHU at FDC Houston, Texas. I was aware that both my security level and a claim of fearfulness, whether true or not, would prompt an investigation by the regional staff.

Looking back, it was not going to happen. The Captain could not risk sending me to Houston to the real SHU for an investigation, because it would prompt an investigation that he could not afford to happen, since he too was having sex with prisoners, something I had not actually known at the time of my reporting. He knew that an investigation would most like eventually lead to an investigation into him as well. It would have been a risky move. But again, I did not know this tidbit of information at the time, or I might have been even more brazen with my words, and actions, while in the lieutenant's office that day.

While on the bench outside the lieutenant's office, everyone who walked by, both staff and other prisoners, were asking me what was going on? Right before the 4:00 p.m. standing count was to take place, CO Cat Lady, as she was referred to by prisoners due to her stories about all her cats named after weather events, such as Stormy, Tornado, and Hurricane, came to take me to the makeshift SHU inside the lieutenant's office.

I asked her why I was being placed in the SHU, and she replied, "I don't know. They just told me to put you in there until after the count." CO Cat Lady was a strange lady indeed. She seemed to enjoy strip-searching prisoners a little too much for my comfort level. She had actually held my underwear in her hands and fondled it, during one of her strip searches of me when I was leaving a visit with my husband. And she never wore disposable gloves when doing strip searches, as the other COs did. She also had ever-changing hair color, and we never knew what color her hair would be, on any given day. Sometimes we even made bets on what color her hair would be the next time she worked. Pink, bright blue, purple, orange, mixed colors, it was a crapshoot.

While I was in the SHU that day, I was brought dinner by a CO I had already caused to be demoted from lieutenant back to CO. This happened after the regional office agreed with me, during one of my Administrative Remedies, that he needed more training for his inappropriate behavior. This was during another incident where I was thrown in the SHU, and threatened to be shipped off the compound, having to do with my Administrative Remedies against staff.

It happened after I had written Ms. V. up regarding the cosmetology class removal. She wrote me up for "threatening staff" because she said I told her I would not stop writing Administrative Remedies against her. I had told her this in a meeting, when she had called me to her office. She had

354

asked me, "Are you going to stop writing Administrative Remedies on me?" I replied, "I will if you stop violating my rights." She then picked up the phone and called security to say I was threatening her. This was the incident that she had later apologized to me about. Writing Administrative Remedies was well within my legal rights and certainly aligned with BOP policy. It is what caused me to be thrown in the SHU that morning, and threatened by the lieutenant on duty, the one I would evidently get demoted after I wrote him up for retaliation.

I had also written this same lieutenant up for forcing me to work in the kitchen at 4:00 a.m. one morning when I had a medical idle, slip form medical that allowed me to miss work due to illness. This was during a time when I had food poisoning and could barely walk, because I was so ill. This same lieutenant had forced me out of bed, made me basically crawl down the stairs from the second story in the unit, and pushed me in a rolling office chair to the kitchen across the compound. I had filed an Administrative Remedy on him for doing this. An idle meant he could not force me to work. However, on that morning he also told me to get up and go to work, or he would throw me in the SHU, and ship me from the compound.

When he came into the SHU on this particular evening, carrying my dinner tray, as I was being held for my PREA reporting, he sarcastically mused, "Looks like you are finally being shipped off this compound." I spitefully replied, "It looks like you have been demoted to delivering trays to inmates in this fake SHU." He was holding my dinner tray at the time. I told him, "I don't want dinner," but he forced me to take the tray through the opening in the middle of the metal door anyway. Once again, in what can only be described, as one of my moments of letting my anger get the best of me, I looked at him straight in the face, as I slammed the tray on the metal sink in the SHU. As the food went everywhere, I said to him in total defiance, "Oopsie, guess you will have to clean that up." Looking back, I'm not even sure why I did this? Again, my anger got the best of me, and I was just so tired by this point. The stress of constantly being retaliated against was beginning to wear on me.

After my embarrassing display of anger, I just sat down on the bunk and started praying. I asked God to show me the way. I was feeling so lost in those moments. Every time I prayed this prayer, I heard God telling me to move forward. So, I always kept going, no matter how tired I got. But move forward how? In prison, I took this to mean God was telling me to keep doing what I was doing.

Maybe because that is what I wanted to hear in those moments. I knew there had to be a purpose for my time in prison. Reflecting back, I clearly see HIS plan. I believe HE also allowed me on this journey to find myself, to entirely give myself over to HIM, and to allow HIM to direct my path. It was time for me to learn to forgive those who had wronged me, and heal from all the anger, and revenge I felt. But at the time, I was still flying by the seat of my own pants.

A few hours later, I was taken from the SHU to the Captain's office. After nothing else worked, the Captain tried to play nice with me. He would not look up at me when I was in his office. He just kept looking down at a piece of paper on his desk. At the time, I assumed he was looking at some sort of report, but I now realize that most likely he just didn't want to make eye contact with me, because he knew he was also having sex with a prisoner, or prisoners.

Maybe he found it hard to look at me, given all that I had just been through reporting the PREA violations, when he was lying to my face at the time. He told me I had been held in the SHU while staff investigated my complaints. And that my complaints were unwarranted. He informed me that he was sending me back to the unit. He told me to give myself a break and stop making reports. I told him what I thought about his staff's investigation, and that I would make sure that it was appropriately investigated by the DOJ PREA staff, and then I left his office.

My bunkie, Rhonda, who had been worried sick, met me

on the compound. She told me the rumor was that I had been shipped. She had not believed the rumor, because no staff member had come to pack out my personal belongings from my prison locker. She was so glad to see me. We returned to the unit together, and I told her everything that had just happened. She was not surprised at all.

The following morning when I was leaving breakfast, and walking across the street to my job in cosmetology, I saw the Warden. I approached her and informed her that she had better get her staff in check. I advised her what had been done to me the prior evening. She explained that the Captain had told her, I was only held for investigation purposes. I told her what I thought of her staff's investigative skills. I said, "Your Captain is a liar." I also informed her that I would put in for a transfer to the camp at Carswell, in Ft. Worth, Texas, and that she needed to make it happen.

The Warden asked me to calm down, and think about it before I put in for a transfer. But I was fed up and needed some peace. I would be going home in a few months, and I just wanted to be left alone. Moral of the story, be careful what you wish for, you just may get it! Little did I know that COVID was about to hit the prison system, and I would be left alone plenty, during my 100 days in what was basically solitary confinement.

At the time, I wasn't sure if the Warden was actually blind to what was going on, or just didn't care. Later that same day, I received the answer to that question. I was approached by a staff member I had come to respect and trust. She came to talk to me at the cosmetology department.

She wanted to know everything I knew about the PREA violations on the compound, and told me she was reporting directly to the Warden. She kept asking me "Is that all you know?" "Are you sure no other staff member is having sex with inmates?" Maybe she knew about the Captain at the time, and wanted me to confirm it for her. But I had told her everything I knew at that moment. She asked that I keep what was going on between us. I told her I would, and I did. While

I did not discuss the investigation with other women on the compound, however, I did report it to one of my state's federal Senators, John Boozman, and the DOJ PREA hotline, for a second time.

Chapter Thirty-Three
Flying On ConAir

In early February 2020, I asked for a transfer to move to Carswell Camp. What happened next was nothing but blatant retaliation by the Captain at FPC Bryan. When I put in for the transfer, I made sure with my case manager that I would be allowed to furlough, by way of my husband, between camps. This was certainly within BOP policy to do so. The case manager assured me I could, since I had the social furlough a few months before, and verified this with the Warden. I made it clear to her that if I was unable to transfer to Carswell, or be furloughed there, that I was not interested in transferring, she agreed. One week later, I would get the shock of my life!

On February 26, 2020, I celebrated my two-year anniversary of being incarcerated. Surprisingly, the time had gone by quickly, once it got going. I celebrated this milestone by cooking dinner for my roommates that evening. Cooking dinner in prison takes a lot of doing. Since our microwaves had been taken some time back, we were left with only hot water jugs to get food hot. It was undoubtedly a labor of love to keep changing out the hot water, until the food reached a temperature hot enough to eat.

That evening I had made one of the dishes we had come to truly enjoy. It was made with instant mashed potatoes that I mixed onion dip into. The potatoes were layered in our plastic bowls as the bottom layer of the dish. I then layered Pancho's shredded beef. I always got a chuckle from seeing my husband's name on this packaging. We often joked that my husband was providing us with meat to eat. On top of the meat, I layered melted queso dip and then shredded cheddar cheese that I had shredded from a block of cheese purchased from the commissary, using the top of a plastic birth control pill container, given to me by another woman, as the grater.

I had also made our favorite "mocktail" as we called them out of cranberry and orange juices, a drink mix packet, a tropical fruit cup with the juice, and several cans of 7 Up. It was a yummy meal, if I must say so myself. And we celebrated that my time was close to coming to an end there. I hoped that I would be transferred to Carswell any day. I watched the weekly BOP counts that we received on CorrLinks to see how the population was at the camp at Carswell. I hoped and prayed each day would be my last at FPC Bryan.

The following day, on February 27, 2020, I was called to the Unit CO's office and told to pack up my property, to be transferred via the United States Marshal Service Airlift, commonly referred to as ConAir. The staff could not tell me where I was being shipped, for security reasons. I felt in my gut that I was on my way to Alabama. This caused a lot of anguish for both my husband, and me, since I called him right away to tell him, before the BOP could cut off my telephone communication, as they often did to prisoners being transferred. I knew in my gut that I was not going to Carswell.

When I put in my transfer, I had been told that my husband would be able to furlough me to the other camp located in Ft. Worth, Texas, just 50 miles up the highway. When trying to find out where I was being transferred, one staff member that I trusted and was close with, told me "Use your gut instincts," when I told her, "I know I'm being shipped to Aliceville, Alabama." This pretty much confirmed what my gut was already telling me. I was being retaliated against and being shipped to Alabama instead of being allowed to furlough to Carswell camp.

That same staff member tried her hardest to get me off of the airlift so that at the very least, I could be driven by my husband to Aliceville. Unfortunately, that was not to be. On the day I was leaving Bryan, that same staff member came up to R&D to tell me goodbye. She told me she would try her best to have me rerouted back to Carswell and informed me that the captain had prevented me from being furloughed.

She said that if the Warden had been on the compound, she felt confident she would have been able to get me off the airlift, and the transfer halted. However, the Warden was gone for a two-week vacation, leaving the captain to call all the shots. True to her word, she kept my husband informed for several days of her efforts to get me rerouted. However, her efforts were fruitless. In the end, she could do nothing to help.

As fate would have it, I was strip-searched on the morning of February 28, 2020, given the worst of clothing and shoes to wear, and then handcuffed, shackled, and belly chained. I was then placed on a bus with a handful of other women to be taken from FPC Bryan to Houston, Texas, where we would meet the US Marshal airlift. As someone who was classified as community custody level, I should have never been placed in that situation. But there I was, being herded like cattle, along with other prisoners, who were being moved between facilities.

It was a very cold day, especially for Texas, and we were wearing short-sleeved shirts and no jacket. BOP staff were bundled up in puffer jackets, and wearing hats and gloves. All I could do was hope that the bus would at least be warm, and it was. It was not the way I had envisioned my transfer, but as we pulled away from the compound, a sense of peace came over me. As I looked back as we drove away, I was not sad to be leaving that place. I was traveling with my friend Ceci. I was thankful to have her on this journey, as she had been on it before, having been moved around in this manner during her criminal case. She told me what to expect.

From Bryan, we rode the bus to Houston, where we were fed a sack lunch of bologna and peanut butter. We were then turned over to the custody of the US Marshal Service for transport on ConAir, headed to the Oklahoma Federal Transfer Center (FTC). US Marshal staff were also bundled up in cold weather gear. However, we were not even given a jacket to fight off the cold.

I saw women coming from county facilities that were wearing even less clothing than I had on. Some even wore orange paper jumpsuits. As I stood on the tarmac that day, shivering to stay warm, I thought of all the changes I would fight for, once I was on the other side of the walls. I never wanted another woman to experience what I felt that day. It is genuinely horrible how prisoners are treated worse than stray animals. We were herded along that day, with no thought to our treatment, or that we were cold. It was also unnerving, flying while handcuffed, shackled, and belly chained. I tried not to think about what would happen in case of an emergency while in flight.

The flight from Houston to Oklahoma City did not take too long. The US Marshal plane flew directly into the basement of the federal transfer center building. This was when the US Marshal's voice came over the loudspeaker to thank us for "flying ConAir that day, and welcomed us to fly again real soon."

I hoped I would never see that airlift again, but I knew this would not be the case, as I knew I would be flown to Aliceville on it in a few days. I had no idea at the time that God had a different plan, or that COVID-19, was about to shut down the entire federal prison system. The Marshal on the loudspeaker also announced a list of names he said had "won the lottery that day."

I had no idea what he was talking about. However, I later learned that the lottery winners had been taken to Grady County jail, since only a limited number of us could be booked into the transfer center that day, due to overcrowding. It was actually us who remained at the federal transfer center (FTC), who had won the lottery. Stories from Grady County are much worse than what I experienced while housed at FTC Oklahoma, as bad as it was.

Once we were escorted off the plane into the bowels of the transfer center, our handcuffs, shackles, and belly chains were removed by US Marshal staff. We were then turned over to BOP staff. As our welcome to Oklahoma gift, we were strip searched again, as if we could have found some contraband while on the US Marshal airlift, handcuffed, shackled, and belly chained?

After all the US Marshal's hardware was removed, and we were searched, we were locked in a dirty, cold cell. The cell had no running water, a toilet in the middle, and no toilet paper. Women from other airlift flights would continue to join us until there were roughly eighteen women. We talked about where we had come from, and listened to each other's horror stories about the treatment of women at those facilities.

Even though the last woman arrived at the transfer center at 3:00 p.m., we were not processed through R&D until after midnight. The eighteen women were made to wait, until three hundred and fifty men were processed ahead of us. This putting men's needs before women's needs, was something I witnessed happen time and time again, while at FTC Oklahoma. I lost count of all the strip searches that day. Reflecting back, I realize just how numb I had become at that point. I no longer cared about stripping down in front of guards, or other women. It had all become so commonplace.

Chapter Thirty-Four
Life In Oklahoma

I could not believe the differences between FPC Bryan and FTC Oklahoma. The staff was not petty like the ones I had experienced while in Bryan. They were just there to do a job, and treated us with respect, for the most part. Surprisingly, the food was so much better than what I had been fed at the camp at Bryan. The most unexpected difference was that the medical staff actually had a bedside manner. Medical staff genuinely seemed interested in my medical care. I had been treated by medical staff for two years at FPC Bryan. Staff, who were indifferent to my needs, unless I started Administrative Remedies to rectify the issue. The staff at the federal transfer center were willing to prescribe needed medicine, and took my health care needs seriously.

A good portion of the COs, and other staff members at FTC Oklahoma, were also reasonable people, who treated us fairly. Again, not how I was accustomed to being treated, while being housed at FPC Bryan. And I believe this was a big part of the reason, I began to heal from my anger while there. However, even some staff at the federal transfer center did not follow BOP Program Statements, which is BOP policy. Being stuck at the transfer center was hard, especially during COVID, and was honestly one of the worst parts of my incarceration. Those three months, during the COVID lockdown, took a toll on my mental health.

Of course, there were some not-so-positive differences at Oklahoma as well. One of the main differences was that I was locked in a cell, behind a metal door, for most of the day. I had never been in a cell before. The staff there also tried to force me to wear used underwear, which I refused. Even Bryan had given me new underwear. I was given one new pair of underwear upon my arrival at Oklahoma.

I was able to purchase another new pair from the commissary. Apparently, there was a "limit of one per inmate," for reasons I can't even fathom. Since I was not about to wear used undies, I resorted to hand washing those two pairs. There was no way I would wear used underwear, with all the diseases that plagued prisons. I knew at Bryan FPC, there were prisoners with Hep C and HIV. I couldn't imagine, and didn't want to find out, what I was being exposed to in Oklahoma. I didn't care that the BOP staff claimed the clothing had been laundered.

I didn't trust the staff or the prison's laundry abilities. The clothes didn't even smell clean, they smelled like other people's body odors, and it was beyond gross. Not to mention, the clothes looked like someone had been sleeping in them. And I knew from ladies that worked in the laundry at Bryan, that not all individuals who work in laundry, used laundry detergent when they wash the clothes. I also knew that everything was washed together and crammed into the washers, so it never really got clean.

While at the transfer center, I learned about the horrors other women had faced while serving time at other women's facilities throughout the BOP. I can't, for the life of me, even to this day, understand why prison staff treat women so horribly. Maybe because most of the staff are men? It would also appear that most women's prisons also have PREA issues, both reported and unreported. So sexual assault of female prisoners, certainly seems to be an issue everywhere within the federal prison system, not just at Bryan. I did not see any actual PREA violations in Oklahoma.

However, I did see a lot of women being exploited by the guards. Before the COVID lockdown, women were flirting and dancing around for the male guards in the guard's office. I assume this is how they got what they wanted, and those women did seem to get their way for the most part. While I did not see any inappropriate touching, or sexual advances by staff at Oklahoma, I witnessed some questionable interactions between female prisoners and male staff. Many other new experiences awaited me at the federal transfer center. I was shocked to learn that prisoners actually talked to each other through the toilets. The "talking" went on all day, and all night long. Female prisoners on the 5th floor, where I was housed, talked to men who were housed on floors above and below us. Their conversations echoed in the walls all night and day. The noise awakened me when I tried to sleep.

It was hard enough to sleep, when the lights in your cell could never be turned off, and shone in your face all night. But the lights, accompanied by all the "ghosts in the walls," was almost too much to bear. Some nights I thought I was about to go insane. Being locked in a room was also a change from what I was accustomed to at the camp. And because my friend, Ceci, had left a few days after we arrived in Oklahoma, I was in a cell by myself, basically solitary confinement.

When I first arrived at the transfer center, I had no idea what all the noise I would hear at night was. Having never spent any time in county jail, I was unaware this was even a thing. Finally, another woman clued me in on "toilet talking." The men above my room, were in the SHU, and would knock on the floors in their cell, which was my ceiling, all night, trying to get me to talk to them. I would have to knock on the walls next to me, to ask the other women, who were talking to their friends in the toilets, to tell the man they were talking to, to tell the men in the cell next to them, to knock it off. I was not going to be talking to them in the toilet, or any other way, for that matter.

At least I finally understood why there was graffiti written inside the toilet in my cell. When the toilet was drained, I guessed inmates doodled as they toilet talked. It was absurd, and disturbing to me. But in prison, you learn to take the attitude of "to each their own." Many things you just turn a blind eye to, because it does not concern you. Toilet talking was one of those things.

However, I have to admit that my curiosity made me ask other prisoners about the desire to talk in a toilet. To accomplish the task, the prisoners in rooms beside, below, and all around me, would drain their toilets, I won't tell you how this is accomplished because it's too embarrassing for me to type, however, I will say that we did not have access to toilet bowl plungers, so use your imagination.

What I will tell you is that many toilets were broken by larger women while draining the water from the toilet. Once the toilet was drained, the women talked to the men who were being housed on other floors, who had also drained their toilets. This caused the echoing in the pipes that ran in the walls throughout the facility and caused what sounded like "ghosts" that I heard talking in the walls all night long. It actually sounded like someone was talking using one of those voice changers. Very eerie.

And as if talking in the toilets doesn't take the cake, enterprising prisoners also went fishing, as it is called, in the toilets. No, we didn't have fish swimming around in the pipes that could be caught for dinner. The fishing I'm referring to was accomplished when a prisoner on one floor used a bed sheet, or several bed sheets tied together, to flush down the toilet, while still holding on to one end of that same bed sheet.

The prisoner who got the bed sheet on the other end, on the floor below, or several floors below, placed a "gift" of food, drugs, notes, or who knows what else, in some sort of plastic, trash bag, baggie, etc., and tied the baggie to the bed sheet on their end, which was then pulled back through the water lines by the person who flushed it initially, and then retrieved through their toilet.

This is also referred to as "kiting." Goodies were sent both ways through the toilets in this manner. I was actually approached by another larger lady who wanted to know if I would give her my worn underwear so she could send it through the toilet. When I asked her why she didn't want to send her own underwear, she commented about our size differences. I kindly refused to give up my used underwear so it could be flushed down the toilet. YES! This really happens. You really just can't make this stuff up. I have been told that kiting is apparently done in county jails, and prisons, across the country.

I have purposely omitted many of the things I saw in prison from this book. In fact, it would take a book all of its own, to describe my entire prison experience. And honestly some things just deserve to be left in prison. Sort of like Vegas, what happens in prison, stays in prison. However, I feel that I have shared enough stories for the reader to get an overview of prison life. What I discovered during my prison stay, was things that were foreign to me, were actually a lifestyle for many.

Chapter Thirty-Five
Surviving COVID-19

A few weeks into my incarceration at FTC Oklahoma, COVID-19 hit the prison systems nationwide. On March 9, 2020, fifteen Democratic Senators sent then BOP Director, Michael Carvajal, a letter, expressing concern about a prison outbreak of the COVID-19 virus. The letter outlined their concerns over the threat of an "unconstrained spread of coronavirus in federal prisons and jails that endanger the federal prison population, correction staff, and the general public." Further concerns were expressed by lawmakers, union officials, and criminal justice advocacy groups, that federal prisons "weren't equipped to manage a spread of the coronavirus in the prison populations."

I had often blogged about the poor medical care prisoners received. Further complicating the matter was that most BOP facilities do not have doctors on staff, and prisoners were treated by Physician Assistants (PAs). I saw this firsthand at FPC Bryan. From speaking to prisoners who have been housed at multiple facilities, I believe this to be true at many other facilities throughout the BOP.

In the twenty-four months I spent at Bryan FPC, we briefly had a doctor on staff, and it was rumored that the one we did have was wearing an ankle monitor. Maybe he was a federal prisoner himself? We never knew. We also had many doctors, that I believe were borrowed from military facilities, who would come around for the day, once every month or so. But there was no way one doctor could treat all 900 plus of us, being housed at the Bryan facility, on one day a month.

During the pandemic, initially, the BOP failed to give us any safety equipment such as masks, hand sanitizer, or other means to protect ourselves against the virus. We did have regular soap, but nothing at the BOP had alcohol as an ingredient. I saw another woman wearing a mask she had made out of a sports bra. I gave her an A for effort. I guess some measure of protection beat none. And the BOP certainly wasn't concerned about us catching the virus, at least not initially.

Eventually, staff did bring in containers of chemicals that prisoners who worked in the unit would spray in the showers, between each shower use, and would use to clean the phones and computer keyboards. But this was after weeks of us having nothing, and only after we were locked down and not allowed out of our cells. And I had my doubts about the effectiveness of such cleaning, since the same rag was being used to wipe all the phones and computer keyboards, spreading germs from one appliance to the other, it appeared.

On March 13, 2020, a nationwide lockdown of the BOP took place. This lockdown was the BOP's response to Attorney General William Barr's memo, calling for the BOP to protect staff and inmates from COVID-19, as it spread like wildfire throughout the prison system. The BOP was certainly not prepared for a national pandemic, or any other national emergency, for that matter.

Sadly, as I am writing this book, we are now over three years into the pandemic. The horror stories I hear from the federal prison system seem to worsen, instead of improving. Apparently, the BOP still can't get its act together. It saddens me to hear of the mistreatment of so many humans at the hands of our government. Prisoners who are captive audiences, with no way to protect themselves from the virus. And as a mental health professional, I worry about the mental health issues this will cause in the long run. Most facilities have been locked down for over three years.

This means prisoners are mostly confined to their cells for most of the time. I do my best to speak out regularly about these issues. I know that spending 100 days in a cell by myself, while housed in Oklahoma, affected my mental health. I now suffer from a high level of anxiety, as well as PTSD, from that experience.

Because of COVID, things at the transfer center were much worse, once the lockdown began. I was in a cell by myself, so I was basically in solitary confinement. The cell had a sink and a toilet. I was locked behind a metal door, with a rectangular-shaped glass window, where guards could look in to do their every few hours wellness checks on prisoners, and to facilitate head counts. There was no shower in the cell, so we were at the mercy of staff to allow us out to take showers. This usually happened every other day, when we were allowed out for thirty minutes to shower, check email, and call our families.

However, several times during the three months that I was locked down during COVID, I was only let out of my cell every five to seven days. I believe this was due to staff shortages, and the BOP's lack of preparedness for the pandemic. My husband would become very worried during these times, because he was not hearing from me. He would call the prison but would be given no information. This was stressful to him. I had no idea at the time that he was calling.

In theory, the BOP was supposed to be locked down tight as of the March 13th national lockdown date. This meant there was no movement of prisoners, in and out of the prison system. But as with most everything I've witnessed with the BOP; this stopping of movement was not quite what it appeared to be.

After the Friday 13th date, we continued to see movement. Prisoners continued to be moved in and out of our unit. From reports from other prisoners who came into our unit from elsewhere, this continued to occur at many facilities, so the prison population was quarantined in name only.

We had two prisoners go out to the hospital and then return to our unit. This was after Oklahoma City became a hotbed for reported cases of COVID-19. And several prisoners left our unit for transfer for court dates, only to be returned later that same day, after they had been exposed to others, outside our unit. Not to mention two prisoners were returned to our unit from the SHU, because staff needed the room in the SHU for male prisoners.

None of these prisoners were quarantined for 14 days, before being returned to our unit, to expose the rest of us. Therefore, we were exposed to whatever they brought into the unit. Since we were mostly locked in our cells, the contact was limited, which was likely the only reason COVID was not spreading in our unit.

Since apparently the BOP couldn't, or didn't want to grasp the seriousness of COVID-19, or the Attorney General's memo, AG Barr again knocked on the hard heads of BOP upper management by issuing further orders. On April 1, 2020, all BOP institutions started a 14-day inmate quarantine nationwide. This was the first time we were locked completely down in our cells for days, with no shower break.

The fact that it was April Fool's Day, was not lost on me, nor apparently on others, as many prisoners, and even staff were acting like fools that day. And the whole thing felt like one big joke, since the quarantine was some sixteen days too late. I had been in Oklahoma since February 28th. The last prisoner that had come into our unit, besides the ones taken and brought back, was on March 13th. We had already all had contact with each other daily in a small area.

And of course, the staff were between units all day long, exposing all of us, to each other, in theory. Staff also went home and out into the public, and then came back to work. Many of the staff were not consistently wearing masks, and we were not even given masks to wear.

On April 2nd, we started being let out of our cells on a rotation basis. The top tier was out at different times than the bottom tier. This was for our 30-minute shower breaks. However, orderlies from both tiers were out all day and were in contact with all of us. And staff continued to go between the units during their shifts, so not much of an actual quarantine was happening. It felt more like punishment than a precaution for health reasons. It also appeared that the federal transfer center was understaffed, for a pandemic situation. But this letting out of cells did not last long, and soon we were locked down permanently. Finally, on April 7th, we were given face masks. As with anything done by the BOP, it was too little too late.

There were many cases of COVID-19 within the prison system by that time. And it was rumored that there were several cases at the transfer center in the men's units. Not surprising, given the continued movement, even after Barr's memo, and the fact that the BOP continued to take new commits and self-surrenders. In efforts to appear in control, the BOP has continued to try to contain, or falsify, the information about the number of virus cases. It has consistently been called out for this by criminal justice advocates, and members of Congress. Many family members continue to speak out. There are many cases of COVID that led to both prisoner and staff deaths.

Because of the transfer center's lack of long-term housing of prisoners, and lack of preparation for COVID-19, we had been locked down since roughly March 13, 2020. I honestly believe the staff at the transfer center just didn't know what to do with us, during the pandemic. I was housed in a cell the size of a small closet. There really was no moving around during that time. Because of this, I lost a lot of my muscle tone, from being locked down in a very small area, with no way to get any movement.

I also suffered from fluorescent pallor, a condition from not being exposed to natural light, for long periods of time. The lights at the transfer center were all fluorescent. They were never allowed to be turned off, so I was constantly under fluorescent lights, for the three months I was housed there. And there was not a window in my cell. When I got home, I was very pale from not seeing any natural light for those three months. I actually looked like a ghost. And my skin had a grayish cast to it.

Being stuck at the transfer center was hard, especially during COVID, and was one of the worst parts of my incarceration. The transfer center is designed to house prisoners briefly while they are going to another prison. It didn't help that the Warden retired right after the March 13, 2020, national lockdown began. The acting Warden was a nice man, and I believe he tried hard to do his very best. He was thrown into a COVID situation, and became the acting Warden, all at the same time. It's also a matter of "right hand, meet left hand," with BOP staff.

Nobody seems to follow the same policies, or even know what the rules are. If you ask ten different staff members a question, you will certainly get ten different answers. This frustrates prisoners who are just trying to follow the rules. While incarcerated, I often blogged about the inconsistency and lack of organization at Bryan FPC. It was no different at the transfer center. After talking with other prisoners, I believe that could be said for the BOP as a whole.

Because of the lockdown, we were fed in our cells, which caused many other issues. Our food was cold, and served past the discard times, on the food cart placards most of the time. This violated BOP Program Statement Food Service 4700.06, and Oklahoma Health Department codes. When I pointed this out to a guard, he replied, "Woman, do you know you are in prison?" I'm pretty sure that fact had not escaped me. However, I was aware that even though I was in prison, I still had rights, and that BOP policies were supposed to be followed. For most of my prison time, I witnessed the BOP refusing to follow its own policies. I was not surprised that the policy was being violated. At the transfer center, we did not have access to commissary food, and the food from the food cart was our only food source, so I had every right to be concerned.

Being the BOP policy gal that I am, I decided to write a BP-8 Administrative Remedy, regarding the mishandling of the food, before an outbreak of food poisoning could occur in our unit. That was the last thing we needed on top of a pandemic. After I wrote the BP-8, the food carts started appearing with the placards erased, so we were unable to know the discard times. However, the food was still cold, causing me to suspect that it was still being served past the allowed safe times.

Due to my complaints, placards were being erased, so we could not know the food had expired, and was past the safe consumption timeframe. I was forced to write another BP-8, to address this issue. Another issue my BP-8 took up was the preferential treatment of the male prisoners over female prisoners. Part of the reason we were being fed late, was that our unit staff went to the male units to help feed them timely, so they would not riot. This violates BOP Program Statement 3420.11 6. and 5200.02 CN-1 Female Offender Handbook. And again, I believe a lot of these issues were caused by understaffing, and lack of preparation for the pandemic, by the BOP.

We were given cold cereal, muffins or other pastry, fruit and milk for breakfast. The fruit we got at Oklahoma was so much better than what I was accustomed to at Bryan, even though it too was often ruined. But I think the staff at the federal transfer center tried hard. And we did get a variety of fruit while I was there. It was not uncommon for staff to bring around boxes of fruit during the day, to hand out as snacks. I appreciated the efforts. For lunch we were given bag lunches of bologna, peanut butter, pie or fruit. The pies were really good and I often see the same individual pies at Kroger.

Unfortunately, this was also when I started having a reaction to the peanut butter. I've gone my entire life eating peanut butter with no problems. But there was something in the peanut butter at the transfer center, that made me break out in a rash, from just touching my lunch bag. I believe it was the oil. The medical staff were nice and gave me shots of Benadryl to calm the itching and rashes. I was thankful I in Oklahoma, as I knew medical staff at FPC Bryan would have ignored me. I was also thankful that after a few days of just bag lunches and dinners, we were served a hot meal at night. Although sometimes it was more luke warm, by the time we got it.

After another few weeks, staff tried to give us a hot meal at lunch as well. Some days it happened, some not. And staff started adding packages of coffee, and drink mixes, for us to also use. It was certainly not an ideal situation, but overall, I have to commend the staff at the federal transfer center for their efforts, led by the new acting Warden. After talking to others who were on lockdown elsewhere during COVID, I think I was lucky, regardless that my situation was not good. Others had it much worse at other facilities.

And I got creative in my survival techniques. I used the Styrofoam trays that we received our food in, to make an ice chest for my room. I took the trays and made a box out of the tray tops, using the sticky part I pulled away from maxi-pads to hold them together. There I was, using the women's camp all-purpose tool, the maxi pad, to build something. I then placed the Styrofoam box in a garbage bag, and another garbage bag inside the Styrofoam box. I then covered the Styrofoam box with another Styrofoam piece, on top of the garbage bag, that contained the ice. The top piece of Styrofoam, and the garbage bag inside the Styrofoam box was removable, so I could replace the ice when it melted. The trash bag that held the box, kept it sturdy, and helped to insulate it. This also kept water from getting on my cell floor, once the ice melted.

It kept ice cold for about a day and a half, depending on the amount of ice I could get each time, and how cold the unit was that particular day. When I was let out of my cell for thirty minutes, to shower, make a phone call, and check my email, I would also try to find time to get ice. Other times the orderlies would bring me small amounts in a garbage bag, that when laid flat, would slide under the small space between the floor, and the cell door. I felt sorry for the orderlies, because they did try to run around and get all of us ice.

The orderlies were out most of the day doing jobs around the unit, such as cleaning, while the rest of us were locked down. They would also take my milk, which came in plastic sealed bags, the same bags we had had at Bryan, and put it in hot water for a few minutes, then slide it under my door, so

I could make coffee. We certainly made do, in the situation in which we found ourselves stuck.

I also used the all-purpose prison tool, maxi-pads, to cover the vent in my room, as it was so cold. I would stand on my chair and stick the maxi pads to the vent. They would blow off about once every day, or so, and I would have to do the same process again. Then another prisoner told me to wet toilet paper and throw it up on the vent. Once the toilet paper dried it did not fall down. It was like a paper mache at that point. Prisoners often make do with what they have available. I found many of the ideas that the ladies came up with to actually be ingenious.

Many things got worse after we were permanently locked down in our cells. The lockdown actually increased the amount of time the toilet talking, and fishing took place, since prisoners were in their cells for more extended periods, with nothing else to occupy their time. This resulted in several issues with entire units, or partial tiers, being flooded due to fishing lines, the sheets, accidentally getting loose in the pipes, resulting in the overflowing of all the toilets. Staff had to run like crazy trying to stop the flooding on multiple floors, and were forced to turn off the water for several hours at a time, while they tried to get the sheets, and other items out of the pipes.

This begs the question why this is allowed in the first place? Many guards even joked with the ladies about talking in the toilets, and seemed to think the matter was funny. Most of the guards worked in all the units, so they knew which prisoners were talking to each other. Guards often brought messages to prisoners, from other prisoners, in the other units. I couldn't wrap my brain around any of it, or understand why this type of behavior was allowed at all? But I have to admit that it was entertaining watching staff running like crazy, trying to figure out where all the water was coming from.

I also saw many prisoners acting out in ways I was not accustomed to, after being at the camp for most of my incarceration, I was used to serving time with minimum security individuals. But in Oklahoma, there were mixed security individuals, all in one unit. The women acted differently there. For example, there were women that would argue through the doors of their cells with other women. They would yell childish things at each other. Things I would not even expect junior high mean girls to say.

Many times, these things included "your mama," even though one of the ladies had made it known that her mother was deceased. Oftentimes, I would try to talk sense into them, through the crack of my own cell door, after it had gone on for so long, that I could no longer stand to listen to it. Many of the women had respect for me, because I was older, and treated everyone respectfully.

One woman who had obvious mental issues, was one that would constantly try to draw attention to herself. This did not help her get along with the other women, which resulted in fights, and arguments. She would often start yelling in the unit in the wee hours of the morning Of course, this woke up the entire unit. Many of the women did not like to be woken up. I was able to calm her, and many times the guard even let me out of my cell, so I could go to her cell door, to talk to her through the door crack, and get her to stop. This letting me out of my cell, especially happened when she would yell ugly things to guards, in the middle of the night, as they did their rounds.

But because of her behavior, other women were not so kind to her. Her cell was located just outside one of the showers, and because of this, she and ladies that did not like each other, would argue while the ladies took a shower. They would knock on her cell door on their way in the shower, and say things to get her agitated. She would in return, yell inappropriate things to them, such as accusing them of "peeing in the shower," which would instigate them even more. Unfortunately, the whole unit was forced to listen to all of this, on a regular basis.

One day I heard the prisoner who was in the cell by the shower, yelling loudly. It sounded like someone was killing her. I was alarmed. But I was locked in my cell, and unable to see what was going on. I would later find out that one of the ladies who was in the shower, that she was arguing with, had thrown a bloody tampon under her door, during a heated argument. I'm not sure if the COVID lockdown had made them lose their minds, or if this is how they normally act? We had, at this point, been locked down for two months.

Or maybe this was the way they normally handled situations? And the staff did nothing to control it. Maybe they couldn't? We were locked down already, and I'm not really sure what else they could have done, in situations like this? The woman that had thrown the bloody tampon under the door, was not even reprimanded.

Even more disturbing than the incident itself, if that is even possible, was the fact that staff did not treat this incident as a blood spill, and sent one of the orderlies into the cell with a mop, and mop bucket to clean it up. This was the same mop, and mop bucket, used to clean the showers, floors, and other areas of the common area, the area where all of us had to go and be in contact with things.

There was no cleaner we had that was equipped to handle a blood spill, this would have had to be brought to the unit, from elsewhere. However, this did not happen. It was concerning, but all I could do was sit back and watch, I was certainly a captive audience, as were the other prisoners in our unit. It is no wonder so many diseases get passed around in prison.

Fortunately, Congress passed the CARES Act, on March 20, 2020. Part of this act directed the BOP to release prisoners to home confinement that met specific criteria, in order to lessen the risk of a COVID outbreak, inside the prison system. I knew I qualified for release under this program. Because staff at the transfer center told us that they could not honor the CARES Act, I was forced to file a pro se Motion for Compassionate Release with the court.

At the same time, I also filed an Administrative Remedy, against the case manager at the federal transfer center, for not placing me on the list for the CARES Act. A week later, I was called into the office and asked to sign home confinement paperwork. When I asked how I was the only woman being picked to do so, I was told "We need to get some of you out of here." Wonder how I got on their radar? I guess for once it paid to be the squeaky wheel, and the BP-8 filer.

God only knows that I had been retaliated against plenty of times for speaking out, and filing Administrative Remedies in the past. At least my policy knowledge was finally paying off, in a positive way. But I was sad that other women did not have the courage to file Administrative Remedies. Therefore, they ended up being stuck at the federal transfer center for months, after I had already made it home, and were forced to make it to their next facility before they were released on the CARES Act.

And of course, COVID is still active in the federal prisons, even today, but since President Biden ended the pandemic, there are no more mandated policies for the BOP to follow, and no more CARES Act releases.

Chapter Thirty-Six
Fighting The Good Fight

After the Jeffrey Epstein case made national headlines, it would have seemed pertinent, that the BOP would have implemented extra security measures within its institutions, and initiated mandatory security training for all BOP staff. However, if the BOP did take those measures, I saw no evidence of it at FTC Oklahoma. The staff there needed a reminder of what can happen, when you neglect your duties in a secure institutional environment. In my unit we had many ladies who had health issues.

Due to the fact that we were actually locked in our cells, during most of the day and all night, we had an emergency buzzer inside our cells. I was forced to write additional Administrative Remedies, because COs were leaving our unit for long periods of time, while we were locked down, which caused prisoners to be unable to get staff when needed, especially if there was an emergency situation, and the buzzer had to be used. This ignoring of the emergency buzzer by certain COs, had been an ongoing issue since I arrived at the transfer center. However, it had gotten progressively worse after the start of the COVID lockdowns.

On April 1, 2020, we were not let out of our cells at all, and the emergency button was ignored each time it went off, for at least thirty-plus minutes at a time. At one point, the buzzer was ignored for fifty-eight minutes, from 6:43 p.m. until 7:41 p.m. I knew from memory, and from studying, and becoming a policy person, while at FPC Bryan, that BOP Program Statement 3420.11 6. stated "Because failure to respond to an emergency may jeopardize the security of the institution, as well as lives of staff or inmates, it is mandatory that employees respond immediately, effectively, and appropriately during all emergency situations." And "Inattention to duty in a correctional environment can result in escapes, assaults, and other incidents. "BOP employees are required to remain fully alert and attentive during duty hours." Notice the words "mandatory and required".

While I understood that many prisoners push the buzzer, just to get the guard's attention, in a non-emergency situation, this did not justify the buzzer being ignored, especially for thirty-plus minutes, and longer, on a regular basis. Staff had no way to know if it was a real emergency or not, unless staff physically went to a prisoner's cell, to do a wellness check. This led me to believe that the BOP had not learned its lesson after Epstein's death, and had not given staff the proper training, regarding prisoner safety issues.

I spoke to the Executive Assistant to the Warden, regarding the matter, when she made her rounds in our unit one day, going door to door, to answer our questions. In the same conversation, I also told her about our food being served cold, and past the discard times, which also went against policy. Her response to me was "You should focus on more positive things instead of wasting your time writing up these issues." Needless to say, I did not take her advice, and immediately filled out a BP-8 Administrative Remedy form. It was obvious that staff just wanted us to sit back, and take it, and had no intention of addressing these issues.

The Unit Team staff apparently took my BP-8 seriously, and referred the emergency buzzer issue to SIA, which is BOP staff internal affairs investigations. I was paid a visit by an SIA staff member. I was requested to sign an affidavit regarding my allegations, so the incident could be referred to the DOJ. to be investigated. This was after SIA staff verified the allegations in my BP-8 by reviewing the camera footage from the April 1, 2020, incident, that I had requested be preserved as evidence.

This would not be the only visit from SIA staff I received during my time at Oklahoma. Shortly before my release, SIA staff also paid me a visit to ask me to sign another affidavit, sent over from the DOJ in Washington, D.C. That affidavit recapped the Administrative Remedies I had written while still being housed at FPC Bryan. These remedies were against a CO who had continuously mistreated us at the camp. I had written the CO up many times, for inhumane treatment. I had contacted my Senator regarding this matter. It appeared from the affidavit that my Senator had actually lodged an investigation.

This particular CO had called us horrible names over the loudspeaker, one such name was a Spanish word, meaning dirty pigs. He was abusive to women who were gay or transgender, made up his own rules to humiliate women, and had made the statement that "all white-collar inmates should be shot," amongst many other degrading things he said and did. He had also almost caused a riot on my last New Year's Eve at Bryan, when he refused to follow the Captain's directive, and allow the ladies out of their cells after the 10:00 p.m. count, so they could watch the ball drop on the television screen.

I would later learn that the CO was escorted from the Bryan compound, and fired. I also received another affidavit from the DOJ, while incarcerated at FTC Oklahoma, that recapped my administrative remedies written while fighting to get back into cosmetology, as well as some of my other allegations of the staff corruption and PREA violations I had seen while at Bryan. At least some of my hard work while in prison paid off, and resulted in change for the better.

Regardless of how bad it was at Oklahoma, there were personal revelations that took place there. Being away from Bryan, locked down with nothing to do, but lay on my bunk all day, alone in my cell, had given me a lot of quiet time with God. I read my bible a lot during this time, and I continuously prayed. I asked God to guide my path going forward.

I knew that getting to Aliceville would be another adjustment period for me. A whole new journey. Shortly after days of praying, I received God's peace with the situation.

And I was given a home confinement date of May 14, 2020. God apparently had other plans, and I would not be going to Aliceville after all. I was going home to my family.

The day the Unit Staff brought me the paperwork to sign, I could not wait to be out of my cell again. I wanted to call my husband and tell him the good news. He actually started crying on the phone when I told him. The amount of relief that both of us felt, knowing that this part of the journey was almost over, was immense. I could feel his emotions through the phone, as we held on to the promise of my release. I'll never forget the sound of Pancho's voice that day on the phone. He could almost not believe it. He just kept saying it, over and over again, in our conversation. "I can't wait for you to be home." I loved hearing the relief in his voice. I could not wait to be in his presence again. To be able to just hug him, and hold him tightly. I longed to feel his arms around me. I wanted to feel safe again.

I asked him to mail me a three-month calendar. I hung the calendar on the wall in my cell, using stickers I took from the fruit we were given each day. Using the calendar, I began to mark off the days. I also used the calendar to document our lockdown. Each day I noted the time we were allowed out of our cells, if any, what food we were served, and when the food was served, and any other events that had taken place that day. In this way I memorialized some of my time in Oklahoma.

But most importantly, I used the time alone in my cell, to work hard to forgive those who had wronged me. I knew the amount of anger I had inside me. I knew I had to let it go. I was trying hard to squelch it before returning home to my family. During my time in Oklahoma, God had revealed to me how my anger had fueled many of the battles I had fought while in prison, as well as during my criminal case.

While the battle at trial had not ended the way I felt it should. I still knew that God is good, even on my worst days. I felt guilty at knowing that I had certainly failed at living out my Christian values, and my faith in many of the situations, along this journey. And I knew that I could no longer rely on my plan. It was time to get back on the plan that God has instore for my life.

While fighting those battles in prison, I had actually helped many women and had made changes in the system, needed changes, yet, I knew that I had done so out of anger at times. One of my biggest regrets was not living more in HIS light while at FPC Bryan. In this way, I felt that I had failed God and my Christian values.

And I felt regret, and guilt, in this failure. It was one of the questions asked of me right after my jury trial, during my conversation with P. Rod in February 2017. "What example would I set as a Christian to my fellow brothers and sisters in Christ, or even to non-believers who may be watching from the outside?" I knew the cost, and yet, I had allowed my anger to control me, on most of this journey.

If I had just focused more on sharing HIS love, and turning the other cheek to the staff corruption, maybe I could have helped many more women come to know HIM. Had I missed the reason God had placed me on this journey altogether? It was a harsh reality, but it was my reality. I felt guilty for this, more than anything else that had happened, during this season of my life. It's a guilt I still struggle with today. And sometimes I wonder if it isn't the devil putting negative thoughts, and self-doubt, in my head? I pray about it a lot.

But in all fairness to myself, at the very least I had been a birthday candle, the birthday candle my dear friend Pam told me to be, on the day before I left for prison. A very dim one at times, there is no doubt, but my light had not gone completely out, in the darkness that is our nation's federal prisons. One thing I knew for certain, was that my past did not need to define my future.

It would take therapy, to completely overcome all the anxiety I knew that I now suffered from, after being on this journey, and all that I had been through, along the way. But I also knew that my God is mighty. With HIS help, I could genuinely feel permanent peace about the situation.

I prayed all day long, for many days in a row, asking God to heal me. I prayed for forgiveness, for how I had treated others along this journey, including some of the staff members at FPC Bryan. I began to feel the peace that only HE can provide. I could feel my heart soften. I could feel the calm that only HE brings, taking over my body, mind, and spirit.

It was during this time that I found true forgiveness for those who had wronged me. And I focused on the future I could have, the one promised to me through God's grace and mercy. It was a time that started my journey towards true restoration. It actually felt good to know I was on my way to finally healing. At this point, I had been dealing with my criminal case for over nine years.

The anger and revenge that I had carried for so long was actually subsiding. Prison had not bound me. My criminal case had not bound me. No, no! It was actually chains of my own choosing that had done that job. But I knew that God still had a plan for my life. And that the rest of my life lay ahead of me. I wanted back on HIS plan.

I thought back to all the moments on this journey that I had been convicted by my faith. I had chosen to ignore God's voice many times, while I continued to go it alone. Taking things into my own hands and following my plan, not HIS. Yet, HE had never given up on me, HIS daughter. HE had continued to try to get my attention all along this journey. And I knew it was HIM that had carried me through it all, even during the times that I had been disobedient to HIS word.

I had come to accept my flaws, but more importantly, I knew that those who had wronged me, were also flawed. The doctors, and the AUSAs, were no different than me. While the mistakes they made were different from the ones I had made, it did not matter in God's eyes. I also realized that the staff I had encountered at the BOP were also flawed. As were many of the ladies, I had served time with. And yet, God still loves all of us.

HE still desires to have a relationship with all of us. HE still wishes for ALL of us, to one day live in heaven with HIM. I had read the book of Philippians so many times while serving time in prison. It was one of my favorite books of the bible. But at that moment, I truly felt like the bible tells us in Philippians 4:12 "I have learned the secret of being content in any and every situation."

On Good Friday, we were still locked down in our cells. And even though it was supposed to be my day for thirty minutes out of my cell, it did not happen, for one reason or another. That Easter would be the first major holiday, during my prison sentence, that I would not be able to speak to my family on the phone. As I already knew that I was not scheduled to be out of my cell on the following day at all. I was feeling sad about missing another holiday with them, but I knew that soon, I would again be celebrating all the holidays with my family, and I held on to those thoughts with all I had.

That evening, I was laying on my bunk, reading the bible in John 19. I was thinking about our church, and imagining the great worship service that was taking place that evening, our annual Remember the Cross celebration. I was sad that I was once again missing it, as it is my favorite service each year. I had no idea that our church was also on lockdown due to COVID, and not having a Good Friday worship service, as we had in the years past.

Suddenly, I felt an urge to praise God in song. I began singing Matthew West's *The God Who Stays*. I'm not really sure why that particular song came to mind? Maybe because it was one that we had frequently sung at Bryan, during service in the Chapel, the last few months I was there? Or maybe because it is a song that I really love.

But for some reason, that was the song I started singing. As I sang, I started singing louder and louder. I suddenly felt led by God to get off of my bunk bed, and go to my metal cell door. I started singing loudly through the crack on the side where the door closed, so that the other ladies in the unit could hear me. When I finished singing, another lady started singing a gospel song that I didn't even recognize. She sang in the most beautiful voice. I could not tell where the voice was coming from, but I listened intently. Her voice moved me. Then more ladies joined in, and one song led to another. It was one of the most powerful moments, out of all the moments, during my twenty-seven months of prison time.

I was healing. My anger was subsiding. I was becoming whole again. I laid back down on my bunk, and I continued to praise God. I thanked HIM for bringing me through this season of life. Even though many times I turned my back on HIS plan, and went it alone. I was really at the end of my prison time! It seemed impossible.

Even as I type it now, this story still stirs so much emotion in me. HE is faithful! HE is good! HE restores! HE heals! HIS goodness and mercy is real! I did not deserve it, but HE gave it to me anyway. Ephesians 2:8 tells us "For by grace you have been saved through faith. And this is not your own doing; it is the gift of God."

I was thankful for HIS many gifts. I was ready to really live the rest of my life with HIS peace. I vowed that going forward, my life would prove to others that God is good. I would live in HIS light. I no longer wanted to be a birthday candle. I was ready for a much brighter light to shine through me.

Chapter Thirty-Seven
Quarantine In The Men's SHU: Home At Last

On May 27, 2020, I finally made it home. I was initially scheduled to be released on May 14, 2020. However, that did not happen. My husband drove five hours to Oklahoma City, Oklahoma, only to be turned away, and told that I could not leave that day. Apparently, on Monday, May 11, 2020, the South-Central Regional Office of the BOP, put out a Memo that informed the medical staff at FTC Oklahoma, that it had not followed CDC guidelines when quarantining prisoners. The memo read, "Inmates had to be in isolation for 14 days before release." Mind you, I had already been in quarantine since April 1, 2020, at least for the most part, since we were being locked in our cells, and only allowed out to shower, email, and make phone calls, for thirty minutes every forty-eight hours. And of course, the BOP was already supposed to be following CDC guidelines when quarantining us.

Unfortunately, I did not find out about the new quarantine memo until around 7:00 p.m. on Wednesday, May 13, 2020, the night before I was to be released. By this time my husband would have already been in Oklahoma, in a hotel room, excited to pick me up the following morning. I was not allowed to call him, to give him this horrible news. In true BOP fashion, he was forced to come to the prison the following morning, only to find out that he would not be allowed to pick me up that day. It would be two days later before I was allowed to make a phone call to him.

On the evening of May 13, 2020, I was laying in my bunk, on what I thought was my last evening in prison, reading the last 150 pages of a book, I had purposely saved to finish that night, anticipating the anxiety I would feel, just knowing I would be going home the following morning. Prisoners count down all their prison lasts. It's a customary thing that is done in every prison in this nation. I had already counted down and turned in my last laundry bag, made what I thought was my last prison phone call, sent my last prison email, eaten what I thought was my last prison breakfast, lunch, and dinner, and had my last 4:00 p.m. stand-up count.

I was only waiting for my last 10:00 p.m. stand-up count to take place, when what looked like a swat team of US Marshals appeared at my cell door. They unlocked my cell door, and told me to get all my personal property. They would not tell me what was going on, or where they were taking me, but knowing how the BOP operates, I knew something was terribly wrong. They took me out of the pod into the hallway. I assume this was done, so the other ladies who had been cheering for me, as I left the unit, and who thought I was going home, would not see what happened next. The Marshals immediately took my personal property from me, and I was handcuffed. I was then told I was going to the SHU for quarantine, and would not be going home the following day. I was then placed in the men's maximum-security SHU with men present in the adjacent cells.

It is against BOP policy, for men and women to be housed together, and highly irregular. I was informed that I would be held for quarantine in the SHU, for 14 more days. I immediately had a meltdown. I went into a full-blown panic attack. I started to feel the old anger beginning to rage inside of me again. I just started praying to God to get me through this situation. I didn't want to start questioning God again. I didn't want to feel the deep seeded anger I had felt for so long.

I wanted peace. I wanted my husband and my family. I wanted to go home! Why was this happening? With God's help, I had just barely made it to a place of forgiveness for those who had wronged me. I had been able to let go of most of the anger and revenge I had held on to for so many years. I did not want to go backwards, in all that I had accomplished, in the last few months. I clung to God's promises, at that moment. And I willed myself to HIS plan. During my time in the SHU, my panic attacks came in waves. Some days I was fine, other days not so much. But I continued to ask God, to see me through, yet another storm.

Men in adjacent cells tried to talk dirty to me, and even threatened me, when I refused to talk to them. One prisoner even threatened to kill my family, if I did not talk to him. The men in the SHU were men that could not be placed in the general prison population, due to behavioral, or other issues. And many of their actions reflected this. Why the BOP thought it was okay to put women in that situation, is beyond me? All I could do was pray. God continued to give me strength and peace in these situations.

I was held in the SHU for fourteen nights and thirteen days. Even though I was kept the extra time, I was still not quarantined correctly. So even though the BOP kept me, they still couldn't get it right. On May 13, 2020, my temperature was taken after 7:00 p.m. Then, roughly thirty minutes to an hour later, it was taken for a second time. Those two temperature checks were falsely logged as a day of quarantine. While I'm appreciative of health services staff calling it a day, since that allowed me to go home a day sooner, it is just another example of how the BOP does precisely what it wants, regardless of the policy, or the CDC guidelines, it is supposed to follow.

When I was taken to the men's SHU on the night of May 13, 2020, I was placed in a dirty cell that still had personal property items, including medical items, left behind from the previous male occupants. There was trash and dirt everywhere, including on the floor, and in the shower. The cell was not sanitized or cleaned, before I was placed in it. At the time, the only prisoners at the federal transfer center, known to be infected with the COVID-19 virus, were men.

It did not make sense to be moved from the women's unit, where I had been housed, since February 28, 2020, to the men's SHU area for quarantine. While held in the SHU, I was not allowed hygiene items. Not even a comb. I did finally receive a comb after seven days into the quarantine period. That comb was snuck in by a female BOP staff member who took pity on my situation.

In the SHU, I was allowed two phone calls per week. I did not have access to a bath towel, and was given a 4X T-Shirt, to use as a towel. After a few days, an actual towel appeared, and only after I complained, to the female doctor who came around to take our daily temperature. The shower curtain did not completely cover my body, as it was designed for men, from the waist down. I had to squat down to take a shower, so my breasts could not be seen, should a male guard do a wellness check, while I was in the shower.

All the clothing in the SHU was too big for me. The smallest size they had was XL. Surprisingly, all the clothing was brand new. Weird! It was the first time I'd ever seen brand new clothing while in prison, and I was shocked to find that SHU prisoners were the ones to get new clothing. Maybe men always got new clothing, and only the women had to wear the old stuff? Or maybe it was just the good old BOP's "Backwards on Purpose," business as usual? Nothing surprises me about the BOP. One of the other things I noticed was that the food was much better quality, and it was served to us still hot. Again, maybe the men always got hot food? And it was just the women that were served lukewarm, or cold food.

A few days into my quarantine in the SHU, the prisoner who had thrown the bloody tampon under the door of the other prisoner was brought to the SHU. She had apparently had an altercation with a guard. The prisoner's door she had thrown the tampon under, was already in the SHU, having been brought there to get her out of the unit, when the constant arguing had become too much for staff to deal with. She was housed in the cell directly beside the cell I was being housed in. Now the staff placed the other prisoner on the other side of her. And so, the nightmare began.

These two women argued with each other constantly, and

did everything they could to aggravate each other. When the prisoner in the middle cell would get quiet, and go to sleep, the other prisoner would pound on the metal shower that was in our cells, to make sure the other prisoner could not sleep.

The same thing happened in return, when the other woman tried to sleep. I remember one night, this went on for so long, that I thought I would lose my mind. Every time I would doze off, it would start all over again. Of course, the men also yelled all night. All I could do was pray for peace, and endure it. And with each of these instances, my anxiety would continue to worsen. I felt like I was living in a nightmare, that I could not escape. And honestly, I was.

We were able to get our two calls a week, when staff would roll the phone down the hallway, and place it outside of our cell. To use the phone, we were required to reach through the trap door, the same trap door guards used to hand us our meal trays, and bring the phone receiver into our cell. The two prisoners would yell as loud as they could, while banging on the metal cell door, in an effort to prevent the other prisoner from getting their voice to go through to connect their call. If the prisoner's voice did connect, they would in turn do the same to prevent the other prisoner from hearing on the phone, during their call.

I had to beg them to stop when it was my turn to use the phone. I needed my voice to go through to connect the call, but also, I did not want my family to hear all that in the background. I knew my husband was already worried. Being in Oklahoma shed new light on the prison system for me. As if I thought things could be any worse than FPC Bryan, I soon found out it could be; being housed in the men's SHU. I actually felt sorry for the prison staff that worked in the SHU. Many of the prisoners treated them harshly. I was being housed with prisoners that could not remain in the general population of the prison, due to their security level, and/or their behavior. The SHU was the last step for them. There was really nothing else the prison could do to them, and they knew this. One evening a prisoner threw urine on the guard, when the guard handed the food tray through the door. Other prisoners constantly yelled nasty things of a sexual nature, that I can't even type in this book. My anxiety continued to increase.

I tried doing breathing exercises. I tried reading. I tried calming my nerves. And I prayed. But no matter what I did, I was anxious with everything that was going on around me. I felt God's presence, and I knew the nightmare would be over soon, and each day, I marked another day off the calendar. I knew that my time in this environment would be short lived. Knowing this, helped me to endure the constant noise. While I could not escape it, I allowed God to provide me with HIS peace.

On May 27, 2020, my husband again showed up to pick me up from the transfer center. This was the day that staff had given me, and told him that he was to pick me up. And the staff had promised me, he would not be turned away this time. I made sure to verify this with several staff members. I asked repeatedly in the days leading up to May 27th. I did so, because I realized that date would be one day shy of my 14-day quarantine time. I had been marking the days off on my calendar.

However, I was not about to look a gift horse in the mouth, and point this out to staff. On the morning of May 27th, another lady who had been in quarantine with me, was called out of our cell to go home, but I was not. I started asking staff what was going on, and I was told that I was not scheduled to leave that day. That is when I totally lost it again.

I did not want my husband to go through that pain again. I certainly was not ready to do it all over again, myself. And I was tired, and ready to go home. Once again, my anger reared its ugly head. I started yelling at staff, and threatening to write Administrative Remedies on them. I told staff that I would file a civil lawsuit against the prison, for being housed with men, in the maximum-security SHU. I knew this was against policy. When I realized how I was acting, and that my anger was once again surfacing, and taking over my body, I just sat down on my bunk and prayed, I prayed to God for peace, as I cried.

Huge crocodile tears ran down my face, as I rocked back and forth, in calming motions. I was not about to allow myself to go back to the angry person I had tried so hard to let go of, during my time in Oklahoma. I asked God to give me HIS peace. And once again, HE provided it. I started reading the bible, to try to take my mind off of what was happening. I tried to lose myself in HIS word.

I could feel my anxiety buzzing throughout my whole body. It actually rang in my ears, and my body felt like it was tingling. A short time later, a nice female doctor came to talk to me. This was the same doctor that tried to get me moved from the SHU, when I was first placed there. She told me, "Mrs. Espejo, just hold on a minute, please give me time to work on this." "I'm going to get you out of here today." And she asked for my husband's cell phone number. She said she would return to update me.

I just kept praying. I just kept asking God to help me with the anger I felt once again. And HE continued to give me the peace that I so desired. Even if I was not going home that day, I felt HIS presence there with me, and I knew that I would be alright, regardless of what was about to happen to me, on that day.

A short time later, the doctor returned to tell me that she had spoken to my husband. While he had been turned away that morning when he came to pick me up, he was still in Oklahoma City, at the hotel. She told me that I was going to go home that day, and that the prison was working on making it happen.

Not too long after she left, a Case Manager Central (CMC) staff member showed up at my cell door. I immediately recognized him, from the rounds he had made in the unit, when he had come by to talk to me during my time in the SHU. He unlocked my cell door, and told me to get my personal belongings. He did not handcuff me, as I left my cell. That was my sign that I was really going home.

Riding down in the elevator, I could not believe it was happening. I was finally going home. My husband was actually outside, waiting to whisk me away. I could not wait to see him. It had been almost four months since I had last laid eyes on him. Four months since I had held his hand, or touched his face. In what appeared to be the basement of the federal transfer center, I was given men's jeans, a white polo shirt, and black imposter converse tennis shoes to put on.

But then I was placed in a cell, and locked in, because I had to wait for my release paperwork to be done. This made my anxiety go up briefly, but once again, I prayed for God's peace, and HE provided it to me. I later realized, once I got my paperwork, that the CMC had been working to get a one-day furlough approved, so that I could leave that day.

After what seemed like forever, I was escorted outside to my husband's vehicle. I was shaking, and full of emotion, as I opened the door, and got into the passenger seat. We briefly hugged each other, but I told my husband to just hurry up and drive. I did not want to be there another minute. I guess I feared the prison would change its mind, and keep me. When we were on the other side of the walls, I asked him to stop the vehicle. I crawled over to him, and as I shook from all the anxiety I felt, I hugged him even longer. I kissed his cheek. I touched his face, and his hair.

As we drove away, I looked back briefly at the massive Federal Transfer Center, with all its concrete blocks, and metal fencing. My emotions were high. I was saddened that I had to leave other women behind, in that horrific situation. But I was thankful to be going home. I never wanted to see that place again! And I thanked God for getting me out of there on that day.

A few minutes away from the prison, Pancho pulled behind a warehouse that was currently not in operation, most likely shut down, due to COVID. I climbed in the backseat and put on the clothes he had brought me. I could not wait another minute to take off the prison clothes I had been given. It was not even women's clothing I was wearing, or that I had worn for the last twenty-seven months of my incarceration.

I looked in the mirror and saw how awful I looked. I was white as a ghost, actually my skin had a gray cast to it. My hair was wild as I had not been able to wash it, due to having no hygiene items in the SHU. Without access to hair conditioner, a hair dryer, and a comb, it would have made it worse to wash it, since shortly before I had left Bryan, I had let another prisoner give me a perm, during our cosmetology classes. Luckily, I still had the hair tie I had made out of the elastic top of a tube sock. I tied my hair up and made the best of it. What a hot mess I must have appeared to all who saw me that day. And yet, I didn't care. I was actually going home to my family!

During the over five-hour drive home, I spent a lot of the time talking on the phone. As you can imagine, many people were waiting for my call that day. But during that time, I just kept looking over at my husband, and occasionally touching his hand, or arm. It was real, I was actually driving down the road with my husband, he was right there within an arm's length from me. I would not be forced to separate from him in a few hours. I was going home with him to stay.

I had dreamed of this day for twenty-seven months. And while it was not like I had imagined it would be in my dreams, given that I was released from the federal transfer center, not the camp, it was a moment I will never forget. My heart was once again full. I never wanted to be away from him again. And even now, years later, I feel anxiety every time my husband has to go out of town for work. It's almost like living my date of self-surrender all over again. Just one of the many scars from my time of incarceration.

One positive thing that has come out of the COVID-19 pandemic, is the light it has shed on the lack of preparedness on behalf of the BOP. The BOP's failure to follow CDC guidelines during the pandemic, and its failure to follow Barr's Memo concerning the release of prisoners under the CARES Act, has brought attention to the mistreatment of prisoners in our nation's prisons.

These same actions by the BOP, caused large amounts of litigation to plague the Courts during the COVID-19 pandemic. This is due to the "we do as we please " attitude, taken by the BOP in response to very deadly situations, at many institutions, as COVID spread like wildfire throughout the prison system. Many prisoners have died due to the BOP's failure to take action. Staff members have died as well.

However, the BOP has taken this same attitude in many other instances, that just did not get the attention COVID-19, has gotten. The BOP has taken the same "we do as we please" attitude, in response to the First Step Act, good-time days, and other legislation. In January 2022, Congress forced the BOP to implement the First Step Act. This resulted in many prisoners getting immediate release, many months past the time they should have been released.

One thing I learned while serving time in prison, is that the BOP thinks it can do as it pleases, regardless of what policy states. Currently, there are ongoing judiciary inquiries into the BOP's COVID-19 responses, and the many PREA violations of female prisoners in its care.

I am hopeful that Congress will implement policies, or pass appropriate laws, to force the needed changes in our prison system. Independent oversight of the BOP is certainly needed, and we must keep fighting for this to happen. It is the only way we will ever see the needed changes take place. Changes that will require humans to be treated as such, regardless that they may be currently incarcerated.

Chapter Thirty-Eight
Living The CARES Act Life

Coming home was difficult for both my family and me. The day I got home, we stopped at Walmart so I could pick up some hygiene items. I became so overwhelmed just trying to pick out a lotion, that I could not function, and had to leave the store. There were just too many choices, and I was unequipped to make a decision at that moment. There were also too many people in the store, and I just wanted to get away from them. I was not the same person that had left for prison. I brought home a lot of anxiety, and Post Traumatic Stress Syndrome (PTSD), with me. The first few months were very hard on all of us. As time has gone on, and with counseling, and God's continued peace, I have gotten better. I have adapted back to my home life, and I feel more normal with each passing day. However, I do not think the anxiety will ever entirely leave me. And I know the scars of prison will not.

When I arrived home, our ten-year old French Bulldog, Olivia, was not doing well. She was at the end of her life, due to health issues. Pancho had not prepared me for how she looked. I knew she had been sick, but when I walked into our home, and saw her, I just burst out crying. My heart sank.

Me being home during this time was a blessing, since Olivia needed constant care, and now had to be fed by hand. I could not believe all that Pancho had been dealing with in my absence. I started to have a new appreciation for him. I tried hard to mend Olivia. I was not ready for another loss in my life. But I was thankful for the little over four months I was able to have with her, before we had to let her go. On the morning I left for prison, I had told both of our dogs, Macklin and Oliva, good-bye, as I thought I would never see them again, except for on video chats, or in photos, due to their age.

But God had another plan, and HE blessed me with those four months to be home to take care of Olivia, before we were forced to put her to sleep. If I had not been home when that choice was made, I would have had one more thing to feel guilty about. But her condition also kept me with constant anxiety, because I knew her time was short, and another loss would soon take place. I had already suffered many losses while away in prison. My mental health was fragile at the time, and I didn't know how I would handle saying good-bye to her. I was not really equipped mentally at the time. It was hard.

Because I was released under the CARES Act, I was required to remain under the constant supervision of the City of Faith Halfway House (HWH), in Little Rock, Arkansas. I wore a GPS ankle monitor, which made wearing pants almost impossible, due to the size of the monitor. I had to follow strict rules, or risk returning to prison. I was only allowed to be no more than 180 feet away from the monitor box that was plugged in on the counter, in our kitchen. This meant I could not even go upstairs in my own home, without risking the monitor showing I was out of bounds. I could not go to my mailbox, or in my own backyard for very far.

I was not allowed to leave my home without permission. I was not allowed to go grocery shopping, or eat at restaurants. I was not even allowed to go to church. When I was first released in May of 2020, I was not allowed to get a job. I was only allowed to leave my home for approved three-hour doctor visits, or when I was called to the halfway house for my weekly reporting.

I was required to report to the HWH through telephone calls to staff between the hours of 8:00 a.m. - 9:00 a.m. each morning, and again between the hours of 8:00 p.m. - 9:00 p.m., each evening. It was very stressful when staff would not answer the phone during these times. Many times, I would have. to call over, and over. again, until someone would answer the phone at the HWH.

This stressed me out, and made my anxiety worse. I also received random calls from staff throughout the day and night, to check to make sure I was home. I never understood why the staff didn't know I was at home, since I was wearing a GPS ankle monitor that I could not take off. The GPS was supposed to show exactly where I was at any given moment. Each night between the hours of 2:00 a.m. - 4:00 a.m. I received at least one phone call, many times, two to three, phone calls.

I was required to have a home phone to receive the calls. My husband still had to be at work the following day, regardless of my situation. When the home phone rang in our bedroom in the middle of the night, it woke him up. I was always on high alert, constantly scared I would miss a phone call, and be returned to prison. This meant I could never fully relax, or sleep. When I returned from prison, my anxiety was already extremely high, from my experiences at the federal transfer center, during COVID.

The constant stress of being fearful of missing a phone call from the HWH, did not help my anxiety get any better. I lived under these conditions for eight months. As I write this paragraph, we are over three years into prisoners being released under the CARES Act. Many of these individuals who have been released for that long, are still wearing ankle monitors, and still live under these stringent conditions.

Sometime in late September, I was called by the halfway house, and told that I had nine days to secure a job, or I would be returned to prison. I had originally been told that I was not allowed to get a job, so I had not even looked for one. Now I had only nine days to get one? My anxiety soared, and I felt the old anger, trying to creep in. I stopped and prayed. Then I text messaged my pastor, P. Rod, to see if he knew anyone at church who needed to hire someone. Within minutes I had a job working at my church. Later, an attorney friend also hired me to do her accounting at her office.

It was actually nice to be able to leave my home each day.

I enjoyed going to work and being around people. It made me feel normal again. Yet it was also stressful because I had to remember to call the halfway house before I left my home to get permission to go to work, as well as call when I arrived at work, to let them know I had arrived. And several times when I called, I was told that it was not on my calendar to leave, and I had to miss work.

I wondered what people who were not working for a friend, or their church did in these situations? The exact process took place when I went to leave work to return home, or had to leave work for any other reason. One human error, and you could be returned to prison. There seemed to be no second chances. But being back at my church made it all worthwhile. I had longed for my church for over two years. Being back in church aided in the healing God had started in me, in that cell all alone, while in Oklahoma City.

I continued to reacclimate to being home. Friends visited me and brought food. We had spa parties, where we invited professional cosmetologists to come into my home, to give us facials, and do our hair, since I was not allowed to go anywhere. We had birthday parties, and dinners, all at my home. My family and I celebrated holidays, and other life events. I started to relax and began to have less anxiety. In early December 2020, I found out that I had been accepted back into my graduate classes.

A therapist that I attended church with agreed to supervise me, so I could finish the last internship required to graduate. I was thankful for his willingness to help me. When I reported to prison, I only needed one class, and the internship, to graduate with my master's degree in Clinical and Mental Health Counseling. I jumped through hoops to get my school approved through the halfway house, and the BOP. I was set to begin classes, and my internship, on January 13, 2021. My long-time goal of becoming a mental health counselor would finally come true. God was continuing to open many doors for me. HIS restoration on this side of the walls was evident.

Upon my return from prison, I had continued to blog,

exposing the mistreatment of inmates left behind, and about criminal justice reform issues in general. And I reported the fraudulent cosmetology hours I had been given at FPC Bryan to the State of Texas Department of Licensing and Regulation (TDLR). An investigation was opened, and I cooperated with the state investigator. True to my word, I became an advocate for those I left behind. I continued speaking out. I appeared on many podcasts, and even had my own radio show that discussed prison issues.

In December 2020, I received an email from my case manager at COF that stated, "any incident report, no matter how minor, would result in pick up by the US Marshal's office and the inmate being returned to prison." This email made me even more anxious. I had already been called by staff several times after having been at work for hours, to ask where I was at? Each time I reminded them that I had called in and reported that I had arrived at work. However, each time, it seemed that staff had failed to notate this in the system, showing me to be an escapee.

I was also given a verbal warning for not turning in the new insurance paperwork on my car when the policy was renewed for the year. Something nobody at the HWH had ever asked me for, or that I was aware they needed. And something I was able to take a photo of with my phone, and text to my case manager, the minute she requested it from me, only after I had been given a verbal warning, from another staff member. I realized that miscommunication could cost me my freedom, and that it was out of my control. This kept my anxiety on high alert.

I also kept in constant contact with many women I met in prison, and had left behind. I emailed them using the BOP's monitored CorrLinks system, sent them cards and books, and tried to keep them encouraged. Nowhere in the rules of home confinement, I was given, did it inform me that by doing so, I was violating a condition of my release. In fact, I had used my real name, and email address, to communicate with these women, through CorrLinks. My husband continued to place money, on the commissary accounts of some of these women, just as he had done, while I was in prison with them.

In December 2020, I was moved to a new case manager at the halfway house, because my original case manager had gone on maternity leave. I liked my new case manager. She was surprised to find out that I had not been allowed to go grocery shopping each week. She immediately allowed me to have a weekly outing of three hours to go to the grocery store. This was very helpful, since my husband worked full-time, and did everything else that needed to be done, such as the grocery shopping, since I was not allowed to leave our home to do these tasks.

I had been concerned since I knew my husband would be out of town during tax season at client locations, sometimes for two weeks at a time. Tax season would be starting shortly after the first of the year. I had wondered how I would manage to accomplish these tasks, especially since our youngest son would return to college after Christmas break. At least now I would be allowed to buy groceries in my husband's absence.

On December 22, 2020, I wrote a blog post titled *The Grinch Resides At Federal Prison Bryan.* This blog post discussed the mistreatment of women I had left behind in prison, who were not allowed phone calls to their families during the Thanksgiving, and Christmas holidays. I knew children waited on those phone calls. This act by the BOP, as punishment to these women, due to COVID being brought into the prison, was inhumane.

Visitation had already been suspended throughout the prison system, for almost a year by this time, due to the pandemic. Now the Warden was taking away phone calls too? It was cruel. A mobile billboard was circling the prison, hired by a non-profit, to bring attention to the matter. I had been sent photos of the mobile billboard that I attached to my blog post. I also used Twitter to bring attention to the matter by tweeting a link to the blog post. Piper Kerman, author of *Orange Is The New Black,* and producer of the Netflix series, by the same name, saw my tweet, and retweeted it on

Christmas Eve. Of course, this made my tweet go viral.

Little did I know at the time, but staff at FPC Bryan were still reading my blog. I'm not really sure what this says about BOP staff? Maybe they were paranoid of what I would tell, once I was on this side of the walls? I had been a strong voice against their corruption, and mistreatment of prisoners while incarcerated. Or maybe they were just curious? I left Bryan in February 2020, almost a year, before the blog post about the mobile billboard occurred.

Later I would find out that the Captain was running around like a chicken with his head cut off, blaming me for the mobile billboard, the day it was circling the prison. He made remarks to the women still incarcerated at the camp, that he would make sure I was punished for sending it to circle the prison. Maybe he was still angry at my PREA violation reporting?

Months later, women who left Bryan would contact me to report to me, and laugh, about the chaos that ensued, when the mobile billboard appeared that day in December 2020. It sounded like a circus, with clowns, the staff, running around, herding the ladies into the units, so they would not get a glimpse of the mobile billboard.

I'm certain that this was to prevent them from knowing that we were out here fighting for them. It was reported that the Captain was sure that I had hired the mobile billboard, and wanted to find a way to prove it. There would have been no proof of this, since I was not the one that was responsible for the mobile billboard's presence at the prison. But as I have seen, through my experience with our criminal justice system, the truth does not really matter anyway. And so, it would seem, that the staff at FPC Bryan set out to have me returned to prison.

The Christmas holidays came and went. It was amazing to be home with my family, and celebrate with them again. We decided to do something different for Christmas that year. Our children made homemade pasta, with several different homemade sauces, for Christmas Eve. It was a fantastic celebration. And since I had started working at my church,

Below Left: *Lynn, Pancho, JT, and Timothy-Christmas Eve 2020, First Christmas Home After Prison*
Below Right: *Our spoiled Frenchie, Macklin-Christmas Eve 2020*

Above: *Pancho and Lynn-Christmas 2020, If you look closely, you can see the ankle monitor poking out of the back right side of my jean leg.*

my church was kind enough to schedule me to work during Sunday mornings. I was required to attend the 10:00 a.m. service as part of my work. I was thankful to my pastors for allowing this to happen. I loved my church, and it felt good to be able to attend weekly services. I was starting to feel some sort of normalcy again. It felt good to continue to heal. I felt God working on me and in me. But unfortunately, that was short lived indeed.

Shortly after Christmas, I received a phone call from my case manager. She had stopped my weekly check-ins to the half-way house when she took over my case, and I was now required to only check in once a month. She was calling to request that I come in for my monthly check-in. However, she was also calling to tell me that she had received an email from my future probation officer, inquiring about the mobile billboard and my blog. She wanted to know if I had hired the mobile billboard to circle the prison? I told her I had not, but asked, "So what if I did?" "What rule would this be violating?" She did not know.

She also asked me about my blog, and informed me that she had been sent a link to that blog. Again, I asked, "What rule is this violating?" The case manager had no idea but replied, "I don't think you can do that." I immediately recapped my previous incident report for blogging while in prison. I made her aware of how the legal staff at the regional office had ruled in my favor. I was allowed to blog by BOP policy. I made it clear to her that I would continue blogging. I told the case manager, "I value my First Amendment rights to free speech."

Finally, she asked me, "Are you communicating with inmates?" I immediately answered "yes." And volunteered that I was also sending them cards and that I had sent over fifty Christmas cards to various women throughout the BOP system, that I met while in prison. I also told her that I kept up with many of them through CorrLinks emails. Her response was, "You can't do that." I once again asked, "What rule is this violating?" The only rules the halfway house had set for those of us on home confinement, were written in black and white, in their orientation manual. The rule clearly stated that "I was not allowed to use my cell phone to communicate with other halfway house residents or text inmates at any institution." I told her that I had not used my cell phone to text anyone, as I was communicating using the BOP's monitored email system, using my laptop.

I also asked, "What about my radio show?" The case manager asked, "What radio show?" And told me she didn't think I was allowed to have a radio show. I was doing the show from my home. I was violating no rule that I was aware of. I had a right to free speech, and I made her quickly aware of these facts. She said she would check with the BOP to see if I could have permission to continue the radio show.

Before we hung up, I requested the name of my future probation officer (PO), and her phone number. I immediately called my future PO. I introduced myself to her, and made her aware that I was calling because I did not want to start off on the wrong foot with her thinking I was a problem. She laughed, and told me she had not understood why the BOP reached out to her, in the first place. She was not supervising me at the moment. Therefore, she had referred the matter to the HWH staff.

She recapped her conversation with the half-way house staff. She had told them, in her opinion, I was not violating any rules. I loved that she was reasonable. I looked forward to having her for my PO. I had heard all the horror stories from other people, about having PO officers who were not reasonable, making their lives miserable. The following day, I was shocked when my cell phone rang, and it was my future Probation Officer, calling me to ask for the gate code to get into my subdivision. She was in the area and wanted to come by my home to meet me.

We had a good visit that day. I asked her who had sent her the email that prompted her email to the HWH? She immediately looked at her email on her phone, and told me the person's name. It was the female SIS officer at FPC

Bryan, Ms. Mitchell. This was certainly interesting, and unprecedented for a BOP employee to contact a PO. Especially since I was released from FTC Oklahoma on the CARES Act, not from FPC Bryan. And because I was on my way to Aliceville when released, my central file, the file that follows prisoners around the BOP system, that contains all their information, would have been in Aliceville, now my home prison of record, since that is where I was transferred when I left Bryan.

Because I was released under the CARES Act while still in Oklahoma, I had never made it to Aliceville. However, my property and central file had. This was clearly more retaliation by Bryan's staff against me. I saw it for what it was, and I got the distinct impression that my future PO saw it that way too. Her parting words to me that day were, "I say if there is something to expose, expose it." I knew I had lucked out in the PO department! Thank you, God. HE was continuing to bless me on this side of the walls.

What I was not aware of at this time, was that TDLR had requested documents from FPC Bryan regarding my reporting of the fraudulent cosmetology hours. FPC Bryan was resisting turning over the documents. I had signed a release form giving TDLR permission to get my records from the prison. The same investigation later led to the prison getting a written warning about the fraudulent hours it was reporting. TDLR proved that false hours had been reported to the State of Texas in my name. I believe my reporting of this fraud had a lot to do with the prison's retaliation, when it made the report on me to my PO, regarding my blog, and the mobile billboard.

I also believe the Captain still had it in for me, due to my PREA reporting. I had learned that after I left Bryan, an investigation did take place. Later, it was rumored that the Chaplin, and the Captain, were escorted from the facility, due to violation of PREA, but no charges have been brought against either of them, to my knowledge. Just another fault in our criminal "in"justice system.

Chapter Thirty-Nine
Staycation At The County Jail

During the holidays I had taken a break from the radio show. I was scheduled to do another show on January 8, 2021. I started asking my case manager about this, when I was called into the half-way house to check-in earlier that week. She said she had still not heard anything from the BOP, so I could not do the show, until it was approved. I continued to email her about this during the week, to inquire if she had an answer yet? She replied, "I'm still waiting, but I will check again on it." I reminded her that I had a show that Friday, and needed an answer.

On the morning of January 8, 2021, I sent the case manager an email, stating that I had not received an answer regarding being allowed to do the radio show that evening. At 2:45 p.m., on that same day, I received an email from Mr. South, Facility Director at City of Faith (COF), that in part read, "Mr. Smith has specifically advised that you refrain from participating in the program." Mr. Smith referred to in the email is the Residential Reentry Manager at the Bureau of Prisons (BOP) offices, in Grand Prairie, Texas." And the program referenced was my radio show *Inside The Walls and Beyond*.

I pushed back, quoting BOP program statement 1480.05, and the City of Faith's Federal Resident Handbook. I provided a link to the decision in the Michael Cohen case, where a federal judge had ruled that the BOP could not make giving up one's freedom of speech a condition of home confinement.

I also made the City of Faith HWH staff aware that I would appeal the decision to the BOP in Washington, D.C., using the BOP's Administrative Remedy process. Apparently, Mr.

Smith at the regional office did not appreciate my policy knowledge, or my value of my first amendment rights to freedom of speech. I believe my email angered him, and in true BOP fashion, he decided to retaliate. I did not do the radio show that Friday evening. However, my listening audience was informed why I was not on the air, and another person did the show for me.

I have repeatedly documented in this book that BOP staff do not like prisoners who are well-versed in BOP policy. BOP staff especially do not like prisoners who dare to speak out against the BOP's violation of policies, and civil rights of prisoners. And most BOP staff are not appropriately trained regarding BOP policy, or just choose not to follow it in general. Regardless, inmates who know the policy, speak out about the violations of said policies, or attempt to hold the BOP accountable, are retaliated against. This has been a pattern I have documented many times during the time I was incarcerated in federal prison, not all of which was written about in this book.

On Monday, January 12, 2021, I was working at my church when I received a phone call from Mr. South of COF. Mr. South instructed me to report to COF immediately, to be picked up by US Marshal Services, and to be transported back to prison. Mr. South informed me "You have received an incident report and are being sent back to prison." I immediately called Pancho to tell him what was going on. He asked, "You are joking, right?" I wished I had been, but unfortunately, I had to inform my husband "This is no joke." "Meet me at the house immediately." "I need you to take me to Little Rock to turn myself in to the HWH."

I followed Mr. South's instruction, and had Pancho drive me to the COF half-way house to self-surrender. On my way to the COF, I called my future PO and told her what was happening. She was shocked that it had been taken this far. She saw no policies I had violated. Once at the HWH, I was served with an incident report (**see Appendix, Document 12**), and my ankle monitor was cut off. The incident report, accused me of emailing inmates, which I had done. However, nowhere in the rules of home confinement was this a violation. I knew the real reason the BOP was retaliating. I had once again tried to hold them accountable to policy, and they were angered at my doing so.

After a lengthy wait, several US Marshals showed up to shackle, handcuff, and place a belly chain on me, so I could be transported to the county jail. Pancho was made to leave the building before this happened, thank goodness. However, when I was escorted out by the US Marshal to his car, I saw Pancho's vehicle sitting down the street watching. It broke my heart to have him see me like that. Just one more nightmare my family was forced to endure. And in that moment, I felt the hot rush of anger again.

Once in the car with the US Marshal, he asked "What did you do to get violated?" "Did you fail a drug test?" I replied, "I don't do drugs?" He said, "Well you don't look like the type." And again asked, "What did you do?" I just handed him the incident report and let him read it for himself. The Marshal was shocked that he was "Returning someone to prison for emails." He said, "I have never heard of such." "What did you really do?" When I explained to him about my blog, the BOP's allegations regarding the billboard, and my radio show, he stated, "I knew there had to be something more to this." "You must have really hit a nerve with whatever you are reporting."

"I've never taken anyone back to prison unless they flunked multiple drug screens." "And while I work for the government, I tell people that it is crooked." Then he asked me, "What is the name of your blog?" The Marshal proceeded to write the name of my blog down, and said "I'm going to read it." I'm fairly certain that he saw the incident report for the retaliation it was. He stayed with me at the county jail, chatting to me about my time in prison, and the corruption I witnessed there, until I was placed in a holding cell several hours later.

While my husband and I had waited at the half-way house for the US Marshal to come take me back to prison that day, multiple COF staff members had approached us to say, "City of Faith did not make the decision to write the incident report." "You have been a model resident for the eight months you have been on home confinement." COF staff reported that "Mr. Smith at the BOP forced us to write the incident Report" and "Move the 300 series incident report to a DHO hearing." This meant the incident report would be decided by the BOP staff Disciplinary Hearing Officer (DHO). Not at the institution level, by COF staff, as is customary for a 300 series incident report. I was not surprised. I had been on the receiving end of retaliation many times before. I recognized it. I was unfortunately aware of how the BOP operated.

What was actually upsetting about this situation, was that the BOP had in December approved me to take the class and participate in the internship I needed to graduate with my master's degree in May 2021. BOP staff were certainly aware that I was due to start those classes on January 13, 2021, the day after BOP staff violated me from the CARES Act, for what should have been a low-level incident report. Staff at the COF and the BOP were aware that my husband had already paid for those classes in full, because I had been required to provide them with proof of payment.

I have no doubt that my placement in the county jail on January 12, 2021, the day before I was to start back to class, was chosen by design, to derail my graduation, and punish me further, for continuing to be a voice against staff corruption and mistreatment of prisoners. So much for the BOP caring about the reentry needs of prisoners, and helping prisoners reintegrate back into society. No such thing as rehabilitation in the BOP.

But this is our system, a system that I continue to bring attention to, in hopes of making changes. I hope one day that families, such as mine, do not have to endure the pain of having their loved one treated in this manner. I wish for a society that makes better choices than just locking up everyone that finds themselves in the crosshairs of the federal government. And for federal prosecutors, BOP staff, and others in the system to be more compassionate and honest.

So as an advocate, I continue to speak out. And I continue to bring attention to the issues, one story at a time.

Chapter Forty
The Granting of My Pro Se Compassionate Release Motion

On December 1, 2020, unbeknownst to the BOP, I amended my motion for compassionate release that I had originally filed in April 2020, while I was stuck at FTC Oklahoma, during the COVID lockdown. While in Oklahoma, I requested the judge grant me compassionate release from prison due to COVID conditions. At that time, I had filed the motion because BOP staff at Oklahoma had repeatedly told us that they were not granting CARES Act releases, from the federal transfer center, which was clearly against the law, and the wishes of Congress. Before the Judge could rule on that motion, I was given a home confinement date by FTC Oklahoma staff, after starting an Administrative Remedy against them, for their failure to grant CARES Act release, to female prisoners at that facility. I had been the only female prisoner to get out on the CARES Act from FTC Oklahoma.

However, when I amended my motion in December, I was now asking to be granted compassionate release for reasons that had nothing to do with my original motion. Now, I requested relief because I wanted to finish my graduate degree, which meant I had to participate in my last internship at a mental health facility. I could not treat patients while wearing an ankle monitor. Secondly, I had been requesting counseling from the COF since early in my release from prison. The BOP had failed to approve counseling for my anxiety and PTSD, even though I had documented proof I had asked many times. I also listed several other reasons, such as my mother's health, and my inability to help care for her, due to being on home confinement. This motion was still pending when I was taken into custody on January 12, 2021, and placed in the county jail.

A few days after being placed in the county jail, a situation that made federal prison look like a cakewalk, the judge's office alerted my PO, that the judge was granting my pro se motion for compassionate release, and releasing me to supervised release. My PO had to inform the court that I was actually at the county jail, having been violated from the CARES Act. My future PO kept Pancho informed of what was going on, while I was in the county jail, since she also communicated with the judge's office. He told me this on our phone call that day.

The judge ordered the government to answer the court about the reasons for my being violated, and gave them only five days to do so. The PO told Pancho that the court would be ruling in my favor, as that is what she was hearing from the court's law clerk. At the same time, I used the jail's electronic tablet that I was able to use for thirty minutes a day, to type an addendum to my motion. I wanted to tell the judge my side of what had transpired. I used email on the tablet to email this information to Pancho, so he could copy and paste my side of the story into a document and file it for me with the court.

When the government answered, its answer was a copy of the incident report written to me by COF, a copy of the rules of home confinement I had signed when I had gone through orientation at COF on May 28, 2020, and a response by the government requesting that the judge deny my motion for compassionate release. The government relied on rule number nine of the BOP's conditions of home detention, which states that "you will not *associate* with other felons while on home confinement." However, the word *association* did not mean talking to, or being friends with other felons.

It means you will not *associate* criminally with other felons. This rule is often mistakenly used, just how the government, and the BOP, were using it against me. Both were trying to apply it as a violation of the rules of home confinement, for me merely talking to other felons by email, as an excuse to violate me.

When the PO sent Pancho the government's response, she mistakenly called it a denial, or at least that is how Pancho understood it. He relayed to me over the phone that the judge had denied my motion, and ruled against me. I went from believing that the judge was going to grant my compassionate release motion, to believing I was still headed back to prison.

While on my way to the half-way house on January 12, 2021, I had calculated how much good time the BOP could take from me for a 309 Incident Report. I understood how the policy worked, and knew how Disciplinary Hearing Officer (DHO) hearings usually turned out. I was prepared to spend the next few months either in the county jail, or being routed through Oklahoma to Aliceville. Knowing how these things go, I felt certain the DHO would take thirty good time days from me, which would change my current BOP outdate, (the date I should have been placed on supervised release, from May 4, 2020, to June 3, 2020.

I was not happy about it, but believed in God's plan for my life. I trusted that God would not allow me to be in this situation, if not for a good reason. And surprisingly, my anger did not rear its ugly head this time. Maybe I saw it as a do-over of sorts? This was my time to share HIS love, and be the light, I had failed at being, so many times on this journey. While at the county jail, it took me over a week to get my hands on a bible. When I did, I immediately turned to the book of Philippians, a book of the bible that had helped me during some of my darkest days in prison.

I immediately read Philippians 4:6-7 "Do not be anxious about anything, but in every situation, by prayer and petition, with thanksgiving, present your requests to God. And the peace of God, which transcends all understanding, will guard your hearts and your minds in Christ Jesus."

I began to thank God for all my many blessings. I praised

HIM in my jail cell. As tears ran down my cheeks, I made my request to go home known to HIM. But at the same time, I spoke to God and said, "I am your willing servant, and am ready to go do your work." I told HIM, "If you are sending me back to prison, then I know there is more work you need me to do, and while I do not want to go, I am ready." I knew that I would not fail HIM this time. I immediately felt HIS peace come over me. I was content with whatever was about to happen. And I prayed for that same peace for my family.

A few days after I made that prayer, on January 26, 2021, Judge Kristine Baker, in the Eastern District of Arkansas, granted my pro se Motion for Compassionate Release. She gave the BOP until 3:00 p.m. the following day, January 27, 2021, to release me from the county jail. On the morning of January 27, at approximately 10:30 a.m., the officer on duty told me to pack up my things, because I was leaving to go home.

I had been counting down the days that the BOP had to bring me before the DHO for the required hearing. I was now on my 15th day in the county jail, and I knew that by policy, the BOP should have had my DHO hearing the previous day. I had not waived my rights to the DHO hearing, and had made that clear to the COF staff. I had also argued during the Community Disciplinary Committee (CDC) hearing, I had over the telephone with the COF staff, around day nine of my time in the county jail, that the incident report was faulty due to technical reasons.

Based on my knowledge of the BOP's Inmate Discipline Policy, I did not believe that Mr. South of the COF could actually write the incident report or sign it, since he did not have access to the BOP's CorrLinks email system. Therefore, he could not have witnessed me "emailing other inmates," as the incident report had charged.

The incident report clearly stated that Mr. South wrote the incident report after he was forwarded the information by the Reentry Services Division, which I understood to be Mr. Smith from the RRM in Dallas, Texas, whom I had angered when

I argued about my rights to continue the radio show. In my addendum to the court, I readily admitted to the Judge that I had actually been emailing with those I left behind in prison, using my real name, and email address.

However, was this really a violation of my conditions of home confinement? I did not think so, and I had already informed the COF staff that this was one of my arguments against the incident report being valid. When the guard told me to pack up that morning, I thought for sure the BOP had dismissed the faulty incident report, and was sending me back to home confinement. During my time in prison, I had beat three false incident reports against me, using my knowledge of policy, as well as helped other prisoners do the same. I knew policy was in my favor and that I had not violated any rules.

I called Pancho to tell him the good news. He had been waiting on my call. He was already aware of what was going on, as he had already been contacted by my PO earlier that morning, with the good news that my pro se motion for compassionate release had actually been granted. I was going straight to supervised release. No more ankle monitor, BOP, or halfway house. The BOP had failed to find me guilty of the incident report, and it's time had run out. The Judge had beat them to the punch with her order to release me. BOP 0, Lynn Espejo 4–the three false incident reports I beat while in prison, and the 309 Incident Report that landed me in the county jail. I was full of anxiety when Pancho picked me up a few hours later.

The experience at the county jail had not been a good one, and it had caused me to regress in the progress I had made in the area of my anxiety. I saw women being horribly mistreated at the jail. Women who said they were suicidal were placed in padded rooms naked. They were not given feminine hygiene products, and were made to use the bathroom in a hole in the middle of the floor. Some mentally ill women were strapped from their necks to their feet, with something resembling a dog leash. I saw mentally ill women have their heads slammed to the concrete floor by the guards, when the women would act out. Some mentally ill prisoners tore up jail property, as the rest of us looked on.

One night we had been forced to listen to the loud noise of the one woman who was being held on murder, as she jumped from her bunk to the table that was welded to the wall, back and forth for hours, until she was finally able to break the table away from the wall. The guard on duty was too scared to go into her cell alone. Apparently, the jail was short-staffed that evening.

The conditions we were kept in were grave. The shower did not have a light in it. One day, I accidentally touched the shower wall, and felt the slime. I realized then why there was no light in the shower. The staff probably didn't want us to know just how filthy the shower really was. I was moved from cell to cell, without any of them being cleaned, and this was at the height of COVID, and before vaccines were available. During my 15 days at the county jail, I only received one change of clothing.

When I arrived and was processed into the jail, my bra, underwear, and socks were taken from me, because they were not white. The jail did not provide replacements for these items. The jail was freezing cold, and there did not seem to be any heat, or the heat did not work correctly. The blanket I was issued was not whole. It was a partial blanket, with many holes in it. It would not even completely cover me. The food we were fed resembled dog food. I never knew what it was, so I did not eat much while at the jail. I always gave my trays away to the other women.

Regardless of the conditions, we made the best of it. I met many nice women there, and was able to share God's love with them. I prayed for, and with many women. One of my most memorable moments, was when we were having out of our cell shower and phone time, one evening. This is the time when many ladies would watch the television that was located near my bunk. I had been moved out into the open common area, where overflow bunks had been set up, due to my good behavior. Individuals that didn't need constant supervision were placed on these bunks, when the cells would get full. I got to know many of the other ladies this way, because of being out in the open when everyone was out of their cells.

One evening a lady was crying, and struggling with being locked up. I asked her if I could pray for her. After I prayed, another woman approached me. She said "You really do know God, don't you?" I replied, "I have a relationship with HIM." She told me that she had never gotten chills before when anyone prayed, but she had when I prayed that evening. I don't even remember what I said in my prayer. I was just asking God to provide peace and understanding, for the woman I was praying with. Now the other lady wanted to know more about my God. I told her HE was her God too. I was able to spend many days discussing the Bible with this same woman, after that evening.

My prayer for the other woman had opened the door for the discussions. Now, she would read a book of the bible each day, and then ask me questions. Some I knew the answer to, some I did not. But I encouraged her to keep reading, praying, and asking God to guide her path. God had used me. I had not failed HIM this time! After I was released from the county jail, I sent her cards to encourage her to continue to seek out God. I never heard back from her, but I do still pray for her.

Months later, I would see another of the ladies I spent time with in the county jail in a public setting. She actually ended up being our waitress at a Mexican restaurant, in a town that is over an hour from my home. She asked, "Do you remember me?" I was unsure. People look so different on this side of the walls.

Even now when the ladies I served time with in prison try to friend me on Facebook, I have to ask myself "Who is that?" The waitress told me, "I remember you because you were nice to me at Pulaski County Jail." She said, "You were the only person that made me feel cared for while I was there, thank you." She had been one of the ladies placed in the suicide cell. I was thankful that God had allowed me to comfort her. I had no idea how much my kindness had meant to her. I realized that HE had actually given me a chance to redeem myself in those moments. It felt good to know I had actually been a light in the darkness and lived out my Christian values for all to see. I had not failed HIM or myself. And I had had HIS peace in that situation.

Later in my advocacy work for another prisoner who was returned from the CARES Act for a minor infraction, much like myself, a lady I had met at the county jail the previous year, ended up being placed in the same cell with the lady I was currently advocating for. They were being held at the Federal Medical Center (FMC) Carswell, in Ft. Worth, Texas. In this way, God allowed our paths to cross again, and us to be reconnected. I am currently advocating for the lady I met in the county jail, who is very ill, and needs to be released under the CARES Act, or Medical Compassionate Release.

Further proof that God always makes a way to use us, if we only allow it. While at the county jail, I had been able to share God's love with her, and help her prepare for federal prison, with my knowledge. Now months later, HE made a way for us to reconnect, just when she needed someone to advocate on her behalf. Who would have thought that those dark fifteen days I spent at the county jail, would allow me to be a voice for so many.

God always knows the plan, even when we don't. HE is faithful!

Chapter Forty-One
Moving Forward

On January 27, 2021, the day I was released from the county jail, I called my graduate advisor to see if I would be allowed in my graduate classes that semester. The classes had started on January 13th, so I had already missed two weeks of classes, and assignments. After hearing my story, my advisor went to bat for me, and I was readmitted to class. I then called the therapist who had agreed to supervise my last internship, to see if I could still intern under him during that semester. He immediately agreed. God continued to open doors even in the midst of all my anxiety and uncertainty, in those moments.

On April 30, 2021, I graduated with my Master's of Science Degree, in Clinical and Mental Health Counseling. As I walked across the football field that day to receive my diploma, with my biggest supporter, my husband Pancho, looking on from the stands, I could hardly believe it was finally happening. I knew that many women I had served time with in prison were also watching me that day via Facebook, where my graduation was being broadcast live.

I fought back the tears as I carried my diploma back to my chair. After everyone had received their diplomas and we were leaving the stadium, I made eye contact with my husband in the bleachers. He was there with our middle son JT, and his wife Rachel, who had accompanied us to my graduation that day. I held my diploma up in the air and did a fist pump with it. Even though it was long overdue, I had just graduated with my master's degree. And I had done so with a 4.0 grade point average (GPA), even while being indicted, and surviving an eight-day jury trial, during part of my time in

Above: *JT, Pancho, Lynn, and Rachel-April, 2021, SAU Master's Degree Graduation,*
Right: *Pancho and Lynn- November 2021, Dream.org Justice Event, Little Rock, Arkansas*

class. It felt amazing. I had actually made it through this life storm.

I had come out better and stronger. And since the granting of my compassionate release motion, I have made great strides in healing the anxiety I suffer from my time in prison, as well as from my trip to the county jail. Aided by the help of the gentleman, my dear friend John, that I interned under that semester, and his care for my mental health during that time. But most importantly, my relationship with God was stronger than ever.

I was mindful that God had carried my family and me through this season of life. I knew we would not have made it during this journey without HIS peace. My marriage was better than ever, even after all we had been through. We were survivors.

I had fought the system. I had stood for what was right. I had managed to heal, and with God's continued help, had learned to let go of the anger and revenge I held onto for so many years. Revenge and anger, that had caused great pain to me, and others. And while I may have lost at trial, I had won in so many other ways. I had made incredible friends, in the darkest of places, while on this journey.

I knew that I had to continue to share my story with others. I wanted to encourage other families on their own journey, through the federal criminal "in" justice system. But more than anything, I wanted to work with women who had been traumatized by that very system. The same system that had also traumatized my family and me. I wanted to help them have the healing of God's promises too. I would be a voice for change, and an advocate for those who found themselves without a voice. I would find a way to expose the dark secret that is our criminal "in"justice system.

On November 23, 2021, I was invited by the criminal justice advocate organization FAMM to go to Washington, D.C., and participate in their *Pardon People Not Turkeys* rally. When I returned home, later that same evening, my friend Retta and her husband visited us at our home. They were spending the night with us, while on their way to Texas, to visit their son for Thanksgiving. It was the first time I had seen Retta, since our days together at FPC Bryan.

As I recapped my Washington D.C. trip, Retta immediately reminded me of one of the conversations we had, while working together in the reentry office, at FPC Bryan. In 2018, I had told Retta about my plan to be a criminal justice advocate for change in the federal system, upon my release from prison. I told her that one of my main goals was to make it to Washington, D.C., to speak out on behalf of those still incarcerated. I had forgotten about that conversation. But there I stood in my own kitchen, talking to my good friend Retta, having returned from doing just that. ONLY GOD!

Retta is just one of the many blessings that came from my journey through our federal criminal "in"justice system.

Top Left: *Lynn-Washington*
D.C. in front of White House, November 2021
Top Right: *My dear friend Retta and I, at my home, November 23, 2021*
Below: *FAMM Pardon People Not Turkeys Rally, November 2021*

Postscript

James 1:12 "Blessed is the man who remains steadfast under trial, for when he has stood the test he will receive the crown of life, which God has promised to those who love him."

After I was granted compassionate release in January 2021, I became known as one of the faces of the CARES Act. I worked diligently to bring attention to this issue, becoming an advocate for others, like myself, who were violated from home confinement for minor infractions. In early June 2021, I was contacted by the fiancé of a pregnant woman who had just been returned to prison from the CARES Act. I immediately took on her case as her advocate, and fought hard for her and her family, bringing national attention to her plight. I feel great satisfaction knowing that I made a difference in her family's journey, if only by providing them with emotional support, information, and advocacy. Unfortunately, she was not quickly released back to the community, as we had hoped she would be, and was ultimately forced to have her baby boy at FMC Carswell. Advocacy work can be heartbreaking in this respect.

However, during this same timeframe, I was able to help bring attention to what was going on with the CARES Act. Ultimately, with the hard work of a lot of advocates, including myself, and criminal justice reform organizations such as Dream.org, FAMM, Color of Change, the ACLU, and others; in December 2021, the Department of Justice rescinded the Trump Administration's OLC Memo, and agreed that no CARES Act person would be returned to prison when the pandemic ended, as was originally set to happen.

And some of the people that had been returned to prison

from the CARES Act, for minor infractions, were able to be released back to home confinement, or received compassionate release, with the help of our advocacy. I am extremely proud of the part I played in this work.

However, I must point out, that I would not have been allowed to do this work, without the support of a wonderful United States Probation Officer, Victoria F., who always encouraged me to excel, and supported my efforts; allowing me to advocate for others caught up in the same system that had held me captive for so many years.

On January 18, 2022, after serving one year on supervised release, and with the support of, and encouragement from that same probation officer, I filed a pro se motion for Early Termination of Supervised Release. Two days later, Judge Baker ordered the government to respond to my motion within 14 days. On February 2, 2022, AUSA Mazzanti filed the government's response, objecting to my early release from supervision, and lodging a litany of false allegations against my character, and our finances. Once again, the government would stop at nothing to continue its false narrative about me, and to keep me in bondage to the broken criminal justice system, for as long as possible.

Regardless that other advocates felt it best that I not address the government's baseless allegations, I knew I had to. I could not allow the government to get by with continuing to lie about my character. And honestly, I would be lying if I said I hadn't felt a lot of anger that day reading what the government, once again, had to say about me. I recognize the anger I still feel at times, as the trauma that will always be with me, due to the journey I have been on, and trauma I will always have to deal with, due to what has happened to my family and me. AUSA Mazzanti's response was another added layer of trauma, and just one more time, I was forced to read the government's lies, in black and white.

As I set out to write my reply, I once again felt that hot anger wash over my body. All I could do was pray for God to give me peace, and the right words to say. I worked very hard to remove the anger from my reply to the government. I wrote, and rewrote, my reply, several times, over the course of the next several days. On February 7, 2022, I drove to the federal courthouse in Little Rock, Arkansas, for what I hoped would be my last time there. I went through the security clearance check point, which caused me to feel some of the same anxiety and angst, I felt during those eight days of my federal jury trial. Again, trauma resurfacing.

At the clerk's office, I filed my reply to the government's response. In the end, I wanted the last words Judge Baker considered to be mine, not AUSA Mazzanti, or any other government prosecutor, for that matter. I was calling the government out one last time, and I must admit, there were no holds barred in my reply. Admittedly it felt good. At that moment I didn't care if I won or lost. I knew I could do another two years on supervised release if necessary, and that God would be there with me as I continued this journey, no matter how the judge ruled. Regardless of the government's continued lies, I know that I am a law-abiding citizen, and always have been.

I promised myself, for the sake of my anxiety, that I would not check the progress of my motion. I prayed, and put my trust in God, laying whatever the judge decided at God's feet. However, on July 12, 2022, I felt prompted by what could only be God, to look on pacer at my case. I could not believe my eyes. Sometime earlier on that same day, Judge Kristine Baker had granted my motion for Early Termination of Supervised Release. I had once again stood up to the government's lies, and this time the judge had ruled in my favor. I felt it fitting that this win be the last entry on the docket in my criminal case. Just one of the many ways God continues to restore me on this side of the walls.

Even though all of our FREEDOM ultimately comes from God, not man, July 12, 2022, was the first time I had felt completely FREE from the government's oppression, in over eleven years! Since my early release from supervision, I have been able to use my experience to help others write motions to also get early release from supervision. But on that day, July 12, 2022, I immediately booked an already planned trip to Washington, D.C., as I was free to go wherever I pleased, without permission from anyone. It felt amazing!

On March 24, 2023, I met my good friend from prison, Carolyn, in Bryan/College Station, Texas. The same place we spent two years together incarcerated. We spent the weekend together, doing real life things. And we had a great time reconnecting. She is certainly a big blessing in my life. Of course, our visit would not have been complete, without a photo in front of the FPC Bryan prison camp (wink wink-see photo, page 444). We never got to take a photo together when we were in prison, but at least we could document ourselves on the right side of those prison walls.

But the biggest blessing from that weekend was our visit to Mrs. Betty's church. Mrs. Betty and her family had made such an impact on us with their volunteerism while we were incarcerated. On that Sunday, Mrs. Betty told us a story of how they had been on the brink of closing down their church, after COVID-19 caused church membership to drop drastically. However, when she received my message that Carolyn and I were coming to visit, and learned just how much they had meant to us in prison, they changed their mind.

Hearing this was further confirmation to me that God does still find a way to use me, even in all my brokenness, to be HIS voice. It was such a blessing to be in Mrs. Betty and her family's presence again, and to spend that time with my dear friend Carolyn, on this side of the walls. Life certainly is much different for both of us now than when we first met, and became fast friends in 2018.

And regardless of my own traumas, my work goes on. I continue to advocate for those I left behind in federal prison, and the ones I meet along the way on their own journeys. I'm grateful that families reach out to me when they have no hope. They trust me to guide them and be a light in the darkness. And I never forget that this is HIS work, not mine. I often speak out about the mistreatment of individuals who are incarcerated, as well as the mental health impact of prison, on those individuals. I have been fortunate enough to be given a platform by several major media outlets, and criminal justice advocacy groups such as Dream.org, LOHM, FAMM, and others. And to be invited to Washington, D.C. on several occasions to advocate for specific issues. I currently sit on the Federal Advisory Council for Dream.org., and the Community Advisory Board for the University of Arkansas Medical Sciences (UAMS) HEALS Lab for Mental Health Research.

And I'm happy to report that my advocacy has helped free several men and women from prison, and for that, I praise God, for allowing me to be the vessel, HE used to speak on their behalf. I cannot tell you the feeling I have when someone is able to walk out from behind those walls! I love celebrating those moments with them. Knowing I had even the smallest part in some of these families being reunited, brings me hope, and immense joy.

I am also an Admin for several Facebook support groups, designed to help those who are headed to federal prison get information, help those newly released from prison get advice, and needed resources, and to help families navigate the federal prison system, while their loved one is away. I have also helped countless women prepare for their own prison journey, many of whom were going to FPC Bryan to serve their time. Though admittedly, reliving my self-surrender day, and time incarcerated there, often triggers my own traumas, from those experiences.

After much prayer and consideration, I chose not to fight the system to get my counseling license, and become the therapist I had so desired to be, mainly because of my own anxiety. I'm too afraid to ever get in a position that could cause me to be charged with another crime. I know the truth does not matter, to an overzealous federal prosecutor, and that it is easy to be accused of wrongdoing. I served time with many therapists who were serving long sentences for commonly practiced billing methods. They told me that they never knew they were violating federal law, until the feds showed up at their doors, and by then it was too late.

And after being released from supervision, each time I attempted to study for my national exams, I felt God pushing me in another direction. Now I use my master's degree to volunteer with women who have suffered from traumas, and addiction, and to speak out about mental health issues related to incarceration. And I continue to be an advocate for the homeless population of Central Arkansas.

Most importantly, I continue to heal and feel more like my "old" self each day. There is no doubt that this journey has changed who I am as a person. I know the trauma and scars from prison, and this season of my life, will always be a part of the "new" person who walked away from that journey. But I am finding ways to channel those traumas into advocacy work, and use them to help others.

It is the plan I believe God has for my life, and that HE allowed this journey to happen, so that I am where I am, at this very moment in time. Each time I'm able to use my experiences to help another person, I see HIS plan more clearly. My pain did have a purpose after all. I am now three years on this side of the walls. And honestly, I love my life. I would not change anything about this journey, even if I could.

Often times, when God allows me to help others on their own journey through our criminal "in"justice system, I refer back to what the bible tells us in 1 Peter 5:10 about suffering, "After you have suffered a little while, the God of all grace, who has called you to his eternal glory in Christ, will himself *restore,* confirm, strengthen, and establish you."

HE is certainly *restoring* me on this side of the walls. May HE *restore* you and your family as well. Thank you for taking the time to read my story. I wish you nothing but God's blessings on your own journey.

Top Left: *JT, Pancho, Lynn, and Timothy-Mother's Day Church Service 2021, First NLR*

Top Right: *Joseph, Lynn, and Timothy-Christmas Morning 2021*

Right: *Pancho, Lynn, and Timothy-Mother's Day Church Service 2022, First NLR*

Above: *Timothy, Lynn, and Pancho-Easter Church Service 2022, First NLR*
Below Left: *Timothy, Pancho, Macklin, Lynn, and Joseph-Christmas 2022*
Below Right: *Pancho, Macklin, and Lynn-Christmas 2022*

Above: *Pancho and Lynn-Christmas Eve Church Service 2022, First NLR*
Below Left: *Pancho and Lynn-Christmas Day Church Service 2022, First NLR*
Below Right: *Pancho and Lynn-Easter Church Service 2023, First NLR*

Above: *My dear friend Carolyn and I-March 2023, Bryan, Texas at Christopher's World Grille,*
Below: *Carolyn and Lynn-with Mrs. Betty and her family, March 2023, Mrs. Betty's Church, Bryan, Texas*

Above: *Carolyn and Lynn-March 2023- In Front of Federal Prison Camp, Bryan, Texas-Standing on the right side of The Walls*

Appendix

Document 1

IN THE UNITED STATES DISTRICT COURT
EASTERN DISTRICT OF ARKANSAS

UNITED STATES OF AMERICA	)	
	)	
v.	)	No. 4:11CR00045 JLH
	)	
LYNN ESPEJO	)	

MOTION TO DISMISS

The United States of America, through Christopher R. Thyer, United States Attorney for the Eastern District of Arkansas, and John E. Bush, Assistant U.S. Attorney for said district, and respectfully states as follows:

1.   The Defendant was indicted on June 8, 2011, of violating Title 18, United States Code, Section 1343, 59 counts.

2.   The United States herein seeks leave of this court and moves to dismiss the Indictment pursuant to Fed. Rules of Crim. Proc. 48(a).

WHEREFORE, by leave of this Court and pursuant to Fed. Rules of Crim. Proc. 48(a), the United States moves to dismiss without prejudice the above referenced Superseding Indictment.

Respectfully submitted,

CHRISTOPHER R. THYER
United States Attorney

By: /s/ John E. Bush
        JOHN E. BUSH (#59193)
        Assistant United States Attorney
        P. O. Box 1229
        Little Rock, AR 72203
        Telephone No. (501) 340-2600
        Email: John.Bush@usdoj.gov

Document 2

My name is Linda Rabatin, Date of Birth 10-1-51, address 22 Victoria Circle, Maumelle, Arkansas. I was employed at Practice Management Services Inc. (PMSI) from approximately September 1997 to July 7, 2011. I was an account Specialist and reported to Lynn Espejo during the time of her employment at PMSI.

For several years my office as well as Lynn Espejo's office was located on the 3rd floor of the Doctors Building at 550 S. University, Little Rock, Arkansas. Sometime in the spring of 2010, the business offices of PMSI located on the third floor were moved to the main office located on the sixth floor. When this was done, all of the records that Lynn Espejo maintained in her office area were moved to the sixth floor. Many of the boxes containing the records she kept were placed into the dressing room of the old x-ray room on the sixth floor. Some of the records were maintained in a file cabinet in her new office on the sixth floor. When Lynn Espejo ceased working at PMSI in early September, 2010, the records referenced above remained at PMSI in the room where they had been stored.

Linda Reynolds became office Manager of PMSI in early February, 2011. I reported to her as I did Lynn Espejo. Sometime after Linda Reynolds's employment, I had the occasion to be with and observe the building maintenance employee enter the small room which contained the records that had been stored by Lynn Espejo. The boxes were stacked very high and upon opening the door to the old dressing room, fell down and made it difficult to get into the room. It was my understanding Linda Reynolds had requested the records in both the old x-ray room and the dressing room were to be accessed.

In later February or early March, 2011, before Mary Cox was terminated, I personally observed workers employed with a paper shredding company remove boxes of records that appeared to be those stored by Lynn Espejo in the old x-ray room and adjoining dressing room and load them into a truck.

Linda Rabatin

STATE OF ARKANSAS)
)
COUNTY OF SALINE)

Subscribed and sworn to before me this 8th day of February, 2012.

My Commission Expires:

April 9, 2017

Notary Public

446

Document 3

Fw: Espejo

Aug 11, 2012 at 5:26 PM
Linda Reynolds <lreynoldspmsi@yahoo.com>
To: lynnespejo@sbcglobal.net <lynnespejo@sbcglobal.net>
1 File51kB

PDF51kB

Espejo Conduct.pdf

Linda Reynolds
Clinic Administrator
PMSI
500 S. University Ave. Ste 615
Little Rock, Ar 72205
Phone 501-666-3666 x112
Fax 501-907-9068
Cell 501-422-9852
----- Forwarded Message -----
From: "Vena, George (USAARE)" <George.Vena@usdoj.gov>
To: lreynoldspmsi@yahoo.com
Sent: Wednesday, May 18, 2011 2:24 PM
Subject: Espejo

Hello Linda,
Here is the document I would like you to look at.   George
<<Espejo Conduct.pdf>>

George C. Vena
Assistant United States Attorney
425 W. Capitol, Ste. 500
Little Rock, AR 72201
george.vena@usdoj.gov

Document 4

G̶M̶a̶i̶l̶ rickholiman2 . <rickholiman@gmail.com>

US v Espejo

Harris, Pat (USAARE)   Sat, Nov 22, 2014 at 11:40
<Pat.Harris@usdoj.gov>   AM
To: Richard Holiman <rickholiman@gmail.com>
Cc: "Dempsey, Jamie (USAARE)" <Jamie.Dempsey@usdoj.gov>

Rick - I believe you or your client know this, but I want to make sure.

Linda Reynolds was interviewed with SA Joe Moore present in
2012. She stated at that time that she believed that Ms. Espejo was
innocent of the theft of PMSI funds. She stated that she had lost her
job at PMSI and had talked with Ms. Espejo about her belief. Ms.
Reynolds also stated that she was asked repeatedly by Dr.
Sanderson to make purchases for him through her personal account,
but she did not do them because Dr. Scott Brown told her not to.

Ms. Reynolds is currently in ADC because she had her state parole
(or probation) revoked. Our office has an open investigation on her
theft from PMSI and I and another Secret Service agent have
interviewed her. She now states that she does not have the same
belief regarding Ms. Espejo's innocence as she did when she first
lost her job at PMSI.

EXHIBIT
19

448

Document 5

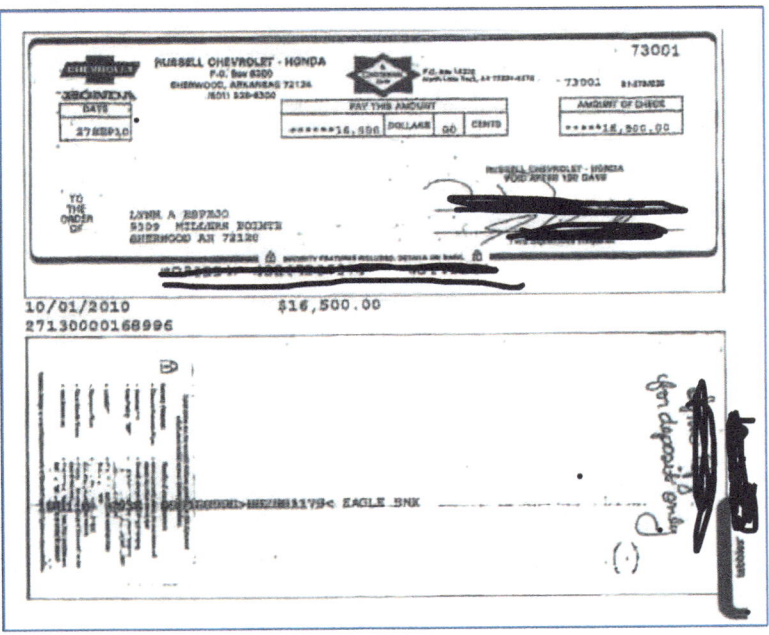

Document 6

Document 7

GF #:	20106010		
Buyer:	Stephen A. Hudgens	SS	
Seller:	Pancho Espejo		8/6/2010
Legal Description:	Miller's Crossing PH 1, Lot 45, Pulaski County		
60)	Proceeds of Sale	$82,744.65	

| 34467 | Check Total | | $82,744.65 |

DEPOSITED WITH:
EAGLE BANK AND TRUST
LITTLE ROCK, ARKANSAS 72221
MEMBER FDIC

LOANS
See Us First
LENDER

This is Your Deposit Receipt

Checks and other items that are received for deposit are subject to the provisions of the Uniform Commercial Code and/or any applicable collection agreement.

Deposit may not be available for immediate withdrawal. The bank symbol, transaction number and amount of deposit are shown to the right.

DDA DEPOSIT

*****82,744.65
Account: 1000000000035600
Transaction 0055
Received 8/6/2010 at 03:41 hm
to drawer 100 on 8/6/2010 business.
Have you came in today?

Document 8

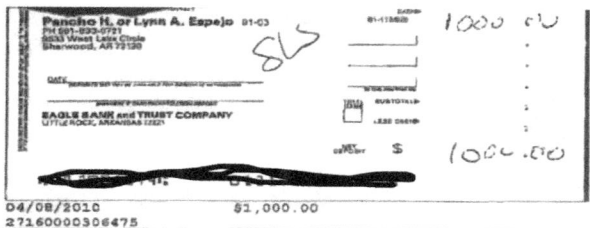

04/08/2010 $1,000.00
2716000030 6475

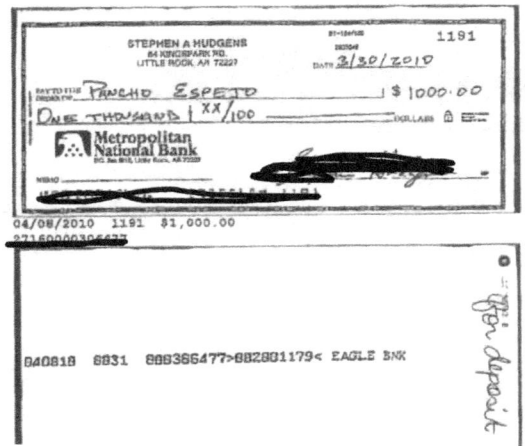

04/08/2010   1191 $1,000.00
2716000030 6475

B40818 8831 888366477>882801179< EAGLE BNK

Document 9

FYI email with letter to Criminal Chief of Justice in DC. I suspect we will immediately see some 'action' from the USATTY here since I am required under the 'Touhey' regulations if a justice 'employee' is subpoenaed to testify.

---------- Forwarded message ----------
From: **rickholiman2 .** <rickholiman@gmail.com>
Date: Tue, Jul 14, 2015 at 1:04 PM
Subject: US vs. Espejo
To: "Thyer, Chris (USAARE)" < >, Pat Harris < >, "john.white2" <John.White2@usdoj.gov>,
"Mazzanti, Stephanie (USAARE)" < >, "Dempsey, Jamie (USAARE)" < >

Attached is a letter faxed and mailed to the Criminal Chief at US Justice regarding our intention to have AUSA John Bush testify at the hearing on July 31st concerning the multiple notebooks of settlement statements I and my client were allowed to review on several occasions with George Vena and later with Bush before the first indictment was dismissed.

Holiman Law Firm, P.A.

Richard E. Holiman
Attorney at Law
212 Center St. Suite 325

Document 10

On Tue, 7/14/15, rickholiman2 . <rickholiman@gmail.com> wrote:

Where do we start with this development? Within an hour of me sending the email with the 'Touhy' letter to US Justice: they're producing the notebooks 'just scanned today.'

On Tue, Jul 14, 2015 at 1:24 PM, Mazzanti, Stephanie (USAARE) < wrote:
Rick – In anticipation of our meeting tomorrow:

There are several notebooks from various doctors, which appear to be the notebooks produced to the United States during the first case. Some of these notebooks were previously scanned and produced in discovery to you. Other notebooks were scanned today and we will provide you with a CD tomorrow (or today if you want to stop by). The only doctor that I don't see a notebook for is Dr. Sanderson.

Also, in Pat's November 7, 2014 letter to you, he inquired as to whether you would prefer paper copies of the 2 boxes of documents from Liles Henry. I don't believe a response was received as to that inquiry. We have scanned the boxes and will have those available for you on CD tomorrow as well. Some portions of those boxes were previously produced in discovery.

Thanks,
Stephanie

Document 11

On Tue, Jul 23, 2015 at 2:10 PM, Mazzanti, Stephanie (USAARE) < wrote:

Rick —I will attempt to answer your questions to the best of my ability below:

The settlement notebooks have been in our office since the dismissal of the first indictment. It was our understanding that you had seen these notebooks when George Vena prosecuted the case. Pat thought that you had copies of the notebooks because he had been at your office and thought he saw notebooks with the same information. Several of those notebooks were scanned and provided to you on CD in October 2014. Those notebooks were placed in a file cabinet in our office. The other unscanned notebooks were stored in a separate drawer in a file cabinet in our office. After the issue regarding production of the notebooks was raised at the May 2015 hearing, Pat went to the file cabinet to make sure we had everything. At that time, the notebooks were brought upstairs (6th floor conference room). A few weeks ago, Jamie and I began going through all documents to determine what had been scanned and whether we could document what had been produced. When we discovered that only a portion of the notebooks had been scanned, we decided to have the others scanned and produced them to you out of an abundance of caution.

Document 12

BP-S205.073 **INCIDENT REPORT (CCC'S)** CDFRM
MAR 10
U.S. DEPARTMENT OF JUSTICE   **FEDERAL BUREAU OF PRISONS**

1. Name of CCC: City of Faith (6ZG)			
Part I - Incident Report			
2. Name of Offender Espejo, Lynn	3. Register Number 26304-009	4. Date of Incident 3 December 2020	5. Time 2:21p
6. Place of Incident HCC Residence	7. Component HCC	8. Type of Offender HOF	

9. Incident
309 : Violating a condition of a community program.

11. Description of Incident (Date: 8 January 2021, Time: 4:18p staff become aware of incident)

On 8 January 2021 at 4:18p, the Bureau of Prisons, Re-Entry Services Division forwarded City of Faith documentation that shows evidence, of inmate Espejo, Lynn, Reg. No. 26304-009 communicating with inmates currently incarcerated in numerous Federal Prisons. Specifically, inmates Breshears, Crystal #31527-045) and Hardman, Kelly #28557-031, housed in FCI Greenville; Lane, Demika (#45413-177, housed in FDC Oklahoma; inmates Dinn, Jenney #54992-177, Keel, Meagan #03518-480 and Trevino, Roxey #23539-479, housed in FPC Bryan. According to TRUVIEW Email Address Center Report inmate Espejo is utilizing e-mail address lynnespejo@sbcglobal.net to communicate with these inmates.

A review of TRUVIEW shows inmate Vasquez, Amber, Reg. No. 49829-177, communicating with Espejo, Lynn, Reg. No. 26304-009, by email address, lynnespejo@sbcglobal.net, on December 3, 2020 at 9:21 PM, Espejo, writes, "The number for the show on Friday, December 4th is 661-451-1451 and it is from 6 - 9 central standard time". On December 5, 2020 at 2:21 PM Vasquez replies, "Lynn we were not able to make it on the phone until after 8. We will try again next week. We have lots of updates including people who've recently filed civil suits and a commutation of sentence aka reduction. Talk with you soon."

12. Signature of Reporting Employee	Date & Time 12 Jan. 21 10:03a	13. Name & Title (Printed) Michael South, Facility Director
14 Incident Report Delivered to Above Offender By		15. Date Incident 16. Time Incident Report Delivered Report Delivered

(Continued below)

Appendix, LINKS

Due to the size of some of the documents I wished to include as proof to back up what I have said in this book, I have chosen to list them as links here instead. If you type the link address in your web browser, you will be able to view these documents. These documents can also be found by going to my blog *Inside The Walls* at https://insidethewallscom.wordpress.com. I regret the inconvenience this may cause to some of my readers, who may not have Internet access.

Link 1
https://insidethewallscom.files.wordpress.com/2018/02/first-please-agreement-offer.pdf

Link 2
https://insidethewallscom.files.wordpress.com/2018/02/shred-it-invoice.pdf

Link 3
https://insidethewallscom.files.wordpress.com/2018/02/linda-reynolds-police-report.pdf

Link 4
https://insidethewallscom.files.wordpress.com/2018/02/construction-loan-amounts-borrowed.pdf

Link 5

https://insidethewallscom.files.wordpress.com/2018/02/closing-papers-west-lake.pdf

Link 6

https://insidethewallscom.files.wordpress.com/2018/02/jeffshortwayemails.pdf

Link 7

https://insidethewallscom.files.wordpress.com/2018/02/letter-criminal-division-chief-us-justice.pdf

Link 8

https://insidethewallscom.files.wordpress.com/2018/02/email-with-2nd-plea-offer.pdf

Link 9

https://insidethewallscom.files.wordpress.com/2018/02/second-plea-agreement.pdf

Link 10

https://insidethewallscom.files.wordpress.com/2018/02/denial-protection-order.pdf

Link 11

https://insidethewallscom.files.wordpress.com/2018/03/immunity-pancho-gov.pdf

Link 12

https://insidethewallscom.files.wordpress.com/2018/02/panchomaritalprivilege-2.pdf

Link 13

https://insidethewallscom.files.wordpress.com/2018/03/order-immunity.pdf

Identification Badge from FPC Bryan-I was required to have this badge around my neck at all times while incarcerated

News Articles About/Quoting Me

The below list is some of the news articles that have discussed me, or that I have been quoted in since 2021. The list is not inclusive of all the news articles I have been discussed or quoted in. During the CARES Act fight to keep already released prisoners at home, I was inundated with requests for comments, due to being remanded from the CARES Act, as well as being an outspoken advocate for others. And again, after the Elizabeth Holmes case broke, since Ms. Holmes was designated to FPC Bryan. Due to this, I lost count of the times my name appeared in a major publication.

https://www.forbes.com/sites/walterpavlo/2021/02/06/inmate-on-home-confinement-spoke-out-on-bureau-of-prisons-policy-and-ended-up-back-in-prison/?sh=75f8f21155ba

https://inquest.org/home-rule/?fbclid=IwAR0t1GIRTh_Jy2k5-uXAxuvQ2r1IsLAOtGXzCoJAb-1fGv1Pc94oMhSKaSM

https://www.washingtonpost.com/local/public-safety/inmates-pandemic-biden-trump-policy/2021/06/25/e89aa28e-d376-11eb-baed-4abcfa380a17_story.html

https://famm.org/famm-to-host-virtual-briefing-on-home-confinement/

https://reason.com/2021/09/17/white-house-offers-clemency-for-drug-offenders-on-home-confinement-but-advocates-say-plan-will-still-send-thousands-back-to-prison/

https://www.prisonlegalnews.org/news/2021/dec/1/federal-prisons-switch-scanning-mail-surveillance-nightmare/

https://people.com/crime/elizabeth-holmes-mother-prison-sentence-theranos-fraud/

https://www.wsj.com/articles/elizabeth-holmes-prison-inmates-3a46a79f?st=l91ibyhm72pz2kc&reflink=article_imessage_share

https://nypost.com/2023/06/01/male-guards-at-elizabeth-holmes-prison-leered-at-women-inmates-in-shower-ex-prisoner/

https://people.com/all-about-elizabeth-holmes-2-kids-7505996

https://www.foxbusiness.com/lifestyle/elizabeth-holmes-prison-what-life-like-texas-facility

Newscasts, Podcasts or Other Videos Lynn Has Appeared

The below list is some of the newscasts, podcasts or other videos I have appeared both before and after prison. The list is not inclusive of all newscasts, podcasts, or videos I have appeared. During the CARES Act fight to keep the already released prisoners at home, and once the Elizabeth Holmes case broke, I was inundated with requests for appearances, unfortunately I lost count of the times I was interviewed.

https://www.youtube.com/watch?v=5yVwDYh2_X0

https://twitter.com/fammfoundation/status/1466769201238994944?s=10

https://www.youtube.com/watch?v=TFgNIKrXzFl

https://www.youtube.com/watch?v=Yn36V1FnWFY&t=1s

https://www.youtube.com/watch?v=xy62m_I0zEk

https://www.youtube.com/watch?v=nES3etk081w

https://www.youtube.com/watch?v=6eonyOABieY

https://www.youtube.com/watch?v=5yVwDYh2_X0

https://lionsofliberty.libsyn.com/website/ff-110-federal-prosecutors-gone-wild

https://www.lionsofliberty.com/episodes/2020/07/17/the-bureau-of-prisons-is-out-of-control-with-lynn-espejo

https://www.lionsofliberty.com/episodes/she-fought-the-bureau-of-prisons-and-won-with-lynn-espejo

https://www.goodmorningamerica.com/news/video/elizabeth-holmes-reports-texas-prison-99718523

https://www.insideedition.com/media/videos/theranos-founder-elizabeth-holmes-to-begin-serving-11-year-prison-sentence-81721

https://www.newsnationnow.com/video/former-inmate-describes-elizabeth-holmes'-new-life-behind-bars-cuomo/8692526/

https://www.youtube.com/watch?v=P4PfqYIQr3U

References

Sniffen, Michael J., (June 23, 2003). Study Examines Prosecutor Misconduct. *Midland Daily News*. Retrieved from https://www.ourmidland.com/news/article/Study-Examines-Prosecutor-Misconduct-7187794.php

Editorial Board, (January 14, 2014). Rampant Prosecutorial Misconduct. *The New York Times*. Retrieved from https://www.nytimes.com/2014/01/05/opinion/sunday/rampant-prosecutorial-misconduct.html

Sallah, Michael, et al, (September 6, 2014). Stop and Seize: Aggressive police take hundreds of millions of dollars from motorists not charged with crimes. *The Washington Post*. Retrieved from https://www.washingtonpost.com/sf/investigative/2014/09/06/stop-and-seize/

Arkansas Business Staff (November 1, 2004). Doctor Sues Accountant for Last-minute Filings. *Arkansas Business*. Retrieved from https://www.arkansasbusiness.com/article/52367/doctor-sues-accountant-for-last-minute-filings

Moritz, Gwen (September 3, 2012). Little Rock Internist Richard Johns Subject of Renewed Police Investigation. *Arkansas Business*. Retrieved from https://www.arkansasbusiness.com/article/86609/little-rock-internist-richard-johns-subject-of-renewed-police-investigation

Moritz, Gwen (August 30, 2017). Richard Johns Sentenced to 9 Years for Selling Painkiller Prescriptions. *Arkansas Business*. Retrieved from https://www.arkansasbusiness.com/article/118542/richard-johns-sentenced-to-9-years-for-selling-painkiller-prescriptions

Moritz, Gwen (September 3, 2012). Doctor Has Twice Reported Nurses Who Complained. *Arkansas Business*. Retrieved from https://www.arkansasbusiness.com/article/86611/doctor-has-twice-reported-nurses-who-complained

Admin, (May 5, 2013). La Santa Muerte. *La Santa Muerte*. Retrieved from https://www.santamuerte.org/english/3846-la-santa-muerte.html

Vincent, Isabel (December 21, 2021). Santa Muerte and five more 'religious' saints worshiped by drug cartels. *New York Post*. Retrieved from https://nypost.com/2021/12/21/religious-saints-of-murders-outlaws-worshiped-by-cartels/

About The Author

 Lynn Espejo lives in Sherwood, Arkansas. She is wife to Pancho, mother to three grown sons, Joseph, JT, and Timothy, and companion to a 14 ½ year old, very spoiled French bulldog, named Macklin. Lynn has a double BBA in Accounting and Finance, and an MS in Clinical & Mental Health Counseling. She spent many years working in the corporate business world, and has owned her own small business. Lynn is a Christ follower. She also volunteers her time working with food pantries, the homeless, and those less fortunate. She and her husband volunteer their time helping with their church's Share Your Lunch (SYL) program. SYL, since its inception in 2017, has provided over 27,000 bags of groceries to individuals and families, as well as weekend backpacks of food to elementary age children, in partnership with local schools in the Central Arkansas area.

Lynn was indicted in the Eastern District of Arkansas on March 2, 2011, however, that indictment was dismissed in May 2012. She was indicted on the same charges on October 8, 2014, after she refused to give up claim to money seized by the federal government during her 2011 indictment, and dared to complain all the way to Washington, D.C., regarding the corruption and prosecutorial misconduct she experienced from staff at the US Attorney's Office in the Eastern District of Arkansas, and a federal agent working for the Internal Revenue Service. She was convicted on February 8, 2017, after an eight-day jury trial, and was sentenced to 45-months in federal prison, of which she served 27 months, before being released to home confinement during COVID-19.

Her blog, *Inside-The-Walls*, started out as a way for her to vent her frustration at being indicted and convicted for a crime she did not commit, and what she saw as a broken criminal justice system. However, it soon became a voice against the corruption, fraud, and violation of prisoner rights she witnessed while incarcerated at Federal Prison Camp (FPC) Bryan located in Bryan, Texas. Many times, Lynn was subjected to retaliation by BOP staff for continuing to blog while incarcerated.

During her incarceration, Lynn taught classes to other women, including classes on women's values, worth, and self-esteem. She also volunteered to tutor prisoners with their college business classes, worked as a clerk in the Reentry Department, and took Cosmetology classes. She gained recognition from other prisoners for her knowledge of BOP Policy, which allowed her to help many women fight false incident reports, and retaliation by BOP staff. During COVID-19, Lynn spent almost 100 days in solitary confinement, and was quarantined in the Men's Maximum-Security Special Housing Unit (SHU) at the Federal Transfer Center in Oklahoma City, Oklahoma, before being released to home confinement under the CARES Act.

Lynn was violated from the CARES Act on January 12, 2021, for a minor infraction of continuing to talk to women she left behind in federal prison, and for advocating against the mistreatment of those women. While being held at the Pulaski County Jail awaiting return to prison, her Pro Se motion for compassionate release was granted on January 26, 2021, by Judge Kristine Baker, and she was released on January 27, 2021. Since that time, she has appeared in many newscasts, news articles, on podcasts, and has become an outspoken advocate for criminal justice reform. She has worked with groups such as FAMM, Dream Corps Justice, and others. She currently sits on the Federal Advisory Council for Dream.org., and the Community Advisory Board for the University of Arkansas Medical Sciences (UAMS) HEALS Lab for Mental Health Research.

On July 12, 2022, Lynn's pro se motion for Early Release from Supervision was granted, after she served a little over a year on supervised release. Since that time, Lynn has used her experience to help others also receive early release from supervision.

Lynn continues to advocate for prisoners and their rights, and wishes to help all women realize their value and worth. She wants to bring awareness to and expose the corruption that is our nation's criminal justice system. Lynn is the Chief Investigative Correspondent for the *Midnight Report*, where she can be found writing stories about criminal justice issues. Lynn's social media platforms *Inside-The-Walls & Beyond* on Facebook and Twitter, focus on women's issues as they journey through the federal criminal "in"justice system. Lynn continues to blog, and speak out against, the BOP's inhumane treatment, of those whose care it is entrusted with. You may contact Lynn at lynnespejo@sbcglobal.net or through her blog at https://insidethewallscom.wordpress.com.

Made in the USA
Coppell, TX
19 August 2023

20482314R00256